EUROPEAN PRACTICE BOOKS

# TAX LAW AND POLICY
# IN THE EEC

**A. J. EASSON,** B.A. (Oxon.), LL.M. (Lond.)
*Professor of Law at*
*Queen's University, Kingston, Canada*

LONDON · ROME · NEW YORK
OCEANA PUBLICATIONS
*1980*

Published in the United States of America
in 1980 by Oceana Publications,
Dobbs Ferry, New York and in
Great Britain by Sweet & Maxwell
Limited, 11 New Fetter Lane, London.
Photoset by Promenade Graphics Ltd., Cheltenham.
Printed in Great Britain by
Hollen Street Press Ltd.,
Slough, Berks.

**British Library Cataloguing in Publication Data**

Easson, Alexander James
    Tax law and policy in the E.E.C.
    1. Taxation—Law and legislation—European
Economic Community countries   [LAW]
    I. Title
    341'.24'2      80–41430

    ISBN 0 379 20711 7

# EUROPEAN PRACTICE BOOKS

## TAX LAW AND POLICY
## IN THE EEC

# PREFACE

As its title indicates, this book is concerned with both the tax law and the tax policy of the European Economic Community.

The tax provisions of the Treaty of Rome and of the Directives adopted by the Council have been a major subject of litigation and a fertile source of the developing jurisprudence of the European Court and that of national courts in relation to Community Law. Few, if any, other areas of the law have made such a contribution to the evolution of the principles of Community Law: the concepts of the supremacy of Community Law and of the direct effect of the provisions of the Treaty and of directives have either been first articulated or have been significantly developed in cases dealing with taxation or with customs duties and charges. The student of Community jurisprudence will find, if undeterred by the sometimes dry and technical subject matter of the cases, that a novel and exciting system of law has emerged from seemingly unpromising disputes over the duties on ureaformaldehyde and akvavit. Not that the subject matter is always dry: as the reader will discover, litigation concerning alcoholic beverages figures most prominently.

As de Tocqueville once observed, there is hardly a single public matter which does not derive from or end in a tax. Virtually every aspect of Community policy has fiscal implications and tax policy has an effect upon all aspects of the Community — on the free movement of goods, persons, services and capital, on agriculture and transport, on competition, economic, regional and social policy, on budgetary policy and on the Community's relations with other states. To study the Community's tax policy is therefore to study the Community itself, in almost its entirety, from one especially important viewpoint.

It is hoped, therefore, that this book will be of interest not only to lawyers and students of law, whether their interests lie in taxation or in community law, but also to economists, political scientists and all students of that exciting creation, the European Communities.

Rather than attempt to provide a detailed description and analysis of each Community directive and proposal, this book seeks to examine the policy reasons for particular decisions, the viability of proposed solutions and the difficulties which have had to be, or remain to be, overcome. Some passages are inevitably technical: it is hoped that these are not excessively so. Others may appear unduly simplistic: if so, the writer can only plead that, given the limitations of space and of his own inadequate knowledge of some aspects of economics or policy, this too was inevitable.

The manuscript was completed early in January, 1980, and is hopefully up to date as at the end of 1979. Subsequently, the Court delivered judgments in the important "alcohol" cases and a number of revisions were made in order to comment upon these.

v

My studies of this subject commenced shortly before British entry into the Community, when I was teaching law at the University of Southampton, and I was fortunate in being encouraged to continue them on coming to Canada in 1976. In the context of our own current debate on "renewed federalism," Canadian interest in the European experience is high and is growing. I hope that this study, of one form of fiscal federalism, will contribute to that debate.

I owe a great debt of gratitude to my friends and former colleagues at Southampton who encouraged me to begin this study, and to my friends and colleagues at Queen's University for their patient help and advice, especially to Professor Nils Ørvik, the Director of the Centre for International Relations at Queen's. To the numerous officers of the Commission, Court of Justice and European Parliament who so generously gave me their time and advice I am also deeply grateful. My special thanks are owed to Mrs. Lynn Freeman, of the Law Library at Queen's, for her expertise in obtaining for me books, articles and papers from all parts of the globe, and to Mrs. Netta Falder for her skill and patience in typing the various versions of this manuscript.

Finally, I wish to express my thanks to the Donner Canadian Foundation for its generous support for the study, in Canada, of the European Communities in general and for my own researches in particular.

*Kingston, Canada.*                                              A. J. Easson
*June, 1980.*

# CONTENTS

# CONTENTS

# TABLE OF CASES

[References are to paragraph numbers.]

## COURT OF JUSTICE OF THE EUROPEAN COMMUNITIES

## NATIONAL COURTS

### Belgium

### France

### Germany

# TABLE OF TREATY PROVISIONS

[References are to paragraph numbers]

xvii

# TABLE OF SECONDARY LEGISLATION

[References are to paragraph numbers]

## REGULATIONS

## DECISIONS AND DIRECTIVES

# TABLE OF SECONDARY LEGISLATION

# ABBREVIATIONS

| | |
|---|---|
| A.F.D.I. | Annuaire Française de Droit International |
| A.J.C.L. | American Journal of Comparative Law |
| A.J.I.L. | American Journal of International Law |
| B.T.R. | British Tax Review |
| C.D.E. | Cahiers de Droit Européen |
| C.L.J. | Cambridge Law Journal |
| C.M.L.R. | Common Market Law Reports |
| C.M.L. Rev. | Common Market Law Review |
| D. St. Z. | Deutsche Steuer Zeitung |
| (EC) Bull. | Bulletin of the European Communities |
| (EC) Gen. Rep. | General Report of the Activities of the European Communities |
| E.C.R. | European Court Reports |
| (EEC) Bull. | Bulletin of the European Economic Community |
| (EEC) Gen. Rep. | General Report of the Activities of the European Economic Community |
| E.L. Rev. | European Law Review |
| E.P. Debs. | Debates of the European Parliament |
| E.P. Docs. | Working Documents of the European Parliament |
| E.T. | European Taxation |
| EuR. | Europarecht |
| Fisc. M.C. | Fiscalité du Marché Commun |
| I.C.L.Q. | International and Comparative Law Quarterly |
| J.B.L. | Journal of Business Law |
| J.C.M.S. | Journal of Common Market Studies |
| J.O. | Journal Officiel des Communautés Européennes |
| J.W.T.L. | Journal of World Trade Law |
| L.C.P. | Law and Contemporary Problems |
| L.I.E.I. | Legal Issues of European Integration |
| L.P.I.B. | Law and Policy in International Business |
| L.Q.R. | Law Quarterly Review |
| N.J.W. | Neue Juristische Wochenschrift |
| N.T.J. | National Tax Journal |
| O.J. | Official Journal of the European Communities |
| P.F. | Public Finance/Finances Publiques |
| R.D.I.D.C. | Revue de Droit International et de Droit Comparé |
| R.I.D.C. | Revue Internationale de Droit Comparé |
| R.I.E. | Revue de l'Intégration Européenne/Journal of European Integration |
| R.I.W. | Recht der Internationalen Wirtschaft |
| R.M.C. | Revue du Marché Commun |
| R.S.F. | Revue de Science Financiere |
| R.T.D.E. | Revue Trimestrielle de Droit Européen |
| S.E.W. | Sociaal-Economische Wetgeving |
| W.D. | Wirtschaftsdienst |
| Z.G.S. | Zeitschrift für die gesamte Staatswissenschaft |

# CHAPTER 1

# THE TAX PROVISIONS IN THE EEC TREATY

## A. INTRODUCTION

**1**   Those articles of the EEC Treaty which are specifically concerned with taxation appear, under the heading "Tax Provisions," in Chapter Two of Title One, headed "Common Rules," of that section of the Treaty devoted to the policy of the Community.[1] It is immediately apparent that the rules on taxation are considerably less detailed than are those on matters such as the customs union and agriculture. As Doctor Hallstein has remarked, "in terms of the Common Market, the chapter on fiscal provisions is formulated in the most limiting kind of language" and the Treaty itself "contains only the most timid of starting points."[2]

**2**   It is perhaps significant that tax policy (if we exclude from that subject customs duties) was not considered by the authors of the Treaty to be one of the "Foundations of the Community,"[3] but rather as part of the common rules and, consequently, ancillary to the main objectives of the Treaty. Thus, as the Court of Justice has emphasised on a number of occasions, the tax provisions seek to fill in any loophole which certain taxation procedures might find in the prescribed prohibition upon customs duties and charges having equivalent effect,[4] and their essential purpose is to contribute to the establishment of a common market which will ensure free trade in goods.[5] Nevertheless, the fact that the tax provisions appear where they do in the general scheme of the Treaty, rather than simply forming a part of the Title on the Free Movement of Goods, indicates that their function is by no means restricted to filling loopholes in the rules relating to customs duties but that they have a more general role to play in assisting the attainment of the wider objectives of the Treaty. In particular, it may be no coincidence that the tax provisions follow on directly from the rules on competition for, as Advocate-General Gand remarked, in the *August Stier* case,[6] the purpose (of Article 95) is to ensure equality of competition. And Article 99, concerning the harmonisation of indirect taxation, immediately precedes the more general chapter on Approximation of Laws, to which it makes express reference, and requires such harmonisation to be "in the interest of the

[1] EEC Treaty, Arts. 85–102. The tax provisions are set out in Arts. 95–99.
[2] W. Hallstein, *Europe in the Making* (1972), pp. 156–157.
[3] Part Two of the Treaty : Arts. 9–84. These "foundations" are the free movement of goods, agriculture, the free movement of persons, services and capital, and transport.
[4] Cases 2 & 3 *Commission* v. *Luxembourg and Belgium (Gingerbread)* [1962] E.C.R. 425, at p. 431. This was the first case in which the Court considered the tax provisions of the Treaty.
[5] Case 31/67 *August Stier* [1968] E.C.R. 235.
[6] Above, at [1968] E.C.R. 164–165.

Common Market." Thus it can be concluded that the tax provisions have, within their own terms, a general applicability to the objectives of the Treaty as a whole and, in particular, to the principles set out in Articles 2 and 3. These read:

3     "2. The Community shall have as its task, by establishing a common market and progressively approximating the economic policies of Member States, to promote throughout the Community a harmonious development of economic activities, a continuous and balanced expansion, an increase in stability, an accelerated raising of the standard of living and closer relations between the States belonging to it.

3. For the purposes set out in Article 2, the activities of the Community shall include, as provided in this Treaty and in accordance with the time-table set out therein:

(*a*)  the elimination, as between Member States, of customs duties and of quantitative restrictions on the import and export of goods, and of all other measures having equivalent effect;

(*b*)  the establishment of a common customs tariff and of a common commercial policy towards third countries;

(*c*)  the abolition, as between Member States, of obstacles to freedom of movement for persons, services and capital;

(*d*)  the adoption of a common policy in the sphere of agriculture;

(*e*)  the adoption of a common policy in the sphere of transport;

(*f*)  the institution of a system ensuring that competition in the common market is not distorted;

(*g*)  the application of procedures by which the economic policies of Member States can be co-ordinated and disequilibria in their balances of payment remedied;

(*h*)  the approximation of the laws of Member States to the extent required for the proper functioning of the common market;

(*i*)  the creation of a European Social Fund in order to improve employment opportunities for workers and to contribute to the raising of their standard of living;

(*j*)  the establishment of a European Investment Bank to facilitate the economic expansion of the Community by opening up fresh resources;

(*k*)  the association of the overseas countries and territories in order to increase trade and to promote jointly economic and social development."

4     All of the above activities, with the possible exception of (j) and (k), would seem to have some relevance to the evolution of a Community policy on taxation and to the scope of the tax provisions as set out in the Treaty. These provisions read as follows:

"95. No Member State shall impose, directly or indirectly, on the products of other Member States any internal taxation of any kind in excess of that imposed directly or indirectly on similar domestic products.

Furthermore, no Member State shall impose on the products of other Member States any internal taxation of such a nature as to afford indirect protection to other products.

Member States shall, not later than at the beginning of the second stage, repeal or amend any provisions existing when this Treaty enters into force which conflict with the preceding rules.

96. Where products are exported to the territory of any Member State, any repayment of internal taxation shall not exceed the internal taxation imposed on them, whether directly or indirectly.

5   97. Member States which levy a turnover tax calculated on a cumulative multi-stage system may, in the case of internal taxation imposed by them on imported products or of repayments allowed by them on exported products, establish average rates for products or groups of products, provided that there is no infringement of the principles laid down in Articles 95 and 96.

Where the average rates established by a Member State do not conform to these principles, the Commission shall address appropriate directives or decisions to the State concerned.

98. In the case of charges other than turnover taxes, excise duties and other forms of indirect taxation, remissions and repayments in respect of exports to other Member States may not be granted and countervailing charges in respect of imports from Member States may not be imposed unless the measures contemplated have been previously approved for a limited period by the Council acting by a qualified majority on a proposal from the Commission.

99. The Commission shall consider how the legislation of the various Member States concerning turnover taxes, excise duties and other forms of indirect taxation, including countervailing measures applicable to trade between Member States, can be harmonised in the interest of the common market.

The Commission shall submit proposals to the Council, which shall act unanimously without prejudice to the provisions of Articles 100 and 101."

In addition, Articles 100 and 101 concern the approximation of laws and administrative provisions generally, including national tax laws,[7] and Article 220, concerning negotiations between Member States, refers expressly to the abolition of double taxation within the Community.[8]

6   Essentially, there appear to be three distinct though related aspects to the above provisions. These are:

(i) The principle of non-discrimination, expressed in Article 95. Member States are not permitted to impose internal taxation upon the products imported from other Member States in excess of that imposed upon similar or competing domestic products. This prohibition serves two functions: it reinforces the ban upon customs duties and like charges, preventing the

[7] See below, Chap. 3, paras. 201–209.
[8] The question of double taxation is discussed in Chapter 3, paras. 293–303.

circumvention of this ban by imposing discriminatory taxation which might have the same effect as a customs duty, and it seeks to ensure conditions of free competition between the products of different Member States by removing distortions created by national tax rules, at least in so far as these relate to the products themselves.

(ii) Articles 95 to 98 set out the basic rules on border tax adjustments, adopting the "destination principle" of taxation.[9] Thus, exports to other Member States may not be subsidised beyond the remission of internal taxes actually imposed on the goods prior to exportation and imports from other Member States may not be subjected to countervailing charges in the form of internal taxes in excess of that borne by the equivalent domestic product. Furthermore, such remissions and countervailing charges are restricted, unless there has been authorisation to the contrary, to indirect taxation. In one sense, of course, the first proposition above can be viewed as merely one of the two parts of this second proposition—that dealing with countervailing charges. That they are in fact distinct propositions can, however, be seen if one supposed that, within the Community, the destination principle of taxation were replaced by the origin principle,[10] *i.e.* that all remissions of tax on exports and countervailing charges on imports were abolished. The prohibition upon discriminatory taxation in Article 95 would remain necessary, for it is by no means restricted to countervailing duties on imports, as will be demonstrated later in this chapter.

(iii) Article 99, calling for the harmonisation of indirect taxation, though it has a major role to play both in the elimination of discriminatory taxation and in the proper functioning of the system of border tax adjustments, has a far more general application, *e.g.* to remove obstacles to free movement, created by differences in national tax systems, even when these are not in themselves discriminatory.[11]

The first two of the above propositions will be considered in the remainder of this chapter, whilst the third will be discussed in Chapter 2.

### B.  THE TAX PROVISIONS AND THE FREE MOVEMENT OF GOODS

**7   (i) The customs union**

One of the foundations of the Community and essential objectives of the Treaty is the creation of a customs union, a goal which was achieved in 1968.[12] The essential features of this customs union are, first, the prohibition

---

[9] The provisions are modelled upon and closely resemble the rules of the General Agreement on Trade and Tariffs (GATT): see below, paras. 81–85.

[10] The concepts of the destination and origin principles are discussed further, at para. 82.

[11] Case 171/78 *Commission* v. *Denmark* (not yet reported), at para. 20 of judgment.

[12] For a comprehensive review of the scope of the customs union, see J. Amphoux, "Customs Legislation in the EEC" (1972) 6 J.W.T.L. 133.

and abolition of all customs duties on imports and exports between Member States[13] and, secondly, the adoption of a common customs tariff in their relations with third countries[14] so that products entering the Community from a third country are in free circulation once the initial import formalities have been complied with and the common tariff has been levied.[15] But, for the customs union to be fully effective, it is also necessary to remove various non-tariff barriers to trade[16] such as quantitative restrictions and measures having an equivalent effect[17] and all charges having an effect equivalent to customs duties on imports or exports.[18] Given the existence of a customs union, it becomes clear that, at the very least, "no member country can be allowed to restore through its internal tax systems the discriminatory treatment of trade with other members which the removal of tariffs, quotas, subsidies and other customs barriers have eliminated."[19] This the tax provisions of the Treaty, in particular Article 95, seek to ensure. As the Court has explained on a number of occasions, Article 95 is "intended to fill in any breaches which a fiscal measure might open up" in the prohibitions laid down by the provisions relating to the free movement of goods.[20]

**8**    However, the rules governing customs duties, quantitative restrictions and charges and measures having equivalent effect and those governing discriminatory taxation, whilst complementary, are by no means the same and cannot be applied simultaneously.[21] In a sense, by permitting internal taxation to be imposed upon an imported product so long as it is not discriminatory, Article 95 can be regarded as a derogation from, as well as a complement to, Articles 9 to 16.[22] Consequently a major problem has been, and still is, to distinguish between those impositions which constitute charges equivalent to customs duties, or measures equivalent to quantitative restrictions, and those which form part of a system of internal taxation. It is this problem which it is proposed to examine in the remainder of this part of the chapter.

[13] Art. 9 (All references are to the EEC Treaty unless otherwise stated).

[14] *Ibid.*

[15] Art. 10.

[16] For a description of the various types of barriers, see C. Mathews, "Non-Tariff Import Barriers and the Kennedy Round" (1964–5) 2 C.M.L. Rev. 403. The process of removing such barriers is a long and continuing one and many still exist within the Community: see (EC) Bull. 10–78, pp. 23–24.

[17] These are prohibited by Art. 30.

[18] Arts. 9, 12, 13, 16.

[19] C.K. Sullivan, in C.S. Shoup ed., *Fiscal Harmonization in Common Markets* (1967), Vol. II, Chap. 7, at p. 46. See also W. Hallstein, *Europe in the Making* (1972), pp. 26–27.

[20] Case 24/68 *Commission* v. *Italy (Statistical Levy)* [1969] E.C.R. 193, at p. 200; Cases 2 & 3/69 *Diamantarbeiders* [1969] E.C.R. 211, at p. 221, and Cases 2 & 3/62 and 31/67 (notes 4 and 5, above).

[21] Case 10/65, *Deutschmann* [1965] E.C.R. 469.

[22] E.P. Burki, "Amélioration ou Altération d'une Formule de la Cour de Justice" (1978) 14 C.D.E. 101, at pp. 109–110.

## (ii) Customs duties and charges having an equivalent effect[23]

9      The customs union prescribed by Article 9 involves the prohibition not only of customs duties on imports and exports between Member States but also of all charges having equivalent effect. Member States are required to refrain from introducing any new charges of that nature, or increasing existing ones,[24] and those charges on imports already in existence when the Treaty entered into force were required to be abolished during the transitional period according to timetables laid down by the Commission.[25] Customs duties on exports and charges having equivalent effect were also required to be abolished not later than the end of the first stage of the transitional period.[26]

10     The prohibition upon equivalent charges has been a major subject of litigation over the years and the Commission has been engaged in a constant struggle to accomplish their elimination.[27] Frequently the Commission has been able to persuade the offending Member State to remove the charge in question but in a number of instances proceedings have been brought by the Commission before the Court under Article 169. Thus, for example, the Court has declared to be invalid the imposition of a fee for the issue of a licence to import gingerbread,[28] a charge for phytosanitary inspection on the import of sheep,[29] a small fee to cover the cost of compilation of statistics on trade levied upon imports and exports,[30] and a tax upon the exportation of art treasures.[31] Other instances have been referred to the Court by national courts, under the preliminary ruling procedure of Article 177. (It should be observed here that, in such proceedings, the Court is requested to rule upon the interpretation of the Treaty and other Community measures and thus does not, as such, expressly rule upon the validity of the domestic measure which is in question in the national proceedings). In these proceedings the Court has considered the compatibility with Articles 9 to 16 of the Treaty of matters such as the imposition of unloading and statistical charges,[32] and

---

[23] For more detailed consideration, see J.K. Bentil, "EEC Commercial Law and Charges having Equivalent Effect to Customs Duties" (1975) 9 J.W.T.L. 458; R. Barents, "Charges of Equivalent Effect to Customs Duties" (1978) 15 C.M.L. Rev. 415; F. Wooldridge and R. Plender, "Charges having an equivalent effect to Customs Duties: a Review of the Cases" (1978) 3 E.L. Rev. 101.

[24] Art. 12.

[25] Art. 13. (The customs union was completed on July 1, 1968).

[26] Art. 16. (*i.e.* by the end of 1961).

[27] See, *e.g.* (EEC) Seventh General Report (1964), p. 24; (EEC) Tenth General Report (1967), p. 67; (EC) Second General Report (1968), p. 24; (EC) Tenth General Report (1976), p. 15; (EC) Eleventh General Report (1977), p. 19.

[28] Cases 2 & 3/62 *Commission* v. *Luxembourg and Belgium* [1962] E.C.R. 425. See also Case 10/65 *Deutschmann* [1965] E.C.R. 469.

[29] Cases 52 & 55/65 *Germany* v. *Commission (Imported Mutton)* [1966] E.C.R. 159; *cf.* Case 89/76 *Commission* v. *Netherlands* [1977] E.C.R. 1355.

[30] Case 24/68 *Commission* v. *Italy (Statistical Levy)* [1969] E.C.R. 193.

[31] Case 7/68 *Commission* v. *Italy (Art Treasures)* [1968] E.C.R. 423.

[32] Case 34/73 *Variola* [1973] E.C.R. 981.

of various fees and charges for public health, phytosanitary and veterinary inspections carried out at frontiers upon imported, or exported, products.[33]

**11** What is of particular relevance, in considering the respective fields of application of the customs and tax provisions of the Treaty, is the interpretation which the Court has put upon Articles 9 to 16 and, especially, the manner in which it has developed the concept of "charges having an effect equivalent to customs duties." Thus, in one of its earlier pronouncements on the subject, the Court declared that:

> ". . . any pecuniary charge, however small and whatever its designation and mode of application, which is imposed unilaterally on domestic or foreign goods by reason of the fact that they cross a frontier . . . constitutes a charge having equivalent effect to a customs duty . . . even if it is not imposed for the benefit of the state."[34]

Again, in *Marimex*,[35] the Court stated:

> "The prohibition, in trade between Member States, of all customs duties and of all charges having equivalent effect refers to all charges demanded on the occasion of or by reason of importation which, imposed specifically on imported products and not on similar domestic products, alter their cost price . . . ."

And in *Bresciani*:[36]

> " . . . any pecuniary charge, whatever its designation and mode of application, which is unilaterally imposed on goods imported from another member state by reason of the fact that they cross a frontier, constitutes a charge having an effect equivalent to a customs duty."

### (iii) Quantitative restrictions and measures having equivalent effect[37]

**12** Like customs duties and equivalent charges, quantitative restrictions on imports[38] and exports,[39] and all measures having equivalent effect, are

---

[33] See, *inter alia*, Case 29/72 *Marimex* [1972] E.C.R. 1309; Case 39/73 *Rewe* [1973] E.C.R. 1039; Case 63/74, *Cadsky* [1975] E.C.R. 281; Case 87/75 *Bresciani* [1976] E.C.R. 129; Case 46/76 *Bauhuis* [1977] E.C.R. 5; Case 70/77 *Simmenthal* [1978] E.C.R. 1453. Of special interest is the recent Case 80/77 *Commissionaires Réunis* [1978] E.C.R. 927, in which a Community Regulation (816/70), authorising a levy on the importation of wine from Italy into France, was declared to be incompatible with Art. 13 and consequently invalid.
[34] Case 24/68 (n. 30, above) at p. 200.
[35] Case 29/72 [1972] E.C.R. at p. 1318. For an essentially similar formulation, see also Case 34/73 *Variola* [1973]E.C.R. at p. 989.
[36] Case 87/75 [1976] E.C.R. at p. 137. See also Case 132/78 *Denkavit Loire* [1979] 3 C.M.L.R. 605.
[37] See further, A.W.H. Meij and J.A. Winter, "Measures having an effect equivalent to Quantitative Restrictions" (1976) 13 C.M.L. Rev. 79; A.C. Page, "The Concept of Measures having an effect equivalent to Quantitative Restrictions" (1977) 2 E.L. Rev. 105. And see the notes by D. Wyatt, (1976) 1 E.L. Rev. 121, 304.
[38] Art. 30.
[39] Art. 34.

prohibited between Member States, subject only to the derogations which are permitted by Article 36 for reasons such as public morality, public policy, public security and the protection of health.[40] Here again, the Court has given a very broad interpretation of the concept of "measures having equivalent effect," so wide in fact that, taken at their face value, it is difficult to reconcile the judgments of the Court with the exercise of those powers which are retained by the Member States over trade matters and which do not have as their primary object the imposition of restrictions on trade. Thus, in *Dassonville*,[41] a case concerned with rules as to the certification of origin of imported whisky, the Court declared that:

"... all trading rules enacted by member states which are capable of hindering, directly or indirectly, actually or potentially, intra-community trade are to be considered as measures having an effect equivalent to quantitative restrictions."

### (iv) The relationship of the concept of "equivalent effect" to that of discriminatory taxation

13    This concept of charges and measures having equivalent effect is clearly formulated in terms which are sufficiently wide to include certain taxes which are imposed when goods are imported into a country. Thus, prior to the adoption of the common system of value-added tax, most Member States levied a turnover equalisation (or compensatory) tax—the German Umsatzausgleichsteuer being the best known example—upon imported goods.[42] Under the cumulative turnover tax system, which applied in all of the original six Member States except France, a product was subjected to tax each time it was the subject of a transaction in the course of its manufacture and marketing. A finished, or partly finished, import was subjected to an equalisation tax to compensate for the fact that a comparable domestic product might already, at that stage, have suffered turnover tax on one or more occasions. Such a tax, being imposed upon a product imported from another Member State, and not upon domestic products, on the occasion of or by reason of importation, would, at first sight, appear to fall squarely within the definition of "charge having equivalent effect" as

---

[40] These derogations are to be construed strictly, as the Court has emphasised on a number of occasions: See Case 7/68 *Commission* v. *Italy (Art Treasures)* [1968] E.C.R. 423; Case 13/68, *Salgoil* [1968] E.C.R. 453; Case 35/76 *Simmenthal* [1976] E.C.R. 1871; Case 153/78 *Commission* v. *Germany* [1980] 1 C.M.L.R. 198, and may not constitute a means of arbitrary discrimination or disguised restriction on trade between Member States: Case 34/79 *Henn and Darby* [1980] 1 C.M.L.R. 246.

[41] Case 8/74 [1974] E.C.R. 837.

[42] Turnover taxes and the value added tax are considered in detail in the next Chapter.

advanced by the Court on a number of occasions.[43] Even the Value-Added Tax, which treats importation as a chargeable event,[44] in that it taxes goods by reason of the fact that they cross frontiers, might seem to come within this concept of a "charge."[45] Yet the Court has also categorically declared that a turnover equalisation tax is to be regarded as an "internal" tax, governed by Article 95, and does not as such fall within the prohibitions of Articles 9 to 13.[46] Moreover, the Treaty itself recognises this, for Article 97 specifically permits the imposition of a turnover equalisation tax, subject to certain conditions, and Article 17(3) permits a Member State to substitute for customs duties of a fiscal nature an internal tax, provided that the latter complies with the provisions of Article 95.[47] Thus, for example, a customs duty formerly imposed for the purpose of raising revenue may validly be converted into an excise duty on the same product.[48]

**14**     This, however, does not solve the problem whether a charge imposed upon imported goods is to be regarded as one equivalent to a customs duty or as part of a system of internal taxation. In one sense, the provisions of Articles 9 to 13 and of Article 95 are complementary and, in practice, alternatively applicable.[49] Yet on numerous occasions the Court has emphatically stated that the provisions are mutually exclusive. Thus, in *Deutschmann*, it stated:

> "A comparison of Articles 13 and 95 shows clearly that they cannot be applied simultaneously, that is, the same charge—or taxation—cannot be governed by both at one and the same time."[50]

---

[43] See the passages quoted from *Marimex* and *Bresciani* (at notes 34 and 35, above).

[44] See the Second VAT Directive, Dir. 67/228, Art. 7 and, now, the Sixth Directive, Dir. 77/388, Art. 10.

[45] This point is well taken by N. Vaulont, "Die Vereinfachung der Verfahren und Förmlichkeiten im innergemeinschaftlichen Warenverkehr . . ." (1977) 12 Eur 1. at p. 12. See also F. Wooldridge and R. Plender, *op. cit.* n. 23, at p. 114. The formulation by the Court, in Case 132/78 *Denkavit Loire* [1979] 3 C.M.L.R. 605, at p. 613, in particular that the chargeable event giving rise to the duty must be identical in the case of both imported and domestic products, if taken literally would seem to imply that the imposition of VAT at the time of importation constitutes a charge equivalent to a customs duty. See also Case 55/79 *Commission* v. *Ireland* (not yet reported).

[46] See especially Case 7/67 *Wöhrmann* [1968] E.C.R. 177, at p. 184; Case 25/67 *Milchkontor* [1968] E.C.R. 207, at p. 220; Case 27/74 *Demag* [1974] E.C.R. 1037, at p. 1046.

[47] See the discussions of this point in Cases 2, 3/62 *Commission* v. *Luxembourg and Belgium* [1962] E.C.R. 425 and in Case 20/67 *Tivoli* [1968] E.C.R. 199, and see the note by K. Mailänder, (1966–67) 4 C.M.L. Rev. 330.

[48] A similar provision applies to the new member states under Art. 38 of the Act of Accession. In the United Kingdom the relationship between customs and excise has historically been far more than merely nominal.

[49] See Mailänder, *op. cit.* above, n. 47.

[50] Case 10/65 [1965] E.C.R. at p. 477. For similar statements, see also Case 57/65 *Lütticke* [1966] E.C.R. 205; Cases 2 & 3/69 *Diamantarbeiders* [1969] E.C.R. 211 (and the note by M. van Empel, (1970) 7 C.M.L. Rev. 74); Case 27/74 *Demag* [1974] E.C.R. 1037; Case 94/74 *IGAV* [1975] E.C.R. 699; Case 77/76 *Cucchi* [1977] E.C.R. 987; Case 78/76 *Steinike & Weinlig* [1977] E.C.R. 595.

It may consequently be of the greatest importance correctly to categorise a particular imposition and it is this relationship, and distinction, between "charges" and "taxes," which must now be examined.[51] It is submitted that the jurisprudence of the Court supports the following propositions:

### (a) The relationship to quantitative restrictions

**15**          Although the imposition of a charge or fee, when goods cross a frontier, may certainly have the effect of hindering intra-community trade, it seems to be established that obstacles of a pecuniary nature do not fall within Article 30 but must rather be considered to be within the scope either of Articles 9 to 16 or of Article 95.[52] It is, however, possible for both Article 30 and Articles 9 to 16 (or perhaps Article 95) to apply, separately, to different aspects of the same obstacle. Thus, a fee for public health inspection of imported goods may constitute a charge equivalent to a customs duty and be invalid,[53] or even be part of an internal system of taxation and valid under Article 95,[54] whilst the requirement to submit to inspection may constitute a measure having effect equivalent to a quantitative restriction, justifiable only on the grounds set out in Article 36.[55]

### (b) Nature of the imposition

The question, therefore, is whether the particular imposition constitutes a "charge" or a "tax." In determining this, the description—charge, duty, fee, levy or tax—is of little importance. As Advocate-General Gand stated in the *Diamantarbeiders* cases: " . . . neither the designation, the technical features nor the purpose pursued by the public authorities is decisive."[56]

Thus, whether the purpose of the imposition is to raise revenue or to deter consumption is not decisive as to its nature;[57] neither is the fact that it is paid to the State or to some other body, such as a local authority or public corporation.[58] And in *AEdle Metaller*, Advocate-General Capotorti

---

[51] This relationship has been the subject of considerable literature. In addition to the works of Barents, Burki, Vaulont, Wooldridge and Plender noted above (at nn. 22, 23, 45), see also H. Ehring, "Zur Abgrenzung der Beihilfsverbot vom Verbot der zollgleichen Abgaben und der inländischen Abgaben . . ." (1974) 9 EuR. 108; J. Tinnion, (1977) 2 E.L. Rev. 359, note.

[52] Case 74/76 *Ianelli & Volpi* [1977] E.C.R. 557; Case 89/76 *Commission* v. *Netherlands* [1977] E.C.R. 1355.

[53] Unless it can be considered to be a proper charge for a service or benefit provided to the importer or exporter, as it might be where the inspection is optional: See Case 46/76 *Bauhuis* [1977] E.C.R. 5 and Case 89/76 (note 52, above).

[54] See Case 35/76 *Simmenthal* [1976] E.C.R. 1871.

[55] This appears to be the view of the Commission: See Eleventh General Report (1977), pp. 17–19.

[56] Cases 2 & 3/69 [1969] E.C.R. at p. 229.

[57] Case 77/72 *Capolongo* [1973] E.C.R. 611.

[58] Case 29/72 *Marimex* [1972] E.C.R. 1309; Case 74/76 *Ianelli & Volpi* [1977] E.C.R. 557.

suggested that a measure might appear to be an internal tax but in reality, by reason of its protective nature, be a charge having an effect equivalent to a customs duty.[59]

**16**  (c)  *Time and place of imposition*

One naturally thinks of customs duties, and equivalent charges, as being imposed at the frontier, at the time of crossing, and internal taxation being imposed within the country. Nevertheless a "charge" does not change its nature simply because it is imposed at some time after the goods have crossed the border,[60] nor, if we accept for the present that a turnover equalisation tax or value-added tax on importation are internal taxes, does a "tax" change its nature by virtue of being imposed at the frontier and by reason of importation

(d)  *Unilateral imposition*

In some of its judgments the Court has suggested that one factor indicative of a "charge" is that it is "unilaterally" imposed upon the products of another Member State.[61] The meaning of this expression is unclear. It might suggest that where the imposition is only upon imported products (or exports) without there being a corresponding tax upon comparable domestic products, then it is unilateral and is a charge equivalent to a customs duty and thus prohibited. However, this is not the case. It is well established that the fact that there is no such comparable domestic product[62] does not prevent a Member State from levying a tax upon that product, *i.e.* a Member State is free to apply its own internal system of taxation, such as excise duties or value-added tax, to any product and is not obliged to exempt an imported product simply because no comparable domestic product exists.[63] Nor does the fact that the comparable domestic product is exempt from tax convert a tax on the imported product into a charge having equivalent effect to a customs duty, though it may, of course, constitute a discrimination prohibited by Article 95.[64] Similarly, a particular tax which applies only to imported products—such as the turnover equalisation tax—may still remain part of a system of internal taxation, *i.e.* it does not matter whether the equalisation tax is imposed under a single turnover tax statute or is contained in a separate enactment as with the Umsatzausgleichsteuer and Umsatzsteuer. It is therefore difficult to know what is intended by "unilaterally,"

[59] Case 142/77 [1978] E.C.R., at p. 1564.
[60] Case 78/76 *Steinike & Weinlig* [1977] E.C.R. 595, at p. 612.
[61] See the quotations from Cases 24/68 and 87/75 (at para. 11 above).
[62] The question of what constitutes a similar domestic product within the meaning of Art. 95 is discussed later in this chapter.
[63] Case 20/67 *Tivoli* [1968] E.C.R. 199; Case 27/67 *Fink-Frucht* [1968] E.C.R. 223; Case 31/67 *August Stier* [1968] E.C.R. 235.
[64] Case 28/67 *Mölkerei Zentrale* [1968] E.C.R. 143.

unless it be that the charge is imposed by one Member State only, as opposed to being reciprocal.[65] Yet the Court does not ever seem to have taken the view that an action which offends the Treaty becomes inoffensive if it is widely practised.

### (e) Similar criteria

17     As we have seen,[66] the Court held, in *Marimex*, that the prohibition on charges having an equivalent effect to customs duties refers to all charges demanded on the occasion of, or by reason of, importation, which are imposed specifically on imported products. It added: "The position would be different only if the pecuniary charges related to a general system of internal dues applied systematically in accordance with the same criteria to domestic products and imported products alike."[67] This insistence upon the "same criteria" recurs in a number of subsequent judgments.[68] It is somewhat puzzling. It seems to suggest that where the obligation is imposed upon the imported product according to criteria different to those which apply to the domestic product, then the imposition is a "charge," and the provisions of Articles 9 to 13 apply. This, however, is not the case, otherwise Article 95 would have little or no scope of application. It is the fact that an internal tax is applied to an imported product in a discriminatory manner, that is, according to different criterion which offends Article 95. This is made abundantly clear in many of the Court's decisions concerning the latter Article.[69] Also, as we have already seen, the fact that a tax is imposed only upon the imported product, as where there is no comparable domestic product, does not prevent its being considered part of a system of internal taxation and does not transform it into a "charge," yet in such a case there can be no "same criteria."

18     What appears to have happened is that the Court, in the test propounded in *Marimex* and the other cases referred to, has telescoped together two separate rules or  principles. The true position seems to be that, first, an imposition on imported products by reason of the fact that they cross a

---

[65] This seems to be suggested in Case 89/76 *Commission* v. *Netherlands* [1977] E.C.R. 1355, where the Court took the view that a fee for phytosanitary inspection on the export of plants was not unilateral, since it was levied in accordance with a Convention on a similar basis to the practice in other member states.

[66] Above, para. 11.

[67] Case 29/72 [1972] E.C.R., at p. 1318.

[68] *e.g.* Case 77/72 *Capolongo* [1973] E.C.R. 611; Case 87/75 *Bresciani* [1976] E.C.R. 129; Case 77/76 *Cucchi* [1977] E.C.R. 987; Case 70/77 *Simmenthal* [1978] E.C.R. 1453; Case 222/78 *ICAP* [1979] 3 C.M.L.R. 475.

[69] Case 7/69 *Commission* v. *Italy (Imported Wool)* [1970] E.C.R. 111; Case 16/69 *Commission* v. *Italy (Eaux de Vie)* [1969] E.C.R. 377; Case 28/69 *Commission* v. *Italy (Cocoa)* [1970] E.C.R. 187; Case 77/69 *Commission* v. *Belgium (Tax on Timber)* [1970] E.C.R. 237; Case 127/75 *Bobie* [1976] E.C.R. 1079; Case 20/76 *Schöttle* [1977] E.C.R. 247; Case 55/79 *Commission* v. *Ireland* [1980] 1 C.M.L.R. 734.

frontier constitutes a charge equivalent to a customs duty, and is consequently invalid, unless it forms part of a general system of internal taxation:
secondly, if it does form part of such a system, it is invalid if it is imposed
according to criteria which are not the same for both imported and domestic
products (where comparable domestic products exist) and *in consequence*
discriminates against the imported *product*.[70] Thus where, because different
criteria are applied, the one product is taxed more heavily than the other, it
does not seem that the excess is to be regarded as a charge equivalent to a
customs duty.[71] The position might, perhaps, be different if, for example, an
imported product was subjected to two distinct impositions of tax, the one
by virtue of importation alone and the other according to criteria similar to
those applying to domestic products. The former imposition might be
regarded as a charge equivalent to a customs duty.[72] In the case of an
imported product it would normally be unimportant whether this were to be
regarded as a "charge" plus a "tax" or as double, discriminatory, taxation.
However, as will be seen later, in the case of an export, or of an import from
a third country, the distinction may be crucial.

### (v)   The "Capolongo exception"

**19**      The foregoing analysis has demonstrated that, the provisions applying to
charges having equivalent effect to customs duties and those applying to
internal taxation being mutually exclusive, the first task is to categorise
correctly a particular imposition as either a "charge" or a "tax." Unfortunately, an analysis of the Court's jurisprudence yields no easy answer as
to how this is to be done.

But even to this initial act of classification there is at least one exception.
In *Capolongo*,[73] a question was referred to the Court by the Pretore of
Conegliano, concerning the interpretation of Articles 13, 92 and 95, in connection with the imposition of a tax upon cardboard containers for eggs
imported from Germany. The tax was imposed on precisely the same basis
as that applicable to domestic cardboard and cellulose containers. The
objection to it, by the importer, was based upon the fact that the proceeds of
the tax were paid to a public corporation whose objects were to promote the
production in Italy and sale of paper and cellulose products. Thus, in effect,
the domestic producer, though paying the same tax, got its money back in
the form of benefits and subsidies in which the importer did not share. Faced
with this question, the Court declared that:

[70] As will be seen in the next section of this chapter, it appears to be necessary to add the
italicised words.
[71] This was argued, and rejected by the Court, in Case 7/67 *Wöhrmann* [1968] E.C.R.
177 and in Case 25/67, *Milchkontor* [1968] E.C.R. 207, see esp. p. 220.
[72] This is suggested by the ruling in the Court in Case 35/76 *Simmenthal* [1976] E.C.R.
1871.
[73] Case 77/72 [1973] E.C.R. 611.

"In the interpretation of the concept 'charge having an effect equivalent to a customs duty on imports', the destination of the financial charges levied must be taken into account. In effect, when such a financial charge or duty is intended exclusively to support activities which specifically profit taxed domestic products, it can follow that the general duty levied according to the same criteria on the imported product and the domestic product nevertheless constitutes for the former a net supplementary tax burden whilst for the latter it constitutes in reality a set-off against benefits or aids previously received.

Consequently, a duty within the general system of internal taxation applying systematically to domestic and imported products according to the same criteria, can nevertheless constitute a charge having an effect equivalent to a customs duty on imports, when such a contribution is intended to support activities which specifically benefit the taxed domestic product."[74]

**20**      This raises the rather disturbing proposition that, even where the tax on the imported and domestic products is ostensibly the same, a court might be required to examine the use to which the proceeds of the tax are put and to hold that, by virtue of a subsidy to the domestic product, the tax constitutes in reality a charge equivalent to a customs duty on imports.[75] However, this is so only where the tax "exclusively" and "specifically" benefits the domestic product and the scope of this exception has been further narrowed in subsequent rulings by the Court. Thus, in *IGAV*,[76] it was stated that this must be the "sole purpose" of the disputed charge and in *Cucchi*[77] and *Interzuccheri*,[78] concerning an Italian surcharge on sugar products, part of which was applied as aid to domestic sugar manufacturers and beet growers, the Court ruled that:

"A duty falling within a general system of internal taxation applying to domestic products as well as to imported products according to the same criteria can constitute a charge having an effect equivalent to a customs duty on imports only if it has the sole purpose of financing activities for the specific advantage of the taxed domestic product, if the taxed product and the domestic product benefiting from it are the same and if the charges imposed on the domestic product are made good in full."[79]

---

[74] [1973] E.C.R. , at p. 623.

[75] it might also, at least in theory, constitute a charge equivalent to a customs duty on exports: See Case 2/73 *Geddo* [1973] E.C.R. 865; Case 51/74 *Van der Hulst* [1975] E.C.R. 79.

[76] Case 94/74 [1975] E.C.R. 699. This case was also concerned with the Italian levy on paper products: see also Case 74/76 *Ianelli & Volpi* [1977] E.C.R. 557.

[77] Case 77/76 [1977] E.C.R. 987.

[78] Case 105/76 [1977] E.C.R. 1029. For comments upon these decisions, see E.P. Burki, (1978) 14 C.D.E. 101; J. Tinnion, (1977) 2 E.L. Rev. 359; J. Usher, "The Consequences of the notion of a Single Market . . . " (1977/2) L.I.E.I. 39.

[79] [1977] E.C.R. at pp. 1010, 1043. See also Case 91/78 *Hansen* [1980] 1 C.M.L.R. 162.

**21**     Consequently, it is not sufficient that the similar domestic product, and perhaps other domestic products as well, receive some part of the charge in the form of aid or subsidy, though elsewhere in these judgments the Court suggests that if the sole purpose is to benefit those particular domestic products it may suffice if the charge is made good even in part.[80]

In any event, the "*Capolongo* exception" now seems to be a very narrow one and there are likely to be very few cases which meet the test.[81] The reason for the exception appears to be that:

> " . . . such a fiscal device would in fact only appear to be a system of internal taxation and accordingly could by reason of its protective character be termed a charge having an effect equivalent to customs duties . . . ."[82]

This explanation, provided by the Court, comes close to the submission of Advocate-General Trabucchi, in *IGAV*,[83] that the Capolongo principle is restricted to a case "involving substantial fraud on the law." A similar view appears in the submission of Advocate-General Capotorti, in *AEdle Metaller*,[84] that a charge which is formally not discriminatory, but which has the sole purpose of financing activities for the specfic advantage of the taxed domestic product would " . . . only appear to be internal taxation whereas in reality, by reason of its protective nature, it could be termed a charge having an effect equivalent to customs duties . . . ."

**22**     The true rationale of the exception thus appears to be that the Court will look beyond the mere form of the imposition in question and will have regard to its substance. If this is the case, then the "substance doctrine" might find other applications apart from the "subsidy-back" situation. In particular, one might question whether, where an internal tax is imposed upon an imported product which has no domestic equivalent (given that a Member State remains free to tax such a product[85]) at a rate which is exorbitant and has a protective nature, this might not also constitute a "charge."[86]

### (vi)   The importance of the distinction

**23**     In many cases the distinction between a "charge" and a "tax" will be unimportant. A provision which discriminates against imported products,

---

[80]  *Ibid.* at pp. 1005, 1041.
[81]  See J. Usher (*op. cit.* n. 78, above).
[82]  |1977| E.C.R. at p. 1005.
[83]  Case 94/74 |1979| E.C.R., at p. 718. See also R. Barents, (1978) 15 C.M.L. Rev. 415.
[84]  Case 142/77 |1978| E.C.R. 1543, at p. 1564.
[85]  See above, paras. 16, 17.
[86]  Some support for this proposition is found in the arguments in Case 20/67 *Tivoli* |1968| E.C.R. 199 and in the submissions of Advocate-General Gand in Case 31/67 *August Stier* |1968| E.C.R. 235.

whether it be classified as a "charge" or as a "tax" will be invalid, at least to the extent to which it discriminates. However, the prohibitions contained in Articles 9 to 16 are not restricted to cases of discrimination[87] and those provisions and Article 95 are governed by different systems. Thus, in *Deutschmann*,[88] the distinction was important because of the difference in the timetables for abolition. This difference has, of course, ceased to be relevant though it will apparently become so again with the accession of Greece to the Community.[89] There are other differences, too, which remain important:

**(a)  Exports.**  Articles 9, 12 and 16 prohibit customs duties on exports and charges having equivalent effect.[90] On the other hand Article 95 refers only to "products of other Member States," *i.e.* to imports. Thus it does not prohibit an internal *tax* which discriminates against exports,[91] though in the recent *AEdle Metaller* case the Court seems to have declared otherwise.[92] This issue will be considered further in the next section of this chapter.[93]

**(b)  External trade.**  Article 95 refers only to the products of other member states: similarly Articles 9 to 16 are concerned with customs duties between Member States. However, the prohibition upon customs duties and charges having equivalent effect has been extended by various Regulations, pursuant to the Common Agricultural Policy and the Common Customs Tariff, and by the Treaties of Yaoundé and Lomé in respect of trade with ACP countries, with the effect that customs duties and equivalent charges are also prohibited in many transactions with non-member States.[94] By contrast, Article 95 has no application to external trade.[95]

**(c)  Extent of the invalidity.**  An internal tax which discriminates against imports is, in Community law, invalid only to the extent of the discrimina-

---

[87] See Case 24/68 *Commission* v. *Italy (Statistical Levy)* [1969] E.C.R. 193; Cases 2 & 3/69 *Diamantarbeiders* [1969] E.C.R. 211.

[88] Case 10/65 [1969] E.C.R. 456, and see K. Mailänder (1966–67) 4 C.M.L. Rev. 330 (note).

[89] Under the Greek Treaty of Accession, Art. 29, existing charges equivalent to customs duties must be progressively abolished by 1986. The provisions of Art. 95 of the EEC Treaty apply immediately.

[90] See Case 2/73 *Geddo* [1973] E.C.R. 865; Case 51/74 *Van Der Hulst* [1975] E.C.R. 79; Case 89/76 *Commission* v. *Netherlands* [1977] E.C.R. 1355.

[91] Case 27/74 *Demag* [1974] E.C.R. 1037.

[92] Case 142/77 [1978] E.C.R. 1543.

[93] See below, at paras, 56–60.

[94] See Case 2/73 *Geddo* [1973] E.C.R. 865; Case 34/73 *Variola* [1973] E.C.R. 981; Cases 37 & 38/73 *Indiamex* [1973] E.C.R 1609; Case 21/75 *Schroeder* [1975] E.C.R. 905; Case 87/75 *Bresciani* [1976] E.C.R. 129; Case 137/77 *Neumann* [1978] E.C.R. 1623; Case 138/77 *Ludwig* [1978] E.C.R. 1645.

[95] Case 7/67 *Wöhrmann* [1968] E.C.R. 177; Case 20/67 *Tivoli* [1968] E.C.R. 199; Case 148/77 *Hansen & Balle* [1978] E.C.R. 1787 (though the prohibition applies to trade with French overseas departments, by virtue of Art. 227 of the Treaty).

tion.[96] By contrast, a provision which constitutes a charge with equivalent effect to a customs duty would seem to be invalid *in toto*,[97] though in some instances it may be possible to sever a provision, one part being regarded as a non-discriminatory internal tax and the other as a "charge".[98]

### C.  THE PROHIBITION OF DISCRIMINATORY TAXATION

**24**    The basic prohibition is set out in the first paragraph of Article 95, which provides that:

> "No Member State shall impose, directly or indirectly, on the products of other Member States any internal taxation of any kind in excess of that imposed directly or indirectly on similar domestic products."

The various parts of this provision require further examination in the light of the Court's jurisprudence.[99]

#### (i)  Internal taxation of any kind

**25**    As has already been observed, in determining whether or not a particular imposition constitutes "taxation," neither the designation, the technical features nor the purpose pursued by the public authorities is decisive.[1] This must necessarily be so for even within a single legal system the distinction between a tax and some other charge of quasi-fiscal nature may be unclear[2] and, within the Community, one country may classify as a tax what another treats as a special charge, fee or levy. Similarly, the fact that it is imposed for the purpose of raising revenue, or is paid to the state rather than to some other body, does not determine the issue.[3] As Advocate-General Roemer has said:

> " . . . fine distinctions of this nature are irrelevent with regard to Article 95; for its application the significant point is the resultant burden,

---

[96] It is for the national law to determine whether the whole tax or only the excess, discriminatory, portion is invalid, but it is clear that Community law will be satisfied in the latter event: Case 34/67 *Lück* [1968] E.C.R. 245, and see below, paras. 77, 78.

[97] For this reason, if for no other, the restriction placed upon the "*Capolongo* principle" is desirable: See J. Tinnion, *op. cit.* above, n. 78.

[98] Case 35/76 *Simmenthal* [1976] E.C.R. 1871.

[99] For comprehensive analyses of the provision, see especially D. Ehle, "Auslegungs-probleme der steuerrechtlichen Vorschriften des EWG-Vertrags" (1967) N.J.W. 1689; H. Ehring, *op. cit.* above, n. 51 and R. Wägenbaur, "Das Verbot steuerlicher Diskriminierung nach dem EWG-Vertrag in Lichte der Rechtsprechung des Gerichtshof" (1969) 3 Eur. 20.

[1] *Per* Advocate-General Gand in Cases 2 & 3/69 *Diamantarbeiders* [1969] E.C.R. 211 at p. 229.

[2] See the arguments of the original plaintiff, concerning the German case law, in Case 10/65 *Deutschmann* [1965] E.C.R. 469 at p. 471.

[3] See above, para. 15.

17

whilst in principle regard is not had for the means by which it is imposed."[4]

Clearly, Article 95 is not restricted to sales or turnover taxes and excise duties: it can apply to special taxes, or quasi-fiscal charges, such as a stamp tax on timber,[5] a contract duty,[6] or a levy on dealings in precious metals.[7]

A further requirement is that it be an "internal" tax but, as we have seen, a turnover equalisation tax imposed upon an import comes within this definition,[8] as may a monopoly equalisation tax[9] and, as cases already discussed demonstrate, a fee for public health or sanitary inspection of imported goods may also form part of a system of internal taxation when certain requirements are met.[10]

### (ii)   Imposed directly or indirectly on products

**26**      The Article speaks of taxation of any kind imposed directly or indirectly on products. In principle it is, therefore, not restricted to those taxes which are commonly called "indirect taxes"[11] and, as the Court has emphasised, the expression "directly or indirectly" is to be given a wide meaning.[12] However, the important words in this context are "on the products." In the great majority of disputes involving Article 95 it is the validity of the tax imposed on the imported product which is in question and the amount of this tax is generally apparent or easily ascertainable. The problem, usually, is to determine the precise tax burden imposed upon the corresponding domestic product. This will be discussed in greater detail later, but here it is necessary to consider which taxes may be taken into account in determining the burden. On the one hand it is clear from the actual wording of the Article that it is not only those taxes directly and specifically imposed upon the actual product which are to be taken into account. Regard must also be had to those taxes imposed on the domestic product at all earlier stages of its manufacture and marketing[13]—something which was, of course, of the greatest importance in determining the burden imposed by a cumulative turnover tax system. On the other hand no account may be taken of non-

---

[4] Case 29/72 *Marimex* [1972] E.C.R. 1309, at p. 1324. (Though perhaps it would be more accurate to say "inconclusive" rather than "irrelevant").

[5] Case 77/69 *Commission* v. *Belgium* [1970] E.C.R. 237.

[6] Case 2/73 *Geddo* [1973] E.C.R. 865.

[7] Case 142/77 *A Edle Metaller* [1978] E.C.R. 1543.

[8] See above, para. 16.

[9] Case 13/70 *Cinzano* [1970] E.C.R. 1089; Case 45/75 *Rewe* [1976] E.C.R. 181; Case 148/77 *Hansen & Balle* [1978] E.C.R. 1787.

[10] See, especially Case 35/76 *Simmenthal* [1976] E.C.R. 1871; Case 46/76 *Bauhuis* [1977] E.C.R. 5.

[11] *Cf.* Art. 98, which specifically refers to indirect taxation.

[12] Case 28/67 *Mölkerei Zentrale* [1968] E.C.R. 143; Case 34/67 *Lück* [1968] E.C.R. 245; Case 55/79 *Commission* v. *Ireland* [1980] 1 C.M.L.R. 734.

[13] Case 28/67 *Mölkerei Zentrale* [1968] E.C.R., at p. 155.

fiscal burdens borne by the domestic product, such as the higher costs of domestic raw materials[14] or higher manufacturing costs.[15]

27    Between these extremes the position is less clear. As Advocate-General Gand pointed out, in *Mölkerei Zentrale*, the manufacture of a product involves various stages and the use of auxiliary materials in packaging, transportation and marketing: "All those factors are combined in the manufacture of the product; internal taxation indirectly imposed on a product must be understood to include charges imposed on all those various elements."[16]

Thus, taxes on raw materials processed or consumed in the course of manufacture, on packaging and on the sale itself are to be taken into account. Even a tax on the transportation of a product, at least in so far as it can be attributed to that product,[17] is included for, as the Court held in *Schöttle*,[18] the concept of tax on a product must be interpreted in a wide sense and includes a tax which has an immediate effect upon the cost of the product. The Court here appears to be on rather dangerous ground. The tax in question was a special road tax, since repealed by Germany, levied on the transportation of goods and assessed on a tonne per kilometre basis. Although the tax applied to the transportation of both imported and domestic goods, it was objected to by the original plaintiff (who had been charged with the tax on the carriage of a load of gravel from a town in Alsace to Stuttgart) on the basis that it discriminated against imported goods, the reason being that there was an exemption from the tax for journeys within a 50 kilometre radius inside Germany but, in the case of international transport, the exemption was restricted to certain border zones. The effect was that a journey of a similar distance wholly within Germany would have been exempt. On a preliminary reference under Article 177 from the German court, the Court ruled that such a tax was included in the concept of taxation imposed indirectly on products within the meaning of Article 95. On the facts of that particular case this is not too difficult to accept: the burden of the tax clearly fell upon that specific load of gravel. Nor should it make any difference whether the person accountable for the tax is the purchaser or the transporter (who happened to be one and the same person in that case) : every tax on products is, in that sense, imposed upon a person. The real difficulty is to distinguish between those taxes which are taxes on products, within the meaning of Article 95, and those which are taxes on producers.[19] There are, after all, many taxes, such as income tax,

[14] Cases 2 & 3/62 *Commission* v. *Luxembourg and Belgium* [1962] E.C.R. 425, especially at pp. 442–443.

[15] Case 28/69 *Commission* v. *Italy (Cocoa)* [1970] E.C.R. 187, 194; Case 169/78 *Commission* v. *Italy* (not yet reported).

[16] [1968] E.C.R. 143, at p. 163.

[17] As will be seen in the next chapter, the adoption of a common system of value added tax solves many of these difficulties.

[18] Case 20/76 [1977] E.C.R. 247.

[19] The distinction, drawn in Germany, between Produktbezogene and Faktorbezogene taxes, seems more appropriate.

corporation tax, property tax, and business taxes which, according to most modern economists, have an effect upon the cost of products, though perhaps not an "immediate" effect in the sense intended by the Court. To what extent, if at all, may such taxes be taken into account in comparing the tax burdens of the products in question?

**28**     This issue was considered in one of the earlier tax cases to come before the Court, in proceedings brought by the Commission against Italy in respect of an alleged infringement of Article 96.[20] Italian law allowed a refund, on the exportation of engineering products, of various domestic taxes borne by those products, including registration, stamp and mortgage duties and charges on licences, concessions, motor vehicles and advertising. Under Article 96 it is provided that, where products are exported to another Member State, any repayment of internal taxation shall not exceed the internal taxation imposed on them, whether directly or indirectly. The Italian government argued that the remitted taxes were "indirect internal taxation", in the sense that they affected the cost of manufacture and the price of the products. The Commission's view, however, was that these were taxes imposed on the undertaking, rather than on the exported products as such. The Court favoured the arguments of the Commission and held that:

> "As used in Article 96, the expression "directly" must be understood to ⸜ refer to taxation imposed on the finished product, whilst the expression "indirectly" refers to taxation imposed during the various stages of production on the raw materials or semi-finished products used in the manufacture of the product. It is clear from the legal measure which introduced them and from the subject matter and nature of the registration, stamp and mortgage duties and the charges on licences and concessions, cars and advertising, that they are *imposed on the producer undertaking . . . rather than on the products as such.*"[21]

In consequence, such taxes could not be the subject of repayment. Although the case was concerned with Article 96, the expression "internal taxation imposed on them, whether directly or indirectly" is essentially the same as that employed in Article 95 and, since the provisions deal with two sides of the same issue, it would seem proper that the expression bear the same meaning in both. One can therefore conclude that the taxes with which Article 95 is concerned are only those taxes imposed, directly or indirectly, upon the product itself—though, as the *Schöttle* case demonstrates, this is to be interpreted widely—and not with forms of direct taxation imposed on the producer.

---

[20] Case 45/64 *Commission* v. *Italy* [1965] E.C.R. 857. Art. 96 will be considered in a later section of this chapter.
[21] [1965] E.C.R., at p. 866. (Italics added).

### (iii) Comparability of the tax burden

**29**     The essential characteristic of the prohibition contained in Article 95 is that the tax burden on an imported product should not exceed that imposed upon the comparable domestic product. It is consequently necessary to take into account not only the rate of the applicable internal tax as applied to both products but also the basis of assessment.[22] That is to say, the effective burden is arrived at by applying the tax rate, expressed as a percentage or as a sum of money, to the relevant tax base, expressed in terms of the value, volume, quantity or other characteristic (*e.g.* alcoholic strength) of the products.

    The application of a higher rate of tax to the imported product than that imposed upon its domestic equivalent consequently constitutes a discrimination against the import unless, by virtue of the fact that the rates are applied to different tax bases, the overall tax burden is not greater. Thus a turnover equalisation tax, imposed at a rate higher than the domestic turnover tax rate, is not discriminatory in so far as it does no more than compensate for the fact that the equivalent domestic product has already borne other charges to the tax at earlier stages in its production.[23]

    Conversely, where the taxes are imposed at the same nominal rate but the criteria for determining the appropriate tax bases are different, this may result in a discrimination against the imported product. As we have seen, the application of different criteria may, in some cases, result in the imposition upon the imported product being classified as a charge equivalent to a customs duty rather than as part of a system of internal taxation.[24] And where the imported product is subjected to a double charge to tax, whilst the domestic product is taxed only once, it may be either that one of the impositions is treated as an equivalent charge[25] or that the taxes are both regarded as internal and that the overall burden, by virtue of the double imposition, is discriminatory.[26]

**30**     Discrimination in the selection of the appropriate tax base may take various forms, as many cases coming before the Court illustrate. For example, the taxes may be calculated at different times or stages of production, as where tax on imported wool was assessed on its value at the time of importation, when it would normally be carded and combed, whilst that on

---

[22] Case 74/76 *Ianelli & Volpi* [1977] E.C.R. 557, at p. 577.

[23] It is clear, from cases such as Case 25/67 *Milchkontor* [1968] E.C.R. 207 and Case 34/67 *Lück* [1968] E.C.R. 245, that, despite the higher rate of equalisation tax, it would be offensive only if, and to the extent that, the overall tax burden were higher on the imported product. The power to fix average compensatory rates, under Art. 97, may be considered as a derogation from the basic principle: See below, para. 88.

[24] See above, paras. 17, 18.

[25] Case 35/76 *Simmenthal* [1976] E.C.R. 1871.

[26] Case 14/72 *FOR* v. *VKS* [1973] E.C.R. 193 (separate taxation on the importation of machinery and its installation—this would not create a problem under the value added tax system).

domestic wool was commonly based upon its value as raw wool.[27] Alcohol seems especially susceptible to discriminatory tax treatment:[28] in one of the earlier cases, Italy was held to have discriminated against imported spirits, which were assessed to tax on the basis of a notional minimum alcohol content of 70 per cent., whereas domestic spirits were assessed according to their actual alcohol content, normally considerably lower.[29] Another form of discrimination occurs where the tax on the imported and domestic product is calculated in the same way, but the latter's tax is reduced by permitting deductions or exemptions which are denied in the case of the imported product, as, for example, where certain production overheads may be deducted from the tax base of the domestic products,[30] or exemptions or lower rates are given to products of small domestic breweries, distilleries or other enterprises.[31] Even different conditions for payment of tax, such as an extended credit period in the case of the domestic product, may constitute a discrimination within the terms of Article 95.[32]

A particular difficulty, in instances of this type, is that the import may be taxed in the same way as some, or most, of the equivalent domestic products but, by virtue of some measure (such as a reduction or exemption for small undertakings) be less favourably treated than other domestic products in the same category. This, essentially, was the problem referred to the Court in the *Bobie* case.[33] The original plaintiffs were importers of beer from Belgium into Germany. Under the German Biersteuergesetz domestic beer was taxed on a sliding scale according to the quantity produced by the particular brewery, the purpose of favouring small breweries being to counteract the tendency towards mergers in the brewing industry. Imported beer, however, had been taxed at a flat rate because the graduated rate was considered inappropriate for imports as the authorities might lack the relevant data. The effect of the system was that imported beer was taxed at a rate somewhat lower than that which might be applied to beer from the largest domestic breweries but well above the lowest rate applicable to small concerns.

[27] Case 7/69 *Commission* v. *Italy* [1970] E.C.R. 111. Similarly, Case 77/69 *Commission* v. *Belgium* [1970] E.C.R. 237, where imported timber would usually be semi-finished, *e.g.* sawn into planks, whereas domestic timber was taxed on its value standing or when felled.
[28] See the examples given, regarding excise duties on alcoholic beverages in (EEC) Tenth General Report (1967) pp. 108–109, and in (EC) Bull. 12–69 pp. 21 *et seq.*
[29] Case 16/69 *Commission* v. *Italy* [1969] E.C.R. 377.
[30] Case 45/75 *Rewe* [1976] E.C.R. 181, concerning the German Monopolausgleich on imported vermouth.
[31] Case 127/75 *Bobie* [1976] E.C.R. 1079; Case 148/77 *Hansen & Balle* [1978] E.C.R. 1787. The exemption for short-haul road transportation, in the *Schöttle* case (above, para. 27) also falls into this category. And see Case 21/79 *Commission* v. *Italy*.
[32] Case 55/79 *Commission* v. *Ireland* [1980] 1 C.M.L.R. 734, in which domestic producers of alcohol were permitted to defer payment of duty, for approximately six weeks, on payment of a very small additional duty. This was considered to constitute a virtually interest-free loan of the duty. See also the question in the European Parliament (E.P.W.Q. 943/78: O.J. 1979, c 68/26) concerning the credit period for payment of excise duty on wines in the United Kingdom.
[33] Case 127/75 [1976] E.C.R. 1079. See the comments of G. Morse, (1976) 1 E.L. Rev. 565.

31    Three possible solutions to the problem present themselves:

(*a*) It should be sufficient that the imported product is not taxed more heavily than the most heavily taxed comparable domestic product. This is unacceptable and contrary to the whole spirit of Article 95, since the theoretical maximum domestic rate might apply to a very small proportion of the domestic production (or even none at all), giving the bulk of domestic products a competitive advantage over imports.

(*b*) The imported product should be taxed at the rate applicable to the typical domestic product, *i.e.* a form of notional "average" rate should be applied.[34] This might be the fairest solution, but Article 97 only permits expressly the establishment of average rates in the case of turnover taxes calculated on a cumulative multi-stage basis and this principle would seem not to be applicable in the case of other taxes.[35]

(*c*) The imported product should not be taxed at a rate higher than the lowest rate applicable to the corresponding domestic product. This achieves the purpose of ensuring that no discrimination exists against the imported product, though at the expense of placing most of the domestic production at a competitive disadvantage.[36] This can perhaps be justified on the ground that a Member State is not obliged to adopt a graduated scale of this type and, if it does not wish to favour imports, it should find some other, legitimate, means of preferring its small producers, such as a lower rate of income tax on the profits of such concerns or some form of state aid, compatible with Articles 92 to 94.

32    Faced with this question, the Court clearly rejected the first solution and appeared to prefer the third. It declared that:

".... although a Member State may apply to the imported product a system of taxation different from the one to which the similar domestic product is subject, it may only do so if the charge to tax on the imported product remains at all times the same as or lower than the charge applicable to the similar domestic product."[37]

This is consistent with its earlier judgment, in *Rewe*, where it held that Article 95 is infringed—

"where the taxation on the imported and domestic products are calculated in a different manner on the basis of different criteria which

[34] This solution had earlier been recommended as an interim measure by the Commission.
[35] See below, para. 88. However, the Court, in Case 55/79 (above, n. 32) appeared to accept that an "average" tax deferral period in the case of Irish beer producers, to allow for "maturing time," would not have been contrary to Art. 95.
[36] In Case 148/77 *Hansen & Balle* [1978] E.C.R. 1787, concerning the taxation of rum imported into Germany, the rate applicable to the import was that which affected 95 per cent. of domestic spirits, only 5 per cent. being taxed at a lower rate. Nevertheless it was held that the imported product was entitled to be taxed at the lower rate.
[37] [1976] E.C.R., at p. 1087.

lead, *if only in certain cases*, to higher taxation being imposed on the imported product."[38]

The Court also rejected the view that a similar graduated scale could be applied to imported beer by treating the importer as though he had been a domestic producer but, though it declined to rule on the compatibility with the Treaty of a further suggested formula, it apparently accepted that a single scale, taking into account the production volume of the foreign brewery, and applied to domestic and imported products alike, would not offend Article 95. This produces a curious result that, though the economic factors in another Member State might be quite different and it might even be desirable to promote concentrations in the particular industry there, competition is distorted as between large and small concerns by making exportation to the state which operates such a graduated system more profitable for the latter. It also appears to suggest that, in determining what constitutes a "similar domestic product," the comparison is made, not with beer, but with beer produced by a brewery of similar size.[39]

**33**     One further question which seems to call for consideration is whether, given that both the rate of tax and the criteria for taxing imported and domestic products are the same, there can yet be discrimination, such as is prohibited by Article 95, by virtue of the choice of the particular criteria. For example, if the wine produced by country A is invariably more expensive, due to higher labour costs, climatic conditions or some such reason, than that produced in country B, then if the latter taxes all wine on an *ad valorem* basis a bottle of wine imported from A will bear more tax than the domestic bottle, whereas if tax is assessed on a volume basis it will not. (The Commission was indeed confronted with a similar problem with respect to the harmonisation of taxes on manufactured tobacco: an *ad valorem* tax discriminated against the "quality" cigarettes favoured by some Member States, a tax based on tobacco weight against those produced in others).[40] One would  suppose that the selection of value, or selling price, as the appropriate tax base could not be criticised: it is, after all, the basis of the common system of value-added tax adopted by the Community and corresponds to what would generally be considered to be equitable in a tax system. The choice of any reasonable tax base, as opposed to an equally reasonable alternative one, would seem to be compatible with Article 95, provided always that it is applied to imported and domestic products alike. It might perhaps be otherwise if the selected criterion was a "perverse" one,

---

[38] [1976] E.C.R., at p. 195. (Italics added). See also Cases 168, 169 and 171/78 *Commission* v. *France, Italy,* and *Denmark* (not yet reported), discussed below at paras. 38–43.

[39] The discriminating drinker, at any rate the English proponents of "real ale," will of course affirm that there is no similarity between the products of large and small breweries, but it is doubtful whether it is this type of comparison that is intended by the Treaty. The concept of "similar products" is discussed below.

[40] See below, Chapter 3, paras. 226–229.

which clearly had the effect of discriminating against imports. Thus far, the Court has not been called to rule on this precise problem, though in the recent action against Denmark,[41] Advocate-General Reischl expressed the opinion that a genuine *ad valorem* tax on spirits, though it would have the result that domestic akvavit would be taxed less heavily than most other imported spirits (the cost of production being lower) would not be prohibited by the Treaty.

It is suggested that the proper question to be asked, under Article 95, is whether the internal tax is imposed upon the imported product in a discriminatory manner, rather than simply whether the actual amount of tax imposed is greater than that on the similar domestic product. But in either event this raises the issue of when two products may be said to be "similar." It is to this issue that we must now turn.

### (iv)  The comparability of products

**34**      The first two paragraphs of Article 95 contain separate, though complimentary, prohibitions. It is provided that:

> "No Member State shall impose, directly or indirectly, on the products of other Member States any internal taxation of any kind in excess of that imposed directly or indirectly *on similar domestic products.*
> Furthermore, no Member State shall impose on the products of other Member States any internal taxation of such a nature as to afford *indirectly protection to other products.*"[42]

The intention underlying these prohibitions is reasonably clear[43]: not only may imported products not be taxed more heavily than similar domestic products but they may also not be taxed in such a way as to afford protection to a competing domestic product. As the Court has explained:

> "The second paragraph of Article 95 is complementary to the first. It prohibits the imposition of any internal tax which imposes a higher charge on an imported than a domestic product which competes with the imported product, although it is not similar to it within the meaning of the first paragraph of Article 95."[44]

Simple though this concept may be, its application gives rise to severe difficulties. The comparison which must be made under the first paragraph is essentially an arithmetical one—a comparison of the tax burden imposed on each product. That under the second paragraph is an economic one—given that different, though competing, products may bear different

---

[41]  Case 171/78 (not yet reported). See below, paras. 38–40.
[42]  Italics added.
[43]  Article 95 appears to be based upon the corresponding provisions of the General Agreement on Trade and Tariffs (GATT), in particular Art. III, para. 2.
[44]  Case 27/67 *Fink Frucht* [1968] E.C.R. 223, at p. 234.

tax burdens, is the difference such as to afford protection to the domestic product, *i.e.* to distort the conditions of fair and free competition?[45] It is consequently necessary to examine the respective scopes of the two paragraphs and the relationship between them.

(a)  *"Similar products"*

**35**     The term is nowhere defined in the Treaty[46] and the jurisprudence of the Court until recently provided little real guidance. In the *Fink-Frucht* reference, the Court stated:

> "Similarity between products within the meaning of the first paragraph of Article 95 exists when the products in question are normally to be considered as coming within the same fiscal, customs or statistical classification, as the case may be."[47]

Again, in the *Cocoa* case:

> " . . . products such as those in question which fall under the same classification for tax purposes must be considered as "similar" within the meaning of Article 95(1)."[48]

And in *Rewe,* the Court declared:

> "The fact that the domestic product and the imported product are or are not classified under the same heading in the Common Customs Tariff constitutes an important factor in this assessment."[49]

**36**     Such a test, especially if it is restricted to the categories of the common customs tariff, does have the advantage of legal certainty and provides a relatively simple guide for national courts to follow,[50] and there is some logic in requiring that those products which are to be treated the same for the purposes of customs duties should also receive the same tax treatment. Nevertheless, Member States might be disconcerted to learn that, in agreeing to a matter of customs classification, they had automatically accepted that the same classifications should apply in their internal tax systems. Moreover, the categories of the common customs tariff itself would seem quite inappropriate in many cases. For example, all private motor vehicles

---

[45] See R. Wägenbaur, *"Le Droit de la Communauté Economique Européene"* (Ed. J. Mégret *et al.*) (1973), Vol. 5, at p. 13 (referred to hereafter as Mégret).

[46] The definition of "like product" in Art. 5 of Reg. 459/68/EEC (concerning dumping) is of minimal assistance.

[47] [1968] E.C.R. 223, at p. 234.

[48] Case 28/69 *Commission* v. *Italy* [1970] E.C.R. 187, at p. 194. If the reference here is to national tax categories this is surely to beg the question.

[49] Case 45/75 [1976] E.C.R. 181, at p. 195.

[50] Thus the Finanzgericht, Hamburg was apparently prepared to accept that imported almonds and domestic walnuts might be "similar," since both were classified as "nuts" in the customs tariff: see *Re Tax on Imported Almonds* [1971] C.M.L.R. 87. But in the current tariff (Reg. 2800/78, Ch. 08.05), the category of nuts is itself sub-divided and different rates of duty are payable: almonds (bitter)—free, almonds (other)—7%, walnuts—8%, pistacchios—2%, etc.

fall into one category, yet most Member States apply graduated rates of vehicle tax or registration fees according to engine size,[51] a practice which is surely both acceptable and, in view of the energy crisis, desirable so long as it is not abused in such a way as to provide an unwarranted protection to domestic vehicles.[52] Conversely, the tariff places rum, whisky and vodka in the same general category, but in different sub-categories, to which different rates of customs duty apply. This fact was most forcefully pointed out by the defendant governments in the actions against *France*, *Italy*, and *Denmark*[53]: indeed, they contended, the fact that different spirits are placed in different sub-categories, with different rates of duty, may be taken as an indication of their dissimilarity. The Commission maintained that these different tariffs are due to reasons of commercial and exchange-rate policy, from which it does not follow that the products are to be regarded as dissimilar from the point of view of the consumer. Not surprisingly, the Court found that these arguments based upon tariff classification[54] were inconclusive, though perhaps the tariff classification was indicative at least of a competitive relationship between the products concerned.[55]

**37**    An alternative approach, and one which the Court has in practice adopted in a number of cases, might be to take the precise imported product in question (and in cases coming before national courts this is easily done, since it is a particular assessment to tax on a particular product which is normally the subject of complaint) and to attempt to determine what *would* have been the tax burden had that product been a domestic product. This has the advantage that it takes into account not only the tax rate applicable to a particular category of products but also the criteria according to which the tax base is determined. Thus, on the importation of a quantity of wool, combed and carded, or of timber, sawn into planks, one enquires what would have been the amount of tax paid on a precisely equivalent domestic product.[56] If the answer is that the tax would have been lower, because the domestic wool or timber would have been taxed on its value in its unprocessed state, then there is a discrimination which offends Article 95.[57] This, however, is to give too restricted a meaning to the term "similar

[51] See E.P.W.Q. 397/78 and the Commission's reply: O.J. 1979, C. 5/3.

[52] As where a country which produces only small cars imposes a steeply rising schedule which discriminates against larger imports: see H. Smit and P. E. Herzog, "*The Law of the European Economic Community*," Vol. 3, pp. 439–440 (referred to hereafter as Smit & Herzog). But, contrary to the opinion of those authors, it is suggested that this is permissible unless the schedule has an artificial, protectionist, character.

[53] Cases 168, 169 and 171/78. Judgments delivered on February 27, 1980 (not yet reported).

[54] Statistical classifications are equally inconclusive, nor could assistance be derived from the decision in Case 185/73 *König* [1974] E.C.R. 607 (which was concerned with the distinction between pure ethyl alcohol — 22.09A — and spirituous beverages — 22.09C).

[55] Case 169/78 para. 31 of judgment.

[56] This also has the advantage of automatically excluding differences which are irrelevant for tax purposes.

[57] Case 7/69 *Commission* v. *Italy* [1970] E.C.R. 111; Case 77/69 *Commission* v. *Belgium* [1970] E.C.R. 237.

products." "Similar" does not mean "identical": it must be given a wide and flexible meaning and applies to products which are not strictly identical but are analogous and comparable in the use to which they are put.[58] Consequently, the existence of a domestic product which is identical to the imported product in question, and is taxed the same, does not prevent the application of Article 95 if there are other "similar," but not identical, domestic products which are taxed less heavily.[59]

38        The problem may be illustrated by the three recent "alcohol" cases, against *France, Italy* and *Denmark*.[60] In each case essentially the same question was raised: does the application of different rates of taxation to different spirituous beverages (by virtue of their being classified differently for tax purposes) constitute an infringement of Article 95, when the effect is that most domestically produced spirits bear a lower tax burden than do most imported spirits?

In the case of *France* the tax system complained of, by the Commission, divided spirits into three main categories: spirits from wine or fruit denominated *d'origine controllée et reglementée* (a category which included cognac, armagnac, calvados etc), spirits from wine or fruit produced by small enterprises distilling their own produce and spirits from cereals (which included gin, whisky and vodka). The total burden of taxes on consumption and production amounted, in 1979, to 6,380 francs per hectolitre, in the case of spirits from cereals; and, 4,270 francs per hectolitre, in the case of spirits from wine or fruit.

Although the French law did not expressly distinguish between different types of spirit on the basis of national origin, by far the greater part of wine- or fruit-based spirits consumed (and taxed) in France are of domestic production and virtually all cereal-based spirits, with the small exception of genièvre, are imported into France.

39        In the case of *Italy* a similar distinction, between spirits made from wine or marc and those made from cereals, was made. In consequence the duty on one litre of grappa was 20 lire, of brandy 60 lire, and of cereal-based spirits such as whisky, 420 lire. Again those spirits of predominantly domestic manufacture bore the lower rates of duty, whilst almost the totality of cereal-based spirits consumed in Italy were imported.

The facts in the case against *Denmark* are of particular interest. The total Danish production of spirits is in the region of 7 million litres a year, of which akvavit constitutes almost 6 million litres. Annual consumption of spirits is around 9 million litres, some 63 per cent. of this being akvavit. Approximately 96 per cent. of that akvavit is of domestic production, the remainder being imported mainly from Germany and Norway. About one-third of other spirits consumed in Denmark are of domestic production, the

---

[58] Cases 168, 169 and 171/78, para 5 in each judgment.
[59] Though the Court avoided giving a direct answer to this question in Case 68/79 *Hans Just* (not yet reported), this conclusion follows necessarily from its decision in Case 171/78.
[60] See n. 53, above.

remainder (notably brandy, gin, rum and whisky) being imported. For tax purposes, akvavit stood alone in one category and all other spirits were taxed approximately 50 per cent. more heavily.

Thus, in each case, the lower tax rate applied to most products of domestic origin, though a small proportion of imports benefitted also from the lower rate: nearly all imported spirits were taxed at the higher rate, though a small proportion of domestic spirits also bore the higher rate.

**40**     It should first be observed that, until such time as the relevant taxes are harmonised, Member States retain the right and the competence to establish their own fiscal categories, provided these do not discriminate between products on the basis of national origin. As the Court itself had declared, in *Hansen & Balle*,

> "At the present stage of its development and in the absence of any unification or harmonisation of the relevant provisions, Community law does not prohibit Member States from granting tax advantages, in the form of exception from or reduction of duties, to certain types of spirits or to certain classes of producers. Indeed, tax advantages of this kind may serve legitimate economic or social purposes, such as the use of certain raw materials by the distilling industry, the continued production of particular spirits of high quality or the continuance of certain classes of undertakings such as agricultural distilleries."[61]

Each of the defendant governments advanced economic or social justifications for their classifications: in *France*, that a legitimate distinction may be drawn between spirits which are primarily aperitifs and those which are digestifs[62]; in *Italy*, the need to compensate for the substantially higher costs of production of wine- and fruit-based spirits[63]; in *Denmark*, the fact that the cost of akvavit was lower than that of most other spirits and that the duty was established to contain an *ad valorem* element. The Commission, however, urged that Article 95 sets out an absolute rule permitting of no exception based upon economic or social policy.[64] The fiscal sovereignty of member States in this regard has been restricted in the interests of internal trade within the Community and, whilst accepting the need for certain corrective mechanisms to take account of economic and social factors, the Commission maintained that these must result from action taken at the Community level and can only function correctly if they are introduced into a market which is neutral from a fiscal point of view.

---

[61] Case 148/77 [1978] E.C.R. 1787 at p. 1806.

[62] Presumably to discourage drinking before meals and encourage it afterwards!

[63] A need recognised by the Council in Reg. 337/79 of February 5, 1979, governing the common organisation of the market in wine.

[64] This would seem to follow from Cases 2 & 3/62 *Commission* v. *Luxembourg and Belgium* [1962] E.C.R. 425; Case 16/69 *Commission* v. *Italy* [1969] E.C.R. 377; Case 28/69 *Commission* v. *Italy* [1970] E.C.R. 187; Case 127/75 *Bobie* [1976] E.C.R. 1079; Case 120/78 *Rewe* [1979] E.C.R. 649.

**41**     In reply to these arguments the Court reminded the parties that, in *Hansen & Balle*, it had emphasised that, though tax differentials are permissible, preferential systems must be extended without discrimination to products coming from other Member States. Thus, it had added:

> ". . . It follows that the special advantages provided by national legislation for certain types of spirits or certain classes of producers could be claimed for imported Community spirits whenever the criteria underlying the first and second paragraphs of Article 95 are satisfied."[65]

The issue therefore turned upon whether or not the products in question were to be regarded as "similar," within the meaning of the first paragraph of Article 95 or, alternatively, as being in competition in such a way as to make the second paragraph applicable. To this question the Commission based its main argument upon the characteristics which are common to all spirits from the point of view of the consumer. Repeating the argument which it had advanced in *Fink-Frucht*, it urged that:

> "In order to establish whether there is similarity, one must first of all enquire whether, in the view of their properties, nature and quality, the products compared afford the same possibilities of utilisation.[66]

And, quoting from the Court's judgment in *Rewe*:

> " . . . in order to determine the meaning of "similar products" it is necessary to compare the taxation of products which, at the same stage of production or marketing, present to consumers analogous characteristics and respond to the same needs."[67]

Thus, according to the Commission,[68] all spirituous beverages are to be regarded as similar for fiscal purposes.[69]

**42**     This notion of similarity, of characteristics and utilisation, was strongly contested by the defendant governments. Distinctions, they maintained, may validly be made between different spirits for a variety of reasons.[70] They are produced by different methods, from different raw materials, are chosen primarily for their distinctive flavour or aroma, are consumed neat or mixed with various dilutants, before or after meals or, in the case of akvavit, with meals. Consumer habits vary widely from one country to

---

[65]  See n. 61, above.
[66]  Case 27/67 [1968] E.C.R. 223, at p. 228.
[67]  Case 45/75[ 1976] E.C.R. 181, at p. 195.
[68]  This was also the conclusion of Advocate-General Reischl, and appeared to be supported by the Court's judgments in Case 16/69 *Commission* v. *Italy* and Case 148/77 *Hansen & Balle* (nn. 61, 64, above).
[69]  This assumption underlies the Commission's proposed directive for the harmonisation of excise duties on alcohol: see chapter 3 para. 235 below.
[70]  The submissions provide a fascinating guide to the drinking habits and preferences of the citizens of the Community. One is surprised to learn that Italians choose their drink primarily for reasons of health!

another and two drinks which might be regarded as alternatives in one country might be put to totally different uses in another.

None of these factors, protested the Commission, ought to have anything to do with fiscal classification. In any event, it would be mistaken to attach importance to purely local or national customs, which may well have evolved as a result of differences in price which, in turn, may be due to the very fiscal discrimination complained of. In this the Commission was supported by Advocate-General Reischl, who submitted that "similar" must be given a Community meaning: one could not risk the evolution of nine separate national interpretations of the term.[71] Thus, for example, the Danish argument that imported akvavit was taxed in the same way as domestic akvavit and other imported spirits in the same way as other domestic spirits must be rejected. For only a minimal proportion of imports to benefit from the favourable treatment accorded to the greater part of the domestic production and for the great majority of similar imported products to be excluded from this benefit constituted, in his opinion, a disguised discrimination forbidden by Article 95.[72]

**43**    The Court, however, was not prepared to go quite so far on this issue. In the case against *Denmark* it concluded that at least some of the other imported products were "similar" to akvavit: these were the products, such as gin and vodka, with characteristics closely resembling akvavit, essentially those with a neutral base and which owe their flavour to aromatic additives.[73] In the case of these products the infraction of the first paragraph of Article 95 was not in doubt.[74] For the rest, the Court turned to the Commission's alternative submission that, even if certain spirits have distinctive qualities and well-defined uses, there exists among spirituous beverages generally a broad capacity for substitution. Thus, even if all spirits may not be "similar" within the meaning of the first paragraph of Article 95, they are all competing products and to tax imported spirits more heavily than domestic spirits constitutes protection within the second paragraph. The Court therefore concluded that:

> "First, there exists among spirits considered as a whole an indeterminate number of drinks which must be regarded as "similar products" in the sense of Article 95, first paragraph, even though it may be difficult to decide this question in particular cases ... Secondly, even when it is not possible to recognise a sufficient degree of similarity between the products concerned, there are nevertheless, in the case of all spirits, characteristics which are sufficiently common for there to

---

[71] The Court accepted this view: para. 11 in each judgment.

[72] The Court had, some years earlier, reached a similar conclusion with regard to the artificial tax classification of cocoa (according to fat content) in Case 28/69, above n. 48.

[73] It was difficult for the Danish government to deny this since, in defining akvavit for tax purposes it had expressly to exclude gin, vodka and wacholder. The Court apparently also found genièvre "similar" to gin, in Case 168/78.

[74] Case 171/78 para. 32 of judgment.

exist, in all cases, a competitive relationship, at least potentially. Thus Article 95, second paragraph, will apply whenever the degree of similarity between different types of spirits is in doubt or is disputed.

It follows from this that Article 95, taken as a whole, applies to all the products in question. It is thus sufficient to examine whether the national fiscal system is of a discriminatory or protective nature, that is to say, if there exists a difference in the rates or methods of taxation and if this difference is susceptible of favouring a particular domestic product. It is in this context that it is necessary to examine, in each of the cases brought by the Commission, the economic relationships between the products concerned and the characteristics of the fiscal system which are the object of the proceedings."[75]

Taking account of all the evidence, the Court concluded that it was not necessary, in order to give judgment, to pronounce on the question whether the products concerned were or were not similar since they stood, without exception, in a competitive relationship with each other. The protective nature of the fiscal systems in all three cases was undeniable, characterised by the fact that the essentially domestic products were found in the favoured categories and the products which were mainly imported were subjected to a heavier tax burden. The fact that some proportion of the domestic production might also bear the heavier tax did not alter the protective nature of the systems, which were all consequently incompatible with Article 95.

**44**    (*b*)    *Other products*

As formulated by the Court in *Fink-Frucht*[76] the essence of the second paragraph is to prohibit discriminations which distort the conditions of free competition between products and, as such, it clearly complements the first paragraph. As already seen, opinions may differ as to which paragraph should apply to a given situation. For example, if one is concerned with the respective taxation of whisky and brandy, a court may conclude that these are similar products within the first paragraph.[77] In reaching such a conclusion, certain characteristics of the two products are discarded as being irrelevant, *e.g.* their colour, taste and smell, but others, such as their use and alcoholic strength, are considered decisive. But in its selection of the relevant characteristics the court is necessarily making a qualitative judgment: *i.e.* characteristics which are considered irrelevant for the purpose of taxation are ignored and, consequently, to decide that the products are "similar" is to decide that they *ought* to be taxed in the same way. The alternative approach is to treat them as dissimilar, but to conclude that, in view of certain common characteristics, it is improper to tax the one more heavily than the other since to do so provides indirect protection to that other.

[75] Paras. 12, 13 in all three judgments (author's translation).
[76] See n. 44, above.
[77] The question is left open by the Court in Cases 168, 169/78, above.

Either way the result is the same. Thus it may not matter whether oranges and apples are regarded as similar, both being fresh fruits, or as dissimilar but competing products, since both may be used in the manufacture of fresh fruit juices,[78] or that hard and soft wheat are similar, or are competing because of the many uses to which both kinds of wheat may be put.[79] In the sense in which it has been considered above, the function of the second paragraph of Article 95 appears to be not only complementary, but also ancillary, to the first paragraph: it prevents evasion of the prohibition on discrimination between comparable products by means of artificial (in a tax sense) classifications. But the scope of the second paragraph does not appear to be restricted to this ancillary role. In the *Fink-Frucht* case, the Court stated that the second paragraph:

> "... forbids the imposition on imported products of any form of taxation 'of such a nature as to afford indirect protection to other products.' Such protection would occur in particular if internal taxation were to impose a heavier burden on an imported product than on a domestic product with which the imported product is, by *reason of one or more economic uses to which it may be put, in competition*, even though the condition of similarity for the purposes of the first paragraph of Article 95 is not fulfilled."[80]

**45**     One method of determining whether or not such competition exists is to ask whether, in one or more of its uses, the domestic product may be substituted for the import.[81] This, of course, is an extremely broad concept for, as the original plaintiffs in the *Fink-Frucht* case pointed out,[82] a broad capacity for substitution exists between products such as umbrellas and raincoats and, on this principle, it is possible that scarcely any product exists which is incapable of being substituted by another. This would lead to the conclusion, at any rate where some products are essentially of domestic origin and others are predominantly imported, either that all those products should be taxed the same or, that in so far as different products might be taxed differently, this should only be in accordance with some sort of principle of proportionality to ensure that competition is not distorted. Such a principle would be virtually impossible for the courts to apply.

Clearly, then, a line has to be drawn somewhere. In the "alcohol" cases, the Court was concerned with products which, if not necessarily "similar", it considered should bear a comparable tax burden if to tax them otherwise would lead to imported products being taxed more heavily than competing

---

[78] See Case 34/62 *Germany* v. *Commission* [1963] E.C.R. 131.

[79] Case 20/67 *Tivoli*, especially the remarks of Advocate-General Gand, at [1968] E.C.R. 199, at p. 175.

[80] [1968] E.C.R. 223, at p. 232. (Italics added).

[81] See Case 148/77 *Hansen & Balle* [1978] E.C.R. 1787, per Advocate-General Capotorti, at p. 1817.

[82] [1968] E.C.R. 223, at p. 229.

domestic products.[83] But what if the products in question are not only dissimilar but lack this close degree of comparability, yet nevertheless are considered to be in competition with each other? This, essentially, was the problem in the recent action against the *United Kingdom*.[84]

**46**    The Commission alleged that the British system of taxing wine was discriminatory and contrary to the second paragraph of Article 95 in that wine, which could properly be regarded as a "product of other Member States" (domestic production being minimal) was taxed considerably more heavily than beer, a product with which it is in competition. The respective duties, in 1977, for a gallon of wine and of beer, were £3.25 and £0.61. Having regard to the difference in alcoholic strength—an average table wine is approximately three times as strong as an average beer—it was not seriously contended that the duties should be the same when assessed on a volume basis. Nevertheless, the Commission submitted that the disparity in tax burdens was considerably greater than would be justified by the difference in strength and consequently afforded protection to the "other product," beer.

The first issue to be determined was whether beer should be regarded as an "other product" within the meaning of the second paragraph of Article 95. It should be noted that the paragraph does not refer to "competing" products: this is the interpretation put upon it by the Court in *Fink-Frucht*.[85] The British government contended that, in Britain, wine is not regarded as being a substitute for, or in competition with, beer. The difference in the alcoholic content is sufficient in itself to make the two drinks fundamentally different: wine is purchased mostly in supermarkets and wine stores and is consumed at home, beer is mainly bought and consumed in pubs.[86] As in the "alcohol" cases, the Commission and the Advocate-General submitted that national habits of consumption cannot be decisive. Taking the Community as a whole, wine and beer meet the same consumer needs, as a table-drink in restaurants and at home and, generally, as a thirst-quencher. This view was accepted by the Court which held that, at least to some extent, the two beverages are capable of meeting identical needs so that it must be acknowledged that there is a certain degree of substitution one for another.[87]

**47**    That being so, it then fell to be considered whether the admitted difference

---

[83] Whether this is also the case when the member state in question produces substantial quantities of both products will be considered later.

[84] Case 170/78 *Commission* v. *United Kingdom* [1980] 1 C.M.L.R. 716. Judgment delivered on February 27, 1980.

[85] See n. 66, above. Nor does it expressly refer to "domestic" products. Taken literally, it could apply where one import is protected against another import. In Case 169/78, the Italian government contended that it be given a very different meaning and applies only where protection is given indirectly to some other product. It seemed to have in mind the type of case where, *e.g.* a tax on imported wine could afford protection to the domestic bottling industry: see Mégret, Vol. 5, pp. 12–13. If so, it is rather surprising that Italy joined, as the intervener, in the action against the United Kingdom.

[86] And, the Court added rather curiously, "in connection with work."

[87] Case 170/78 para. 14 of judgment.

in duty was such as to afford protection to domestic beer. This, in turn, involved two questions: given the dissimilarity of the products, was the tax differential discriminatory and, if so, did it afford protection to beer?

The British government firstly denied any element of discrimination in the tax system. In view of the difference in alcoholic strength a straight comparison on a volume basis was clearly inappropriate. Taking into account the widely different ways in which the two drinks are sold, in relation to total consumer expenditure the taxes on beer and wine were almost the same. Alternatively, having regard to the manner in which they are consumed, the tax on a normal (four and a half ounce) glass of wine was approximately equal to that on a pint of beer. By contrast, the Commission based its calculation upon the retail price in supermarkets and upon the respective alcohol strengths of wine and beer: in each case, wine was taxed more heavily, approximately in the ratio 5:3. Thus, whether or not the British system should be regarded as discriminatory seemed to depend upon which criterion should be applied in order to determine the appropriate tax relationship between the two products.

**48**     It was on this point that the Court ultimately found it impossible to deliver judgment. As the Court stated:

> "Of the criteria put forward by the parties, the only factor which may enable an appropriate and somewhat objective comparison to be made consists therefore in an appraisal of the incidence of the tax burden in relation to the alcoholic strength of the beverages in question ... according to the only criterion whereby an objective, although imperfect, comparison can be made between the rates of tax applied to wine and beer, it seems that wine is subject in the United Kingdom to a tax burden which is relatively heavier than that imposed on beer ... However, in view of the uncertainties remaining both as to the characteristics of the competitive relationship between wine and beer and as to the question of the appropriate tax ratio between the two products from the point of view of the whole of the Community, the Court considers that it is unable to give a ruling at this stage on the failure to fulfil its obligations under the Treaty for which the United Kingdom is criticised. It therefore requests the Commission and the United Kingdom to resume examination of the question at issue in the light of the foregoing considerations and to report to the Court [before December 31, 1980] either on any solution of the dispute which they have reached or on their respective viewpoints, taking into consideration the legal factors arising from this judgment."[88]

**49**     The second part of the question concerned the protective nature of the British tax system. The defendant government argued that for many years wine had been taxed comparatively (on the basis of alcoholic strength) less

---

[88] *Ibid.* paras. 19, 20, 24 of judgment.

heavily than beer; the discrimination in favour of beer, if any existed, dated only from around 1974,[89] yet since then domestic consumption of wine had risen considerably more quickly than that of beer.[90] This was an argument which Advocate-General Reischl had found convincing. He concluded that the evidence did not support a finding that the difference in tax burdens had had a protective effect and could be shown to have influenced the behaviour of consumers. On this basis he would have rejected the action as unfounded. The Court, however, agreed with the Commission stating:

> "It is however appropriate to emphasise that [the second paragraph of Article 95] is linked to the 'nature' of the tax system in question so that it is impossible to require in each case that the protective effect should be shown statistically. It is sufficient . . . for it to be shown that a given tax mechanism is likely, in view of its inherent characteristics, to bring about the protective effect referred to by the Treaty."[91]

The position, then, remains in some doubt, at least until final judgment is delivered in the *United Kingdom* case. The following tentative conclusions may be advanced:

**50**      (i)   "Similar," in the first paragraph of Article 95, is to be given a broader meaning than "identical." Thus, for example, domestic akvavit is to be regarded as similar not only to imported akvavit but also to some other imported spirits, such as gin and vodka. It is therefore no defence that identical imported and domestic products are taxed the same if other similar, but not identical, imports do not partake of the same advantage.[92]

(ii)   The scope of the first paragraph remains unclear. It appears that a number of spirituous beverages are to be regarded as "similar": akvavit and gin, presumably whisky and whiskey (Scotch and Irish), cognac and branntwein, would fall into this category. It also seems that other spirits are not similar in this sense: thus, whether brandy and whisky fall within the first or second paragraph of Article 95 is not certain.

(iii)   This, the Court appears to say, is unimportant since they are all competing products and as such subject to the prohibition in the second paragraph. One question is consequently resolved, the two paragraphs of Article 95 are not mutually exclusive. Even if an imported product is taxed the same as a similar domestic product (as with "other" spirits imported into

---

[89] It was this comparative increase in the tax on wine, subsequent to British entry into the Community and contrary to the Commission's Recommendation 76/2 of December 5, 1975 (O.J. 1976, L 2/13) which particularly seemed to offend the Commission. The purpose of the Recommendation, however, was to reduce the Community's "wine lake" and it was not as such concerned with discriminatory taxation.

[90] In Cases 168 & 169/78, the French and Italian governments had similarly pointed to the rapid increase in consumption of imported whisky in those two countries.

[91] Para. 10 of judgment. This is consistent with the Court's jurisprudence relating to Art. 85 of the Treaty. *i.e.* that it is not necessary to prove an actual effect on trade.

[92] This appears to conflict with the view expressed in *Bobie* (above, para. 30) that beer from foreign breweries may validly be compared to beer from larger domestic breweries, rather than beer generally.

Denmark) the second paragraph applies if they are nevertheless taxed more heavily than some other competing domestic product.[93]

**51**      (iv)   There now appear to be two classes of "competing" product for the purposes of the second paragraph: those which are almost "similar" and should be taxed in the same way (*e.g.* spirits) and those which are 'dissimilar" and need not be taxed in the same way but whose respective taxation should bear a proper relationship to the relevant differences (*e.g.* wine and beer). This, in turn, gives rise to a number of problems. For example, when should two different products be regarded as "almost similar," in the sense described above? Some spirits, notably certain fruit-based liqueurs, have a significantly lower alcoholic strength than others. How should fortified, or sparkling wines be regarded in relation to table wines? The problem may be avoided if all alcoholic beverages are taxed in accordance with alcoholic strength, but Member States may find this solution excessively complicated. It may be more convenient to tax on the basis of volume, classifying alcoholic beverages into a number of categories, *e.g.* beers, table wines, fortified wines, spirits. Even assuming that these categories are taxed in a proper relationship to each other (on the basis of the average alcoholic strength of each category) there will still be difficult borderline cases.

**52**      (v)   Products which are "dissimilar," but which are in competition with each other, should be taxed in such a way that there is no tendency to afford protection to one of those products, *i.e.* they should be taxed in accordance with some principle of proportionality. But on what basis is the proper tax relationship between "dissimilar" products to be determined? The question has been left open by the Court, though it indicated that, in the case of wine and beer, it considered alcoholic strength to be the only reasonably satisfactory criterion. Is this necessarily so? It has been suggested, for example, that an *ad valorem* basis would be equally acceptable.[94] And what would be the appropriate criteria for determining the proper tax relationship between products such as coal and oil, motor cycles and cars, umbrellas and raincoats?

(vi)   In the *United Kingdom* case, the Court adopted a wide interpretation of the second paragraph of Article 95. It appears to apply whenever products are in competition, either partially or potentially and where there is a potential for the substitution of products for one another.[95] But, as the Danish government submitted, the only true competitor for akvavit is beer[96]

---

[93] The contrary was suggested by Advocate-General Gand in Case 27/67 *Fink Frucht* [1968] E.C.R. 223, at pp. 170–1.

[94] Thus, on the basis of the figures given by the United Kingdom government, it would seem that to abolish specific excise duties on beer and wine and to replace these by an additional VAT rate of, say, 20 per cent., would preserve the existing differential between the two drinks, but in a non-discriminatory manner.

[95] Paras. 5 and 6 of judgment.

[96] It is also probable that, in the United Kingdom, the greatest degree of competition is between beer and whisky.

and other studies have shown that, in many parts of the Community, wine is in competition with soft drinks, coffee and tea.[97] Must one conclude that the taxation of all beverages must be in some proper relationship and is the same true of other competing products such as oil, coal and natural gas? If so, the implications are enormous.

53      (vii) In rejecting the submissions of Advocate-General Reischl, the Court ruled that it is not necessary to establish, on the basis of statistical or other evidence, the fact that a domestic product has been protected. It is sufficient that the tax system in question is likely to bring about a protective effect. This may simplify matters for national courts and, more particularly, for individual plaintiffs.[98] The Court appeared to assume that a difference in the relative tax burden upon two competing products, at any rate if substantial, is in itself likely to have this effect. What, however, would be the position if the imported product was taxed only a little more heavily?[99] Under the first paragraph of Article 95, it is sufficient if the imported product, if only in certain cases, is taxed at all more heavily than a similar domestic product.[1] It is submitted that such a slight difference, especially if it occurred only in a few cases or if the difference between the products in question was substantial, would be insufficient to be likely to provide protection. Consequently, the meaning of "similar" and, perhaps, also the degree of similarity will remain vital in many cases.

54      Finally, it must be observed that five of the six judgments delivered by the Court on February 27, 1980, related to proceedings against Member States under Article 169 of the Treaty.[2] It seems important to remember this for a number of reasons. Firstly, the Court was concerned essentially with the question whether the tax systems of the Member States concerned infringed Article 95. Although, as will be considered later, Article 95 is capable of producing direct effects and may be applied to individual cases, it seems that in proceedings under Article 169, the Court has to consider the protective effect of a tax system, or a particular tax rule, as a whole. It may be insufficient to constitute an infraction of the Treaty that, in certain cases, an import is taxed more heavily than a competing domestic product if, in general, the tax has no protective effect.[3] Secondly, the offensive nature of the provisions in question was that they benefited products which were

---

[97] See (EC) Bull. S. 7–78, p. 15 and, generally, U. Wasserman, "The International Wine Trade" (1971) 5 J.W.T.L. 83.
[98] On a related question concerning the burden of proof under Art. 86 of the Treaty, see the comments of D. Wyatt, (1977) 2 E.L. Rev. 122.
[99] According to various criteria suggested by the United Kingdom government, wine was taxed from 4 to 11 per cent. more heavily than beer. According to the Commission's criteria, from 50 to 60 per cent. more heavily.
[1] Case 45/75 *Rewe* [1976] E.C.R. 181; Case 127/75 *Bobie* [1976] E.C.R. 1079.
[2] The sixth, Case 68/79 *Hans Just*, is considered further at paras. 79, 80.
[3] For example, if an average wine is taxed in a proper relationship with an average beer it might be unimportant that a weaker wine is taxed disproportionately more heavily than a stronger beer.

predominantly of domestic production to the detriment of most similar or competing imports. The Court expressly repeated what it had said in *Hansen & Balle*,[4] that Member States are not precluded from granting tax advantages to certain types of spirits, provided such advantages may be claimed by imported products also. This, however, raises perhaps the most difficult issue of all. The crucial point, in the actions against *France*, *Italy*, the *United Kingdom* and *Denmark*, was that the privileged tax category applied to most beverages of domestic production, though some imports benefitted from the same privilege, and the heavier tax category applied to products which were mostly imported, though some domestic products also suffered the imposition. It was not difficult to conclude, though of course the Court did not express this, that the tax systems had been designed to favour domestic, as opposed to imported, product, rather than one product as opposed to another.[5] It would seem to be implied that, in proceedings under Article 169, a member state would not be considered to be in breach of its Treaty obligations if it discriminated between two products, *both* (or neither) of which it produced in substantial quantities. Thus Germany, for example, would be permitted to discriminate, from the point of view of taxation, between wine- and cereal-based spirits, Italy (and indeed all wine-producing countries) between wine and beer.[6] Perhaps the United Kingdom might be permitted to discriminate between oil and coal, whereas Luxembourg might not.

**55**     This, of course, produces some curious results. Having been at pains to establish that the concepts of "similar" and "competing" products must be given a single, Community, meaning, the Court has apparently succeeded in establishing that tax rules may validly be imposed by one Member State but that another Member State may be precluded from adopting identical rules. Moreover, it appears to have introduced a question of percentages: the Court may have been justified in considering the Italian production of whisky, or even the British production of wine, as insignificant, but Danish production accounted for 30 per cent. of "other spirits." At what point, therefore, is a particular product determined to be "domestic" or "imported?"[7] Again, if there are more than two tax categories in question,

---

[4]  Case 148/77 [1978] E.C.R. 1787.

[5]  In the case of the United Kingdom, this was strongly disputed. Before entry into the Community, the customs duty on wine had probably been intended to afford protection to Commonwealth wine rather than to domestic beer. The aggravation of the discrimination, from 1974 onwards, may have owed more to internal political considerations, notably a preference for taxing "luxury" goods rather than everyday commodities.

[6]  This is clearly permitted by the Commission's most recent proposals for the harmonisation of excise duties: see below, Chapter 3, para. 237.

[7]  It is also necessary to bear in mind that "products of a member state" includes imported raw materials processed in a member state : Case 28/69 *Commission* v. *Italy* [1970] E.C.R. 187. See also the decision of the Finanzgericht, Münster in *Re Import of Finished Textiles* [1969] C.M.L.R. 261, and consider the problem raised by Case 179/78 *Rivoira* (not yet reported), where Spanish grapes imported into Italy and processed there were held to be products of Italy.

what determines the choice of the appropriate comparison? Should wine be compared to beer, cider, whisky or tea, or to all of them?

These are problems which the Court may be able to resolve, though with difficulty, in the context of proceedings under Article 169. They appear even more intractable when they fall to be considered by a national judge in the course of proceedings brought by an individual complainant.[8] They would also appear to have major implications for the Commission's policy of harmonisation of excise duties.[9]

### (v) The scope of Article 95

**56** According to the plain wording of Article 95, it prohibits discrimination only against "the products of other Member States", *i.e.* products imported from other Member States. It would consequently not appear to apply to discriminations against imports from third countries, against exports of domestic products or against the domestic products themselves.

### (a) *External trade*

It is well established that Article 95 relates only to products originating in other Member States and does not apply to imports from a third country.[10] For this reason it has sometimes been important to distinguish between internal taxation and charges having an effect equivalent to customs duties.[11] In a recent pronouncement on the subject, the Court stated:

> "The EEC Treaty does not include any provision prohibiting discrimination in the application of internal taxation to products imported from non-member countries, subject however to any treaty provisions which may be in force between the Community and the country of origin of a given product."[12]

It must, however, be remembered that the notion of "products of other Member States" is given a wide meaning, and includes any product which has been manufactured or processed in some way in a Member State, even though the raw material, or the product itself at some earlier stage of manufacture or processing, originated from outside the Community.[13]

---

[8] This problem is considered further, below, at paras. 69–71.

[9] See below, Chapter 3, paras, 239–242.

[10] Case 7/67 *Wöhrmann* [1968] E.C.R. 177 (milk powders from Austria); Case 20/67 *Tivoli* [1968] E.C.R. 199 (wheat from U.S.A.). See also the decisions of the Finanzgerichte of Nürnberg and of Berlin, in *Re Siamese Tapioca Meal* [1964] C.M.L.R. 310; *Re Hungarian Eggs* [1967] C.M.L.R. 346.

[11] See para. 23, above.

[12] Case 148/77 *Hansen & Balle* [1978] E.C.R., at p. 1810. By virtue of Art. 227(2), it was held that Art. 95 does apply to goods coming from the French overseas departments (rum from Guadeloupe). The Commission had previously thought otherwise: See (EC) Bull. 1/80, pp. 23–24. See now Dirs. 80/368, 369.

[13] See n. 7 above.

*(b)* *Exports*

It would similarly appear that Article 95 does not prohibit the less favourable taxation of domestic products which are exported. In the *Geddo* case,[14] Advocate-General Trabucchi submitted that nothing in the Treaty imposes a general obligation on Member States to reimburse taxes and domestic charges when products on which they have been paid are exported. And in *Demag*,[15] the Court held that a temporary German economic measure which reduced the amount of the refund in respect of domestic turnover taxes given on the exportation of products did not offend Article 95. Article 96,[16] which prohibits a Member State from refunding on exportation any amount in excess of the domestic tax borne by the product in question, does not prevent it from refunding a smaller amount.

**57**     More recently, however, in *AEdle Metaller*,[17] the original plaintiff contended that an internal levy, imposed upon precious metals, which was not refunded in the case of exported products and did not benefit those products as it did those sold domestically, constituted an obstacle to international trade and was invalid. The levy, being imposed upon all domestic products alike, whether exported or not, did not appear to be a charge equivalent to a customs duty on exports. However, regarding the applicability of Article 95, Advocate-General Capotorti submitted that:

"The literal wording of that provision in fact establishes a relationship between the charges applied to national products and those applied to similar products imported from other Member States. Its field of application might however appear not to cover a case, such as that to which the court making the reference refers, which involves the treatment for tax purposes of exported national products which is alleged to be discriminatory compared with the treatment of the same products sold in the producer State. In the oral stage of these proceedings the representative of the Danish government expressed himself to this effect. There is no doubt that the Treaty intended to ensure equal treatment for tax purposes for national products and products from other member states in the legal system of each Member State. If equality were not however uniformly ensured with regard to the same national products in the sense that the same fiscal charge had to be imposed on those marketed in the producer State and those exported to other Member States it would be necessary to recognize that there was a serious lacuna or at least a surprising lack of harmony in the system of the Treaty and in particular in the system of freedom of movement of

[14] Case 2/73 [1973] E.C.R. 865, at p. 892.
[15] Case 27/74 [1974] E.C.R. 1037.
[16] See para. 92, below.
[17] Case 142/77 [1978] E.C.R. 1543.

goods between the Member States. The lacuna would exist if, on the basis of an absolutely literal and restrictive interpretation of Article 95, it were held that each Member State were free to impose from the tax point of view a heavier burden on products intended for export than on products sold on the domestic market. Such treatment might seem to be abstract theory in periods characterized by a plentiful supply of products or even merely by domestic economic policies designed to stimulate exports. It might however become a reality and threaten the principle of the freedom of movement of goods within the Community in periods of shortages (perhaps in certain sectors) of products and of national policies preoccupied by excessive exports. Through discriminatory application of the weapon of tax each Member State would in fact be able to discourage exports of products in short supply, if such conduct could not be penalized under the Community legal system; assuming that in theory it would fall outside the prohibition laid down in Article 95 and that, moreover, since it constitutes genuine internal taxation it would automatically fall outside the field of application of Article 16 of the EEC Treaty.

**58**    I therefore consider that in order to avoid the above-mentioned serious lacuna in the system of the movement of goods within the Community it is necessary to regard the charges levied on exported products as coming within the field of application of the first paragraph of Article 95.

Within the system of the Treaty it would be illogical to hold that the intention was to leave the Member States free as regards the discriminatory application of the weapon of tax to exports. In reality, in view of the general economic situation at the date on which the Treaty was drafted and adopted the real danger from the point of view of the exercise of the powers of taxation of the Member States was that of discriminatory treatment against products from other States of the Community. As far as national products for export were concerned the problems were quite different; they consisted in the large number of facilities, incentives and aids by means of which each state sought to promote its own exports. It therefore seems reasonable to consider that in drafting Article 95 the more urgent requirements at that time were taken into account and that in the meantime the possibility of a discriminatory use of the weapon of tax against exports which could have arisen, in a different economic context, has been forgotten.

The basic characteristic of the principle of the freedom of movement of goods between the member states and the need to guarantee fully the effectiveness of the provisions laid down in the Treaty must however lead to an extension of the provision laid down in Article 95 by analogy also to the case of charges imposed on exported goods. The analogy is justified by the fact that the function which the provision is required to perform is the same in this case as in that of charges imposed on imported goods; to avoid any tax treatment forming on obstacle to actual freedom of trade through discrimination based on the origin or destination of the products. Moreover, if the secondary function of the provision laid down in Article 95 with regard to the prohibition on customs duties and charges having equivalent effect is taken into account it seems reasonable to consider that it must fully perform that function and therefore apply to obstacles which may be placed not only in the way of imports but also of exports, as occurs in the case of all provisions coming within the customs union."[18]

**59**    This, it might be objected, is to take the teleological approach to interpretation well beyond its permissible limits. Nevertheless, the Court appeared to accept this reasoning, at least in part. It held:

"The wording of Article 95 refers only to the discriminatory application of systems of internal taxation to products imported from other member states.

The application of the same systems of taxation to exports is referred to in Articles 96 to 98 from the point of view of the repayment of excessive taxation which may distort conditions of trade within the common market.

It follows from a comparison of those provisions that the aim of the Treaty in this field is to guarantee generally the neutrality of systems of internal taxation with regard to intra-Community trade whenever an economic transaction going beyond the frontiers of a Member State at the same time constitutes the chargeable event giving rise to a fiscal charge within the context of such a system.

It therefore seems necessary to interpret Article 95 as meaning that the rule against discrimination which forms the basis of that provision also applies when the export of a product constitutes, within the context of a system of internal taxation, the chargeable event giving rise to a fiscal charge.

**60**    It would in fact be incompatible with the system of the tax provisions laid down in the Treaty to acknowledge that Member States, in the absence of an express prohibition laid down in the Treaty, are free to apply in a discriminatory manner a system of internal taxation to products intended for export to other member states.

Although it is true that as a general rule the States have no interest in curbing their exports by measures of that kind, it is however impossible to rule out the possibility of such discrimination in cases such as the export of rare products which are particularly valuable or especially sought after.

It is therefore appropriate to hold, as the Court of Justice has

---

[18] *Ibid.* at pp. 1565–1567.

already indicated in its judgment of 23 January 1975[19] that Article 95, considered in conjunction with the other tax provisions laid down in the Treaty, must be interpreted as also prohibiting any tax discrimination against products intended for export to other Member States."[20]

It will, however, be observed that the Court restricts the application of Article 95 to exports to those cases where it is the exportation itself which constitutes the chargeable event giving rise to the fiscal charge. Thus, where (as in the case in point) the Member State taxes all domestic products alike and simply does not refund the tax when a product is exported, no contravention of Article 95 occurs, even though that product may be taxed on importation into the country of destination and thus bear a double burden of taxation. The decision is thus consistent with that in the *Demag* case.[21] It had, of course, long been established that a specific charge on exportation might constitute a charge equivalent to a customs duty and thus be prohibited by Article 16.[22] Nevertheless, this decision, and that in *Van der Hulst*,[23] to which the Court and Advocate-General referred, appear to go considerably further and to hold that, even when the charge in question clearly forms part of a system of internal taxation, it is not permitted to tax more heavily exported goods than those destined for the home market. Such an interpretation, it is submitted, is not justified by the plain wording of Article 95.

**61**    (c)   *Domestic products*

Given this broad interpretation of Article 95, it remains to ask whether there is anything in that provision to prohibit the discriminatory taxation of domestic products. In the passage quoted above, Advocate-General Capotorti suggests that the intention of the Treaty was to ensure the equal treatment for tax purposes for national products and products from other Member States in the legal system of each Member State. Can a domestic producer or merchant complain if his product must bear a heavier tax burden than an equivalent imported product? The answer would appear to be "no."[24] As was seen in the *Bobie* case,[25] if a domestic product is taxed according to a graduated rate, an import may not be taxed at a rate higher than the lowest rate applicable to the equivalent domestic product. It follows

---

[19] Case 51/74 *Van der Hulst* [1975] E.C.R. 79, para. 34 of judgment.
[20] [1978] E.C.R., at pp. 1557–1558.
[21] Above, n. 15. At any rate, it is not inconsistent.
[22] Case 7/68 *Commission* v. *Italy* (*Art Treasures*) [1968] E.C.R. 423; Case 18/71 *di Porro* [1971] E.C.R. 811, and see above para. 22.
[23] Above, n. 19. See also Case 46/76 *Bauhuis* [1977] E.C.R. 5, at p. 17, though that judgment as a whole scarcely supports the proposition.
[24] Case 86/78 *Distilleries Peureux* (not yet reported); Case 68/79 *Hans Just* (not yet reported).
[25] Case 127/75 [1976] E.C.R. 1079, see paras. 30–32, above.

that some at least of the domestic products must necessarily be taxed more heavily than the equivalent import.[26] Furthermore, nothing in the wording of Article 95 suggests that this is forbidden—if the wording is to be regarded as having any importance.[27]

**62**     Of greater concern is the question whether a domestic producer may complain against a national provision which discriminates against imported products and against his own domestic products in favour of some other competing domestic product. As has been established, a tax system which discriminates between two competing products, one of which is largely imported and the other largely domestic, contravenes Article 95. Clearly, if the Member State removes the discrimination against the former *product*, at the request of the Commission or following a judgment of the Court, the domestic producer benefits from its removal in the same way as does the foreign producer or the importer. Since, however, it is apparently only the discrimination against the import, rather than against the particular category of product, which is prohibited, the Member State could legitimately lower the tax only on those products which are imported and could retain the higher tax on the domestic production. And since, in proceedings before a national court, it is for that court to determine how the domestic law shall be applied in order to conform with the Treaty, as properly interpreted,[28] it is open to that court to hold that the discriminatory tax is invalid only to the extent that it applies to imports. Thus, in its recent decision in *Hans Just*,[29] the Court expressly ruled, in answer to the question posed by the *Østre Landsret*, that the benefit of Article 95 may not be claimed by the domestic producers of the Member State in question.[30]

### (vi)  The relationship of Article 95 to other Treaty provisions

**63**     The relationship between Article 95 and the provisions on customs duties and quantitative restrictions (Articles 9–36) has already been discussed. Certain other Treaty provisions interact with Article 95 and call for a brief comment:

---

[26] This is also supported by Case 20/76 *Schöttle* [1977] E.C.R. 247, and by Case 148/77 *Hansen & Balle* [1978] E.C.R. 1787.

[27] Nor does Art. 7 apply, since this relates only to discrimination on the grounds of nationality of persons. For a consideration of whether a Member State may discriminate against its own nationals, see Case 1/78 *Kenny* [1978] E.C.R. 1510; Case 175/78 *Saunders* [1979] 2 C.M.L.R. 216, and the note by D. Wyatt, (1978) 3 E.L. Rev. 488.

[28] Case 34/67 *Lück* [1968] E.C.R. 245. This issue is discussed further, at paras. 77–80, below.

[29] Case 68/79, judgment delivered on February 27, 1980 (not yet reported).

[30] Para. 15 of judgment. This, of course, is so only under Community law. If, for example, a provision of national constitutional law invalidated all laws which were contrary to the Treaty then the domestic producer might indirectly, by virtue of his own national law, claim the benefit of Art. 95.

## (a)  State monopolies[31]

Article 37 requires that Member States shall progressively adjust any state monopoly of a commercial character so as to ensure that no discrimination regarding the conditions under which goods are procured and marketed exists between nationals of Member States, and shall refrain from introducing any new measure which is contrary to those principles or which restricts the scope of the provisions dealing with the abolition of customs duties and quantitative restrictions between Member States. Such state monopolies have been a common feature in many European economic systems: important and typical examples are the monoplies on tobacco in France and Italy, on alcohol in Germany and on petrol in France.[32] Such a monopoly gives a state, or the particular body which exercises the monopoly within a state, effective control over the types and quantities of the goods purchased and sold and over the price of those goods, and the "mark-up" which is taken by the monopoly may be regarded, in certain circumstances, as having an effect similar to a tax or excise duty. A major purpose of Article 37 is to prevent a state monopoly being operated in such a way as to discriminate against the products of other Member States. Particular problems arise when a product imported from another Member State is subjected to a tax or charge[33] which is intended to correspond to, or compensate for, the charge imposed upon the equivalent domestic product by virtue of its being subjected to the monopoly. Essentially, such a charge must conform with the principles both of Article 37 and of Article 95, *i.e.* the fact that the product is subject to a state monopoly, and thus Article 37, does not relieve a Member State from its duty not to impose discriminatory taxation on that product and, if there is imposed upon it a charge which the domestic product does not have to bear, or a higher charge than that borne by the domestic product, Article 13 or Article 95 will apply.[34] On the other hand, a charge levied on an import which is not discriminatory does not constitute a "new measure" within the meaning of Article 37(2),[35] though the fact that a national measure complies with Article 95 does not necessarily imply that it is valid in relation to Article 37.[36] Such might be the case where, though the charges on  imports and domestic products were similar, the monopoly was operated in a manner which benefited only the domestic product.

[31] See further, M. Waelbroeck, in Mégret, Vol. 1, pp. 121 *et seq.*
[32] It may be remarked that these products are also, in many member states, the most important sources of excise duties: see below, Chapter 3, paras. 220–225.
[33] *e.g.* the German Monopolausgleich.
[34] Case 45/75 *Rewe* [1976] E.C.R. 181: Case 91/75 *Miritz* [1976] E.C.R. 217, and see also Case 148/77 *Hansen & Balle* [1978] E.C.R. 1787; Case 91/78 *Hansen* [1980] 1 C.M.L.R. 162 and the note by D. Wyatt (1976) 1 E.L. Rev. 307.
[35] Case 13/70 *Cinzano* [1970] E.C.R. 1089.
[36] Case 45/75 *Rewe* [1976] E.C.R., at p. 197; Case 91/78 *Hansen* [1980] 1 C.M.L.R. 162.

**64**   *(b)   State aids*[37]

State aids to particular industries, products or regions are not *per se* incompatible with the Common Market. The general principle is stated thus:

> "Save as otherwise provided in this Treaty, any aid granted by a Member State or through state resources in any form whatsoever which distorts or threatens to distort competition by favouring certain undertakings or the production of certain goods shall, in so far as it affects trade between Member States, be incompatible with the Common Market."[38]

Article 92 goes on to "provide otherwise" by declaring certain types of aid to be compatible (*e.g.* aid to make good the damage caused by natural disasters or exceptional occurrences) and stipulating other aids which *may* be considered to be compatible (*e.g.* aid to promote the economic development of areas where the standard of living is low or unemployment is high), including aids specifically authorised by the Council.[39] One form which state aids commonly take is the granting of tax exemptions or privileges to certain types of enterprise, certain industries or regions.[40] These may or may not be valid as aids and, as they do not generally relate to specific products, Article 95 is normally not involved. Where, however, an aid benefits a specific product,[41] then not only the provisions of Articles 92 to 94 but also those of Articles 95, or of Articles 9 to 16, may be involved. Thus:

**65**   (1)   Where imported and domestic products are subjected to the same charges, but these charges have the sole purpose of financing activities for the specific advantage of the domestic product and, in its case are made good in full, then the charge on the imported product may be treated as a charge equivalent to a customs duty, under what may be termed the "*Capolongo* exception."[42]

(2)   Where the imported product is not taxed more heavily than the domestic product, but the domestic product receives a benefit which is not accorded to the import then, even though the *Capolongo* exception does not apply (because there is no complete identity of products or the charge is not

---

[37] See further Mégret, Vol. 4, pp. 379 *et seq.* : Smit & Herzog, Vol. 3, pp. 3–381 *et seq.* : H. Ehring, *op. cit.* p. 10, n. 51, above : P. Mathijsen, "State aids, state monopolies and public enterprises in the Common Market" (1972) 14 L. & C.P. 376.

[38] Art. 92(1).

[39] See G. Schrans, "National and Regional Aid to Industry under the EEC Treaty" (1973) 10 C.M.L. Rev. 174; A. Dashwood, "Control of State Aids in the EEC . . ." (1975) 12 C.M.L. Rev. 43.

[40] See, *e.g.* Case 173/73 *Commission* v. *Italy* [1974] E.C.R. 709 (reductions in family allowance contributions in certain industries).

[41] It would seem that a distinction must be drawn, though it may sometimes be difficult to do so, between an aid benefiting a product and one benefiting a producer, in much the same way as it is necessary to distinguish between taxes imposed on products and on producers: see above, paras. 26–28.

[42] See above, paras. 19–22, and see Case 91/78 *Hansen* [1980] 1 C.M.L.R. 162.

made good in full) it is legitimate to consider the use to which the tax is put.[43] Consequently, if the effect is to remit part of the tax on the domestic product it can be said that the product bears a smaller tax burden than does the import and Article 95 is applicable.

(3) Where imported and domestic products are taxed alike, but some part of the proceeds is applied to benefit the domestic *producer* or industry, though it cannot be said that the domestic *product* itself bears a reduced tax burden, then Article 95 does not appear to be infringed and the validity of the aid in question must be judged according to Articles 92 and 93 alone.

A state aid must comply both with Articles 92 and 93 and with Article 95. As the Court has held:

> "The fact that a national measure complies with the requirements of Article 95 does not imply that it is valid in relation to other provisions, such as those of Articles 92 and 93."[44]

Similarly, the fact that an aid itself is valid does not permit it to be financed in a discriminatory manner.[45]

**66**    (c)  *Other Treaty provisions*

What has been said in the context of state monopolies and state aids illustrates a general principle of Community law. Actions by a Member State in relation to a subject matter which is specifically governed by the Treaty or by some subsequent Community legislation must nevertheless accord with the basic requirement of non-discrimination, such as that contained in Article 95. For example, if a particular product is within the scope of a Common Market organisation in agriculture and the relevant agricultural provisions permit a measure of discretion to member States, such discretion must be construed strictly and may only be exercised subject to the rules contained in Article 95.[46] And although economic policy remains essentially a matter for national governments,[47] the policies pursued by Member States must not be inconsistent with the Treaty or with Community law.[48] As the Court held, in an early case, the abolition of customs duties and charges having equivalent effects constitutes a fundamental principle of the Common Market and, thus, any possible exception must be strictly construed and must be clearly laid down.[49] (It would, however, seem that a Member State might be competent to take actions which were con-

---

[43]  Case 51/74 *Van der Hulst* [1975] E.C.R. 79.
[44]  Case 47/69 *France* v. *Commission (Aids to Textiles)* [1970] E.C.R. 487, at p. 494.
[45]  Case 77/76 *Cucchi* [1977] E.C.R. 987, 1003.
[46]  Case 16/69 *Commission* v. *Italy (Eaux de Vie)* [1969] E.C.R. 377.
[47]  Arts. 103, 104. See Chapter 4, paras. 402–404, below.
[48]  Case 31/74 *Galli* [1975] E.C.R. 47; Case 154/77 *Dechmann* [1978] E.C.R. 1473.
[49]  Cases, 90 & 91/63 *Commission* v. *Luxembourg and Belgium* [1964] E.C.R. 625, 633.

trary to a fundamental Treaty provision in the event of a sudden balance of payments crisis, so long as it complied with the provisions of Article 109.)

It is suggested that the prohibition of discriminatory taxation in Article 95 is a "fundamental principle" of the Common Market[50]: it certainly can be no less fundamental than the prohibition of discrimination between producers or consumers contained in Article 40(3). If this is indeed the case, then this principle is binding, not only on the Member States, but also on the Community Institutions themselves. Consequently, any regulation or directive of the Council or Commission must conform with this principle and, to the extent that it does not do so, will be invalid.[51] Thus a directive for the harmonisation of taxes, adopted pursuant to Article 99 or 100, must be consistent with the general principle contained in Article 95.[52] This makes the task of the Commission difficult in drafting proposals for directives—especially for the harmonisation of excise duties on alcoholic drinks—for, as discussed above, the extent to which Article 95 applies to the relative tax burdens upon competing products remains a matter of some doubt. Grave legal uncertainty will exist if the validity of a directive, and of the national legislation which faithfully implements it, is open to challenge in this manner.

## D. THE LEGAL EFFECTS OF ARTICLE 95

### (i) Failure by Member States to fulfil a Treaty obligation[53]

**67** A Member State whose tax laws or practices discriminate against products from other Member States is in breach of its obligation under Article 95 and proceedings may be brought against that state by the Commission under Article 169.[54] If the Court finds that the state has failed to fulfil its obligation, the state is required to take the necessary measures to comply with the judgment of the Court, *i.e.* to repeal or modify the offending provision so as to remove the discrimination.[55] Generally the Commission

[50] In Case 171/78 *Commission* v. *Denmark*, at Para. 20 of the judgment, the Court expressly referred to Art. 95 as a "fundamental requirement." See also Case 21/79, *Commission* v. *Italy*.

[51] See, *e.g.* Cases 80 & 81/77 *Commissionaires Réunis* [1978] E.C.R. 927; Cases 103, 145/77 *Scholten Honig* [1978] E.C.R. 2037 (the isoglucose cases); Case 117/76 *Ruckdeschel* [1977] E.C.R. 1427.

[52] Case 5/77 *Tedeschi* [1977] E.C.R. 1555, supports this contention. See also M. Prouzet, "La Politique de la CEE en Matière d'Harmonisation des Impôts Indirects" (1972) 49 R.D.I.D.C., 151, 159, and R. Wägenbaur, in Mégret, Vol. 5, p. 14. See further Chapter 3, paras. 239–242, below.

[53] Generally, see A. Barav, "Failure of Member States to fulfil their obligations under Community Law" (1975) 12 C.M.L. Rev. 369; H. G. Schermers, "The Law as it stands against Treaty violations by States" (1974/2) L.I.E.I. 111.

[54] Proceedings could also be brought by another Member State, under Art. 170, and the validity of a national law may also be tested in other proceedings, *e.g.* where a Member State contests the legality of a ruling of the Commission: See Cases 52 & 55/65 *Germany* v. *Commission* [1966] E.C.R. 159.

[55] Art. 171. See, *e.g.* Case 16/69 *Commission* v. *Italy* [1969] E.C.R. 377; Case 77/69 *Commission* v. *Belgium* [1970] E.C.R. 237. The State may choose the method of remedying its breach; Case 21/79 *Commission* v. *Italy*.

acts on the basis of complaints received, from individuals or from other Member States and, if the provision complained of appears to offend, attempts to persuade the defaulting state to remedy the position. If persuasion fails, the Commission, after giving the state the opportunity to submit its observations, delivers a reasoned opinion, stating why it considers the state to be in breach of its obligation and requiring it to take remedial action. Only if the state fails to comply with this request will proceedings be commenced before the Court. In practice, only a small proportion of Treaty violations are condemned by the Court in this manner. The Commission may be successful in securing compliance without recourse to legal proceedings, will normally resort to such action only after it has become plain that persuasion will not prevail and, among the hundreds of complaints which it investigates,[56] is necessarily selective in deciding with which to proceed. It would seem that the cases which reach the Court are normally concerned with the more significant abuses or are to be regarded as important test cases. In view of the extensive preliminary stages it is also clear that a violation may continue for a considerable time before it is pronounced upon by the Court. The recent proceedings in respect of the discriminatory taxation of alcohol[57] were the culmination of many years of effort on the part of the Commission.[58]

**68**     Proceedings under Article 169 are, consequently, a rather less than efficient means of removing discriminatory taxation. Such proceedings are, however, of crucial importance. It is only in this way that the Court of Justice specifically examines and rules upon the validity of national laws. Thus, one can learn from the Court's decisions in these cases precisely what does constitute a breach of Article 95 and also the factors which the Court considers should be taken into account in reaching such a conclusion. Of special significance is the way in which the Court refuses to restrict itself to a mere literal examination of the national law but, rather, will consider the nature and the economic effects of the tax in question,[59] how it is applied in practice,[60] the actual characteristics of the product,[61] the economic circumstances in a particular industry,[62] and the uses to which the tax revenues are put.[63] From these decisions national courts receive guidance, not only as to

[56] See (EC) Eleventh General Report (1977) pp. 12, 13.
[57] Above, paras. 38–55.
[58] Complaints of these, and similar, practices dates back to 1963 or earlier: see (EEC) Sixth General Report (1963), p. 78; (EEC) Tenth General Report (1967), p. 108; (EC) Third General Report (1969), p. 78; (EC) Eleventh General Report (1977), p. 116. Further proceedings have been commenced, against Belgium, France, Italy, Luxembourg and the Netherlands, in respect of the taxation of alcohol, fortified wines, beer, tobacco, petroleum products and sugar: see (EC) Thirteenth General Report (1979), p. 109.
[59] Case 45/64 *Commission* v. *Italy* [1965] E.C.R. 857.
[60] Case 77/69 *Commission* v. *Belgium* [1970] E.C.R. 237.
[61] Case 28/69 *Commission* v. *Italy* [1970] E.C.R. 187.
[62] Case 7/69 *Commission* v. *Italy* [1970] E.C.R. 111.
[63] Case 89/76 *Commission* v. *Netherlands* [1977] E.C.R. 1355.

the proper interpretation of Article 95, but also as to the manner in which it should be applied to particular fact situations.[64]

### (ii) Actions in national courts: the preliminary reference procedure

**69**     If individuals who were adversely affected by those discriminatory tax provisions prohibited by Article 95 were restricted to laying their complaints before the Commission and awaiting the outcome of proceedings under Article 169, their grievances would be long in obtaining redress. However, the principles of direct effect and of the supremacy of Community law are able to provide a far swifter remedy, for an individual may challenge the validity of a law of a Member State in the national courts of that state,[65] on the ground that it is contrary to Community law. This necessarily raises a question of the proper interpretation of the Treaty, or other Community Act, and, under Article 177, a court or tribunal of a Member State may, or if it is a court of final resort, must, refer the question to the Court of Justice to give a ruling thereon.[66] Unlike the Article 169 procedure, the Court does not, in giving a preliminary ruling, pronounce upon the validity or proper interpretation of the national law in dispute.[67] But the question may be phrased by the national court, or rephrased by the Court of Justice, in such a way that it is possible for the latter to declare that a national provision, which had a particular effect, *would* be contrary to Community law and be invalid.[68] It would, of course, still be for the national court to determine whether or not that provision *did* have such an effect. The jurisprudence concerning Article 95, its proper interpretation and its effect, consists of those decisions of the Court of Justice which have applied it under Article 169, its rulings as to its interpretation under Article 177, and the decisions of national courts which have interpreted it, with or without the aid of a preliminary ruling, and have applied it in domestic proceedings.

**70**     However, the recent decisions of the Court in the "alcohol" cases raise a doubt as to whether the principles of law which it expresses in proceedings under Article 169 are necessarily always applicable in actions by individuals before their national courts. As has been suggested above,[69] in actions alleging breach by a Member State of its Treaty obligations, the Court is concer-

---

[64] See however the remarks below, at para. 70.

[65] Or, perhaps, even in the courts of another Member State: see Case 104/79 *Foglia* v. *Novello* (not yet reported).

[66] See further, J. L. Mashaw, "Ensuring the observance of Law in the Interpretation and Application of the EEC Treaty . . . " (1970) 7 C.M.L. Rev. 258, 423: H. G. Schermers, "The Law as it stands on Preliminary Rulings" (1974/1) L.I.E.I. 93: A. Barav, "Some aspects of the Preliminary Ruling Procedure in EEC Law" (1977) 2 E.L. Rev. 3.

[67] Case 74/72 *FOR* v. *VKS* [1973] E.C.R. 193. An exception to this occurs where the national law in question has been declared, in Art. 169 proceedings, to be contrary to the Treaty: see Case 68/79 *Hans Just* (not yet reported).

[68] See, *e.g.* Case 13/78 *Eggers* [1978] E.C.R. 1935; Case 83/78 *Redmond* [1978] E.C.R. 2347.

[69] At. para. 54.

ned more with the effect as a whole of the provision or system in question. In the national court the question concerns the effect of the provision in a particular case. Thus, as cases such as *Bobie*[70] illustrate, it is sufficient that an individual demonstrate that the tax imposed upon a particular product imported from another Member State is greater than that imposed upon a similar domestic product, even though other similar domestic products may be taxed as heavily as, or more heavily than the imported product. As pointed out, the actions against *France, Italy* and *Denmark* succeeded essentially because the lower tax rate applied to predominantly domestic products and the higher rate to predominantly imported products. It was therefore suggested that it would be permissible, in the context of Article 169, for a country such as Germany to tax wine-based spirits more heavily than cereal-based spirits, since it produces both in substantial quantities, or for Italy to tax beer more heavily than wine.[71]

**71**     The problem arises, however, that a German importer of French brandy (or an Italian importer of British beer) might claim that the tax imposed upon the imported product was greater than that upon a similar or competing domestic product. If the Court has declared that the two products which are being compared[72] are "similar," or at any rate should bear an equivalent or proportionate tax burden, is it possible for the national court not to allow such a claim, or must it also consider whether its own government is in breach of the Treaty?[73]

It is submitted that, by insisting upon a "Community" meaning of the concepts of "similar" and "competing" products, the result is that although a member state which produces substantial quantities of both products which are being compared, and taxes them differently or disproportionately, would apparently not be condemned in proceedings under Article 169, an importer of the disadvantaged product into that country would still be entitled to invoke the protection of Article 95. Thus, the fiscal sovereignty which the Court reaffirmed to exist in principle is, in fact, illusory, except that domestic products and producers may continue to be discriminated against. This is all the more serious since it is now clear that Article 95 applies also to the *relative* taxation of dissimilar but competing products. There must be many cases, in all Member States, where different but competing products are not taxed in a proper relationship to each other, for economic or social reasons or for no reason at all: all of these cases are potential subjects for litigation. One thing does seem to be clear: it will require many references to the Court under Article 177 before the problems raised by its latest decisions are resolved.

[70] Case 127/75 [1976] E.C.R. 1079.
[71] This is the view taken by the Commission.
[72] And is the Plaintiff free to choose with which particular domestic product his import should be compared?
[73] It would be contrary to the entire jurisprudence of the Court to require that the national system must first have been condemned by the Court : see below.

### (iii) The direct effect of Article 95

**72**    In its landmark judgment in the *Tariefcommissie* case[74] the Court established that a Treaty provision (in that case Article 12), in addition to imposing obligations upon Member States, may, in certain circumstances, confer rights which are directly enforceable by individuals in national courts.[75] The *Tariefcommissie* case was concerned with an appeal, in a Dutch court by a Dutch importer of chemicals from Germany, against an assessment to customs duty. It was claimed that, by virtue of a reclassification of products in the Dutch customs tariff, the duty on ureaformaldehyde had been increased and that this was contrary to Article 12, which provides that member States shall refrain from introducing, as between themselves, any new customs duties and from increasing those which they already levy. The Court held that the Article sets out a clear and unconditional prohibition which is perfectly suited by its nature to produce direct effects in the legal relations between the Member States and their citizens.

**73**    The principle was first applied to Article 95, a few years later, in the *Lütticke* case.[76] The Lütticke company, whose contribution to Community jurisprudence in its numerous recourses to litigation was wryly acknowledged in another case,[77] challenged an assessment by the German authorities to turnover equalisation tax (Umsatzausgleichsteuer) on the importation from Luxembourg of a quantity of powdered milk. It alleged that the tax was prohibited under Article 95, since the domestic product was exempt from turnover tax. The German court, the Finanzgericht Saarland, referred the issue to the Court of Justice and specifically asked if Article 95(1) has direct effects and creates for the individual rights to which national courts should give effect. It further asked if similar effects were created by Article 95(3) (providing that Member States shall, not later than at the beginning of the second stage,[78] repeal or amend any provisions existing at the time when the Treaty entered into force which conflict with the rules set out in the first two paragraphs). It was strenuously argued by the German government, with support from the Belgian and Dutch governments, that Article 95, being expressly addressed to the Member States, could not give rise to rights enforceable by individuals and that any violation of its rules by a Member State could only be remedied by recourse to Article 169. It was further argued, in relation to the third paragraph, that, unlike the first

---

[74] Case 26/62 *Van Gend en Loos* [1963] E.C.R. 1.

[75] An abundance of scholarly literature exists on this subject. See, in particular, G. Bebr, "Directly Applicable provisions of Community Law ..." (1970) 19 I.C.L.Q. 257; A. Dashwood, "The principle of Direct Effect in European Community Law" (1977–8) 16 J.C.M.S. 229; J. A. Winter, "Direct Applicability and Direct Effect ..." (1972) 9 C.M.L. Rev. 425.

[76] Case 57/65 [1966] E.C.R. 205. See the note by K. Mailänder, in (1966–67) 4 C.M.L. Rev. 330.

[77] *Per* Advocate-General Dutheiller de Lamothe, in Case 4/69 *Lütticke* v. *Commission* [1971] E.C.R. 325, at pp. 339–340.

[78] *i.e.* not later than January 1, 1962.

paragraph which imposes a "standstill obligation" (*i.e.* not to introduce a tax contrary to the provisions of the Article), the third paragraph imposes a positive obligation to act (*i.e.* to repeal existing laws which do not conform). The Court held, however, that Article 95(1) lays down a general and permanent Community rule and states a prohibition of discrimination which constitutes a clear and unconditional obligation which is legally complete and consequently capable of producing direct effects in the legal relations between the Member States and their subjects. The fact that the Article designates the Member States as subject to the obligation does not mean that individuals cannot benefit from it. As to the third paragraph, whilst it involves an obligation to act, in the sense that existing discriminations must be eliminated or corrected, that obligation does not leave the Member States any discretion, except that it be done at some time prior to the specified date. It follows that, in the case of pre-existing discriminations, the general prohibition in Article 95 has direct effect only as from that date.

74      The impact of the *Lütticke* decision was enormous. Whereas previously complaints against discriminatory taxes had been made to the Commission, which sought to persuade the offending states to remedy the situation or ultimately commenced proceedings under Article 169, it now became clear that a far more effective and swift remedy was available—an individual could simply refuse to pay the tax and could contest its validity in the national courts.[79] In Germany especially the effect of the decision was horrendous: some 330,000 petitions were lodged by importers and 22,000 tax appeals initiated in the national courts.[80] Many of these appeals were founded upon what was subsequently shown to be a mistaken application of the direct effect principle to Article 97,[81] but meanwhile German courts produced conflicting judgments and in some cases even appeared to question the correctness of the decision of the Court of Justice.[82] In the event, the Bundesfinanzhof, the supreme German tax court, asked the Court of Justice to reconsider its decision in *Lütticke* and to clarify the position with regard to Article 97.

75      This reference, in the *Mölkerei Zentrale* case,[83] together with six other references from German courts, was ruled upon by the Court of Justice in April, 1968. The Court confirmed its decision in *Lütticke*, stating:

[79] See the comments of the Commission in (EEC) Tenth General Report (1967), at p. 106. For a comparison of the effectiveness of the two remedies, contrast Case 7/68 *Commission* v. *Italy* [1968] E.C.R. 423 (art treasures) and Case 18/71 *Eunomia di Porro* [1971] E.C.R. 811.

[80] See P. Hay, "Supremacy of Community Law in National Courts" (1968) 16 A.J.C.L. 524; C. W. Timmermans, (1968–69) 6 C.M.L. Rev. 132 (note).

[81] See below, para. 89.

[82] See, in particular, the *Powdered Milk* cases in the Finanzgerichte of Düsseldorf and Saarland, and in the Bundesfinanzhof: [1967] C.M.L.R. 107, 319, 326, and the notes by K. Hopt, (1966–67) 4 C.M.L. Rev. 450; (1967–68) 5 C.M.L. Rev. 73; (1970) 7 C.M.L. Rev. 87; (1971) 8 C.M.L. Rev. 97.

[83] Case 28/67 [1968] E.C.R. 143. See the note by C. W. Timmermans, *op. cit.* above, n. 80.

"The first paragraph of Article 95 contains a prohibition against discrimination, constituting a clear and unconditional obligation ... This prohibition is therefore complete, legally perfect and consequently capable of producing direct effects on the legal relationships between Member States and persons within their jurisdiction."[84]

The Court further confirmed, notably in the *Fink-Frucht* case,[85] that the second paragraph of Article 95 also produces direct effects. Notwithstanding that, as was pointed out by the German government, the meaning of Article 95 is far from clear, especially as to what constitute "similar" and "other" products, the Court urged that the obligation is unconditional, requiring no implementing action of the part of Member States, and:

"Although the provision involves the evaluation of economic factors, this does not exclude the right and duty of national courts to ensure that the rules of the Treaty are observed ... "[86]

76      Implicit in the ruling that Article 95 produces direct effects, which can be relied upon by individuals in their national courts, is that national laws, including those enacted subsequent to the Treaty, are subordinate to the prohibition and may not be applied to the extent that they offend Article 95. As the Court has recently reaffirmed in *Simmenthal*,[87] a national court which is called upon to apply provisions of Community law is under a duty to give full effect to those provisions, if necessary by refusing to apply conflicting provisions of national legislation, notwithstanding that the national provisions were enacted at a later date than the Community provisions. That is the position according to Community law: it has been accepted, occasionally with some hesitation or reservation, by the national courts of those Member States which have been confronted with the dilemma.[88] Though British courts have not as yet been compelled to choose between the supremacy of Parliament and of Community law, it would seem from recent utterances that they would be prepared to accord precedence to directly applicable provisions of Community law (by which apparently is meant those provisions which have direct effect) over a conflicting national law, at any rate where the national law does not expressly exclude the application of Community law.[89]

[84]  |1968| E.C.R., at p. 153.
[85]  Case 27/67 |1968| E.C.R. 223. This is also implicit in its decision in Case 68/79 *Hans Just* (not yet reported) in which the effects of the first and second paragraphs were considered together.
[86]  *Ibid.* at p. 232.
[87]  Case 106/77 |1978| E.C.R. 629.
[88]  See, especially, the decisions of the Belgian Cour d'Appel, in *Fromageries "Le Ski"* |1970| C.M.L.R. 219 and of the French Cour de Cassation, in *Cafés Jacques Vabre* |1975| 2 C.M.L.R. 336. And see G. Bebr, "How supreme is Community Law in the national courts?" (1974) 11 C.M.L. Rev. 3.
[89]  See the remarks of Lord Hailsham of St. Marylebone in *The Siskina* |1978| 1 C.M.L.R. 190 (House of Lords) and of Lord Denning M.R. in *Macarthys Ltd.* v. *Smith* |1979| 3 C.M.L.R. 44 (Court of Appeal).

### (iv)    The application of Article 95 by national courts

77    Under the preliminary reference procedure the Court of Justice is restricted to ruling on the interpretation of the Treaty: it does not determine the validity or otherwise of the national law in question, neither does it determine the issue between the parties to the action. These are matters for the national courts alone, though where a Community provision is applicable it must be applied in accordance with the principles of Community law. The national court may have to decide whether the imposition in question is an internal tax or is a charge with equivalent effect to a customs duty[90] and, if it is a tax, whether or not it is discriminatory.[91] It may also have to determine if products are "similar," or are competing, within the meaning of Article 95.[92]

The Court of Justice has further ruled that:

"... when internal taxation is incompatible with the first paragraph of Article 95 only beyond a certain amount, it is for the national court to decide, *according to the rules of its national law*, whether this illegality affects the taxation as a whole or only so much of it as exceeds that amount."[93]

According to Community law, if a national court finds that an imported product has been taxed more heavily than a similar domestic product, it is entitled, if its own law permits, to reduce the tax assessed on the import to the level of that on the domestic product. National law, however, may not permit such forms of "judicial legislation" and the court may have no alternative but to discharge the assessment entirely. This may produce the further anomalous result that, until such time as the national legislature enacts an amending law which complies with Article 95, the imported product will enjoy an advantage by way of total exemption.

78    An additional result of the fact that the national law is invalid only to the extent to which it offends Article 95, as opposed to being invalid *if* it offends the article, is that the national courts may continue to apply the law in situations where to do so is not contrary to the prohibition. For example, the German Federal Tax Court has held that a turnover equalisation tax, which discriminates against imports from Member States, may nevertheless continue to be applied to products from third countries.[94] If we return to the example discussed previously,[95] where one product, which is mainly

---

[90] Case 77/76 *Cucchi* [1977] E.C.R. 987, and see the decision of the Dutch *Tariefcommissie* in *Van Gend en Loos* [1970] C.M.L.R. 1.
[91] *Cafès Jacques Vabre*, above, n. 88.
[92] *Imported Almonds* [1971] C.M.L.R. 87, decision of the Finanzgericht Hamburg.
[93] Case 28/67 *Mölkerei Zentrale* [1968] E.C.R. 143, at p. 154, (italics added). See also Case 34/67 *Lück* [1968] E.C.R. 245, and the judgment of the Bundesfinanzhof in *Mölkerei Zentrale* [1969] C.M.L.R. 300.
[94] See *Lütticke* [1969] C.M.L.R. 221 (Bundesfinanzhof).
[95] At paras. 61, 62, above.

imported but of which there is a small domestic production, is taxed in such a manner as to afford protection to another product, the production of which is mainly domestic, then, although the tax assessed upon the importer is improper (to the extent to which it is discriminatory) this is not necessarily so of the tax assessed upon the home producer. A Member State may, it seems, validly discriminate as between its domestic products and producers,[96] and a tax assessment on a domestic producer would therefore not offend Article 95 even if a similar assessment made against an importer would do so.

Finally, where a tax has been paid which was invalidly imposed, it is a question of national law whether or not it can be recovered. It is clear that a law which is contrary to Article 95 is invalid to that extent, and will always have been invalid[97] and does not merely become invalid when declared to be so by the Court.[98] But recovery of the tax may nevertheless depend upon national rules such as limitation periods.

**79**     The question was expressly referred to the Court in the recent case of *Hans Just*.[99] The Danish company, Hans Just I/S, had been assessed to tax on the importation of six litres of akvavit and 2,159 litres of other spirits, under the law which was subsequently condemned by the Court in the action against *Denmark*.[1] The tax was paid under protest and the company sought recovery of some 200,000 krone claiming that the rate of tax on the other spirits should not have been greater than that on the akvavit. The Danish Government doubtless feared a flood of claims similar to that which had occurred in Germany following the *Lütticke* decision[2] and was concerned that it should not be exposed to claims going back to the beginning of 1973,[3] which might amount to 1,000 million Kroner. It urged that, under Danish law, the question of recovery of taxes wrongfully levied or paid in error is a matter for the national judge and depends upon whether or not the applicant has suffered detriment. In the particular case, it was alleged, the Just company had suffered no such detriment since it had merely served as an agent of collection and had passed the burden of tax on to the consumer. To permit it to recover the tax in such circumstances would constitute unjust enrichment and would offend one of the cornerstones of the principles of Danish law.

[96] This seems implicit in decisions such as that in Case 127/75 *Bobie* [1976] E.C.R. 1079 and has now been confirmed by the Court in Case 68/79 *Hans Just*, see para 62, above.

[97] At least since the beginning of the second stage in 1962 (Art. 95(3)), or since accession to the Community, or the expiration of any transitional period, in the case of a new member state.

[98] Case 77/76 *Cucchi* [1977] E.C.R. 987; Case 105/76 *Interzuccheri* [1977] E.C.R. 1029.

[99] Case 68/79 (not yet reported).

[1] Case 171/78 above, paras. 38, 39.

[2] Above, paras. 73, 74.

[3] Or to 1975, the normal Danish limitation period being five years. In the United Kingdom, the relevant limitation period is three months: Customs and Excise Management Act 1979, s. 127.

**80**      Earlier jurisprudence of the Court might have suggested that the principle of direct effect would demand repayment of the tax.[4] However,[5] the Court held that, in the absence of Community rules on the question of recovery of national taxes improperly levied, it rests with the internal legal order of each Member State to prescribe the competent courts and to lay down the procedural rules of law designed to ensure the protection of rights which the parties derive from the direct effect of Community law, on the understanding that these rules may not be less favourable than those governing a similar action of an internal nature and that in no event may they operate in such a manner as to render impossible, in practice, the exercise of those rights which the national courts are obliged to protect. Thus, Community law does not demand the making of restitution of taxes which have been improperly levied in conditions which would involve the unjust enrichment of the person in whose favour the right exists, but nor (added the Court) would it be contrary to Community law if courts, according to their national laws, also took into account the detriment which an importer may have suffered as a result of discriminatory or protective fiscal measures.[6]

As a result, it may be complained that the protection afforded by Article 95 to individuals may vary considerably from one Member State to another. Limitation periods may be long or short and the principle of unjust enrichment may apply to some claims and not to others. Moreover, since Article 95 applies essentially to taxes on products, the burden of which is passed on to the consumer, the acceptance of the unjust enrichment principle may come perilously close to rendering impossible in practice the exercise of those rights which the Court declared must be protected.

## E.   THE TAX PROVISIONS AND BORDER TAX ADJUSTMENTS

### (i)   The taxation of goods in international trade

**81**      Where goods are produced, or partly produced, in one country (A) and are sold in another country (B), a fundamental issue is to determine which country, A or B, should tax those goods. In the absence of special rules governing international transactions of this kind, a variety of solutions is available. The goods may be taxed only in Country A, only in B, in neither, or in both, and, in the latter case, they may be taxed fully in both or only partly. This depends, essentially, upon the type of taxation levied upon goods in each country, and the stage or stages at which it is levied. Suppose,

---

[4] This would seem to follow from Case 106/77 *Simmenthal* [1978] E.C.R. 629, and see the remarks of Advocate-General Reischl in Case 77/76 *Cucchi* [1977] E.C.R. 987, at p. 1020.

[5] Applying the principle established in Case 33/76 *Rewe* and Case 45/76 *Comet* [1976] E.L.R. 1989; see the comments of D. Wyatt, (1977) 2 E.L. Rev. 122.

[6] The appellant company alleged that it had suffered detriment in that its volume of imports and sales had been affected by virtue of the higher after-tax price. How such a detriment might be measured the Court did not indicate.

for example, that a particular article goes through the following stages on its way to the ultimate consumer: the raw materials are sold to a manufacturer in country A, the manufacturer produces the finished article and sells it to a wholesaler-importer in country B, who sells it to a retailer who, in turn, sells it to a consumer in country B. If the countries each impose a single-stage sales tax the tax burden borne by the product will depend upon the stages at which the tax is imposed in each country. Thus, if both countries impose a manufacturer's sales tax, it will be taxed in A. If both apply a wholesale sales tax, it will be taxed in B. If A has a manufacturer's sales tax and B has a wholesale sales tax, it will be taxed twice, once in each country. If the tax systems are reversed, it will be taxed in neither. If the countries impose multi-stage turnover taxes, levying tax on each transaction, then the first two transactions will be taxed in A and the third and fourth in B.[7] Further combinations are possible, where one country uses a multi-stage system and the other a single-stage system. The above merely demonstrates that the tax burden borne by a product in a transaction of this kind varies according to the tax system adopted by each country and, of course, according to the rate of tax applied. Unless both system and rate are the same in each country, the tax burden on the article imported into country B and consumed there will differ from that borne by a similar domestically produced article.[8] Competition between the imported and domestic articles is consequently likely to be distorted by virtue of the differences in the amount of tax which each has borne.

### (a) The "origin" and "destination" principles[9]

**82**    According to traditional theory, an article which is traded across a frontier may be taxed according to one of two jurisdictional principles—the origin principle or the destination principle. It may be taxed either where it is produced or where it is consumed. This, however, is a gross oversimplification.

**Origin principle.** The real essence of the origin principle is that the tax on an article applies equally to all domestically produced values regardless of the ultimate destination of the article and does not apply to values produced abroad. Thus exports are taxed up to their export value in the same way as articles sold on the domestic market while imports are exempt from tax up to their import value.[10] In effect no adjustments are made by virtue of the fact that the article is exported or imported. Since no adjust-

---

[7] A multi-stage turnover tax is not, of course, necessarily levied at every stage. It may, *e.g.* not apply at the retail stage.

[8] Unless the difference in system and rate cancel each other out.

[9] For a comprehensive analysis of these principles, see H. Möller, "Ursprüngs-und Bestimmungslandprinzip" (1968) 27 *Finanzarchiv* 385; H. Shibata, in C. S. Shoup (ed.), *Fiscal Harmonisation in Common Markets* (1967), Vol. I, Chapter 2 (referred to hereafter as Shoup, *Fiscal Harmonization*).

[10] C. K. Sullivan, in Shoup, *Fiscal Harmonization*, Vol. II, at p. 21.

ments are made, there is no need for tax frontiers. On the other hand, differences between national tax systems, or rates of tax, will affect the tax burden as between imported and domestically produced articles (as demonstrated above) and these tax differentials will be reflected in prices, thus distorting the conditions of competition. Goods imported from a low-tax country will be able to undercut those produced in a country where the tax is higher,[11] causing trade deficits in the latter unless it takes steps to counteract this effect by reducing the real costs of domestic production or the rate of exchange of its currency.[12] As neither of these solutions is attractive,[13] it is widely accepted that the origin principle is only suitable when applied between countries with identical, or closely similar, tax systems and rates.

**Destination principle.** The alternative theory is to tax all products alike where they are consumed, regardless of their country of origin. Thus, although an article has been imported, it is taxed as if it had been produced in the country of its ultimate destination. The normal corollary of this is that articles which are produced in a country and are destined for export are not taxed in the country of production. The advantage of this system is that all goods, when finally sold to the consumer, should have borne the same tax burden, *i.e.* that imposed by the country of destination, regardless of where they were originally produced and competition between domestic and imported products is not distorted by tax differences. The chief disadvantage is that the destination principle requires a system of border tax adjustments: on exportation the tax already borne by the article in the country of production is remitted, and on importation a compensatory tax is imposed in order to equalise the tax burden on that article with that borne by the corresponding domestic product.

83  (b)  *The provisions of GATT*[14]

In international transactions between countries with widely differing tax systems and rates, the destination principle is more appropriate and this is recognised in the General Agreement on Tariffs and Trade.[15] With regard to imports, Article III of the Agreement provides:

[11] Though small differences in tax may be absorbed by higher transportation costs: see W. M. McNie, in Shoup, *Fiscal Harmonization*, Vol. I, Chap. 3.

[12] See the analysis in the *Report on the problems raised by the different Turnover Tax systems applied within the Common Market*: ECSC High Authority, 1953 (referred to hereafter as the Tinbergen Report).

[13] And major exchange rate adjustments would be contrary to the proposals for economic and monetary union in the Community: See Chapter 4, paras. 408, 409, below.

[14] General Agreement on Tariffs and Trade, a multilateral agreement signed on October 30, 1947, and adhered to by the great majority of the world's trading nations.

[15] For analysis of the border tax adjustment rules in GATT, see R. H. Floyd, "GATT Provisions on Border Tax Adjustments" (1973) 7 J.W.T.L. 489; M. Leontiades, "The Logic of Border Taxes" (1966) 19 N.T.J. 173; M. von Steinaecker, *Domestic Taxation and Foreign Trade . . .* (1973), Chap. 6.

"1. The contracting parties recognise that internal taxes . . . should not be applied to imported . . . products so as to afford protection to domestic production.

2. The products of the territory of any contracting party imported into the territory of any other contracting party shall not be subject, directly or indirectly, to internal taxes . . . in excess of those applied, directly or indirectly, to like domestic products. Moreover, no contracting party shall otherwise apply internal taxes . . . to imported . . . products in a manner contrary to the principles set forth in paragraph 1.

Article II further provides:

"2. Nothing in this Article shall prevent any contracting party from imposing at any time on the importation of any product:

> (a) a charge equivalent to an internal tax imposed consistently with the provisions of paragraph 2 of Article III in respect of the like domestic product or in respect of an article from which the imported product has been manufactured or produced in whole or in part; . . . "

As regards exports, Article XVI restricts the granting of subsidies, but an Addendum provides that:

> "The exemption of an exported product from duties or taxes borne by the like product when destined for domestic consumption, or the remission of such duties or taxes in amounts not in excess of those which have accrued, shall not be deemed to be a subsidy."[16]

The application of the destination principle is therefore permissive, rather than mandatory. Contracting parties may impose compensatory taxes on imports and may exempt from tax, or remit taxes on, exports, but there is no requirement that they do so. It should be added that Member States of the Community are subject, as contracting parties, to the rules of the GATT in their trade with non-Member States.[17]

**84**     (c)   *Direct and indirect taxes*

The GATT refers only to those taxes which are "imposed upon," "applied to," or "borne by" a particular product.[18] This, of course, raises

---

[16] The edited extracts from the GATT are quoted from Appendix II of M. von Steinaecker, *op. cit.* above.

[17] As to the legal effects of the GATT rules, see R. E. Hudec, *"The GATT Legal System and World Trade Diplomacy"* (1975), especially Chap. 3, and J. H. Jackson, "The Puzzle of GATT" (1967) 1 J.W.T.L. 131. The Finanzgericht Hamburg held, in *Re Chilean Apples* (decision of October 29, 1966, translated in (1971) 65 A.J.I.L. 627) that, unlike Art. 95, the rules of the GATT are not, in German law, self-executing and are not enforceable by individuals. See further, S. A. Riesenfeld, "The Doctrine of Self-Executing Treaties and GATT" (1971) 65 A.J.I.L. 548; M. Waelbroeck, "Effect of GATT within the legal order of the EEC" (1974) 8 J.W.T.L. 614, and G. Bebr, *op. cit.* (at pp. 257–261), above, at p. 55, n. 75.

[18] *Cf.* Arts. 95–98, EEC, referring to tax "imposed on" products.

again the question of which taxes are imposed on, or borne by, products, whether directly or indirectly.[19] The apparent intention of the GATT rules, and it would seem of the EEC rules, is that border tax adjustments may be made only in respect of indirect taxation, such as sales or turnover taxes and excise duties, and not in respect of direct taxes, such as income or business profits taxes, property taxes or social insurance contributions, for these are regarded as being imposed upon the producer rather than upon the product.[20] The rationale for this distinction appears to be founded on the traditional view that indirect taxes are fully shifted forward to the consumer in the price of the product, whereas the burden of direct taxation remains with the producer and is borne by the enterprise, its owners, shareholders or employees. Modern economic theory would suggest that neither assumption is wholly correct: a producer may choose to absorb some part of an increase in indirect taxation rather than to pass it on to the consumer in the form of higher prices and risk a reduction in total sales and profits, and will similarly seek to shift forward an increase in direct taxation if able to do so, rather than reduce net profits, dividends or wages.[21]

**85**      This distinction, between direct and indirect taxes, raises two problems. First, the question of classification itself: is a particular tax one which it is permitted, under either GATT or EEC rules, to remit on exportation or impose on importation?[22] For example, is a tax imposed upon transportation generally to be regarded as a tax on the goods which happen to be transported?[23] And how should other types of business tax and even value-added tax be classified?[24] Secondly, in so far as the economic effects of direct and indirect taxes may be much less different than is implied by the distinction, the destination principle, in seeking to remove one form of distortion to competition, may introduce another distortion. A country which relies heavily upon direct taxation and imposes a relatively low indirect tax on goods, such as the United States of America,[25] may be at a disadvantage as against a country where direct taxation is low and indirect

---

[19]   See above, paras. 26–28.
[20]   See R.W. Rosendahl, "Border Tax Adjustments: Problems and Proposals" (1970) 2 L.P.I.B. 85: R.E. Latimer, "The Border Tax Adjustment Question" (1968) 16 Can. Tax Jo. 409, and see the Report of the GATT Working Party on Subsidies, approved by the Contracting Parties on November 13, 1960.
[21]   See P.B. Feller, "Mutiny against the Bounty: an Examination of Subsidies, Border Tax Adjustments and the Resurgence of the Countervailing Duty Law" (1969) 1 L.P.I.B. 17.
[22]   For a comprehensive analysis of this problem, see "*Méthodes et moyens pour établir une nouvelle classification des impôts . . .*" EC Commission, Série Concurrence — Rapprochement des Législations, No. 13, 1970 (the Hesse Report).
[23]   See the discussion of Case 20/76 *Schöttle*, at para. 27, above.
[24]   See Chapter 2, para. 107, below. The classification of a tax will frequently depend upon the form in which it is imposed, rather than upon its economic effects. Thus, the former British Selective Employment Tax would seem to have been a (direct) payroll tax though essentially it performed the role of an (indirect) sales tax on the performance of services.
[25]   See M. B. Krauss, "Border Tax Adjustments: a potential Trans-Atlantic Trade Dispute" (1976) 10 J.W.T.L. 145; G. M. Grossman, "Alternative Border Tax Policies" (1978) 12 J.W.T.L. 452.

taxation is high. The same is true for different Member States within the Community. To give but one example, if country A finances its social security system by means of large social insurance contributions or payroll taxes, whereas country B finances these out of general revenue derived from high sales taxes, the conditions of trade are distorted in favour of the products of country B. Suppose that an article is sold in country B at a price of 125, comprised of 100 as the cost of production and 25 sales tax. The same article produced in country A is also sold there at 125, being 120 cost of production,[26] plus (approximately) 5 sales tax, *i.e.* assuming sales tax at 25 per cent. in country B and at 4 per cent. in country A. If the cost of transportation between the two countries is 5, then the article exported from B to A will sell in A at 109 (cost 100, transportation 5, sales tax 4), whereas the article exported from A to B will sell at 156 (cost 120, transportation 5, sales tax 31). The obvious conclusion is that any large disparity between countries, in the proportions in which each relies on direct and indirect taxation, is likely to distort the conditions of competition.

## (ii)   Border tax adjustments in the European Community

**86**   (a)   *The Coal and Steel Community*

The ECSC Treaty has little to say on the subject of taxation, apart from the general prohibition on import and export duties and charges having equivalent effect and upon subsidies or aids granted by Member States and special levies imposed by them.[27] The question of border tax adjustments was not dealt with at all, though the Community had been in existence for less than a year before the issue arose, in what came to be known as the "ECSC Tax Dispute."[28] The main parties to the dispute were France, which applied a value-added tax at fairly high rates, and Germany, which applied a cumulative turnover tax at relatively low rates. Not unnaturally, France favoured the adoption of the destination principle, Germany supported the origin principle. Faced with this problem, the High Authority set up, in March 1953, a Committee to examine the question. This Committee, under the chairmanship of Professor Tinbergen, reported back in little over one month.[29] It concluded that for a general tax, whether direct or indirect, either system might be adopted without distorting the conditions of

[26] The cost being greater due to higher profits and payroll taxes.
[27] ECSC Treaty, Art 4(2), (c). Arts. 60 and 67, dealing respectively with pricing policy and competition, contain general rules which have some application to tax provisions. See also Arts. 2 and 11 of the Convention on the Transitional Provisions. For an analysis of these provisions, see R. Regul and W. Renner, *Finances and Taxes in European Integration* (1966), Chap. 2.
[28] For full descriptions, see R. Regul and W. Renner (*op. cit.* above); J. E. Meade, H. H. Liesner and S. J. Wells, *Case Studies in European Economic Union* ..." (1962) Chap. 4; G. Schmolders, "*Turnover Taxes*" (1966), Part V.
[29] The Tinbergen Report, above, n. 12.

competition,[30] provided that the same system of tax was applied to all industries and products, nor was it necessary to adopt the same system (origin or destination) for all taxes.[31] But to apply the origin principle to some products and the destination principle to others would cause distortion, where some degree of substitution between these products was possible, unless all member states agreed to adopt the same rate of general turnover tax and imposed it on the same basis.[32] Since the latter solution was highly improbable in the short term and since only the coal and steel industries came within the scope of the Treaty, this constituted a recommendation to retain the destination principle which was being applied in their external trade by all the Member States. This recommendation was adopted by the High Authority in a Decision of May 2, 1953.[33]

*(b)   The Economic Community*

As already mentioned in the introductory section of this chapter, Articles 95 to 98 apply, or rather permit the application of, the destination principle in intra-Community trade. These provisions will now be considered.

### (iii)   Compensatory taxes on imports

87      The essential feature of the destination principle is that goods are taxed in the country where they are consumed, regardless of their origin. Thus imported goods are subjected to the tax of the country into which they are imported. As we have seen, Article 95 permits this, provided that the imported product is not taxed more heavily than the similar, or competing, domestic product. It has been further pointed out[34] that this rule would remain necessary even if the destination principle, and the system of border tax adjustments, were to be abandoned.

A major problem in applying Article 95 is caused by the difficulty of calculating the precise amount of tax which has been imposed upon the corresponding domestic product. This was especially so in the case of those Member States which applied a cumulative system of turnover tax, as did five of the original six members.[35] Where turnover tax was payable upon each transaction when a product changed hands in the course of its produc-

---

[30] Though there might be other effects, *e.g.* on balance of trade and payments.

[31] Thus the destination principle could apply to indirect taxes and the origin principle to direct taxes. However, as the Neumark Report (see Chapter 2 paras. 109–111, below) points out (at p. 146) it is misleading to talk in terms of origin and destination principles in relation to direct taxes.

[32] Tinbergen Report, pp. 25–27. For a full analysis of the recommendations, see the works cited in n. 28, above, and for a shorter comment (by a member of the committee) see W. B. Reddaway, "The Implications of a Free Trade Area for British Taxation" [1958] B.T.R. 71.

[33] Dec. 30/53/ECSC (J.O. 1953, 109).

[34] At Para. 6, above.

[35] See para. 13, above.

tion and marketing, one domestic product might have been taxed  several times—on sales by the producer of the raw material, by the manufacturer, by the wholesaler—whereas another domestic product might not have been taxed at all, because the manufacturer produced his own raw materials and retailed the product himself. At what rate, then, should a foreign product be taxed? The general rule, established by the Court, is that it should not be taxed more heavily than the least-heavily taxed domestic product to which it corresponds.[36]

**88**     However, by way of what may be regarded as a derogation from the basic principle of Article 95, Article 97 provides that Member States which levy a turnover tax calculated on a cumulative multi-stage tax system may, in the case of internal taxation imposed by them on imported products,[37] establish average rates for products or groups of products, though it adds the proviso that there shall be no infringement of the principles laid down in Articles 95 and 96. As the Court of Justice has explained:

> "The object of Article 97 with regard to imports is to ensure that equalisation taxes imposed within the framework of a cumulative multi-stage tax system are in conformity with the principles of Article 95. Having regard to the special characteristics of this system of taxation, the economic effects of which may very often only be calculated approximately, the Treaty allows Member States to take certain measures of a flat-rate nature consisting in the determination of average rates of tax on the importation of specific products or groups of products. Such a system necessarily implies, on the part of the states which apply it, the exercise of a discretion . . ."[38]

Two conditions must be met in order for Article 97 to apply.[39] First, the Member State must levy a cumulative-type turnover tax. Since no Member State now does so, the Article may be regarded as a dead-letter, though it will become applicable again when the Community is further enlarged, unless new members have adopted the value-added tax system.[40] The intention of Article 97 would seem to be that average rates may be adopted only with respect to the turnover tax: thus average rates may not be established for other forms of tax, even though similar problems of calculation may apply.[41]

---

[36] Case 127/75 *Bobie*: see above, pp. 30–32.

[37] Art. 97 also applies to the calculation of remissions of tax on exports: see below, para. 92.

[38] Case 4/69 *Lütticke* [1971] E.C.R. 325, at p. 337. See also Case 29/68 *Milchkontor* [1969] E.C.R., at p. 181.

[39] Case 28/67 *Mölkerei Zentrale* [1968] E.C.R. 143; Case 29/68 *Milchkontor* above.

[40] By the Treaty of Accession of Greece (O.J. 1979, L. 291), Greece may defer adoption of the VAT until the beginning of 1984. Until then, Art. 97 will be applicable.

[41] *Cf.* the Commission's suggestion in Case 127/75 *Bobie* [1976] E.C.R. 1079, above para. 31, and the Court's comments in Case 55/79 *Commission v. Ireland* [1980] 1 C.M.L.R..

**89**     The second condition is that the Member State must have established average rates. According to the jurisprudence of the Court of Justice and of the national courts (in particular the German courts), an "average rate" need not have been expressly adopted pursuant to Article 97: a rate fixed before the Treaty came into force may nevertheless be a genuine average.[42] According to Community law, a declaration by a Member State that a particular rate has been established as an average rate is sufficient proof[43] though it still remains for the national court to determine what constitutes an average rate and whether or not its government has availed itself of the opportunity to fix an average rate.[44] An average rate may consequently be valid even though it imposes a higher tax burden on an import than on the corresponding domestic product (which, as an average, it must of necessity sometimes do), and Article 97 does not require an exact balance to be struck in the case of each product, though neither does it authorise a purely arbitrary rate.[45]

As has been mentioned, the legal effect of Article 97 was, for sometime, a matter of considerable controversy.[46] Article 97 permits a measure of discretion to the Member States and this discretion, so long as it is exercised properly, precludes the possibility of the direct effect of the Article.[47] If a Member State has established an average rate and that rate is considered to be contrary to the principles of Article 95, it is essentially for the Commission to take the appropriate action.[48] Nevertheless, the meaning of the proviso to Article 97 is unclear[49] and subsequent decisions of the Court suggest that, where there is a clear prohibition subject to a limited discretion on the part of Member States to derogate therefrom, then, if the Member State exceeds the limits of this discretion, the fundamental prohibition retains its direct effect.[50]

---

[42] Case 29/68 *Milchkontor*, above: *Lütticke* [1969] C.M.L.R. 221, decision of the Bundesfinanzhof.

[43] Case 29/68 *Milchkontor*, at p. 183.

[44] Case 28/67 *Mölkerei Zentrale*, above, and see the decisions of the German Bundesfinanzhof in *Lütticke*, n. 42, above, and *Mölkerei Zentrale* [1969] C.M.L.R. 300. In another case, the Finanzgericht Münster held that a rate was not an "average" since no calculations of prior charges had been made: *Re Import of Finished Textiles* [1969] C.M.L.R. 261.

[45] Case 29/68 *Milchkontor*, above; *Re Import of Finished Textiles*, above: *Re Adjustment Tax on Petrol* [1966] C.M.L.R. 409, Finanzgericht Hamburg.

[46] See above, para. 74, and see R. Wägenbaur, (*op. cit.* p. 17, n. 99) at (1969). 3 EuR, pp. 25 *et. seq.*, and the various authorities cited there at p. 25, n. 30.

[47] This was clearly stated in Case 57/65 *Lütticke* [1966] E.C.R. 205, at p. 211, though apparently overlooked by many. It was reaffirmed in Case 28/67 *Mölkerei Zentrale*, above, and in Case 34/67 *Lück* [1968] E.C.R. 245.

[48] *e.g.* under Art. 169: see Cases 28/67, 29/68 and 4/69 above. In the latter case, an attempt to obtain damages against the Commission for failure to take action was unsuccessful.

[49] See the discussion in Case 25/67 *Milchkontor* [1968] E.C.R. 207, and contrast the decisions in *Re Tax on Imported Almonds* [1971] C.M.L.R. 87 (Finanzgericht Hamburg) and in *Re Tax on Imported Distilling Wine* [1971] C.M.L.R. 435 (Finanzgericht Bremen).

[50] See, *e.g.* Case 153/78 *Commission* v. *Germany* [1980] 1 C.M.L.R. 198.

**90**     From the beginning, compensatory turnover taxes on imports, whether or not established as averages, caused considerable difficulty and there were frequent complaints of "over-compensation" which discriminated against imported products. In 1960, the Council established a Consultative Procedure[51] by which Member States agreed in principle to refrain from further increases in countervailing duties unless such modifications could be justified for technical reasons. This "standstill agreement" did not work very well in practice, Member States occasionally giving a rather wide meaning to "technical,"[52] and on a number of occasions the Commission had recourse to the issue of directives to offending Member States under the second paragraph of the Article.[53] Finally, a general Directive was adopted in 1968,[54] establishing a common method of calculating average rates though, as the Council had by then adopted the Directives whereby the cumulative turnover tax was to be replaced by a common system of value-added tax, the "average rate" Directive was already almost redundant and soon became so.[55]

**91**     Countervailing charges, or compensatory taxes, imposed upon imports are further subject to Article 98. This provides that, in the case of charges other than turnover taxes, excise duties and other forms of indirect taxation, countervailing charges in respect of imports from Member States may not be imposed unless the measures contemplated have been previously approved for a limited period by the Council acting by a qualified majority on a proposal from the Commission. Since no such authorisation has been given, the provision can be dealt with briefly. The effect of Article 98 is that a countervailing charge on an import may not compensate for any direct taxation borne by the corresponding domestic product, unless this is expressly authorised. This prohibition is in accordance with the principles of Article 95 though it may be viewed both as imposing a further restriction and as providing a permissible derogation. On the one hand, in so far as a direct tax can be considered to be imposed on a domestic product at all,[56] it is nevertheless forbidden to take this into account, without authorisation, in assessing the tax burden on an imported product, notwithstanding that to do so might not be contrary to Article 95. On the other hand, approval may be given to take direct taxes into account. This can be interpreted in one of two ways: approval may be given only in respect of those direct taxes which can be shown to be imposed on the domestic product and would therefore

[51] Decision of June 21, (1960): see (EEC) Bull. 5–60, p. 34; (EEC) Fourth General Report (1960), p. 79.
[52] See the comments of Mr. H. v.d. Groeben in (EEC) Bull. 1–63, p. 6.
[53] *e.g.* that addressed to Germany (J.O. 1962, p. 2215) requesting the amendment of certain duties. The Commission also gave a number of authorisations to modify or impose countervailing duties: see (EEC) Bull. 11–62, p. 35; 12–62, p. 12.
[54] Dir. 68/221 of April 30, 1968.
[55] It becomes relevant again with the accession of Greece: see the Treaty of Accession of Greece, Art. 21 and Annex I, Title VI.
[56] See paras. 26–28, above.

otherwise properly be taken into account under Article 95, or approval may be given to compensate for the burden of direct taxes which may be reflected in the price of the domestic product although not imposed, directly or indirectly upon that product as such. The former construction would seem to be too narrow. In the first place, since it will rarely if ever be possible to regard a direct tax as being imposed on a product (in the sense in which the Court has interpreted Article 95), there would be very little scope for the exercise of the authorisation procedure. Secondly, unlike Article 97, there is no proviso in Article 98 that the principles of Article 95 be observed. Thirdly, although Article 95 may be considered to be a fundamental principle of the Treaty,[57] when the Chapter of the Treaty is read as a whole the approval procedure appears as an express power to derogate from the general rule, for otherwise the restriction—that approval be given for a limited period only—would seem pointless. It is perhaps surprising, therefore, that those Member States which have complained that their comparatively heavy reliance on direct taxation places their producers at a competitive disadvantage have not had recourse to the procedure in Article 98. The reason may be that, in the long term, it is more effective to reduce the burden of direct taxes on producers and to resort increasingly to indirect taxes on products—a trend which is discernible in a number of Member States.

### (iv)   The remission of taxes on exports

**92**     Given that a product imported into a Member State may be subjected to countervailing duties, that product is liable to suffer a double imposition unless the taxes imposed upon it in the exporting Member State are remitted, or it is otherwise exempted from such taxes. This is permitted by Article 96 to the extent that any repayment of tax does not exceed the tax which has been imposed on the product, directly or indirectly. Article 96 is thus the counterpart to Article 95 and should be interpreted similarly.[58]

The Article is both permissive and prohibitory. A Member State may remit internal taxation on exported products, but is not required to do so,[59] even though the failure to do so may result in double taxation.[60] It is prohibited from remitting internal taxation in excess of that actually imposed on the product and to do so is therefore a breach of its obligations under the Treaty.[61] In theory, this prohibition is clear and complete in itself and is capable of producing direct effects. It is, however, difficult to imagine

---

[57] See para. 66, above.

[58] See para. 28, above. As Art. 96 concerns only the refunding of taxes on a particular product, no comparison of tax burdens is necessary.

[59] Case 2/73 *Geddo* [1973] E.C.R. 865; Case 27/74 *Demag* [1974] E.C.R. 1037.

[60] To impose a tax or charge in the event of exportation, by contrast, may be prohibited by Art. 16 as a charge with equivalent effect to a customs duty on exports (above, para. 23) or, perhaps, as a discrimination within Art. 95 (above, paras. 57–60).

[61] Case 45/64 *Commission* v. *Italy* [1965] E.C.R. 857 (above, para. 28).

an exporter challenging a refund of tax made to him on the ground that the amount was excessive, or to see what other person might have a cause of action. Producers in other Member States might complain, to the Commission, that this constituted an improper subsidy to a competitor but would otherwise have no legal redress. It is unlikely that a Member State would challenge the validity of its own laws or practice in this way in order to recover an excessive refund, nor is it clear that the doctrine of direct effect can be relied upon by a Member State in respect of its own default.

Articles 97 and 98 apply equally to the repayment of taxes on exportation as to the imposition of taxes on imported products. Thus where, because of the employment of a cumulative turnover tax system, it is impossible to calculate the precise amount of internal tax borne by the product which is to be exported, the repayment may be made—or could, prior to the replacement of cumulative turnover tax systems by the common system of value added-tax—on the basis of an average rate established for that purpose.[62] And Article 98 forbids, except with previous approval of the Council, any remission or repayment to be made in respect of direct taxes. Thus, in *Commission* v. *Italy*,[63] Italy was apparently in breach of Article 98, as well as Article 96, since it had remitted not only indirect taxes imposed on the producer, rather than on the product, but also some direct taxes.

## F.   CONCLUSIONS

**93**   The interpretation and application of Articles 95 to 98 have given rise to considerable difficulties and will no doubt continue to do so, despite the extensive jurisprudence which has been developed by the Court of Justice and by national courts. It might have been hoped that the Court would resolve most of these problems in delivering judgment in the recent "alcohol" cases; instead, the difficulties seem to have multiplied.

One of the major problems has been the calculation of the precise amount of tax imposed upon domestic products. Differences in national tax systems, the application of different taxes at different stages to different tax bases, especially under cumulative-type turnover tax systems, had rendered this task almost impossible. A solution to the problem could only be found in the harmonisation of national systems of turnover tax: it seems clear that the harmonisation of excise duties similarly presents the only rational solution to the problems highlighted by the "alcohol" cases. It is this subject—the harmonisation of taxes—which will be considered in the two following Chapters.

### [The Next Paragraph is 101]

---

[62] The rate must have been established as an average rate: see Case 45/64 *Commission* v. *Italy*, above.
[63] Case 45/64, above.

CHAPTER 2

# THE HARMONISATION OF TURNOVER TAXES: THE COMMON SYSTEM OF VALUE ADDED TAX

## A. THE NEED FOR HARMONISATION

**101**  The authors of the EEC Treaty were already well aware of the difficulties caused by the existence of different systems of indirect taxation in the Member States and of the particular problems created by the cumulative multistage type of turnover tax.[1] These problems had been demonstrated in the ECSC "tax dispute"[2] and there was also the experience of the Benelux Union, which had been wrestling for some years with the question of excise duties.[3] It was therefore anticipated that some harmonisation of the national systems of indirect taxation would be necessary, and Article 99 provided:

> "The Commission shall consider how the legislation of the various Member States concerning turnover taxes, excise duties and other forms of indirect taxation, including countervailing measures applicable to trade between Member States, can be harmonised in the interest of the common market."

The provision is mandatory. The Commission is directed to consider how, not "if," such taxes can be harmonised,[4] and "the Commission shall submit proposals to the Council, which shall act unanimously without prejudice to the provisions of Articles 100 and 101."[5]

**102**  The disadvantages of the cumulative, or "cascade," type of multi-stage turnover tax have already been demonstrated in Chapter 1. Under such a system it is difficult to calculate the precise tax burden borne by a particular product, which makes it almost impossible to operate a truly non-discriminatory system to satisfy the requirements of Article 95. Similarly, the calculation of the appropriate countervailing charges on imports and remissions on exports becomes impossible without recourse to average rates, which themselves constitute a form of derogation from the principles of the Treaty. Such average rates inevitably lead to disputes as to whether a Member State is over, or under compensating for domestic taxation—

---

[1] Secretariat of the Intergovernmental Committee created by the Messina Conference, *Rapport des chefs de delegation aux Ministres des affaires étrangers* (The Spaak Report), Brussels, 1956, especially pp. 65, 68.

[2] Chapter 1, para. 86, above.

[3] An excellent description is given in J. E. Meade, H. H. Liesner and S. J. Wells, "*Case Studies in European Union . . .*" (1962), Chapter 2.

[4] See the observations of the Internal Market Committee of the European Parliament, *Rapport sur la proposition de la Commission . . . concernant une Directive en matière d'harmonisation des legislations des Etats membres relatives aux taxes sur le chiffre d'affaires*, E.P. Doc. 56, 1963, at p. 34 (referred to hereafter as the Deringer Report).

[5] The meaning of this second paragraph is considered in Chapter 3, at paras. 205, 206, below.

disputes which are scarcely conducive to the harmonious development of the Community. A further objection to the cascade system, one founded rather upon the competition philosophy of the Community than upon the tax principles, is that a multi-stage system causes distortions by providing an incentive to the vertical integration of industries. If an article is to be taxed each time it changes hands in the course of its production and marketing, then the fewer times it changes hands the smaller the tax burden. Manufacturers are therefore encouraged to acquire control of the production of raw materials or of wholesale or retail outlets, retail organisations to acquire control of their suppliers, and so on. It was therefore apparent that it was not only the differences between the various national turnover tax systems which needed to be eliminated, but that the cascade system itself would have to be replaced.[6]

If there was general agreement in principle that the cumulative turnover tax should go, it was less clear what type of system should be adopted as a replacement.[7] The nature of the objections to the turnover tax indicated that the replacement must be either a single-stage sales tax or a multi-stage non-cumulative tax. It was also clear that the chosen replacement should be a general sales tax, applying to all types of goods, and perhaps also to the provision of services, subject only to specific exemptions.

**103**    Single-stage sales taxes may be classified according to the stage of production or marketing of the goods at which the tax is imposed.[8] A *manufacturer's sales tax* is one applied, essentially, on the sale of an article by the manufacturer, normally but not necessarily to a wholesaler : a *wholesale sales tax* is one applied on the sales made by a wholesaler or, more accurately, at the transaction prior to that at which the article reaches the consumer : a *retail sales tax* is applied on the sale to the consumer. Each system has advantages and disadvantages. As a general rule, where the tax is imposed at an early stage the number of taxpayers, *e.g.* of manufacturers, is fewer. This facilitates administration, the cost of collection of the tax is lower and there is less likelihood of tax evasion. By contrast, the tax base is smaller (the market value of the article increasing as it progresses along the chain of production and marketing), rates of tax must be correspondingly higher and the tax has probably less flexibility as an economic tool. More serious, from the point of view of the Community's tax principles, is the possibility of distortions and discriminations. The incidence of tax may vary according to the degree to which a particular industry is integrated and according to the stage of production at which the article becomes subject to

[6] See the comments of H. van der Groeben (a member of the Commission) in (EC) Bull. 2–70, p. 26.

[7] See C. S. Shoup, *Fiscal Harmonisation*, Vol. II, Introduction; C. K. Sullivan, in Chapter 8 of that work, and the same author's "*The Search for Tax Principles in the European Economic Community*" (1963).

[8] For a comprehensive study, see J. F. Due, "*Sales Taxation*" (1957) and for a shorter, but illuminating analysis, see S. S. Surrey, "Implications of Tax Harmonisation in the European Common Market" (1968) 46 *Taxes*, 398.

the tax, *i.e.* according to how much value is added before and after the taxable event. Moreover, where a product is imported from another Member State in a more advanced state than that at which the corresponding domestic product is taxed, discrimination will occur contrary to the principles of Article 95. This is especially so where the tax is applied at the manufacturer, or pre-manufacturer, stage.[9]

**104**      A single-stage tax imposed at a later stage, especially one imposed at the retail stage, is much to be preferred in this respect. But a retail sales tax requires that there be a much greater number of taxable persons (retailers) who are accountable. The costs of administration and collection will be greater, a heavy burden is placed upon small retail businesses which may lack the requisite book-keeping and accounting facilities and the likelihood of tax evasion is greatly increased.

A multi-stage non-cumulative turnover tax also possesses some of the above advantages and disadvantages. Under such a system the tax is imposed at each stage, or on each transaction, but is non-cumulative in the sense that, at each stage subsequent to the first, the tax paid at an earlier stage is taken into account by taxing only the value added since the previous stage, hence the name "value added tax."

## B.   THE THEORY AND PRACTICE OF VALUE ADDED TAX

**105**    Although its widespread adoption has been a comparatively recent phenomenon, the antecedents of the value added tax can be traced back at least to the period immediately following the first World War.[10] A value added tax was introduced in France in 1954, though it may be considered to have evolved in that country through a series of reforms of the turnover tax system, notably in 1936 and 1948.[11] Roughly simultaneously, its adoption by Japan was advocated by a mission, led by Professor Carl S. Shoup, whose study has been a major influence,[12] despite the fact that Japan ultimately did not follow the mission's recommendations.

The value added tax, as introduced in France and as subsequently adopted by the EEC, may be regarded as an improved type of turnover tax, the improvement consisting of the removal of the cumulative features of the latter tax. Like the turnover tax, it is imposed at a number of stages, upon transactions each time an article changes hands in the course of its production and marketing. But since the tax is imposed only upon the value added

[9] See Case 7/69 *Commission* v. *Italy* [1970] E.C.R. 111 (imported wool): Case 77/69 *Commission* v. *Belgium* [1970] E.C.R. 237 (imported timber).

[10] Of the many excellent works on the subject, see especially P. Derouin, "*La Taxe sur la Valeur Ajoutée dans la CEE*" (1977); C. K. Sullivan, "*The Tax on Value Added*" (1965); A. A. Tait, "*Value Added Tax*" (1972).

[11] J. F. Due, (*op. cit.* above, n. 8) Chapter 7.

[12] See C. K. Sullivan, (*op. cit.* above, n. 10) Chapter 3, and M. Bronfenbrenner, "The Japanese Value-Added Sales Tax" (1950) 3 N.T.J. 298.

since the previous taxable event, the total tax burden should remain the same regardless of the number of times an article is taxed. In theory this may be achieved in one of two ways : the amount of the value added may be calculated and the tax rate applied only to that value, or the tax may be calculated on the value of the article itself at any taxable stage and a credit given for any tax which it has previously borne. In practice, however, it is misleading to relate the tax to any specific article : whichever method is employed, the tax is payable by taxable persons, *i.e.* by businesses, upon the value added by that business over the chosen accounting period. The value added, essentially, is the difference between total output (sales), and the input of raw materials, including those consumed in the course of production (purchases), and is therefore to be equated with wages and profits. If the amount of value added is to be calculated, this can be done either by adding wages and profits (the additive method) or by subtracting inputs from outputs (the subtractive method). Alternatively (the other method referred to above, which might be termed the tax-from-tax method) tax may be charged on the total sales of a business, less the tax paid by that business on its total purchases.

**106**  It should be noted that the end results produced by the different systems are not necessarily the same. For example, if food is taxed at one rate but restaurant meals are taxed at a higher rate, under the methods which calculate value added, part of the total—the value added in producing the food—will be taxed at the lower rate, and the remainder—the value added by the restaurant—will be taxed at the higher rate. But if the tax-from-tax method is employed, the total amount will be taxed at the higher rate, the tax paid previously at the lower rate (on the purchase of food by the restaurant) being simply credited against the tax calculated on the total. It is therefore the tax rate applicable at the final taxable stage which determines the total amount of tax payable.

This fact is of the greatest importance in appreciating the effects of exemptions. An exemption at an earlier tax stage does not, under the tax-from-tax method, affect the total tax burden on a particular product. Consequently, if food is an exempt product, or the farmer who supplies it is an exempt person, but the restaurant meal is taxable, the earlier exemption will simply mean that there is no tax to credit against the final assessment. If, however, the food or the farmer is taxable but the meal is exempt, then the final transaction is not a taxable event but the meal will still have borne whatever tax was imposed previously.[13] This should be contrasted with the "zero-rating" system, whereby a particular supply is a taxable event but the applicable tax rate is zero. This, if it is the final taxable event, means that the total tax burden is also zero, for the supplier remains entitled to a credit for tax paid in respect of inputs. Such a system is commonly applied to exports,

---

[13] If a taxable person supplies both taxable and exempt goods or services, an allocation of the tax on inputs between taxable and exempt supplies will be necessary.

the effect being to remit any tax previously imposed upon the exported product as permitted by Article 96.[14]

**107**     The distinction between the calculation of value added method and the tax-from-tax method is also important conceptually. As stated above, where the value added by a particular enterprise over a given period is calculated, the result is equal to the sum of wages and profits. Viewed in this light the base corresponds, roughly, to the notion of business income[15] and the value added tax is seen as an "income-type" tax. It is in this sense that it has been perceived as a form of, or as an alternative to, a business income tax[16] or to a payroll tax.[17] Where the tax-from-tax method is employed, the value added tax appears as a form of sales tax, or a consumption type tax : the tax is imposed upon the ultimate sale of goods or provision of services, though it is in part collected at earlier stages. This distinction, between an income-type and consumption-type tax, is sometimes made with respect to capital expenditures.[18] Where a business purchases capital goods such as plant or machinery which may have a working life of several years, an income-type tax would normally require this expenditure to be written-off over that period as the value of those goods depreciates. Thus an income-type of value added tax would seem to require that only a part of the purchase be treated as a deductible input in computing value added. A consumption-type tax, where consumption is equated with income less savings or investment, should permit an immediate deduction of the entire expenditure.

As mentioned earlier in this chapter, the value added tax was perceived in Europe[19] as an alternative to the cumulative, multi-stage, turnover tax, *i.e.* essentially as a consumption-type tax. As such, it has a number of advantages, which stem largely from its non-cumulative nature.[20] The burden of taxes indirectly imposed upon a product in the course of its production, *e.g.* on materials consumed in the course of manufacture, on transportation or on packaging, is automatically subsumed into the eventual tax burden imposed at the final taxable stage, thus removing the difficulties in determining the total tax burden on a product in order to establish whether or not discrimination exists within the meaning of Article

---

[14]  See above, Chapter 1, para. 92.

[15]  The major difference from the normal tax base for the purposes of business income tax is that the latter normally permits wages to be treated as a deductible expense.

[16]  C. S. Shoup, "Theory and Background of the Value-Added Tax," Proceedings of the National Tax Association, May 1956. In the United Kingdom, the Richardson Committee considered VAT as a replacement for corporate income tax: 1964 Cmnd. 2300, and see A. R. Prest, "A Value Added Tax coupled with a reduction in taxes on business profits" 1963 B.T.R. 336.

[17]  W. H. Oakland, "The theory of the Value Added Tax: a comparison of tax bases" (1967) 20 N.T.J. 119; *cf.* C. S. Shoup "Consumption Tax and Wages Type and Consumption Type of Value Added Tax" (1968) 21 N.T.J. 153.

[18]  See C. K. Sullivan, (*op. cit.* above, n. 10) at pp. 22–30; S. S. Han and G. K. Shaw, "Value Added Tax: the economic consequences" (1970) 4 J.W.T.L. 548.

[19]  Except perhaps initially in Britain : see n. 16, above.

[20]  See further, T. Georgakopoulos, in D. Dosser ed. *British Taxation and the Common Market* (1973), Chapter 2, and C. K. Sullivan, (*op. cit.* above, n. 10) Chapter 4.

95. Similarly, the calculation of the appropriate border tax adjust-ments—remissions on exports and countervailing charges on imports—is greatly simplified. Moreover, the value added tax is economically neutral in the sense that it neither encourages nor discourages the vertical integration of industries.

**108** Some of these advantages are shared by single-stage sales taxes. In general, a sales tax imposed at the same stage as the final taxable stage under a value added tax system has a similar effect, though even here the single-stage tax does not take into account other taxes which have been imposed indirectly upon a product. The main advantage of a single-stage sales tax is its simplicity and the fact that, at whatever stage it is imposed, it necessarily involves a smaller number of taxpayers than a comparable value added tax or, of course, than a multi-stage turnover tax. The value added tax is more complex, but there is inherent in it a self-enforcing factor. In so far as supplies are made between taxable persons, *e.g.* from manufacturer to wholesaler, the cross-checking of tax returns is facilitated and where a tax-able person makes a purchase he will have an incentive to ensure that the correct tax is charged on his purchase in order to be entitled to deduct that tax from the tax which he must pay on his sales. Only at the retail stage, where a supply is made to a non-taxable person, is there a serious risk of tax evasion and here the extent of the risk is less than under a retail sales tax since, under a value added tax, some of the tax will already have been collected at earlier stages and only the tax in respect of the value added in the final phase is likely to be lost.[21]

This latter factor weighed heavily with several of the Member States of the Community. Tax evasion by small businesses was perceived as a major problem and a value added tax, especially one extending to the retail stage, was considered preferable to a single-stage sales tax for this reason. Further-more, since France already had a value added tax and the other members applied cumulative turnover taxes, which share with value added tax the disadvantages of complexity and of a greater number of taxpayers, the adoption of a common system of value added tax was not expected to create any major new difficulties.

## C. The Directives of 1967

### (i) The preliminary studies

**109** In accordance with Article 99, requiring the Commission to consider how national legislation concerning turnover taxes, excise duties and other forms of indirect taxation might be harmonised, work on this subject commenced almost immediately. A working group of the Commission was set up and, reporting in late 1959, concluded that the maintenance of the diversity of

---

[21] See J. F. Due, *Sales Taxation*, Chapter 17; S. S. Surrey, *op. cit.* above, n. 8; G. S. A. Wheatcroft, "Some Administrative Problems of an Added Value Tax" 1963 B.T.R. 348.

national tax systems was clearly prejudicial to the good working of the Common Market and that the harmonisation of turnover tax systems was especially desirable. Following a meeting between Commission experts and senior officials of the national governments, a Fiscal and Financial Committee was set up, in April 1960, under the chairmanship of Professor Fritz Neumark and consisting of experts from all the member states,[22] to consider to what extent national fiscal differences hindered the establishment of the Common Market and how such differences might be eliminated. The report of the Committee was adopted in July 1962.[23]

The Committee's terms of reference, and its report, were not confined to the question of turnover taxes. It considered also the problems created by differences in excise duties, other indirect taxes, the taxation of company profits and distributions, personal income tax, international double taxation and fiscal policy generally. Its main conclusion[24] was that tax harmonisation should be considered as a dynamic process. The proper functioning of the Common Market would eventually require some measure of harmonisation of most, or all, of these taxes but that it would be necessary to proceed in stages. Without suggesting any precise timetable, the Committee proposed that harmonisation should proceed in three stages.

**110**    During the first phase, the most urgent need was the reform of the turnover tax systems and this should be followed as soon as possible by the abolition of fiscal frontiers in respect of turnover taxes. The methods and level of taxation of dividends and interest should be harmonised and international double-taxation treaties recast.[25] In the second phase, company taxation would have to be reformed and there would be some harmonisation of personal income tax. Harmonisation or abolition of special excise duties would also be required. In the third phase, co-ordination of national tax administrations would be necessary, financial compensation measures operated at Community level from a common fund might be required and a special Community tax court would be created.

Turnover tax, however, was perceived as the most immediate problem and the various alternatives were studied in detail by three separate Sub-Groups. To Sub-Group A was referred the question of the possibility of the removal of tax frontiers and the need for physical inspections at borders to administer the system of border tax adjustments in relation to turnover taxes. Sub-Group B was given the task of considering the adoption of a common single-stage general sales tax, to apply at a stage prior to the retail stage and, if necessary, to be combined with a separate tax on retail sales. Sub-Group C considered the possibility of a common single-stage tax at the

[22] Professor Shoup, of the United States, was also a member.
[23] An unofficial translation into English was prepared by Dr. H. Thurston and published by the International Bureau of Fiscal Documentation : *The EEC Reports on Tax Harmonisation* (Amsterdam 1963). Included are the reports of the Sub-Groups (see below).
[24] *EEC Reports on Tax Harmonisation*, pp. 153–156.
[25] Most of these aims have yet to be achieved and the Community remains a long way from completing this first phase.

production stage, with a separate retail tax and of a common tax on value added, again with a separate tax at the retail stage if required.

**111**    Two points merit special attention. First, a major preoccupation was the desire to abolish tax frontiers. It was widely felt that much of the benefit derived from the prohibition upon customs duties would be lost if frontier inspections were still to be required by reason of border tax adjustments, and that the maintenance of such frontiers would have an adverse psychological effect, as well as hindering intra-Community trade, and was fundamentally inconsistent with the principles of the Common Market. Secondly, it was assumed that it would not, at least in the short term, be possible to apply any common system of turnover tax to the retail stage. Strong resistance to this existed in several Member States, (especially those where there were large numbers of small retail businesses) for pyschological, technical and political reasons.

The choice was therefore presented as one, essentially, between a single-stage sales tax at either the manufacturer or wholesale stage, or a value added tax, in each case with the possibility of a separate, non-harmonised, tax at the retail level. Sub-Group B concluded that a wholesale sales tax, though easy to apply and avoiding many of the disadvantages of the cumulative turnover tax, nevertheless gave rise to problems of neutrality, could cause distortions, and would inevitably result in considerable evasion, and could not be considered to constitute a satisfactory and final solution.[26] Sub-Group C was even less enthusiastic about a single tax at the production stage and recommended that, of the systems considered, a tax on value added met most closely the relevant criteria.[27]

### (ii)  The Commission's proposed Directive

**112**    In the light of these recommendations the Commission submitted to the Council, on November 5, 1962, a proposal for a Directive for the harmonisation amongst Member States of turnover tax legislation.[28] In the view of the Commission, as it appears in the Preamble to the draft Directive, it was evident from the studies which had been made that harmonisation must culminate in the adoption of a common system of value added tax, to be applied at all stages of production and wholesale trade, leaving to the Member States the option whether to impose independently a supplementary tax on retail sales or to extend the system of value added tax to retail trade. As this would require considerable modifications of national laws and would have far-reaching budgetary, economic and social conse-

---

[26] *EEC Reports on Tax Harmonisation*, p. 44.
[27] *Ibid.* pp. 73–74.
[28] Doc. IV/COM (62) 217 : (EEC) Bull. S. 12–62. For an analysis of the proposed directive, see K. V. Antal, "Harmonisation of Turnover Taxes in the Common Market" (1963–64) 1 C.M.L. Rev. 41.

quences, it was desirable to carry out the operation in stages. The Commission proposed two stages:

(1) During the first stage, within three years of the Directive, Member States would replace the multi-stage cumulative turnover tax by a non-cumulative system of their choice. This might be either a single-stage system or a value added tax. Member States would be free to fix independently a supplementary tax at the retail stage. During this period they would also remove standard-rate compensatory measures on imports and exports.

(2) During a further transitional period, Member States would be required to introduce a common value added tax system, extending to the wholesale stage, again remaining free to apply a separate tax at the retail stage or to include retail sales in the value added tax. During this second stage, the Commission would submit further proposals with a view to the abolition of countervailing charges on imports and drawbacks on exports, *i.e.* to adopt the "origin principle" and thereby remove tax frontiers.

The proposed Directive gave no details as to the structure of the common system of value added tax : this was to be worked out before the end of the first transitional period.

**113**     The proposal was transmitted by the Council to the European Parliament and to the Economic and Social Committee for their opinions. These, whilst welcoming the intention to harmonise turnover taxes, were strongly critical of the actual proposal.[29] In particular, the Internal Market Committee of the Parliament, under the chairmanship of M. Arved Deringer, prepared a lengthy report[30] in which the whole question of the harmonisation of taxes was reviewed. The Deringer Report emphasised the importance of the early removal of all tax frontiers and regretted that the problems of excise duties had not been tackled simultaneously. Of special interest is the Committee's interpretation of Article 99[31]: this, in their view, requires not only that the turnover taxes, excise duties and other indirect taxes of the Member States be harmonised, but that they be harmonised in their relationship to each other. No attempt had been made to do this and, as the Committee prophetically observed:

"On this basis, it will still be necessary in twenty years' time to open one's case between Emmerich and Arnhem, Wasserbillig and Trier, between Erquelines and Jeumont, between Strasbourg and Kehl, Ventimiglia and Menton, to prove to customs that one has not wrapped cigars inside one's pyjamas."[32]

[29] J.O. 1963, No. 157, p. 2631 (Parliament) : J.O. 1964, No. 158, p. 2512 (E.S.C.).
[30] Parlement Européen : Documents de Séance 1963–64, No. 56, referred to hereafter as the Deringer Report.
[31] Deringer Report, p. 33.
[32] *Ibid.* p. 35.

The report further rejected the proposal of an intermediate stage, during which Member States might adopt a single-stage tax, and urged instead that the Community should proceed directly to the adoption of a common system of value added tax.[33] There seemed little point in changing to a single-stage system as a temporary measure if the value added tax would ultimately be adopted generally.

**114**　This latter objection was accepted by the Commission, which had in any event not considered the two-phase operation to be the ideal solution but had proposed it in order to meet objections which some of the national governments had raised.[34] In consequence, the Commission revised its draft, which it re-submitted to the Council in June 1964, and proposed instead that a common system of value added tax be adopted by all Member States not later than the end of 1967, though its entry into force could be deferred until the end of 1969 in order to give the Member States adequate time to prepare the necessary executive measures. To proceed directly to the common system, however, required that the structure and details of that system be prepared immediately, rather than during a transitional period. The Commission therefore outlined the main features of this system in its revised draft and promised a second proposed directive concerning the structure. In response to the urgings of the Parliament, the Commission further undertook to submit proposals, by the end of 1968, for the abolition of tax frontiers.

The proposal for a Second Directive was duly submitted to the Council on April 14, 1965.[35] As the Commission explained, the temporary subsistence of fiscal frontiers would permit the maintenance of certain differences in the methods of taxing value added in the Member States. These differences might later have to disappear but meanwhile a certain measure of discretion could be left to the Member States, notably with regard to the taxation of the retail stage, of small businesses and of agricultural products. The two Directives were adopted, with some amendments, on April 11, 1967.[36]

### (iii)　The Directives

**115**　The underlying philosophy of the Community is clearly set out in the Preamble to the First Directive. The main objective of the Treaty is to establish, within the framework of an economic union, a common market within which there is healthy competition and whose characteristics are similar to those of a domestic market. The attainment of this objective presupposes the application in Member States of legislation concerning turnover taxes such as will not distort conditions of competition or hinder the free movement of

---

[33] This was also advocated by the ESC : see (EEC) Bull. 9, 10–63, p. 50.
[34] See the explanatory memorandum accompanying the Commission's revised proposal : (EEC) Bull. S. 7–64.
[35] Doc. IV/COM (65) 144: (EEC) Bull. S. 5–65.
[36] Dir. 67/227/EEC and Dir. 67/228/EEC.

goods and services within the Common Market. From the studies it is clear that such harmonisation must result in the abolition of cumulative multi-stage taxes and the adoption of a common system of value added tax. Such a system achieves the highest degree of simplicity and of neutrality when the tax is levied in as general a manner as possible and when its scope covers all stages of production and distribution and the provision of services. It would therefore be in the interest of the common market and of Member States to adopt a common system applying to the retail stage. At that time, however, this met with practical or political difficulties in some Member States and it was therefore permitted to apply the system only up to and including the wholesale stage, applying if appropriate a separate tax to the retail stage. Even without the harmonisation of rates and exemptions this ought to achieve neutrality in competition, since within each country similar goods would bear the same tax burdens, whatever the length of the production and distribution chain, and in international trade the amount of the tax burden borne by goods would be known so that an exact equalisation of that amount might be ensured. Consequently, in the first stage of harmonisation envisaged by the Directives, Member States were to remain free to fix their own rates and, to a lesser extent, their exemptions,[37] though further proposals were to be prepared with a view to adopting the "origin principle." The First Directive therefore required the Member States to adopt, not later than January 1, 1970,[38] a common system of value added tax, involving the application to goods and services of a "general tax on consumption" exactly proportional to the price of the goods and services, whatever the number of transactions which take place in the production and distribution process before the stage at which tax is charged.[39]

**116** The details of this common system were set out in the Second Directive.[40] This provided that the value added tax should apply to:

    (a) the supply of goods or the provision of services within the territory of the country by a taxable person against payment, and

    (b) the importation of goods.[41]

The expressions "supply of goods," "provision of services" and "importation of goods" were further defined,[42] and a "taxable person" was stated to be "any person who independently and habitually engages in transactions pertaining to the activities of producers, traders or persons providing services, whether or not for gain."[43] The tax should be calculated on the basis of the consideration or price for the supply of the goods or provision of the services or, in the case of importation, on the customs value of the

---

[37] See Dir. 67/228, Art. 10.
[38] Dir. 67/227, Art. 1. This was later extended to January 1, 1972.
[39] *Ibid.* Art. 2. This also provided for the use of the "tax-from-tax" method.
[40] For a comprehensive analysis of the provisions of the directive, see the special issue of *European Taxation*, "The Common System of Tax on Value Added" (1967) 7 E.T. 148.
[41] Dir. 67/228, Art. 2.
[42] *Ibid.* Arts. 5, 6, 7.
[43] Art. 4.

goods.[44] A taxable person would be required to keep proper accounts and to issue an invoice in respect of goods supplied and services provided by him to another taxable person,[45] and be authorised to deduct from the tax for which he is liable the value added tax invoiced to him or paid in respect of his purchases and imports.[46] In the case of the purchase of capital goods, Member States might permit an immediate deduction of the full amount of the tax or require this to be spread over a period of years.[47]

The system adopted, therefore, employed a tax-from-tax method : in practice, a trader retains a copy of each invoice issued by him on his sales and of each invoice issued to him on his purchases, and pays the amount of tax calculated on sales less the tax already paid on purchases during the appropriate accounting period. Regarding international trade, imported goods were required to be taxed at the same rate as that applied internally to the supply of goods[48] and the exportation of goods was required to be exempted.[49]

Within this basic framework, Member States were free to establish their own standard rate of tax and to subject certain goods or services to increased or reduced rates[50] and, subject to consultations, to determine their own exemptions,[51] to adopt special measures in exceptional cases to simplify procedures or prevent frauds[52] and to apply special systems to small undertakings whose subjection to the normal system would meet with difficulties.[53] Further proposals were to be made for applying value added tax to agricultural products and Member States were meanwhile permitted to apply special systems to the agricultural sector.[54]

### (iv) Implementation of the Directives

**117**     The two Directives were adopted unanimously by the Council and therefore agreed to by all the Member States at that time. Nevertheless, adoption of the necessary legislation proved to be a far from simple matter in some of the Member States.

### (a) The existing Member States.

France had already possessed a value added tax for many years and consequently only needed to make a number of adaptations to its existing

[44] Art. 8.
[45] Art. 12.
[46] Art. 11.
[47] Arts. 11, 17.
[48] Art. 9(3).
[49] Art. 10(1).
[50] Art. 9. The Preamble, however, makes it clear that the application of zero-rates should be strictly limited.
[51] Art. 10.
[52] Art. 13.
[53] Art. 14.
[54] Art. 15.

system, though it chose to extend the system to the retail stage, albeit in a modified form.[55] Germany, too, was prompt in implementing the Directive and the new system entered into force there in 1968.[56] In fact, German experts, and the federal government, had decided some years earlier that reform of the turnover tax system was urgently needed and that value added tax offered the most desirable solution.[57] An earlier Bill to that end had been introduced in 1964 and the attitude of German members of the various Community institutions has been described as "aggressively positive."[58] The outcome was that the Community, at Bonn's prompting, had now required the German government to do something which it had wanted to do in any event and which, at the time, fully accorded with what was perceived as the national economic interest. A further impetus to the adoption of value added tax was provided by the mass of litigation which had been provoked in Germany by the decision of the Court of Justice in the *Lütticke* case.[59] Thus Germany required no prompting to comply with its obligations under the Directives.

**118**     The tax was introduced in the Netherlands at the beginning of 1969[60] and in Luxembourg a year later.[61] Major difficulties, however, were encountered by Belgium and Italy. The introduction of the tax in the Netherlands had coincided with a period of increasing inflation and price rises were considerably larger than had been forecast, whether or not due to the new tax. Government forecasts[62] suggested a similar steep increase in consumer prices in Belgium. Additionally, it was feared that the new tax might have serious budgetary repercussions since much of the revenue from the existing turnover tax was collected by means of pre-paid stamps and the change to the new system would cause a gap in the flow of revenue. Psychological factors also weighed with the Belgian government. A value added tax which replaces a multi-stage turnover tax will necessarily be imposed at a higher rate, if it is to provide the same amount of revenue, since the latter is cumulative whereas the former is not.

Unsophisticated electors, especially in a time of general inflation, are unlikely to appreciate this fact. There was, consequently, some reluctance on the part of Belgium to make the change immediately and, in the event, it proved necessary to extend the deadline for implementation until January 1,

---

[55] For details of the French system, see G. Egret, in *Value Added Tax in the Enlarged Common Market* (G. S. A. Wheatcroft ed., 1973), Chapter 4.

[56] See T. Knatz, "Value Added Tax : Practice and Planning" 1970 B.T.R. 292.

[57] This was, at least in part, a result of the German experience in the ECSC tax dispute.

[58] D. J. Puchala and C. F. Lankowski, "The Politics of Fiscal Harmonisation in the European Communities" (1977) 15 J.C.M.S. 155, 164.

[59] See Chap. 1 para. 74, above.

[60] See A. E. de Moor, in Wheatcroft (*op. cit.* n. 55), Chapter 6 : (1968) 8 E.T. 30.

[61] See (1969) 9 E.T. 119.

[62] An excellent analysis is given by Y. Guillaume and J. Waelbroeck, "Impact of the Added Value Tax on an Economy : the case of Belgium" (1972) 3 *European Economic Review* 91.

1972, by means of a Third Directive.[63] The Belgian value added tax came into force in 1971.

Even more serious difficulties confronted the Italian government.[64] A chaotic regime of unco-ordinated taxes had evolved over the years and the need for general fiscal reform was clearly recognised. Proposals for a value added tax had been made in 1965 as part of a general plan of reform and the Italian government had no difficulty in agreeing, in principle, to the adoption of the Directives. The problems of implementation were essentially political : the value added tax was included in a package of tax reforms, many of which encountered hostility for different reasons, and was itself variously opposed on grounds that it was inflationary, regressive, involved a heavy administrative burden on small businesses and, though this was rarely articulated, was less easy to evade. Given the delicate balance necessary to maintain coalition governments in Italy, prompt implementation was impossible and two further Directives[65] were necessary, extending the time limit for Italy, before value added tax was eventually introduced in 1973.

### (b) The new Member States

**119**     In negotiating membership of the Community, Denmark, Ireland and the United Kingdom were already aware that, as members, they would be obliged to adopt the value added tax system. Indeed Denmark had introduced the system in 1967, some days before the adoption of the Directives themselves.[66] The contents of the Directives were, however, well known by the Danish government and the legislation conformed closely to their principles. Indeed, Denmark could be said to have been the first country to introduce a fully comprehensive value added tax.[67] The tax replaced a single-stage wholesale sales tax (as opposed to a cumulative multi-stage turnover tax) and was introduced primarily in order to raise revenue. Clearly, the possibility of accession to the Community was a factor in the choice of the tax and in the form which it took, though Denmark would quite probably have adopted a value added tax in any event since there was a general trend in this direction in the Scandinavian countries and it was shortly afterwards adopted in Sweden and in Norway.[68]

[63]  Dir. 69/463/EEC of December 9, 1969.
[64]  See Puchala and Lankowski, (op. cit. n. 58).
[65]  Fourth and Fifth VAT Directives, 71/401 and 72/250, of December 20, 1971 and July 4, 1972. These were addressed to the Italian government alone.
[66]  See F. Stranger, in Wheatcroft (op. cit. n. 55), Chapter 3 : C. S. Shoup, "Experience with the Value Added Tax in Denmark and prospects in Sweden" (1969) 28 Finanzarchiv, 236.
[67]  C. S. Shoup, op. cit. above.
[68]  Membership of the Community may also have been a factor in Norway, but not in Sweden : See M. Norr and N. Hornhammer, "The Value Added Tax in Sweden" (1970) 70 Columbia L. Rev. 379. VAT has been introduced in other non-member European countries, notably in Austria, and is proposed for Switzerland.

Ireland likewise introduced value added tax before accession, in November, 1972,[69] though the form of the tax, designed to alter as little as possible the incidence of the existing taxes, clearly indicated that compliance with the Directives was the main, or sole, reason. In the United Kingdom a value added tax had been advocated for some years, though chiefly as an alternative to corporate income tax,[70] and its adoption was formally proposed by the government in 1971.[71] Somewhat surprisingly, since previous studies had shown little enthusiasm for value added tax, the then government proclaimed an intention to adopt the tax on its own merits and not simply in order to comply with Community objections.[72] Although strong fears were expressed as to the social consequences of value added tax due to its perceived inflationary and regressive effects,[73] its introduction in Britain coincided with a desire to reduce the burden of direct, income, taxes and to rely more upon indirect taxation.

In consequence, with the adoption of value added tax by Italy and by the United Kingdom,[74] the year 1973 saw the common system applied throughout the Community, albeit some three or four years later than had originally been anticipated.

## D.   THE SIXTH DIRECTIVE

### (i)   The Inadequacies of the 1967 Directives

**120**     The 1967 Directives were clearly conceived as constituting a first stage in the evolution of a common Community system of value added tax and, as such, they left a number of matters to be dealt with in subsequent Directives and, at least temporarily, permitted a broad discretion in some areas to the Member States. In addition, most of the Member States, in adopting implementing legislation, derogated to some extent even from the basic framework as laid down in the Directives. Thus, in 1973, there really existed nine separate and different systems of national laws rather than one common Community system.[75] This situation was largely tolerated by the Commission, for until the first two Directives had been implemented by Italy and

---

[69] See G. S. A. Wheatcroft (*op. cit.* n. 55) Chapter 8: (1973) 13 E.T. 308.

[70] The Richardson Committee, in 1964, had been unenthusiastic; see p. 74, n. 16, above.

[71] Green Paper *Value Added Tax* Cmnd. 4621 : see P. Lawton, "Value Added Tax" [1971] B.T.R. 171.

[72] A. J. Easson, "The British Tax Reforms—a step towards Harmonisation" (1971) 8 C.M.L. Rev. 325.

[73] P. Stephenson, "Problems and Political Implications for the United Kingdom of introducing the EEC Value Added Tax" (1970) 8 J.C.M.S. 305. These fears were partly allayed by the zero-rating of food and certain other essential commodities.

[74] For descriptions of the British system, see R. S. Nock and M. A. Pickering, "The Shape of Value Added Tax" [1972] B.T.R. 70; H. H. Mainprice, "Value Added Tax after three years" [1976] B.T.R. 230.

[75] See P. Derouin, (*op. cit.* n. 10) in the Conclusions to Part One.

by the new Member States it seemed inappropriate to take any action—other than drawing attention to derogations and exhorting that they be removed—against those Member States which had, to a great extent, complied with their obligations.[76] Subsequently the Commission began to pursue a more active policy and in a few cases initiated proceedings under Article 169 against Member States for non-fulfilment of their obligations[77]: however, it was apparent that such derogations were best remedied by a further measure of harmonisation.

The major problem areas, which had been identified in the 1967 Directives, or became apparent soon afterwards, were:

*(a) The retail stage*

**121**  As we have seen, it was originally thought that the application of value added tax to the retail trade would cause considerable problems in some Member States and might not be necessary, and the original proposals left to the Member States the option to apply instead some separate form of taxation at this stage. By 1967, however, it had been agreed in principle that the retail stage should be included though this remained discretionary,[78] and in 1969 the Council went further, recognising and urging that the system should extend to the retail stage.[79] Probably the major objection to its inclusion had been that it would be difficult to apply to the many small businesses engaged at this level, but since it was permitted in any event to exempt small businesses entirely from the system, or to apply special rules to them,[80] it appeared more logical to make special provision for small retailers on the ground that they were small, rather than that they were involved in retail trade.

*(b) Agriculture*

As with small businesses and the retail trade there were economic, technical and psychological objections to the inclusion of farmers and of agricultural products within the common value added tax system. This was acknowledged in the Second Directive[81] and the six original Member States all introduced special systems for agriculture, which varied in numerous details.[82] As envisaged, a further proposed Directive was prepared by the

---

[76]  P. Nasini, "Harmonisation of National Systems of VAT," (1973) 13 E.T. 39, and in Wheatcroft (ed.), (*op. cit.* n. 55) Chapter 9.

[77]  See (EC) Tenth General Report (1976), p. 106.

[78]  Dir. 67/227, Art. 2, paras. 3 and 4.

[79]  Council Resolution of December 9, 1969 : J.O. 1969, C 163/1.

[80]  Dir. 67/228, Art. 14.

[81]  *Ibid.* Art. 15.

[82]  *Etudes des problèmes particuliers posés par l'application de la taxe sur la valeur ajoutée au secteur agricole. . . .* Commission, Etudes : Série Concurrence—Rapprochement des Législations, No. 24 (1973) Vermand Report.

Commission[83] : this advocated a single, uniform, flat-rate system to be applied to the agricultural sector. However, it soon became apparent that such a system would have to await a general approximation of tax rates and that, until then, national differences would have to persist.

(c)   *Special types of business*

**122**     As conceived by the Directives, the value added tax is a general, consumption-type, tax, which should apply to all supplies of goods and provisions of services. Nevertheless, there are certain types of transaction which do not lend themselves readily to integration into   the system. Transactions involving immovables present difficulties, since whilst building construction and the letting of land or premises may properly be regarded as the supply of goods or as the provision of services—though it is not always clear which — land itself, being a commodity which is not consumed, does not seem  appropriate for inclusion.[84] Similarly, financial operations, such as banking and credit transactions and insurance, by their nature present problems and, if they are to be within the system at all, call for special treatment.[85] Further difficulties exist in the case of used and second-hand goods, antiques and works of art.[86]

(d)   *Exemptions*

Exemptions from the tax varied widely from one Member State to another, especially with regard to the treatment of small undertakings.[87] Other disparities arose as a result of the different definitions adopted in national legislation for taxable supplies and taxable persons.[88] Some Member States, notably the United Kingdom and the Republic of Ireland, had extensive recourse to zero-rating, notwithstanding that this practice appears to be contrary to the Second Directive.[89]

---

[83] Submitted to the Council on February 26, 1968 : see (EC) Bull. 4–68, p. 36.

[84] *Rapport sur l'application de la TVA aux opérations immobilieres au sein de la Communauté.* Commission, Etudes : Série Concurrence—Rapprochement des Législations, No. 21 (1971) (Bours Report.) See also L. S. Bartlett, in (1974) 14 E.T. 302 and P. G. Willoughby, "VAT : an analysis of some of the problems involving Land and Premises" 1973 B.T.R. 288.

[85] *Les opérations financieres et bancaires et la taxe sur la valeur ajoutée.* Commission, Etudes : Série Concurrence—Rapprochement des Législations, No. 22 (1973) (Hutchings Report).

[86] See below, paras. 133, 134.

[87] *Etudes sur l'application de la taxe sur la valeur ajoutée aux petites entreprises . . .* Commission, Etudes : Série Concurrence—Rapprochement des Législations, No. 23 (1973) (Kauffmann Report). For details, see the Commission's reply to EPWQ 532/78 : O.J. 1979, C 92/1.

[88] P. Derouin, (*op. cit.* n. 10) Chapters 2 and 3.

[89] Dir. 67/228, Preamble and Art. 9, para. 2 : and see P. Guieu, "L'Uniformisation des Systèmes Nationaux de TVA" (1974) 178 R.M.C. 437, 446.

### (e)  Deduction of tax on inputs

**123**     The general principles of value added tax require that a trader, in accounting for the tax on the goods or services supplied or performed by him, be permitted to deduct any tax invoiced to him in respect of his business purchases.[90] Whilst some departure from this principle was permitted in the case of purchases of capital goods,[91] some Member States were operating this derogation in an unduly restrictive manner.[92] And in some other Member States, notably France, a "buffer rule" prevented a full deduction of input taxes where this might result in a trader receiving a tax refund.[93]

### (f)  Territoriality and the provision of services

Perhaps the most serious problem, from the point of view of its distorting effects upon intra-Community commerce, concerned the treatment of services performed across frontiers. If, for example, a lawyer in country A gave advice to, or acted for, a business client in country B, should the service be treated as having been performed in A, or exported to B?[94] If tax is payable in A, and if the foreign business can obtain neither a refund of that tax from the authorities there nor a deduction for it from his own authorities, this may result in double taxation, for the cost of those services will be included in the bill provided by the business to its own client, and, as such, will be taxed again.[95] The national rules as to where and when services were deemed to be performed, whether a supply was one of goods or of services and whether there was deemed to be an exportation, varied considerably, resulting in double taxation in many cases and thus impeding the freedom to supply services within the Community.[96]

### (ii)  VAT and the community budget

**124**     Given the immediate objectives of the 1967 Directives, these national differences, with the exception of the various rules on the performance of services, caused little or no distortion to competition and to intra-

---

[90]  Dir. 67/228, Art. 11.

[91]  *Ibid.* Art. 17.

[92]  See Case 51/76, *Verbond van Nederlandse Ondernemingen* [1977] E.C.R. 113.

[93]  See (EC) Sixth General Report (1972), p. 67.

[94]  See the decisions of the Dutch tax court, noted in (1978) 18 E.T. 108, (1979) 19 E.T. 130. And see below, para. 127.

[95]  And see the decision of the *Finanzgericht Baden-Wurttemberg* in *Re Foreign Value Added Tax* [1975] 2 C.M.L.R. 326 (car repairs carried out in France for a German customer taxed as a service in France and taxed on the value of materials on re-importation into Germany).

[96]  See G. Kolling, "Services and the Sixth VAT Directive" (1974) 14 E.T. 79; P. Derouin, "E.G. Territorialitätsregeln für Dienstleistungen bei der Mehrwertsteuer" 1976 *Intertax*, 291, 392: P.W. de Voil, "U.K. VAT: Services performed across tax frontiers" 1976 *Intertax*, 372.

Community trade. Similar goods or services sold or performed within the territory of a Member State bore the same tax burden, regardless of country of origin, and the major problem of calculating the appropriate border tax adjustments on imports and exports was essentially solved. Such distortions as remained were now among the least of the obstacles to free competition within the Community.[97] There were, however, other pressing reasons for further harmonisation of value added tax.

The Community's budget was originally financed, in accordance with Article 200 of the EEC Treaty, by financial contributions from the Member States. However, Article 201 provided that the Commission should examine the conditions under which those financial contributions might be replaced by the Community's "own resources," and required the Commission to submit proposals to that end. The original proposals, submitted in 1965, provided for financing by means of the proceeds of the common customs duties and agricultural levies,[98] but it became apparent that additional sources of finance would be required to meet the needs of the Community.[99] The Council's Decision of April 21, 1970[1] provided that, as from the beginning of 1975, the budget should be financed entirely from the Communities'[2] own resources, which should include, in addition to customs duties and agricultural levies, revenue

> "accruing from the value added tax and obtained by applying a rate not exceeding 1 per cent. to an assessment basis which is determined in a uniform manner for Member States according to Community rules."[3]

The Decision therefore required that a uniform tax base be established : tax rates within the Member States could continue to vary, but exemptions—of persons and of transactions—would require further harmonisation. Since the Community's revenue was to derive from the application of a single rate of tax, to be fixed annually in the budget resolution, it was necessary, in order to ensure that Member States each contributed their fair share, that that rate be applied to essentially the same transactions throughout the Community. Thus a number of national differences which, in themselves, had little or no effect upon the conditions of competition in the Common Market,[4] and might otherwise have been tolerated, were required to be eliminated in order to secure an equitable distribution of the fiscal burden as between Member States. Another consideration, from the point of view of

---

[97] P. Derouin, (*op. cit.* n. 10) at p. 289.
[98] (EEC) Bull. 5–65, p. 10.
[99] See I. E. Drucker, *Financing the European Communities* (1975), pp. 245 *et seq.*
[1] Dec. 70/243.
[2] The budget covers the expenditure not only of the EEC but also of Euratom and, in part, of the ECSC. See D. Strasser, *The Finances of Europe* (1977).
[3] Dec. 70/243, Art. 4.
[4] *e.g.* in the taxation of transactions in immovables: see the Bours Report (n. 84, above) at p. 157.

the Community, was that if the basis of assessment could be standardised by reducing the number of permitted exemptions, this would enlarge the tax base and correspondingly increase the revenue to the Community from the application of the Community rate.[5]


### (iii)  The Sixth Directive[6]

**125**      The Decision of April 21, 1970, had called for the full implementation of the system of own resources as from the commencement of the 1975 financial year. The delays, on the part of Belgium and Italy, in implementing the 1967 Directives and the accession of the new Member States at the beginning of 1973 upset this timetable and it was not until mid-1973 that the Commission was able to submit its proposals for a Sixth Directive.[7] Various amendments were proposed by the Parliament and the Economic and Social Committee,[8] in the light of which (though it would appear that the reactions of the Member States themselves were more influential), the Commission submitted an amended proposal.[9] Despite the urgency of the matter, from the point of view of the Community's budget, progress remained slow and the shortfall in revenue had to be made good by means of financial contributions from the Member States.[10] The Member States appeared to be especially reluctant to surrender their autonomy with respect to the determination of the tax base and the exceptions which they would permit and, ultimately, it was necessary to reach a compromise whereby the Directive would permit a greater degree of flexibility, in return for which it was accepted that some form of correcting mechanism would be required to take into account differences in the national tax bases in order to calculate what should be a proper and equitable tax yield in each country.[11]

The Sixth Directive was eventually adopted by the Council on May 17, 1977. It replaces the Second Directive, and consequently repeats many of its

---

[5]  P. Guieu, (*op. cit.* n. 89, above) at p. 438.

[6]  Dir. 77/388 of May 17, 1977: For detailed considerations of the provisions of this Directive, see R. Goergen, "The decision of the Council of Ministers of the Community on the proposal for a Sixth Directive on VAT," (1977) E.T. 48: P. Guieu, "E.C; Sixth Council Directive on VAT," 1977 *Intertax* 245: J. Reugebrink, "The Sixth Directive for the Harmonisation of Value Added Tax," (1978) 15 C.M.L. Rev. 309.

[7]  The proposal was transmitted to the Council on June 29, 1973: O.J. 1973, C 80. See the Commission's explanatory memorandum, in (EC) Bull. S. 11–73 and, for comments, see P. Guieu, (*op. cit.* n. 89) and G. N. Glover and C. Levy, "The new draft Directive for the Harmonisation of Value Added Tax" 1974 B.T.R. 206.

[8]  O.J. 1974, C 40/34 (E.P.) : C 139/15 (ESC). Of particular interest is the report of the Parliament's Committee on Budgets: E.P. Docs. 360/73 (referred to hereafter as the Notenboom Report).

[9]  O.J. 1974, C 121/34.

[10]  Calculated on the basis of gross national product, in accordance with Dec. 70/243, art. 4(2).

[11]  E.C. Bull. 11–75, pp. 27–28, and see below, para. 135.

provisions with only minor amendments, and repeals part of the First Directive notably the provision which permitted the application of a separate tax to the retail trade.[12] The tax applies to the supply of goods or services effected for consideration within the territory of a Member State by a taxable person acting as such and to the importation of goods.[13]

"Taxable person" means any person who independently[14] carries out in any place any economic activity—which is specified to comprise all activities of producers, traders and persons supplying services including mining and agricultural activities and activities of the professions— whatever the purpose or results of that activity.[15] Consistently with the overall concept of the value added tax as a tax on consumption, it is irrelevant whether or not the supply is made for profit. The professions are included (they had formerly been widely exempted in some Member States) and the tax applies to agricultural activities, though by Article 25 special arrangements may still be made for farmers. Member States may also treat as a taxable person anyone who carries out such a transaction, even though only on an occasional basis.[16] States, regional and local government authorities and other public bodies are not normally considered to be taxable persons in respect of activities engaged in in that capacity, though this exemption does not apply to certain specified activities such as the provision of utilities and transportation.[17]

**126**    "Supply of goods" is stated to mean the transfer of the right to dispose of tangible property as owner.[18] Also included are transfers made in connection with a compulsory purchase or under a contract for hire purchase or conditional sale.[19] The self-supply of goods by a taxable person, or other appropriation for non-business use, is also treated as a taxable supply.[20] In addition, Member States are permitted to treat as taxable supplies certain other transactions, notably the transfer of interests in immovable property. This particular problem has, therefore, been left unresolved.[21]

Goods are treated as being supplied at the place where the goods are

---

[12] Dir. 67/227, Art. 2, para. 4: see Dir. 77/388, Art. 36.

[13] Dir. 77/388, Art. 2. Note that the tax applies to goods imported by a private individual, though a number of exemptions are provided by other Directives: see below, Chapter 3, paras. 245–251.

[14] Associated enterprises may be treated as a single, independent entity: cf. Cases 181, 229/78, van Paasen [1979] E.C.R. 2063, interpreting the corresponding provision in the Second Directive.

[15] Ibid. Art. 4.

[16] Ibid. Art. 4, para. 3. This provision is essentially aimed at occasional transactions in land and buildings.

[17] Ibid. Art. 4, para. 5. This could result in some disparities as between Member States, for the size of the public sector and the type of activities engaged in varies from one country to another: see the provisos to para. 5, and Annex D.

[18] Art. 5. Tangible property includes electricity, gas, heat, refrigeration, etc.

[19] Art. 5, para. 4.

[20] Art. 5, para. 6.

[21] See above, para. 122.

when the supply takes place or, if they are transported (whether by the seller or purchaser), where the transportation commences.[22]

127    "Supply of Services" is defined residually to mean any transaction which does not constitute a supply of goods, and includes an assignment of intangible property.[23] A major problem under the Second Directive had been the different national rules determining where a service is supplied.[24] A common rule is now established by the Sixth Directive, which provides that the place where a service is supplied shall be deemed to be the place where the supplier has established his business or has a fixed establishment from which the service is supplied.[25] To this general principle, however, there are a large number of exceptions: thus services supplied in connection with immovable property, such as the services of estate agents and architects, are deemed to be performed where the property is situated.[26] Many other services, such as those connected with cultural, artistic, sporting, scientific, educational or entertainment activities, or work performed on tangible movable property are deemed to be performed where they are physically carried out. Yet a further category of services, when performed for customers established in another country,[27] are taxable in the country where the customer has his establishment. These include the services of consultants, lawyers and accountants, banking, financial and insurance transactions, advertising services and services in connection with transfers and assignments of copyrights, patents, licences, trade marks and similar rights.

Where services are performed by a taxable person whose place of establishment is in country A for a customer whose business is in country B, then:

(a) If the service is deemed to be provided in B there should be no possibility of double taxation. If tax is imposed in B, the customer, being himself a taxable person, will be entitled to deduct the tax invoiced to him in respect of the service from the tax for which he is accountable in respect of his own supplies. No doubt there will be many instances where tax is not in fact imposed on the service, since the provider is not a registered taxable person in country B.[28] This will not lead to evasion, however, since the

---

[22] Art. 8. But if installed by or on behalf of the supplier, they are treated as supplied where installed. Member States are required, where goods are installed by a foreign supplier, to take steps to avoid double taxation: *cf.* Case 74/72, *FOR.* v. *VKS* [1973] E.C.R. 193.

[23] Art. 6. The use of business assets and the self-supply of services are also taxable: *ibid.* para. 2.

[24] Above, para. 123. See also J. Bonafons, "La Taxation des prestations de services dans la proposition de la sixième directive" (1974) 179 R.M.C. 467.

[25] Art. 9, para. 1.

[26] Thus, in the example given by Reugebrink (*op. cit.* n. 6), at p. 315, where a Dutch housepainter paints a house in Germany, the supply would now be deemed to take place in Germany. Formerly, it would have been taxable in both countries.

[27] But if the customer is in another Member State, only if he is himself a taxable person: Art. 9, para. 2(*e*).

[28] But see Art. 21(1)(*b*).

service will in effect be taxed when the recipient passes the cost on to his own customers.

(*b*) If the service is deemed to be provided in A, and is taxed there, there is a possibility of double taxation unless the customer in B is entitled to a deduction for, or a refund of, that tax. Double taxation may be prevented by:

(1) permitting the customer to deduct, against the tax assessed in B, the tax paid in A. This practice, which is consistent with the "origin" rather than with the "destination" principle, has not been adopted;

(2) treating the supply in A to a foreign customer as an exportation of the service, so that no tax is in fact charged. It is provided in Article 15 that certain supplies of services, in particular those consisting of work on movable property which is re-exported,[29] are to be exempted as exports.[30];

(3) allowing the customer to obtain, from the tax authorities in A, a refund of the tax invoiced to him. This is required by Article 17(3) of the Directive.[31]

**128** Rates of tax, expressed as a percentage of the taxable amount,[32] are fixed by the Member States and are not required to be harmonised. Member States are permitted to apply increased rates or reduced rates to certain categories of supplies, as determined by them, but the Directive requires that reduced rates shall be fixed at such a level as to permit the deduction of the whole of the tax imposed upon inputs.[33] For example, if small businesses are to be allowed to apply a reduced rate to their supplies, this rate should not be so low that they are unable to absorb the tax imposed upon their purchases at the full rate. The reason for this requirement appears to derive from an objection to the granting of tax refunds.[34] If so, it seems hard to justify since the burden of the tax falls ultimately upon the consumer and the taxable person is, in effect, merely an unpaid tax official who collects the money. As such it should be of no consequence whether that person accounts for tax collected or receives a refund in respect of over-collection.[35] The objection to zero-rating also seems to have the same derivation. Essentially, zero rates are simply an extreme form of reduced rating (*i.e.* unlike exemptions, zero rated transactions are within the framework of the

---

[29] *e.g.* car repairs: *cf. Re Foreign Value Added Tax* [1975] 2 C.M.L.R. 326.

[30] *Cf.* the United Kingdom rule that a supply to an overseas resident of any service not used by that person in the United Kingdom is zero-rated: Finance Act 1972, Sched. 4, Group 9, and see *Commissioners of Customs and Excise* v. *G. & B. Practical Management Development Ltd.* (n. 19 ET 66).

[31] See also the Eighth Directive, Dir. 79/1072, para 135 below.

[32] As defined in Art. 11.

[33] Art. 12, para. 4.

[34] Hence the so-called "buffer rule" formerly applied in some Member States: see para. 123, above.

[35] See Reugebrink (*op. cit.* n. 6) at p. 313.

tax system[36]) and by their nature must result in a remission of taxes imposed at earlier stages.[37] Nevertheless, the Directive treats zero rates as incompatible with the system, though Member States are permitted to retain those zero-ratings which were in force at the end of 1975, if applied for clearly defined social reasons and for the benefit of the final consumer, until such time as tax frontiers are abolished or such earlier date as is fixed by the Council.[38] One other possible objection to zero-rating should be mentioned: the main purpose of the Sixth Directive was to achieve a common basis of assessment throughout the Community in order to secure an equitable division, among the Member States, of the budget revenue deriving from VAT-based own resources. Transactions which are zero-rated should, like those which are subject to reduced rates, form part of the basis of assessment to which the Community rate of tax is applied. This in itself should not cause problems, since those transactions remain within the tax system and tax returns are still made in respect thereof, so that a member state can calculate the amount of tax due to the Community.[39] If a Member State persists in zero-rating transactions then, in effect, it will be subsidising those transactions (to the extent of the Community tax imposed on them) out of its revenue from taxed transactions.[40] Difficulties arise, however, if zero-rating is used as an alternative to exemption, since exempt transactions do not form a part of the Community tax base and do not provide the Community with "own resources."

*Exemptions*

**129**    In order to achieve a harmonised basis of assessment for budgetary purposes it was considered necessary to standardise the exemptions, which had varied considerably from one country to another. Article 13 of the Directive sets out a long list of those transactions which Member States are required to exempt. These include matters such as postal services, medical, social, educational and cultural services. Also exempt, under certain conditions, are certain financial and credit transactions and transactions in immovable property. Importations of goods which, if supplied within the country, would be exempt are also required to be exempted as are certain

---

[36] See above, para. 106, *cf.* the *Notenboom Report* (at p. 30) which objected that zero-rates do not really constitute genuine taxation. The Parliament, however, considered that zero-rates do not vitiate the system: O.J. 1974, C. 40/34, at p. 35.

[37] There will, of course, not necessarily be a refund, as where a trader makes both zero-rated and standard-rated supplies and the latter are sufficient to absorb all the input taxes.

[38] Art. 28, para. 2.

[39] Reg. 2892/77, Arts. 2, 4: see below, para. 135.

[40] Or, indeed, out of any other revenue. Thus it is arguable that it is not necessary to have identical VAT coverage so long as the tax base, to which the Community rate is applied, can be estimated accurately on a comparable basis from national accounts data. See the comments of A. R. Prest and of D. Dosser in G. Denton (ed.), *Economic and Monetary Union in Europe* (1974), Chaps. 6 and 7, at pp. 94, 109.

temporary and other kinds of importations.[41] As was the case under the Second Directive, exports are required to be exempted and, in this case, exemption means zero-rated, since the supplier is entitled to a deduction or refund of the tax previously paid.[42]

*Deductions*

The basic principle is retained that a taxable person has a right to deduct, from the tax for which he is accountable in respect of his supplies, the tax invoiced to him on goods or services supplied to, or imported by, him but only in so far as those goods or services are used for the purposes of his taxable transactions.[43] One purpose of this restriction is clear: no deduction is permitted in respect of goods or services supplied for a non-business purpose, such as the personal use of the trader himself. However, the goods or services must also be used for the purposes of his taxable transactions[44]: thus it would seem that no deduction may be given for goods or services supplied in respect of exempt transactions. A trader who makes both taxable and exempt supplies may consequently deduct only the tax in respect of the purchases used by him in connection with the taxable supplies and in some cases an apportionment of input tax will be necessary, as where goods purchased are used for the purposes of both types of supply.[45] This restriction does not, of course, apply to exported supplies or to other zero-rated supplies, where these are permitted. Member States are still permitted, subject to consultation, to exclude capital goods from the system of deductions or to spread the deduction over a period of five years.[46]

*Small Undertakings*

**130**     Member States apply a wide variety of special provisions in the case of small businesses. These may take the form of a flat-rate tax, lower or graduated rates, or complete exemption from the system. Similarly, the definition of what constitutes a "small" undertaking varies considerably.[47] For the present, Member States are permitted to retain existing schemes and to introduce exemptions, or increase existing exemptions, for undertakings

---

[41]  Art. 14. See also the Prop. Dir. of June 13, 1980 (O.J. 1980, C 171/8.
[42]  Arts. 15, 16 and 17, para. 3.
[43]  Art. 17, para 2.
[44]  *Cf*. Dir. 67/228, Art. 11, which said "for the purposes of his undertaking" : on this point, see Reugebrink, (*op. cit*. n. 6) at p. 317.
[45]  Art. 17, para. 5.
[46]  Art. 17, para. 6: art. 20. By Art. 20, para. 4, Member States may define the concept of capital goods: *cf*. Case 51/76 *Verbond van Nederlandse Ondernemingen* |1977| E.C.R. 113.
[47]  See the Kaufmann Report and, for more recent details, the Commission's reply to EPWQ 532/78: O.J. 1979, C 92/1.

whose annual turnover does not exceed 5,000 units of account.[48] During the course of preparation of the Sixth Directive it became apparent that it would not be possible to reach agreement on a common scheme to be applied to small undertakings and consequently a form of "standstill" compromise was reached, though the Directive envisages that further harmonisation will be necessary. The present situation is unsatisfactory in a number of respects. There is some justification for the exemption of, or application of a special scheme to, small undertakings since the administrative burden of value added tax, with its relatively complex accounting requirements, bears disproportionately heavily upon them. But annual turnover is not necessarily the best indication of size or of the ability to bear this burden, and an exemption on this basis may distort competition between different enterprises.[49] Moreover, the proportion of large and small businesses varies considerably from one country to another, and the wide divergence of national rules[50] prevents the attainment of a uniform basis of assessment and causes budgetary problems.

*Farmers*

**131**    Similar problems exist in the agricultural sector. Despite the intention avowed in the Second Directive,[51] to prepare "as soon as possible," directives on common procedures applicable to agriculture, it has still not been possible, in most Member States, to bring farmers within the value added tax system and Member States remain free to apply their own special systems.[52] Again, taking into account the differences in the national treatment of agriculture and the relative importance of the agricultural sector in the various Member States, the desired neutrality in the tax base is impaired and budgetary difficulties are caused.

*Value Added Tax Committee*

The Sixth Directive[53] establishes an Advisory Committee on value added tax, consisting of representatives from each Member State and from the Commission, to examine questions raised by the Commission or by a Member State concerning the application of the Community provisions on value added tax. In addition, a number of the provisions of the Directive which

[48] Art. 24. For Member States which already had an exemption limit in excess of 5,000 u.a., notably the United Kingdom, that limit may be retained but may only be increased in order to maintain its value in real terms. For the provisions applying to Greece, see the Treaty of Accession of Greece, Art. 128 and Annex VIII.

[49] On this point, see Notenboom Report.

[50] The exemption limit in the United Kingdom is more than 10 times higher than that in Denmark.

[51] Dir. 67/228, Art. 15.

[52] Dir. 77/388, Art. 25.

[53] Art. 29.

leave a margin of discretion to the Member States as to the manner in which the rules are implemented provide for consultation with the Committee. Though the Committee has been given no power to make binding regulations, as the Commission's proposal originally intended, it can nevertheless be expected to play an important role in limiting national derogations from the principles of the Directive and in the further harmonisation of value added tax.

### (iv)   Implementation of the Sixth Directive

**132**     The "own resources" Decision had anticipated that the proposed new budgetary system would commence in 1975. As we have seen, this was not possible as regards the value added tax portion of revenue due to the delays in preparing and adopting the Sixth Directive. When finally adopted, in May 1977, this required Member States to adopt the necessary laws, regulations and administrative provisions by January 1, 1978, at the latest,[54] so that the own resources system could be fully operational in the financial year 1978. Yet again expectations were frustrated, for only two Member States, Belgium and the United Kingdom, succeeded in meeting the deadline. As a result, a further directive, the Ninth[55] Directive, had to be adopted, authorising the remaining seven states to defer implementation until January 1, 1979, at the latest.[56] Even so, four Member States—Germany, Ireland, Italy and Luxembourg—were unable to meet the new deadline,[57] though all had adopted the necessary measures by the end of 1979.

The "own resources" Decision[58] provided that where the rules determining the uniform basis for assessing the value added tax, *i.e.* those contained in the Sixth Directive, have not yet been applied in all Member States but have been applied in at least three of them, the Community VAT rate should apply to the implementing states but, as to those states which had failed to implement, financial contributions should be made by them, calculated on the basis of their relative gross national products. The result, consequently, was that for the financial year 1978, since only two Member States had implemented the Directive, all Member States made gross national product-based financial contributions: for the financial year 1979, by the commencement of which five Member States had adopted the necessary legislation, the VAT-based system of "own resources" operated for the first time, though under a mixed system with some Member States continuing to make

---

[54]   Art. 1.

[55]   In the meanwhile, two further directives, the Seventh and Eighth, had been proposed but had not then been adopted.

[56]   Dir. 78/583 of June 26, 1978.

[57]   (EC) Twelfth General Report (1978) pp. 118–119. Proceedings under Art. 169 have been commenced against Germany (Case 132/79).

[58]   Dec. 70/243, Art. 4(2).

financial contributions.[59] For the financial year 1980 (when the budget is eventually adopted) all Member States will make VAT-based contributions.[60]

## E. THE FURTHER HARMONISATION OF VAT

**133** The urgent need to adopt the Sixth Directive, in order to put into effect the budgetary provisions concerning value added tax, made it necessary to leave a number of matters outstanding, to be dealt with in subsequent Directives. Consequently, since the adoption of the Sixth Directive, a number of additional proposals have been prepared.

### (i) Proposed Seventh Directive[61]

One problem, essentially technical in nature, to which it had not been possible to devise a satisfactory solution in time for inclusion in the Sixth Directive, concerned the appropriate treatment of used and second-hand goods, works of art, antiques and other collectors' items. Article 32 of the Directive entrusted the Commission with the task of reviewing the problems and preparing fresh proposals, until the adoption of which Member States would remain free to apply their own special schemes.

Three major difficulties were apparent:

(*a*) the definition of "used goods." A distinction clearly needs to be made between those used goods which have reached the final consumer and those which have not. For example, a motor vehicle which has been purchased by a trader, as a "capital good" for use in his business, and is later sold by him, should remain within the general system of value added tax. The trader will have benefited by a deduction of the tax on his input and should consequently be taxed on the proceeds of subsequent sale. Where, by contrast, the vehicle has been purchased for private use it has completed its "commercial cycle" : it is less clear whether, if it enters a second "commercial cycle" by being re-sold to a dealer some years later, that second cycle should also be taxable.[61a] Moreover, used goods which have reached the consumer do not all share similar characteristics. Some, such as most consumer durables, depreciate in value, others, such as antiques or works of art, tend to appreciate. Some used goods normally change hands privately, others commonly do so through a commercial intermediary, such as an art or car dealer.

[59] (EC) Twelfth General Report (1978), pp. 55–57.
[60] By the Treaty of Accession of Greece, Art. 145, Greece is given until the beginning of 1984 to adopt the necessary VAT legislation. Until then, it will make g.n.p.-based contributions as provided for in Dec. 70/243: Treaty of Accession of Greece, Art. 127.
[61] Proposal submitted to the Council on January 11, 1978: O.J. 1978, C 26/2.
[61a] *Cf.* the *non bis in idem* argument in Case 21/79 *Commission* v. *Italy* (1980) 2 C.M.L.R. 613, 623.

(b) the application of tax to used goods. A problem of double taxation arises where goods which have already reached the final consumer are subsequently purchased by a taxable person with a view to resale.[62] The goods will already have borne tax, yet, if the normal system is to apply, none of this will be deductible on the re-sale by the dealer.

(c) the status of the seller. If sales of used goods by taxable persons are to be taxable but sales by private individuals are not, this will lead to market distortions and, probably, to widespread tax evasion.

The Commission concluded that the total exemption of used goods from the value added tax system, though theoretically justifiable, would result in a substantial loss of tax revenue for some Member States and would also lead to distortions of competition. On the other hand, the normal system was inappropriate, since it also would lead to distortions and to double taxation. Consequently, a special scheme was proposed whereby, according to the type of goods involved, a taxable person reselling could be authorised to deduct from the tax chargeable on the resale price a notional amount of tax calculated on the basis of his purchase price or, alternatively, the taxable amount on resale could be a standard percentage of the selling price, rather than the full price.

Neither the Economic and Social Committee[63] nor the Parliament[64] was enthusiastic about the proposal and, as a result, the Commission submitted a revised proposal,[65] introducing a third scheme, whereby the actual value added (i.e. the dealer's mark-up) would be taxable and permitting a taxable person to choose, in some but not all cases, the appropriate scheme.

### (ii)   Eighth Directive[66]

**134**     Another matter expressly left over by the Sixth Directive[67] for further action concerned the right of a taxable person to a deduction or refund of tax invoiced to him and paid in another Member State. In the case of a supply of goods this should not normally occur, since exportations of goods are required to be exempted, but in the case of services, in particular the services of international carriers and those provided to exhibitors at international trade fairs, double taxation can occur where a service is deemed to be performed in one Member State on behalf of a customer established in

---

[62] e.g. a used car sold to, or taken in part exchange by a car dealer: see EPWQ 714/78; O.J. 1979, C 60/6.

[63] O.J. 1978, C 269/21. The ESC rejected the proposal altogether, considering it too complex and (rather unrealistically) advocated that the general VAT rules should apply. Their opinion contains useful details of the special schemes applying in each Member State.

[64] O.J. 1974, C 93/7, and see Doc. 647/78. The Parliament agreed with the Commission that the general system was not appropriate, but was critical of the flat-rate proposals and advocated a more flexible approach.

[65] Submitted on May 16, 1979: O.J. 1979, C 136/8.

[66] Dir. 79/1072 of December 6, 1979.

[67] Dir. 77/388, Art. 17(3).

another Member State. The Directive lays down the procedure whereby, on presentation of the appropriate documentary evidence, a refund of tax can be obtained.

### (iii)  Proposed Tenth Directive[68]

This proposes to amend and supplement Article 9 of the Sixth Directive and is concerned with the hiring-out of movable tangible property, other than forms of transport. In effect, the supply is deemed to take place where the property is situated at the time it is actually made available to the customer.

### (iv)  Further Harmonisation[68a]

**135**    As we have seen, the Sixth Directive was unable to resolve a number of other issues and a margin of discretion was left to the Member States until such time as harmonised rules can be adopted. The major remaining problems relate to the treatment of farmers and small undertakings and to zero-rating. All of these have some significance from the point of view of the Community's budget, for the differences in national rules prevent the establishment of a common basis of assessment for the Community's share of the value added tax. It is consequently necessary, for the present, in ascertaining the amount of revenue due to the Community, to make certain estimations, based upon available data, of the tax which would be payable in respect of farmers and small undertakings, and in zero-rated transactions, if a uniform basis were applicable throughout the Community.[69] This state of affairs is not entirely satisfactory, for it could give rise to conflict between the Commission and the Member States and it is contrary to the basic principles of the system of "own resources" in that it involves the collection of revenue from the Member States themselves, rather than merely employing them as collectors of the Community's revenue.[70]

The Sixth Directive provides for the submission of further proposals on these subjects—in the case of farmers within five years[71] and, in the case of small undertakings and zero-rating, to take effect at a date "which shall not be later than that on which the charging of tax on imports and the remission of tax on exports in trade between the member States are abolished."[72]

[68] Proposal submitted to the Council on April 11, 1979: O.J. 1979, C. 116/4. The opinion of the Economic and Social Committee on this proposal provides a useful illustration of the problems involved: O.J. 1979, C. 297/16. See also the comments and criticisms of the Parliament: O.J. 1980, C 4/63.

[68a] An Eleventh Directive, 80/368, excludes French overseas departments from the scope of Dir. 77/388. See also n. 41, above.

[69] Reg. 2892/77, Arts. 4, 5, 9. See J. P. Bouquin, "Les Resources Propres des Communautés Européennes," (1978) 218 R.M.C. 321.

[70] Whether this principle or the amounts involved are sufficient to justify further harmonisation may, of course, be questioned. See also the comment at n. 40, above.

[71] Dir. 77/388, Art. 25, para. 11.

[72] *Ibid.* Art. 24, para. 2; Art. 28, para 2.

## F.  VAT AND THE ABOLITION OF TAX FRONTIERS

**136**    From the very beginning a major objective of the harmonisation of turn-over taxes has been perceived to be the eventual removal of tax frontiers.[73] Although not expressly listed as an objective of the Treaty, the existence of internal frontiers has always been considered to be incompatible with the very notion of a common market and to be undesirable for political and psychological reasons. The aim, of abolishing such frontiers, has been explicitly proclaimed in the Commission's first proposed Directive, in the first two Directives of 1967[74] and in the Sixth Directive.[75] Initially, the hope was that tax frontiers would disappear simultaneously with the achievement of the customs union in 1968.[76] Gradually, the anticipated date was pushed back to 1970 or 1971,[77] and it soon became apparent that its attainment would be far from simple, if possible at all.[78]

Tax frontiers are necessary, or thought to be necessary, because of the adoption of the destination principle in intra-Community and international trade.[79] Internal indirect taxes are remitted when goods are exported and are imposed upon imported goods at the point of importation. Thus, it is normally assumed,[80] despite the abolition of internal customs duties it remains necessary to check goods at frontiers, both to impose the tax of the importing country and to ensure that goods have been exported so as to qualify for a refund of tax by the exporting country. Only, it was believed, by changing over to the origin principle, would the need for tax frontiers disappear: thus the First Directive speaks of "the aim of abolishing the imposition of tax on importation and the remission of tax on exportation in trade between Member States, whilst ensuring the neutrality of those taxes as regards the origin of the goods or services."[81]

### (i)  VAT and the origin principle

**137**    The theory of the origin and destination principles has been discussed in Chapter 1: the origin principle assumes that goods will be taxed where they are produced or, rather, where value is added regardless of where they are eventually consumed, the destination principle that they will be taxed where

---

[73] See above, paras. 109–111.

[74] Dir. 67/227, Art. 4: Dir 67/228, Art. 19.

[75] Dir. 77/388, Art. 35.

[76] Deringer Report, p. 32, and see (EEC) Bull. 12–63, p. 8.

[77] "Initiative 1964", (EEC) Bull. 11–64, p. 5: the Barre Plan, (EC) Bull. S3–70, p. 9.

[78] A recent study suggests 1995 as a realistic target date: Report of the ESC Section for Economic and Financial Questions, Doc. CES 846/78, point 4.2.2.3. (referred to hereafter as the Fredersdorf Report).

[79] Chapter 1, para. 82, above.

[80] This was the conclusion of the majority of Sub-Group A: *The EEC Reports on Tax Harmonisation*: paras. 109–111, above.

[81] Dir. 67/227, Art. 4. See also Dir. 77/388, Arts. 24(2), 28(2).

consumed, regardless of where they were originally produced. The value added tax, however, especially where it extends to the retail stage, does not fit neatly into either category.[82] The essence of value added tax is that tax is charged at each stage of production and marketing upon the value added in the course of that stage. Where value added tax applies at the final retail stage, as it now does in the Community, goods, whether domestically produced or imported, will necessarily be taxed in, and at the rate fixed by, the country where they are consumed, *i.e.* the country of destination. If the system of border tax adjustments, associated with the destination principle, is abandoned so that remission of tax is no longer made upon exportation and importation ceases to be a taxable event, the natural result of the value added tax would be to allocate the tax between the countries concerned in proportion to the value added in each.[83]

Under the tax-from-tax method,[84] assuming that the country of importation allows a credit against its own tax for the tax already paid in the country of exportation (which would normally be the tax invoiced to the importer by the exporter), the effect would be two-fold. The total tax burden on the final product would be determined, as it now is, by the rate applicable at the final, retail, stage but tax revenues would accrue to the two countries according to the value added in each instead of, as now, accruing entirely to the importing country. This seems entirely equitable, at least where tax rates are the same in both countries, but problems arise where the tax rates are different.

**138**     Suppose that an article is manufactured in country A and exported to country B, where it is packaged and sold to the ultimate consumer, and that the value added in each country is 100, *i.e.* the article is sold to the importer for 100 (exclusive of tax) and to the consumer for 200 (exclusive of tax). If the tax rate is the same—say 10 per cent—in each country, then,

  (*a*) the tax paid in country A will be $100 \times 10\% = 10$ :
  (*b*) the tax paid in country B will be $200 \times 10\% = 20$, less a credit of
       $10 = 10$.

But if the tax rates are different—say 20 per cent in A and 10 per cent. in B—then,

  (*c*) the tax paid in country A will be $100 \times 20\% = 20$ :
  (*d*) the tax paid in country B will be $200 \times 10\% = 20$, less a credit of
       $20 = 0$.[85]

---

[82] For a penetrating analysis, see D. Biehl, *"Ausführland-Prinzip, Einführland-Prinzip and Gemeinsamer Markt-Prinzip. Ein Beitrag zur Theorie der Steuerharmonisierung"* (1968), and for a concise summary, see N. Andel *et al.*, *"Steuerharmonisierung: Bericht der Facharbeitsgruppe"* in *"Möglichkeiten und Grenzen einer Europäischen Union"* (1975), at pp. 75 *et seq.*, (referred to hereafter as the Andel Report).

[83] This is termed the *Wertschöpfungsland-Prinzip* in the *Andel Report*, p. 80, *i.e.* the principle of allocating tax according to where the value is created.

[84] *i.e.* tax is imposed upon total sales and a credit given for tax on purchases.

[85] And if the rate in A was still higher, or was lower in B, a refund would have to be given by B for tax paid in A.

It will be seen that the price paid, and the tax borne, by the ultimate consumer is the same in each case (200 + 20(tax) =220), that this is determined by the tax rate applied in country B, and that the price and tax are precisely the same as they would be if the article had been entirely produced in Country B. Thus the value added tax system, when it extends to the retail stage, ensures that, even where countries apply different tax rates, competition between domestic and imported products is not distorted, provided the importing country is willing to give a full credit for the tax paid in the exporting country; *i.e.* the system is neutral as regards the consumer.[86] So far as the exporting country is concerned the system is also neutral: tax is paid, at that country's rate, on the value added there, whether or not the product is exported. It is only the importing country which is affected by differences in tax rates: if a product is imported from a higher tax country it suffers a reduction in revenue, if from a lower tax country it obtains an increase in revenue. By contrast, if the base-on-base method were employed (*i.e.* the amount of value added at each stage calculated and the appropriate rate applied to that amount) then, if tax rates were different in the two countries, the system would be neutral as regards the allocation of tax revenue but consumer prices would be affected.

**139**     Three possible solutions present themselves:

(1) to do nothing, on the assumption that losses and gains will largely cancel each other out. Since the system is neutral as regards both the consumer and the importer himself, products may equally well be imported from low-tax countries as from high-tax countries. A possible objection to this is that, if a country imposes high rates of VAT and correspondingly lower rates of business profits tax, personal income tax or payroll tax,[87] production costs (before tax) will be lower there and that country may enjoy a competitive advantage:

(2) to restrict the tax credit in the importing country to the rate of tax applied there, and to require the exporting country to refund the balance to the importer or retailer. In principle the exporting country should not object to this since, under the present destination principle, it now refunds the entire amount of tax which it has received. However, such a system would lead to considerable administrative complexities. A more acceptable alternative would be for the importing country to grant the full tax credit and to recover the balance directly from the government of the exporting country. Though much simpler, even this would require that tax returns identify the

---

[86] This is not the case, however, where goods are imported by the eventual consumer: see below.

[87] Or if it uses the revenue from the increased VAT receipts to finance expenditure which benefits its domestic industry, *e.g.* development grants, regional aids, state pensions etc.

country of origin of imported goods and the amounts of tax borne in the exporting country.[88]

(3) rates of tax could be harmonised.

From the beginning the assumption has been that a change to the origin principle would require a fairly close approximation of tax rates.[89] This was the conclusion of the early studies[90] though, as has been seen, these were largely based on the assumption either that there would be a common single-stage tax or, in any event, that the common system would not extend to the retail stage. As demonstrated above, where the VAT system includes retail transactions the existence of different rates of tax does not, of itself, cause distortions in the conditions of competition. To this statement, however, one important qualification must be made. Where goods are imported by the final consumer, *i.e.* a consumer resident in country B purchases goods from a retailer in country A and himself transports them back to country B, or where he purchases the goods from a foreign mail-order retailer, any substantial difference in VAT rates will have an effect.

## (ii)   The approximation of tax rates

**140**      Most of the difficulties associated with the adoption of the origin principle disappear if national tax rates are closely aligned.[91] The real question is whether such harmonisation is feasible in the foreseeable future. It may be objected that the Community succeeded, at a relatively early stage, in abolishing internal customs duties and in adopting a common external tariff. However, customs duties played a far less important role in the national fiscal systems than does the value added tax.[92] The value added tax constitutes an important component in the revenue of all Member States, though the degree of importance varies widely, and rates of tax vary even more.[93]

[88] Some writers take the view that, as VAT is essentially a tax on consumption, tax should be levied only in the country of consumption and on the full value, wherever added. They therefore assume that the importing government, having given credit for tax paid in the exporting country, would recover the *entire* amount of this tax by means of some "clearing-house" system: see J. Reugebrink (1978) 15 C.M.L. Rev. at pp. 310–311; Th. W. Vogelaar, "Tax Harmonisation in the European Community" (1970) 7 C.M.L. Rev. at p. 331. The effect of this would seem to be to preserve the "destination" principle, whilst abolishing border checks: see below.

[89] See (EEC) Eighth General Report (1965), p. 110: (EEC) Ninth General Report (1966), p. 107: (EC) Bull. S5–73, p. 14.

[90] Especially the Tinbergen Report, the Neumark Report and the report of Sub-Group C: see the *EEC Reports on Tax Harmonisation* especially pp. 76, 146.

[91] Increased transportation costs would permit some divergence without undue distortion. It is assumed that the harmonisation of technical standards, *e.g.* labelling, electrical wiring, etc, would greatly reduce or eliminate non-tax costs.

[92] See Appendix A, Table 3, and see K.V. Antal,"Harmonisation of Turnover Taxes in the Common Market" (1963–64) 1 C.M.L. Rev. 41, 49: C.K. Sullivan, "Indirect Tax Systems in the European Economic Community and the United Kingdom," Shoup, *Fiscal Harmonisation*, Chapter 8, p. 104.

[93] Standard rates vary from approximately 10 to 20 per cent: see Appendix A, Table 3.

Any attempt to approximate the rates of VAT is therefore likely to meet with strong resistance from most Member States. In the first place, if rates were fixed by the Community, rather than at the national level, this would involve the surrender of a major degree of fiscal autonomy on the part of Member States, and governments tend to guard their fiscal sovereignty even more jealously than their sovereignty over other aspects of economic and social life. Even were the proposed Community rates to be generally accept-able, Member States would lose the power to make subsequent adjustments for economic or social reasons, except presumably within fairly narrow stipulated limits. Since changes in value added tax tend to have fairly rapid economic consequences, this autonomy is considered to be essential to enable countries to stimulate or restrict demand and generally to deal with short term economic problems. A study of national VAT rates since 1973 shows that these have changed frequently and substantially[94]: this does, however, demonstrate that major changes can be and are made[95] and one might add that, on balance, the changes have tended to be towards a Com-munity average rather than away from it. Nevertheless, Member States could scarcely be expected to abandon the power to vary VAT rates unless a far higher degree of economic union existed than at present and the loss of fiscal sovereignty would have to be balanced by some form of Community mechanism to assist Member States in times of economic difficulties.[96]

**141**     Even were Member States to agree that their hands should be tied for the future—changes could of course be made at the Community level, but it is unlikely that this could be done swiftly and probable that, at any given time, some Member States would be worried about inflation and others about stagnation so that no agreement could be reached as to the direction in which the change should be made—it would first be necessary to reach agreement as to what should initially be the appropriate rate or rates. Tax systems are rarely the product of comprehensive reform, designed to achieve an ideal level of taxation and balance between different taxes. They tend to evolve in response to various economic, political and social pres-sures and philosophies and these philosophies vary widely from one Mem-ber State to another.[97] To fix a particular level of VAT necessitates making some judgment as to what constitutes a proper balance between indirect and direct taxation. Some Member States rely heavily upon indirect taxation[98] :

[94] The United Kingdom, for example, recently increased its standard rate from 8 to 15 per cent.
[95] See the Fredersdorf Report, point 2.1.15.
[96] W. Albers, "Steuerharmonisierung in der EWG—Wünsch und Wirklichkeit" (1973) 11 W.D. 593, 598. And see Chapter 4, paras. 407, 416, 441, below.
[97] See *Conséquences budgétaires, économiques et sociales de l'harmonisation des taux de la TVA dans la CEE;* Commission, Etudes: Série Concurrence—Rapprochement des Législations, 1970, No. 16 (report of the Europa Institut, Utrecht, referred to hereafter as the Utrecht Report). See also M. Krauss, "The Anti-Economics of the European Common Market. . . ." (1973) 7 J.W.T.L. 555.
[98] See Appendix A, Table 2.

this may be due to voter hostility towards direct, personal income taxes, to a tax administration or a level of "tax dishonesty" which makes direct taxes more difficult to collect or simply, in the case of less affluent states, to the fact that income taxes cannot yield sufficient revenue without the rates being unconscionably high. It may also be due to a conviction that high rates of personal taxation stifle individual initiative or that, under the rules of the GATT, high rates of indirect taxation, which are imposed on imports and remitted from exports, assist towards a favourable balance of external trade.[99] Other Member States prefer to rely more upon direct taxes, believing that indirect taxes are essentially regressive by nature, bear proportionately more heavily upon the poor than upon the rich (since they tax consumption and exclude savings) and are socially undesirable, as well as being inflationary. Moreover, rates of both indirect and direct taxes are affected by the overall level of taxation, which in turn reflects perceptions as to what should be the size and scope of public expenditure.

**142**   In addition, most Member States apply more than one rate of value added tax[1]: various essential commodities, such as food, bear reduced rates and luxuries are commonly subjected to increased rates. Again, national perceptions as to what constitute the necessities and the luxuries of life vary considerably. One objective of multiple-rating is clearly an attempt to make the tax less regressive—the poor spend proportionately more on food and less on jewellery than do the rich. In practice, however, it is not uncommon for exemptions or lower rates to apply also to goods and services which may be more heavily used by upper income groups.[2] It may well be, therefore, that a multiplicity of rates does little or nothing to secure an overall progressive, or non-regressive, effect.[3] Most studies have suggested that, if and when rates are eventually harmonised, this is likely to be around the level of 15 per cent. for the standard rate, with a reduced rate of, perhaps, 8 per cent. on an agreed range of essential goods,[4] and that zero-rating would not be permitted. If, as has been suggested, reduced rates have very little social or economic effect, then it may well be preferable to adopt a single rate of, say, 12 per cent. The advantages, in administrative terms and from the point of view of neutrality, of a single rate of tax are considerable[5]: thus, if it is ever possible to reach agreement on a harmonised rate structure it would seem to be worthwhile attempting to achieve an optimum structure rather than simply aiming for an average.

[99] See below, Chapter 3, paras. 334, 335.
[1] If the zero-rates in Denmark and the United Kingdom are treated as reduced rates, all members do so: see Appendix A, Table 3.
[2] *e.g.* books, cultural activities, postal services.
[3] See the Notenboom Report (E.P. Docs. 360/73), pp. 32 *et seq.* and the study, *Impact of tax changes on Income Distribution*: Institute of Fiscal Studies (1971).
[4] See the *Utrecht Report*, and see C.K. Sullivan, "Potential Rates of Value Added Tax in the European Community" in Shoup, *Fiscal Harmonization*, Chapter 9.
[5] C.K. Sullivan, *The Tax on Value Added* (1965), Chapter 6: A. A. Tait, *Value Added Tax* (1972), Chapter 5.

**143**      In any event, whether a dual or single-rate structure is eventually to be adopted, and at whatever level the rates are fixed, there must inevitably be serious economic repercussions for some Member States.[6] On the basis of current rates of tax, Luxembourg, Germany and the United Kingdom[7] would experience an increase in rates and in revenue from value added tax. If the governments of those countries could blame the increase on Brussels and, simultaneously, take the credit for reductions in other taxes, such as personal income tax, such a change might be politically feasible. Belgium, France, Ireland and Italy, on the other hand, would have to increase direct taxes or excise duties to compensate for the loss of revenue. This would probably be more difficult politically and perhaps also administratively, since some of those countries appear to experience considerable difficulty in collecting direct taxes.

Given the diversity of national rate structures, of reliance upon value added tax, and of tax philosophies in general, the economic consequences of the approximation of rates (even if this were to be acomplished by stages), and the difficulty of finding a time when the economic and political conditions in all nine (or 12) Member States might permit such a step to be taken, it is hard to see how this aim can be achieved until considerably greater progress has been made towards economic and monetary union and the development of a common economic policy.[8] If that is indeed so, then it seems worth considering whether it might be possible to remove tax frontiers without proceeding to a harmonisation of VAT rates.

**(iii)   The removal of tax frontiers without approximation of rates**

**144**      This might be possible in one of two ways:

*(a)   Origin principle*

As we have seen, one major difficulty in adopting the origin principle without approximating tax rates is that the allocation of tax revenue between states may be distorted.[9] This could be overcome by a system of accounting and compensation between national tax authorities: it would require a fairly high level of administrative efficiency and of co-operation between tax authorities, but any additional burden would be compensated for by the fact that the existing administrative controls at frontiers would be

[6] These are reviewed in the Fredersdorf Report, para. 2.3.

[7] Because of the abolition of zero-rating: the effect of harmonisation will be far less than it might otherwise have been since the recent near-doubling of the standard rate.

[8] The Benelux Union, with only three members whose cultural economic and political differences are far fewer, has been striving without great success to harmonise its excise duty rates since 1948: see J. E. Meade, H. H. Liesner and S. J. Wells, "Case Studies in European Economic Union . . ." (1962), Chapter II.

[9] Even when tax rates are the same, a change from the destination to the original principle may have serious economic repercussions. See below, para. 148.

done away with. Another possible solution might be to adopt a single, common, rate of tax for all transactions prior to the retail stage and to leave Member States free to fix their own rate or rates applicable to the final stage.[10] This would also achieve neutrality as to the consumer price, but at the expense of introducing a further complexity into the national systems. Though this should not be a major problem, since exemptions and reduced rates already apply frequently at the retail stage, it would probably be necessary to fix the standard pre-retail rate at a fairly high level, in order to discourage tax fraud, and this would result in some mis-allocation of tax revenue between exporting and importing states.

**145**   The other major problem concerns retail sales made to consumers who are resident in another Member State. Different tax rates would lead to a certain amount of cross-border shopping and to intra-Community mail-order sales. Special rules could doubtless be devised to deal with mail-order business, treating the sale as being made in the country of the consumer. In the case of cross-border shopping it should be noted that some relaxation of the rules already exists and that individuals are permitted to import small quantities of goods and certain items of personal-use property free of value added tax which is normally imposed on importation.[11] Whether existing controls could be removed completely is another matter. It is no doubt true that only a small proportion of imports are made by consumers and, given the increased cost and inconvenience of shopping in another country, differences in tax rates would have to be substantial before any Member State suffered an appreciable loss of tax revenue.[12] But retailers whose businesses are located in frontier areas of high-tax countries might well be seriously affected.

**146**   This raises another possibility : the problem would vary greatly from one Member State to another. Ireland and the United Kingdom, without common land-frontiers with other Member States, would be little affected and a comparatively small proportion of Italy's trade with other members crosses the frontier with France. These are three of the Member States for whom an approximation of tax rates would have most serious consequences, but for whom the abolition of tax frontiers would cause the least difficulty. A closer alignment of rates would clearly be necessary in the more central regions of the Community, but some divergence would still be possible. It might therefore be possible to agree upon the removal of tax frontiers, leaving each Member State free to fix its own tax rates. A state which wished to retain a relatively high rate would then have to weigh against the increased revenue

[10] The Neumark Committee, and Sub-Groups B and C, anticipated that there would be a separate tax, or rate of tax, at the retail stage: see *The EEC Reports on Tax Harmonization* and, for other proposals along these lines, see S.S. Han and G. K. Shaw, "Turnover Tax Harmonization in the European Community" (1968) 2 J.W.T.L. 97, at p. 106: C. S. Shoup in *Fiscal Harmonization*, Vol. 2, p. xv: A. A. Tait, *Value Added Tax*, pp. 67–68.

[11] See below, Chapter 3, paras. 245–251. See also the Prop. Dir. of June 13, 1980 (O.J. 1980, C 171/8).

[12] G. M. Grossman, "Alternative Border Tax Policies" (1978) 12 J.W.T.L. 452.

this would yield the possible tax loss it would suffer as a result of cross-border consumer purchases. No doubt this would lead to a degree of "spontaneous harmonisation" of rates in some parts of the Community,[13] but member States would retain the freedom to diverge from the Community norm to the extent to which they saw fit and, more important, would preserve their freedom of action for the future.

### (b)   Destination principle

147        The alternative, which has apparently been rejected by the Commission[14] but which merits fresh consideration, would be to abolish tax frontiers in the sense that physical checks at borders would be dispensed with, whilst retaining the destination principle. This possibility was considered by Sub-Group A,[15] the majority of whom concluded that there would be serious problems of tax fraud if rates differed widely. It is true that such a solution would require a greater degree of administrative efficiency and of co-operation and trust between national tax authorities than presently exists[16]: this is, in any event, desirable. In one sense, of course, this solution would not result in the removal of tax frontiers as such. Rather, it would remove the need for physical checks at borders and, with it, one of the obstacles to intra-Community trade,[17] and substitute a system of checks made internally.[18]

So far as imports are concerned, other than imports made by consumers, this should not give rise to any great difficulty. At present an importer of goods pays tax at the moment of importation and receives a credit for that tax on the subsequent disposal of the goods by him. Thus, the only effect of removing the charge to tax at importation would be a deferral of payment.[19] Border checks, however, ensure that no refund of tax is made to an exporter unless goods are actually exported. The border check would therefore have to be replaced by a system of verification, perhaps by "matching" the invoices of exporter and importer, requiring the co-operation of the national tax authorities concerned. Apart from administrative considerations the only problem which would be created by such a system would be that of

---

[13]  See G. Schmolders, "Turnover Taxes" (1966), at pp. 71–72.

[14]  See above, para. 136.

[15]  The *EEC Reports on Tax Harmonization*, pp. 14–22.

[16]  Andel Report, p. 78. However, the adoption of Dir. 79/1070 of December 6, 1979, which extends mutual assistance of national tax authorities to cover VAT, marks a promising step in this direction.

[17]  As Albers (n. 96 above) points out, it is these physical frontiers which make possible the existence of other technical and administrative obstacles.

[18]  Fredersdorf Report, para. 3.2.: J. Reugebrink (1978) 15 C.M.L. Rev. 309. For internal purposes, reliance is normally placed upon a trader's tax return, reinforced by cross-checking and occasional spot checks. It is not clear that Intra-Community transactions would require a greater degree of vigilance.

[19]  *Cf.* Case 55/79, *Commission* v. *Ireland* [1980] 1 C.M.L.R. 734, and the comments at Chapter 1, para. 30 above.

direct importation by consumers. Here, the difficulties would appear to be the same as those already outlined above and, again, one might expect that there would be some "spontaneous harmonisation" of rates.

**148**    The retention of the destination principle coupled with the abolition of physical checks at borders is not necessarily inconsistent with the notion of a common market. Indeed, federal states such as Canada and the United States apply a form of destination principle to provincial or state sales taxes without the need for internal frontiers. Moreover, a number of other advantages flow from the retention of the destination principle:

(1) It would avoid the economic consequences of a change to the origin principle. Although the origin principle secures what would appear to be a more equitable division of tax revenues between exporting and importing states—under the destination principle the entire revenue goes to the importing state—a change to the origin principle would benefit those states which have a favourable balance of trade within the Community, to the detriment of those which have an unfavourable balance. This is so whether or not rates are harmonised;

(2) The destination principle would continue to apply to extra-Community trade. If a "mixed" system were to apply, *i.e.* an origin system for trade within the Community and a destination system for external trade, then, whether or not tax rates were harmonised, considerable problems arise.[20] To modify the illustration given above,[21] if an article is manufactured in country A and is finished in country B and then exported to country X (being outside the Community), then, if the value added in each producing country is 100, and the tax rate in each is 10 per cent., under an origin system country A will receive 10 in tax revenue, and country B will receive nothing (exports outside the Community being zero-rated) and moreover will give a credit for the tax paid in A. By contrast, under the destination principle neither country receives any revenue. And if an article manufactured in country X is imported into country A, finished or packaged there, and then sold in country B, country A will receive tax revenue in respect of the value added in X, as well as in A.

It would therefore seem that a "mixed" system is only appropriate when a high degree of economic union has been attained and adequate mechanisms exist, at the Community level, to compensate for what may be no more than accidents of geography. For example, a "mixed" system would cause no problem at all where the entire proceeds from the value added tax accrued to the Community's budget, but it is hard to envisage how it could operate without necessitating the most complex adjustments and a heavy administrative burden.

---

[20] See D. Dosser, "Economic Analysis of Tax Harmonisation," in Shoup, *Fiscal Harmonization* Chapter 1, pp. 61 *et seq.*
[21] At para. 138.

### (iv)   Conclusions

**149**    In summary, the following propositions can be stated briefly:

(*a*) The removal of tax frontiers is a desirable goal, for political and psychological reasons and because the abolition of border checks for tax purposes would assist in removing other obstacles to free trade which are able to persist by virtue of the existence of frontier controls.

(*b*) An alignment of national rates of VAT would greatly facilitate the abolition of tax frontiers. However, the harmonisation of tax rates would involve a major surrender of fiscal autonomy on the part of Member States and would have serious budgetary, economic, political and social consequences for many of them. It therefore seems unlikely that a harmonisation of tax rates will be possible in the near future.

(*c*) The removal of tax frontiers, as regards VAT, is feasible without the harmonisation of rates, though it would probably lead to some spontaneous alignment of rates. This is to be preferred to formal alignment, since it will be limited to that which is strictly necessary and will leave a far greater degree of control and discretion in the hands of the national governments.

(*d*) Tax frontiers could be removed with the adoption of the origin principle. Without harmonisation of rates, this would require a complex, and perhaps contentious, system of accounting and compensation between Member States.

**150**    (*e*) The adoption of the origin principle would also have major economic consequences, operating to the benefit of those Member States which already have favourable trade balances with their neighbours. There would also be major difficulties in applying a "mixed system," with the origin principle adopted for intra-Community trade and the destination principle continuing to apply to external trade.

(*f*) Physical checks at borders could be abolished while retaining the destination principle in intra-Community trade. Some alignment of tax rates might still be needed, to deal with the problem of direct importations by consumers, but this could be done spontaneously by those Member States which considered it necessary to do so. In addition, the efficiency of some national tax administrations would have to be improved and a greater degree of co-operation between authorities would be required.

(*g*) The problems of harmonising excise duties to an extent sufficient to permit the removal of "excise duty frontiers" are probably considerably greater.[22] As these are commonly single-stage taxes (usually imposed at the manufacturer stage), the approximation of rates would seem to be essential yet the differences in national excise duty rates are far greater than is the case with VAT. There would seem to be little to be gained from abolishing

---

[22] See below, Chapter 3, paras. 243–244.

VAT-frontiers, so long as border checks have to be retained in respect of excise duties,[23] or for non-tax reasons.[24]

The abolition of fiscal frontiers would consequently seem to remain a rather distant objective: at least until then, the question of harmonisation of the rates of value added tax does not arise.

### [The Next Paragraph is 201]

---

[23] Deringer Report, pp. 32 *et seq.*; Fredersdorf Report, para. 4.2.2.1, and see G. Sessa and A Vitali, *La Politica Fiscale della Communita Economica Europea* (1969), Chapter 8, who conclude that the abolition of tax frontiers also requires some harmonisation of direct taxes.

[24] In particular, in connection with monetary compensatory amounts under the Common Market for agricultural products.

# CHAPTER 3

# THE HARMONISATION OF OTHER TAXES

## A.   THE OBJECTIVES AND MEANS OF TAX HARMONISATION

**201**   As was seen in the previous chapter, Article 99 of the Treaty requires that the Commission consider how the legislation of the various Member States concerning turnover taxes, excise duties and other forms of indirect taxation can be harmonised in the interest of the Common Market. Articles 100–102 relate to the approximation of laws in general, and provide a legal basis for the harmonisation of other forms of taxation. It is with the scope of these Articles, and their inter-relationship, that the first part of this chapter will be concerned.

### (i)   The Treaty provisions

**202**   It is immediately apparent that the Treaty provides expressly for the harmonisation of indirect taxes whereas the laws governing direct taxation are treated in the same way as any other laws—their approximation is required only in so far as they directly affect the establishment or functioning of the Common Market. This naturally raises the question of the proper distinction between indirect and direct taxation.[1]: fortunately, the provisions of Articles 99 and 100 are complementary and the problem of classifying a particular tax can therefore be avoided by basing the appropriate measure upon the juridical foundations of both Articles, as have been the majority of tax harmonisation directives so far adopted.[2]

The wording of Article 99 is rather curious: the Commission is required to consider how the national legislation can be harmonised and to submit proposals to the Council, "which shall act unanimously without prejudice to the provisions of Articles 100 and 101."[3] These provide:

"100. The Council shall, acting unanimously on a proposal from the Commission, issue Directives for the approximation of such provisions laid down by law, regulation or administrative action in Member States as directly affect the establishment or functioning of the Common Market.

The Assembly and the Economic and Social Committee shall be consulted in the case of directives whose implementation would, in one or more Member States, involve the amendment of legislation.

---

[1] See above, Chapter 1, paras. 25–28.

[2] Four Directives, concerned solely with turnover taxes and excise duties, have been adopted pursuant to Art. 99 alone. One, dealing with mutual assistance between tax authorities, is based only on Art. 100. Two other measures, concerning taxes relating to transport, are based upon Arts. 75 and 99.

[3] Recourse to the original Dutch, French, German and Italian texts does not afford any clarification.

101. Where the Commission finds that a difference between the provisions laid down by law, regulation or administrative action in Member States is distorting the conditions of competition in the Common Market and that the resultant distortion needs to be eliminated, it shall consult the Member States concerned.

If such consultation does not result in an agreement eliminating the distortion in question, the Council shall, on a proposal from the Commission, acting unanimously during the first stage and by a qualified majority thereafter, issue the necessary Directives. The Commission and the Council may take any other appropriate measures provided for in this Treaty."

A number of points would seem to call for comment:

(a) Article 99 refers to "legislation," Articles 100 and 101 to "provisions laid down by law, regulation or administrative action," Thus, the harmonisation of the administrative procedures of national tax authorities would seem to fall within Article 100, even if it related to indirect taxes.[4]

(b) Article 99 provides for "harmonisation," Article 100 for "approximation." These terms will be discussed later.

(c) Under Article 99 the Commission must consider how indirect taxes can be harmonised "in the interest of the Common Market." The requirement, to harmonise these taxes, appears to be mandatory: it is not a question of whether or not they should be harmonised, but how they can be harmonised. The qualification is that this harmonisation should be in the interest of the Common Market. By contrast, the general power of approximation in Article 100 is restricted to those provisions which "directly affect the establishment or functioning of the Common Market" and, in Article 101, to differences which distort "the conditions of competition in the Common Market."

**203**   Some distinction can perhaps be drawn between Articles 100 and 101: a distinction was clearly intended, since the former requires unanimity in the Council whereas the latter requires, after the end of the first stage, only a qualified majority. As the discussion in the previous chapter (of the application of the origin principle to value added tax) has shown, it is possible to have a situation which is neutral as regards competition but could be said to affect the proper functioning of the Common Market because of its budgetary effects. As to the distinction between Articles 99 and 100, there appears to be at least a presumption that indirect taxes should be harmonised, whereas it must be shown that direct taxes directly affect the establishment or functioning of the Common Market. Thus, there can be no "harmonisation for harmonisation's sake." But indirect taxes must still be harmonised "in the interest of the common market" and it is difficult to see

---

[4] See Dir. 77/799 of December 19, 1977 and Dir. 79/1070 of December 6, 1979, below, para. 310. But Dirs. 69/169, 78/1032, 78/1033 (relating to exemptions in international travel) were adopted pursuant to Art. 99 alone yet refer to laws, Regulations and administrative action.

how this can be done if the functioning of the common market is not affected.

Mention may here be made of Article 235, which some commentators[5] have suggested may also have an application to tax harmonisation. This provides:

> "If action by the Community should prove necessary to attain, in the course of the operation of the Common Market, one of the objectives of the Community and this Treaty has not provided the necessary powers, the Council shall, acting unanimously on a proposal from the Commission and after consulting the Assembly, take the appropriate measures."

**204**        By Article 2, the objectives of the Community are stated to be the promotion of "a harmonious development of economic activities, a continuous and balanced expansion, an increase in stability, an accelerated raising of the standard of living and closer relations between the states belonging to it." This is to be achieved by two means—by establishing a common market and by progressively approximating the economic policies of Member States. Thus, the objectives of the Community are broader than those of the Common Market and, consequently, the harmonisation of tax provisions, insofar as it is concerned only with the approximation of economic policy rather than with the functioning of the Common Market, appears to be a proper matter for action under Article 235 rather than under Articles 99 or 100. Whether such a distinction can reasonably be drawn is another matter. The problem of classification can in any event be avoided by adopting a directive pursuant to both Articles 100 and 235,[6] thereby disarming objections that a particular measure is outside the scope of the Common Market. More important is the fact that Article 235 is not confined to the approximation of laws. Thus, where approximation has already been achieved and what is really required is reform, recourse to Article 235 may be appropriate.

**205**        It may also be remarked that whereas Article 100 specifies the instrument which must be employed for approximation, namely the Directive, Article 235 simply provides for "the appropriate measures." Although the directive is normally most appropriate, and is indeed specifically designed for the task of approximation, there may be instances, particularly if uniformity is the only satisfactory solution, where the use of a Regulation would be desirable. The question may therefore be raised whether, if the Community wished to employ a Regulation for the purposes of approximating tax laws, rather

---

[5] *e.g.* the Fredersdorf Report, at para. 2.2.7., and H-D. Hoppner, "Die EG-Steuerharmonisierung" (1977) 12 EuR 122, at p. 128. For a consideration of the relationship between Arts. 100 and 235, see I. E. Schwartz, "Le pouvoir normatif de la Communauté, notamment en vertu de l'article 235 . . ." (1976) 197 R.M.C. 280.

[6] As has been done in a number of instances concerning the approximation of other areas of law.

than a Directive,[7] it could do so pursuant to Article 235, on the ground that Article 100 did not provide the necessary power, *i.e.* to issue a Regulation. It is suggested that the answer should be "no": if the Treaty does provide the power to take action and stipulates the instrument by which this should be done, then it is clearly intended that the action should only be taken in that manner and recourse to Article 235 is precluded.[8] If a greater freedom of choice as to instrument is required then the Treaty should be amended to permit this.[9]

**206**    (*d*) Unlike Article 100, Article 99 does not expressly stipulate the instrument to be used for harmonisation. This brings us to the curiously worded second paragraph of Article 99.[10] However one tries, it is difficult to make sense of the words "without prejudice to the provisions of Articles 100 and 101."

One possible interpretation is that the proviso simply makes it clear that the harmonisation of taxes is not restricted to indirect taxes and that other taxes may be approximated under the general powers in Articles 100 and 101. This would mean that, in the case of indirect taxes under Article 99, the Council and Commission are not restricted to the use of Directives and may adopt instead Regulations or Decisions.[11] Another possibility is that the proviso qualifies the preceding word "unanimously": thus, after the end of the first stage, a qualified majority would suffice if the proposed measure was designed to eliminate a difference which was found to be distorting the conditions of competition.[12] A third possibility is that all the requirements of Articles 100 and 101 apply, *i.e.* as to choice of instrument and the necessary

---

[7] Where a choice of instrument is available, the Commission has tended to prefer the Regulation : *c.f.* Dir. 74/651 and Reg. 3301/74, both of December 19, 1974. See A. J. Easson, "The Direct Effect of EEC Directives" (1979) 28 I.C.L.Q. 319, at p. 345.

[8] See P. Soldatos and M. Vandersanden, in *"Les Instruments du Rapprochement des Législations dans la Communauté Economique Européenne* (Institut d'Etudes Européennes, Bruxelles, 1976), at p. 113 : A. J. Easson, above, n.7. But *cf.* Case 8/73 *Massey-Ferguson* [1973] E.C.R. 897.

[9] As suggested by the Commission, in its *Report on European Union*, (EC) Bull. S. 5–75, p. 13. See also (EC) Bull. S. 7–78, points 51, 52. It may also be noted that, unlike Art. 100, Art. 235 does not require consultation of the ESC. The wise course would nevertheless be to consult that body, both for the benefit of its advice and to avoid any question as to the validity of the measure in question.

[10] The meaning of the proviso is discussed *inter alia*, by N. Andel, "Die Harmonisierung der Steuern im Gemeinsamen Markt" (1971) 30 *Finanzarchiv*, 224 at p. 239 : F. Hellinger, "Harmonisierung der Steuern nach den allgemeinen Rechtsangleichungsvorschriften des EWG-Vertags" (1976) 6 R.I.W. 363 : H-D Höppner, *op. cit.* above n. 5 : H. P. Ipsen, *"Europäisches Gemeinschafts-recht"* (1972), at p. 709 : M. Prouzet, "La Politique de la CEE en matière d'Harmonisation des Impôts Indirects" (1972) 49 R.D.I.D.C. 151, at p. 162 : I. E. Schwartz, "Zur Konzeption der Rechtsangleichung in der Europäischen Wirtschaftsgemeinschaft" in *Probleme des Europäischen Rechts : Festschrift für W. Hallstein* (1966) : R. Wägenbaur, "Les Fondements Juridiques d'une Politique Fiscale des Communautés Européennes," (1975) 67 *Revue de Science Financière* 5, at p. 12.

[11] See Höppner, Prouzet and Wägenbaur, *cf.* Hellinger, *op. cit.* above.

[12] See Andel, Hellinger, Ipsen *op. cit.* and the Fredersdorf Report, at para. 2.2.3. But in that case, the proviso would need only to have referred to Art. 101.

consultations, save that it is not necessary, in the case of indirect taxes, to show that the establishment or functioning of the Common Market is directly affected or that the conditions of competition are being distorted,[13] since this is implicitly presumed by Article 99.[14] It must be confessed that none of these interpretations[15] is particularly convincing: if any of them had been intended it would have been easy to state so expressly. In practice, the first problem—whether or not a Directive is prescribed—has been resolved by always having recourse to Directives[16] which, by their nature, are better adapted to the harmonisation of laws, though at some later stage when uniformity is required it may be desirable to employ Regulations.[17]

(e) The consultation requirements in the three Articles are different. Article 100 requires consultation of the European Parliament and of the Economic and Social Committee, Article 101 of the Member States concerned, and Article 99 does not expressly require consultation at all, though this may be the effect of the proviso. With regard to Article 99 it is interesting to note that, with one exception,[18] all the Directives have only been adopted after consulting both bodies. Article 101 would appear to be primarily designed to deal with specific distortions on the part of a single Member State (though it is not so restricted) to be removed if possible by negotiations with that State or, if this cannot be achieved, by the issue of a Directive or other appropriate measure.[19]

(f) As already pointed out, Article 100 requires unanimity on the part of the Council, whereas Article 101 permits the use of a qualified majority. Whilst the proviso to Article 99 may permit a qualified majority to act with respect to indirect taxes if there is a distortion of the conditions of competition (which will frequently be the reason for desiring to act), it is in practice most unlikely that any attempt would be made to do so. The harmonisation of laws requires the fullest co-operation on the part of all Member States in making the necessary amendments to their existing laws and in ensuring subsequent compliance. Until such time as the Treaty is amended to permit Community legislation generally by a qualified majority, it would seem highly inappropriate to attempt to force upon a reluctant member any

---

[13] Unless it is wished to proceed by qualified majority only.

[14] See Hellinger *op. cit.*

[15] Or others, *e.g.* that Directives are required but that consultation is not, or vice-versa.

[16] Regs. 3060, 3061/74 (see below, para. 248) relates to customs duties, and Dec. 65/271, which affects taxation on transport, is not really a measure of harmonisation and is, in any event, validly based upon Art. 75. However, the first proposal for the harmonisation of taxes on tobacco was initially made in the form of a Regulation : see below, para. 228.

[17] Wägenbaur *op. cit.*

[18] Dir. 69/169 (see below, para. 246) on exemptions from turnover taxes and excise duties on importation of goods in international travel. Subsequent Directives on this subject have followed consultations.

[19] Normally consultations have been sufficient. See, *e.g.* the recourse to Arts. 101, 102 in response to German proposals to increase the turnover equalisation tax : (EEC) Bull. 2–64, p. 33.

measure, in such a sensitive area as taxation,[20] especially upon the basis of an ambiguous Treaty provision.

### (ii) Harmonisation and approximation

**207**    Whether any distinction may be drawn between the terms "harmonisation," in Article 99,[21] and "approximation" in Article 100,[22] has been the subject of much discussion.[23] Neither a textual analysis nor a schematic interpretation of the Treaty would suggest that any meaningful distinction can, or should, be made. Read in their context, what is important is the expressed objective: indirect taxes should be harmonised "in the interests of the Common Market," approximation is required of provisions "which affect the . . . functioning of the Common Market," co-ordination should be "to the necessary extent" to render safeguards equivalent.[24] The emphasis is upon the end to be achieved, rather than upon the degree of assimilation required to achieve it. Nevertheless, a number of questions remain:

(*a*) Is total unification of tax laws permitted under Articles 99 and 100? The Treaty nowhere uses the expression "unification,"[25] though where the use of Regulations is allowed for this can clearly be achieved. But where Directives alone are prescribed it may be that the choice of form and method which it must leave to Member States[26] precludes the possibility of unification.[27] In practice, however, some Directives (notably those concerned with technical standards) are so detailed as to leave little or no discretion to the Member States. Whether or not this is permissible,[28] it is most

[20] Thus, although the Commission has suggested that, following enlargement of the Community, Art. 100 should be amended to permit recourse to action by qualified majority in most cases, it specifically stated that *tax* harmonisation should continue to require unanimity : (EC) Bull. S. 2–78, p. 18.

[21] The expression also appears in Art. 117.

[22] And in Arts. 3(h), 27 and 117. The expression "co-ordination" is used in Arts. 54, 56, 57 and 70.

[23] See *e.g.* N. Catalano, "La Communauté économique européenne et l'unification, le rapprochement et l'harmonisation des droits des Etats membres" (1961) 13 R.I.D.C. 5 : A. J. Easson, "Approximation and Unification of Laws in the EEC" (1979) 2 RIE/JEI, 375 : N. Lochner, "Was bedeuten die Begriffe Harmonisierung, Koordinierung und gemeinsame Politik in den europäischen Vertragen?" (1962) 118 Z.G.S. 35 : R. Monaco, "Comparaison et rapprochement des législations dans le Marché commun" (1960) 12 R.I.D.C. 61 : G. Sessa and A. Vitale, *La Politica Fiscale della Communita Economica Europea* (1969), Chap. 4, at pp. 100 *et seq.* : Th. W. Vogelaar, "Het nader tot elkaar brengen van de nationale Wetgevingen . . ." (1974) 22 S.E.W. 299.

[24] Art. 54 (3) (*g*).

[25] The French and Italian texts of Art. 117(1) ("égalisation" and "parificazione") perhaps suggest that there is a higher degree of uniformity than mere "rapprochement" or "ravvicinamento."

[26] Art. 189.

[27] See P. Leleux, "Le Rapprochement des Législations dans la CEE" (1968) 4 C.D.E. 129, 153 : J. Mégret, "La Technique Communautaire d'Harmonisation des Législations" (1967) 10 R.M.C. 181, 188.

[28] See W. C. van Binsbergen, "Kan een Richtlijn tot Aanpassing der Wetgevingen . . . in Details treden? (1961) 2 S.E.W. 216.

unlikely that the validity of such a Directive, adopted unanimously by the Council, would ever be challenged on this ground. If, therefore, the only satisfactory solution to a particular problem requires the adoption of uniform national laws it is submitted that this is not prevented by the Treaty.

**208**     (b) Is the Community's legislative capacity restricted to doing only that which is strictly necessary in order to achieve the prescribed objective? This in turn depends, of course, on what the prescribed objective is perceived to be—the interest, establishment or functioning of the Common Market is a fairly elastic notion. Clearly, tax harmonisation is not an aim which must be pursued for its own sake: it is merely an instrument which serves to promote the process of economic, social and political integration in the Community.[29] As one member of the Commission has said: "We do not want harmonisation for the sake of harmonisation. Rather do we want harmonisation where it is essential to the Common Market."[30] But the same spokesman pointed out on another occasion: " . . . The purpose of approximating legislation is not to find an arithmetical average [between divergent national provisions], but to adapt them to the requirements of the proper functioning of the Common Market."[31]

Significantly, M von der Groeben took, as an example of this approach, the first Directive on Value Added Tax. Even if the "cascade" type of turnover tax system had been in force in all six Member States it would still have been possible to introduce the VAT, that being the only neutral system. In that case, the "arithmetical average" approach could not have achieved the desired result in any event, since the distortions were inherent in the "cascade" system by its very nature. What remains to be resolved is whether the Council and Commission can do more than that which is simply necessary, e.g. to remove a particular distortion, and can engage in more radical reforms. As the Fredersdorf Report points out,[32] viewed solely from a technical angle the aim is to find what is the minimum amount of tax harmonisation required by the Treaty and its objectives. Viewed from what it describes as the "political" angle, harmonisation affords the opportunity to make the tax system simpler and easier to understand and administer and to make it more in keeping with social justice and maximum fairness of competition.[33] Since such aims are clearly consistent with the interests and proper functioning of the Common Market, and since Articles 99 and 100

---

[29] K. Schneider, "Tax Harmonization Policy from the point of view of the Commission," D. Dosser (ed.) *"British Taxation and the Common Market"* (1973), at p. 131 : See also G. Close, "Harmonisation of laws : use or abuse of the powers under the EEC Treaty" (1978) 3 E.L. Rev. 461.

[30] H.v.d. Groeben, "Harmonisation of turnover taxes in the Community" (statement in the European Parliament), (EEC) Bull. 12–63, p. 10.

[31] (EC) Bull. 2–70, at p. 26.

[32] Para. 4.1.1.

[33] Para. 4.2.1. See also Th. W. Vogelaar, "Evolution du droit fiscal Européen" (1972) 55 Fisc. M.C. 105.

contain no express limitation to that which is "necessary," there is no reason why "harmony" should not also mean "reform."

**209**     (c) An allied question is whether, if "harmony" already exists, in the sense that no significant differences remain between the national laws, the Treaty provides any basis for further action. Suppose, for example, that the exemptions from VAT have been harmonised and have become identical in all Member States. How can these exemptions be changed thereafter? A Member State cannot do so unilaterally, for to do so would be to create a distortion and is thus contrary to Article 102, as well as constituting a derogation from the original measure of harmonisation. Thus action can only be taken collectively at Community level and even here the juridical basis for such action is unclear, since harmonisation under Article 99 seems inappropriate when national provisions are already in unison, albeit off key.[34] Presumably Article 235 provides the necessary powers, but this requires unanimity and the legislative process in the Community is a slow and laborious one. It is bad enough that it takes many years of difficult negotiation before an acceptable solution can be reached and divergent national laws harmonised. At least in the meanwhile Member States retain a certain freedom of action.[35] It will be intolerable if, once harmonisation is achieved and this freedom of action disappears, the process of reform must be equally prolonged.

### (iii)   The Commission's policy with respect to tax harmonisation

**210**     It is convenient to deal with the Commission's policy in three parts: its philosophy of what tax harmonisation means, the means which it has adopted to reach its perceived objectives and the specific objectives which it has set itself.

### (a)   Philosophy

To recurrent accusations of devotion to harmonisation for its own sake,[36] the Commission has consistently avowed that it regards it solely as a means to an end, an essential tool for achieving the real objectives of the Treaty. Thus, although it admits to having a tax "policy," this policy is of a secondary or complementary nature and is subordinate to the major policy objectives of the Community.[37] Nevertheless, as these major objectives have

---

[34] See the comment of C. W. A. Timmermans, "Directives : their effect within National Legal Systems" (1979) 16 C.M.L. Rev. 533, at p. 551.

[35] Restricted by Arts. 5(2) and 102.

[36] See the Twenty-second Report of the House of Lords Select Committee, 1978 H.L. 131, the comments in (1978) 15 C.M.L. Rev. 1, 389, and M. Seidel, "Ziele und Ausmass der Rechtsangleichung in der EWG — zur britischen Auffassung" (1979) 14 EuR 171.

[37] Th. W. Vogelaar, "Tax Harmonization in the European Community" (1970) 7 C.M.L. Rev. 323, 330 : R. Wägenbaur, (op. cit. above, n.10) p. 10.

evolved, or the perception of their relative importance has changed, so have there been changes in the subordinate tax policy.

In the early years of the Community two themes predominated—the removal of distortions to competition and the abolition of tax frontiers, the latter tending to be emphasised more strongly by the Parliament. To quote Mr. von der Groeben again, the Commission view was that:

> "Harmonisation does not mean that the tax systems must be made uniform, but only that they must be mutually adapted to the extent that this is necessary to make them neutral from the point of view of competition and thus to bring the tax systems into line with the competition system of the Community."[38]

Tax policy was thus regarded, by the Commission, principally as an aspect of competition policy.[39] Two developments, around the year 1970, marked a change in emphasis—the "own resources" decision,[40] in effect providing the Community with its own sources of revenue and power of taxation, and the decision to proceed towards an economic and monetary union,[41] requiring co-ordination, at Community level, of the economic policies of the Member States. These made it clear that the Community's tax policy must serve a number of different objectives, that there are goals other than the attainment of neutrality and the removal of obstacles to competition and that regard must also be had to the budgetary, economic and social functions of taxation.[42] The budgetary role of tax harmonisation has clearly been recognised by the Commission and was the main reason for the Sixth Value Added Tax Directive[43]: it is perhaps too early to judge to what extent economic and social factors have also influenced the policy of the Commission.

### (b) Modus operandi

**211**　It was clearly not possible initially to draw up a grand overall strategy for tax policy and harmonisation. As tax policy is merely an instrument for achieving the objectives of the Community the process of harmonisation must necessarily be an evolutionary one. This does not of course mean that the policy must always be a passive one, reacting only to progress already

[38] "Policy on competition in the EEC," (EEC) Bull. 7, 8–61, p. 15.

[39] No doubt this was, at least in part, due to the internal structure of the Commission and the division of competence among the various Directorate-Generals.

[40] Dec. 70/243 : see above, Chapter 2, para. 124.

[41] See below, Chapter 4, paras. 408–416.

[42] See D. Dosser, "Introduction to the Theory and Practice of Tax Harmonisation," *British Taxation and the Common Market* (1973), Chap. 1 : B. M. Veenhof, "Harmonisation fiscale et coordination des politiques dans les Communautés Européennes" (1972) 53–54 Fisc. M.C. 75.

[43] Chapter 2, para. 125 above.

achieved in other fields which renders further harmonisation necessary. A constructive tax policy must accompany such progress, not merely follow it, and at times it must anticipate developments. Nevertheless, fiscal autonomy is jealously guarded by the Member States, tax harmonisation is a prolonged and difficult process and it is difficult to persuade the Council to adopt any tax measure until the need to do so has become obvious and pressing.

Tax harmonisation therefore involves a determination of priorities. Even within the framework of an overall strategy the approach is necessarily piecemeal: the Commission proceeds according to the so-called "salami tactics," by stages, moving towards the eventual goal.[44] A pattern has emerged, clearly discernible in the harmonisation of value added tax but, as will be seen later in this chapter, applicable also to other taxes, of harmonising first the tax system, then the tax base and finally, if necessary, the tax rates.

### (c)  The scope of tax harmonisation

212      All taxes by their nature have an effect upon economic life. Potentially, all are candidates for harmonisation since differences in taxation may affect decisions such as where to buy or sell goods, where to set up business, where to invest, where to work or where to live. But clearly some taxes are more significant than others, some national differences create major obstacles to the establishment and functioning of the Common Market, others are of little consequence. Some national differences may tend to be balanced by others, so that the harmonisation of one tax could increase distortions and itself create the need to harmonise other taxes. Harmonisation in other fields, *e.g.* in company law, may necessitate the harmonisation of taxes as well.[45]

Both Articles 99 and 100 require that any action which is to be taken must be founded upon a proposal from the Commission. Thus it is the Commission which must assess the relative urgency and competing priorities, having regard also to the technical and political feasibility of any proposed action. The Treaty itself provides an indication of the perceived priorities in singling out turnover taxes and excise duties as subjects for harmonisation. Nor surprisingly, therefore, the Commission first turned its attention to the problem of turnover taxes though, despite the mandate in Article 99 and the urgings of the Parliament,[46] it was not until 1970 that any serious start was made with regard to excise duties. In a wide-ranging study the Neumark Committee, in 1962, considered the need, and made recommendations, for

---

[44] (EEC) Bull. 1–63, p. 5 : (EEC) Sixth General Report (1963), p. 76.

[45] Thus it is generally considered that the proposed European Company can only become a reality if the laws governing the taxation of company profits and reconstructions are also harmonised : see below, paras. 291, 292.

[46] See Chapter 2, para. 113, above.

the harmonisation of other taxes, in particular the taxation of company
profits and distributions, of investment income, of transfers of capital, of
motor vehicles and transport, of personal income and even of wealth and
inheritances.[47] In most of these fields little progress has been made. Apart
from the value added tax, Directives have been adopted in connection with
excise duties (though so far only those relating to tobacco), with tax-free
allowances for private importations of goods, with taxes upon the formation
of company capital, with taxes relating to transport and with mutual
assistance between national tax authorities. Further proposals have been
prepared and submitted to the Council in connection with most of these subjects and additional proposals deal with the taxation of company profits and
distributions, the taxation of corporate mergers and reconstructions and of
associated companies, and the taxation of transactions in securities. As yet,
no action has been considered necessary regarding the taxation of personal
income and wealth.[47a] These Directives and proposals will be considered
in later parts of this chapter.[48]

### (iv)  The Directive

**213**        First, however, it seems appropriate to consider briefly the legal nature of
the Directive[49] and the role of Community law in the process of harmonisation. Whether or not harmonisation of indirect taxes under Article 99 is
limited to the use of Directives, it is this instrument which has invariably
been used in the past. According to Article 189, "A Directive shall be binding, as to the result to be achieved, upon each Member State to which it is
addressed, but shall leave to the national authorities the choice of form and
methods."

### (a)  Implementation[50]

Directives are addressed to the Member States, not necessarily to all of
them, requiring those States to take whatever measures are necessary in
order to bring their laws and practices into conformity with the rules and
principles set out in the Directive, within the prescribed time limit. Member
States are given a choice, both of form and method. They may therefore
select the appropriate instrument—statute, regulation, *loi*, *decret*,

---

[47] *The EEC Reports on Tax Harmonisation*, especially pp. 153 *et seq.*
[47a] Apart from the taxation of income of migrant workers—Prop. Dir. of December 21,
1979 (O.J. 1980, C 21/6).
[48] The Commission's proposal for action are set out in its *Action Programme for
Taxation*, (EC) Bull. 7, 8–75, pp. 14 *et seq.*, and more recently in a statement by the Com-
missioner, Mr. Burke, "Harmonization of Taxation in Europe" 1979 *Intertax* 46.
[49] For comprehensive studies, see N. Weber, *"Die Richtlinie im EWG-Vertrag"* (1974) :
D. de Ripainsel-Landy and A. Gerard, in *"Les Instruments du Rapprochement . . ."* (above,
n. 8), Chapter 3.
[50] See further, M. Ayral, "La Transposition des directives dans les droits nationaux"
(1977) 210 R.M.C. 411.

etc.[51]—and the appropriate terminology, provided this is consistent with the Directive. As we have seen,[52] in the case of the first two Directives on value added tax, several Member States failed to adopt the necessary legislation within the time allowed and even after implementation there were numerous examples of derogations from the prescribed rules. Initially, the Commission did little to rectify this state of affairs, other than to point out to Member States the errors of their ways and politely suggest that they should take steps to comply with their obligations. In part this was due to the fact that not until 1973 had all the Member States adopted the common system. It therefore seemed inappropriate to commence proceedings against those States which had done so, but had failed to comply with the Directives in all respects. Moreover, it was evident that further changes would become necessary once the Sixth Directive was adopted.[53] More recently, however, the Commission has pursued a more vigorous policy towards the implementation of Directives, and delayed or incomplete incorporation of Directives into national law is likely to lead to infringement proceedings under Article 169.[54]

### (b)    The direct effect of directives[55]

**214**     It is clear that a Member State which fails to implement a Directive, either by not adopting the necessary legislation within the time permitted or by adopting legislation which does not fully conform with the requirements of the Directive, is in breach of its obligations under the Treaty. In addition, it is now well established that provisions contained in a directive addressed to Member States may impose obligations upon those States which give rise to corresponding rights in individual citizens, *i.e.* Directives may have direct effect.[56] Thus, where a Member State has failed to implement a Directive, or its purported implementation is defective, then, insofar as a provision of that

---

[51] The choice is probably not entirely a free one. For example, if the existing law were contained in a statute, to alter it by a mere departmental circular leaving the unamended statute on the books, would be misleading and unsatisfactory : Case 167/73 *Commission* v. *France* [1974] E.C.R. 359.

[52] Chapter 2, paras. 117–119.

[53] P. Nasini, "The Efforts of the EEC Commission to achieve a better balance among the National VAT Systems," in G. S. A. Wheatcroft (ed.), *"Value Added Tax in the enlarged Common Market"* (1973) Chap. 9 : but *cf.* Case 111/76 *Van Hazel* [1977] E.C.R. 901.

[54] Approximately one-half of the 68 infringement proceedings commenced in 1977 concerned the failure to implement Directives : (EC) Eleventh General Report (1977), p. 13. See also Chapter 2, para. 132, above.

[55] See A. J. Easson, *op. cit.* above, n. 7; C. W. A. Timmermans *op. cit.* above, n. 34; D. Wyatt, "The Direct Applicability of Regulations and Directives" 1977 C.L.J. 216.

[56] Case 9/70 *Grad* [1970] E.C.R. 825; Case 33/70 *SACE* [1970] E.C.R. 1213; Case 41/74 *Van Duyn* [1974] E.C.R. 1337; Case 51/76 *Verbond van Nederlandse Ondernemingen* [1977] E.C.R. 113; Case 38/77 *Enka* [1977] E.C.R. 2203; Case 21/78 *Delkvist* [1978] E.C.R. 2327; Case 161/78 *Ratti* [1980] 1 C.M.L.R. 96; *cf.* the decision of the French Conseil d'Etat in *Cohn-Bendit* [1980] 1 C.M.L.R. 543.

Directive is capable of creating direct effects,[57] an individual may rely upon it in his national courts. The point is well illustrated by the *Verbond* case,[58] which concerned the Second Value Added Tax Directive. The original plaintiff, the Federation of Dutch Industries, had purchased a printer and a stock of reply cards, on which it had paid VAT. It attempted to deduct this tax from the tax due on its supplies, but the Dutch tax authorities disallowed the deduction in part on the basis that the printer and cards were "capital goods" and could not be fully deducted in the year of purchase. The Dutch authorities relied upon the Dutch law of 1968, which had been introduced in order to comply with the Second Directive. The plaintiff contended, however, that he should be allowed a full deduction by virtue of Article 11 of the Directive, which provided:

> "1. Where goods and services are used for the purposes of his undertaking, the taxable person shall be authorised to deduct from the tax for which he is liable:
> (*a*) value added tax invoiced to him in respect of goods supplied to him or in respect of services rendered to him; . . . "

215     To the objection that Article 17 of the Directive permitted a modification of this rule in the case of capital goods, the plaintiff contended that the goods in question were not capital goods within the meaning of the Directive. The Dutch Supreme Court, considering that the case raised questions of Community law to which it was necessary to have an answer, referred the matter to the European Court under Article 177 of the Treaty and asked (a) what was the meaning of "capital goods" in the Directive, and (b) whether the Directive gave rise to rights enforceable by an individual in his national courts? The Court gave its interpretation of the expression and ruled that:

> " . . . in the case of goods purchased . . . and intended to be used for the purposes of the undertaking which do not belong to the category of capital goods within the meaning of Article 17 of the Directive, it is the duty of the national court before which the rule as to immediate deduction set out in Article 11 of the Directive is invoked to take those facts into account insofar as a national implementing measure falls outside the limits of the margin of the discretion left to the Member States."[59]

---

[57] The test for determining whether or not this is so—clarity, unconditionality, etc.—would seem to be the same as for Treaty provisions : see Chapter 1, paras. 72–76 above, and see A. J. Easson, "Can Directives impose obligations on Individuals?" (1979) 4 E.L. Rev., at p. 74, *cf.* C. W. A. Timmermans, (*op. cit.* above, n. 34) and see Case 148/78 *Ratti* (above), and the note by J. Usher in (1979) 4 E.L. Rev. 270.

[58] Above, n. 56. For comments, see P. Duffy, (1978) 41 M.L.R. 219 : N. M. Hunnings, (1978) 15 C.M.L. Rev. 487 : G. Morse, (1977) 2 E.L. Rev. 236.

[59] [1977] E.C.R., at p. 126. See also Case 21/78 *Delkvist* [1979] 1 C.M.L.R. 372; Case 126/78 *Nederlandse Spoorwegen* [1980] 1 C.M.L.R. 144; Case 148/78 *Ratti* [1980] 1 C.M.L.R. 96; Cases 181, 229/78, *Van Paasen* [1979] E.C.R. 2063.

In the light of this ruling, the Dutch Supreme Court subsequently held that the goods in question were not capital goods, within the meaning of the Directives as interpreted by the European Court, and that consequently the plaintiff was entitled to a full deduction of the input tax.[60]

**216**    Of particular significance is the fact that, though the Directive left a margin of discretion to the Member States—whether or not to accord special treatment to capital goods and which categories of capital goods should receive this treatment—the Member State may act only within the limits of this discretion. The right of an individual to deduct input tax, given by Article 11 of the Directive, is clear and (where the goods are not capital goods) unqualified and may be relied upon by an individual in the national courts.

In the *Verbond* case, the Dutch Government had introduced legislation purporting to implement the Directive. The result is the same where a Member State has failed to introduce the necessary measures within the prescribed time limit.[61] There is thus a sanction for non-implementation of a Directive which may be far more immediate and compelling than the threat of proceedings under Article 169—the risk that an individual may validly refuse to pay a tax which is contrary to the directive.

### (c)   The interpretation of directives

**217**    Where an individual, in an action before a national court, relies upon an alleged right created by a provision in a Directive, this necessarily raises a question as to the proper interpretation of that provision—a question which the national court may, or should[62] refer to the European Court under Article 177. Such is clearly the case where the Member State has failed to adopt any implementing legislation, but the same is true where national legislation has been adopted and it is claimed that this legislation does not accord with the Directive. The national judge is not restricted to applying the national law alone[63] but should, where necessary, request an interpretation of the Directive[64] in order to interpret the national law in accordance

---

[60] Judgment of the *Hoge Raad,* No. 17, 833 of November 30, 1977 : See (1978) 18 E.T. 103. But contrast the Sixth VAT Directive, 77/388, Art. 20, which permits the Member States to define the concept of capital goods.

[61] Case 9/70 *Grad* : Case 33/70 *SACE* (above, n. 56) : Case 130/78 *Salumificio* [1979] 3 C.M.L.R. 561.

[62] If it is a court of final resort.

[63] *Cf.* the decision of the Leeds VAT Tribunal, in *Re Processed Vegetable Growers* [1974] 1 C.M.L.R. 113 and the recent decision of the French Conseil d'Etat in *Cohn-Bendit* (above n. 56). For persuasive criticisms of the latter case, see M. Simon and F. E. Dowrick, "Effect of EEC Directives in France" (1979) 95 L.Q.R. 376; J. Boulouis, "L'applicabilité directe des directives. A propos d'un arret Cohn-Bendit du Conseil d'Etat" (1979) 225 R.M.C. 104, the note of G. Isaac in (1979) 15 C.D.E. 265 and the editorial note in (1979) 4 E.L. Rev. 65.

[64] Case 32/74 *Haaga* [1974] E.C.R. 1201 : Case 111/75 *Mazzalai*; [1976] E.C.R. 657 : Case 13/77 *Inno* [1977] E.C.R. 2115. See further, A. Barav, "Some Aspects of the Preliminary Ruling Procedure in EEC Law" (1977) 2 E.L. Rev. 3 : N. M. Hunnings, "Value Added Tax and EEC Directives" 1977 J.B.L. 289.

with the Directive, if this is possible, or, if not, to apply the Directive in those instances where it creates enforceable rights.

Since by no means all provisions of all Directives are capable of producing direct effects it seems advisable for the national court to also ask specifically whether or not the provision in question gives rise to enforceable rights in circumstances such as those in issue.[65] Usually it will only be if a right is alleged to exist, based on the directive, that the interpretation of the Directive will be necessary, but this will not necessarily be so and the Court has made it clear that the preliminary reference procedure is not restricted to those provisions of directives which are alleged to have direct effect.[66]

### (d)   The validity of directives

It is submitted that Directives for the harmonisation of taxes, like all secondary legislation of the Community, must be in conformity with the fundamental principles of Community law. One such fundamental principle is that contained in Article 95 of the Treaty. Directives may consequently not derogate from the prohibition against discriminatory taxation : this issue is considered further in the context of the proposed Directives for the harmonisation of excise duties on alcoholic beverages.[67]

### B.   EXCISE DUTIES

### (i)   The need for harmonisation

**218**   The need to harmonise the special excise duties existing in the various Member States was clearly recognised by the authors of the Treaty and excise duties, together with turnover taxes, are expressly mentioned in Article 99. From the earliest days of the Community the intention has been avowed to harmonise these duties[68] and the Neumark and Deringer Committees[69] both urged that work on excise duties must parallel that on turnover taxes. Yet, whilst progress in the field of turnover taxes has been substantial (with the adoption of the common system of value added tax), remarkably little has been accomplished with regard to excise duties.

It is clear, from their very nature, that Community policy requires the

---

[65] As was done in the *Verbond* case : Case 51/76 [1977] E.C.R. 113.

[66] Case 111/75 *Mazzalai* [1976] E.C.R. at p. 665. See also Case 90/76 *Ameyde* [1977] E.C.R. 1091; Case 145/78 *Augustijn* Case 146/78 *Wattenberg* [1979] 3 C.M.L.R. 516 and the decision of the Netherlands Hoge Raad in *KKF Gooiland* v. *Cetra Nederland NV* [1979] 2 C.M.L.R. 189.

[67] Below, paras. 239–242.

[68] A working party was set up to study the question as early as 1960 : (EEC) Third General Report (1960), p. 126.

[69] See above, Chapter 2, paras. 109, 113.

harmonisation of excise duties.[70] For the most part, such taxes are single-stage taxes applied at a stage of production prior to the final retail sale[71] and, as such, they necessarily make it difficult to calculate the appropriate countervailing duties on imports and remissions on exports consistently with the principles of Articles 95 and 96. Moreover, it should be observed that Article 97, which permits the establishment of average rates of cumulative turnover taxes, does not apply to excise duties: thus, according to Article 95, an imported product may not be taxed at a level higher than the lowest tax burden imposed upon a similar domestic product.[72] Calculation of the respective tax burdens may itself prove difficult where the basis for the assessment of the national tax is one which does not permit a simple comparison between the domestic product, taxed at a particular stage of manufacture, and the imported product, taxed at the time of importation in its finished state.[73] Problems of this nature, it would seem, can only be satisfactorily solved by harmonisation of the appropriate bases of assessment.[74] Further, since these special excise duties are imposed upon specific products, or categories of product, the classification of particular products and their inclusion or exclusion is likely, as has been seen in Chapter 1,[75] to lead to discriminations, intentional or otherwise, between domestic and imported products and to raise the difficult question as to when products are to be considered as "similar" or "competing" within the meaning of Article 95.

**219**      The case for harmonising excise duties is therefore clear and, at first sight, it is hard to understand why harmonisation has proved so difficult to achieve.[76] All of the Member States impose excise duties and nearly all of them derive more than 90 per cent. of their excise revenue from three main sources—tobacco, alcoholic beverages and fuel oils.[77] Although some Member States, notably Italy, impose excise duties on many other products —such as coffee, tea, sugar, matches, lighters and playing cards—only the

---

[70] The expression is employed here in a broad sense to include those special taxes, such as monopoly equalisation taxes, which are imposed on particular categories of products, as opposed to sales taxes of a general nature such as the VAT.

[71] Commonly at the manufacturing stage.

[72] Case 127/75 *Bobie* [1972] E.C.R. 1079. But contrast the interim solution proposed by the Commission in that case, which appears to involve the establishment of a form of average rate.

[73] *e.g.* the taxation of beer, in some Member States, on the basis of worts (as opposed to alcoholic content)—see J. Dodsworth "Excise Duties," D. Dosser (ed.), *"British Taxation and the Common Market,"* Chap. 3, at pp. 73–77—or where, as in the *Bobie* case (Chapter 1, paras. 30–33 tax is assessed on a graduated scale according to the size of the producing enterprise : see further the question of Mr. Schworer in the European Parliament; EPWQ 861/77, O.J. 1978, C. 64/10.

[74] See the Commission's reply to EPWQ 540/76, O.J. 1976, C.300/33.

[75] In particular, see Cases 168–171/78, discussed at paras. 38–43 above.

[76] However the experience of the Benelux nations over the past 30 years of endeavour in this field has been far from encouraging : see H. G. M. Wardenier, "Benelux : Excise Tax Convention" (1977) *Intertax* 351.

[77] See App. A, Table 4, and J. Dodsworth (*op. cit.* n. 73) at p. 62 : (EC) Bull. S. 3/72.

duties on coffee[78] and on sugar[79] are of any great budgetary significance. Nevertheless within this apparently similar framework major disparities exist between one Member State and another, reflecting basic differences in philosophy, social attitudes and patterns of consumption. Thus, for example, wine may be considered a staple commodity in one Member State and a luxury in another. In some Member States there is a substantial domestic production of commodities such as tobacco and wine: in others these are mainly imported.[80] The problem is further complicated by the fact that, in several Member States, products such as tobacco and alcohol are subject to state monopolies and thus also within the provisions of Article 37 of the Treaty, and that the harmonisation of taxes on wine, tobacco and fuel oils cannot be approached in isolation but must be considered in the wider context of the overall policy of the Community with regard to agricultural products, to energy sources and to transportation.[81]

### (ii)   The Commission's programme

**220**     Despite the fact that studies had commenced some 12 years earlier, it was not until 1972 that the Commission was able to present its programme for a general harmonisation of excise duties.[82] On March 7, 1972, the Commission submitted to the Council a number of proposed Directives for the harmonisation of excise duties and indirect taxes (other than VAT) which are levied directly or indirectly on the consumption of products. Four of these proposals related to alcoholic beverages and will be considered later. The other took the form of a "framework" Directive, setting out the general policy towards the harmonisation of excise duties. Simultaneously, a proposed decision, establishing a "Committee on Excise Duties," was submitted.[83] The essential feature of the proposed policy was that harmonisation should proceed in stages: first, the structures of the various excise duties should be harmonised and, later, the rates of duty would have to be aligned in order to facilitate the removal of tax frontiers. This method of proceeding by stages follows that earlier adopted in the case of VAT: it

---

[78] In Germany and Italy.

[79] In Italy.

[80] Upon accession, the new Member States were permitted to replace customs duties of a fiscal nature on imported products with internal taxes conforming with Art. 95 : Act of Accession, Art. 38 and see Commission Decs. 73/199 and 73/200, of February 27, 1973, authorising the United Kingdom and Ireland to retain customs duties of a fiscal nature for a limited period on certain products (mainly tobacco, alcohol and mineral oils).

[81] See the comments of M. Prouzet, "La Politique de la CEE en matière d'harmonisation des Impôts Indirects" (1972) 49 R.D.I.D.C. 151.

[82] Meanwhile a proposal for the harmonisation of taxes on manufactured tobacco had been submitted, in 1967, and was adopted later in 1972, and a proposed Directive relating to mineral oil had been submitted in 1971 : see below.

[83] The texts of the proposals, with the Commission's explanatory memorandum are set out in (EC) Bull. S.3/72. The proposals are discussed extensively by J. Dodsworth, (*op. cit.* above, n. 73).

also appears to be modelled in part upon the "framework" agreement adopted by the Benelux nations, with regard to excise duties, as early as 1950.[84]

**221**     As already mentioned, all the Member States impose special excise duties upon certain categories of products. Among the six original Member States these duties applied to some 28 different categories. The first task, therefore, was to determine in respect of which products excise duties were to be maintained and harmonised at Community level. In the opinion of the Commission the primary aim of an excise duty is to raise revenue, though there may be a subsidiary aim to reduce consumption of those products which may be regarded as being detrimental to health. It was therefore proposed that only those excise duties whose yields were significant and justified the costs of collection should be retained: in addition, those duties should not affect essential products,. *i.e.* those that "are virtually indispensable for living," and should avoid affecting, whenever possible, those products which are used as raw materials by industry. Considerations of common economic policy should also be taken into account.

**222**     Consequently, according to the proposed Directive, Member States will be required to subject the following products to harmonised excise duties (methods of harmonising these duties to be the subject of further directives to be adopted by the Council):

mineral oils;

manufactured tobaccos;

alcohol;

beer; and

wine.[85]

As to the duties on other categories of products three possible solutions presented themselves; such duties could be abolished entirely throughout the Community, Member States might be permitted to impose duties on some or all of these categories, or further categories might be selected for subsequent harmonisation. The most attractive solution would clearly be the abolition of all other excise duties and such a solution would seem to be entirely practicable since these duties have very little budgetary significance in any of the Member States.[86] Of these other duties only those upon coffee (in Germany and Italy) and on sugar (in Italy and the Netherlands) could be considered to be of importance and these should be abolished in any event, according to the criteria established by the Commission: coffee, since it is

---

[84] See J. E. Meade, H. H. Liesner, S. J. Wells, *"Case Studies in European Economic Union : the Mechanics of Integration"* (1962), Chap. 2.

[85] Art. 3 of the Proposed Directive, which proposed that this should be done by January 1, 1974 at the latest.

[86] In the original six Member States excise duties accounted for between 22 per cent. (France) and 41 per cent. (Italy) of revenue from indirect taxes. Only in Italy (4 per cent.) and Germany (2 per cent.) did duties on the "other" categories account for more than 1 per cent. of total indirect tax revenue : see the Annexes to (EC) Bull. S. 3/72.

largely imported from developing countries, and sugar, since it is an essential product and a raw material in industry.[87] Other duties on various categories of manufactured goods might better be incorporated into the general system of value added tax, *e.g.* by subjecting them to a higher, "luxury," rate of VAT.[88] This latter, however, would not be an attractive long-term solution since it is envisaged that ultimately the rates of VAT will be harmonised and probably restricted to a "normal" and a "reduced" rate only.[89]

223     However, it appears that at least some of these other duties could be retained by one or more Member States, at least for the time being, without causing any serious difficulties. The Commission therefore proposed, in its draft Directive, the following compromise:

(*a*) Member States will be free to maintain their existing duties, subject to the harmonisation of the five major duties.[90]

(*b*) By the time that taxes on imports and tax rebates on exports have been abolished, all other duties are to be abolished unless these affect only one product or group of products and are so arranged that, if necessary, they involve, in intra-Community trade, neither taxes on imports and tax rebates on exports nor border controls.[91]

(*c*) After adoption of the Directive a Member State wishing to change the rates of duties in force must inform the Commission of its intention and the Commission will, if necessary, consult the (proposed) Committee on Excise Duties and may recommend appropriate measures to the Member States concerned.[92]

(*d*) Notwithstanding the above provision, Member States shall retain the freedom to introduce new duties provided that these only affect one product or group of products and do not involve, in trade between Member States, border tax adjustments or border controls.[93]

(*e*) The directive shall not preclude the introduction, at Community level, of harmonised duties on categories other than the five major ones.[94]

224     The effect of this compromise appears to be twofold: until such time as tax frontiers within the Community are removed, existing duties may be retained. Although not expressly stated in the proposed Directive, it is sub-

---

[87] (EC) Bull. S. 3/72, pp. 9, 10. The same holds true for duties on cocoa, tea and salt.

[88] This could be done with products such as gramophone records, matches and playing cards if a Member State desired to continue to impose additional tax upon such items. A similar solution could be adopted for other "special" consumer taxes, *e.g.* that on private cars in the Netherlands. Of the new Member States Denmark, in particular, imposes a number of such special taxes on "luxury" goods.

[89] Denmark would probably also be reluctant to sacrifice the purity of its single-rate VAT system by introducing an additional luxury rate.

[90] Proposed Dir., Arts. 2 and 3.

[91] *Ibid.* Art. 4.

[92] *Ibid.* Art. 5.

[93] *Ibid.* Art. 6.

[94] *Ibid.* Art. 8.

mitted that any countervailing duties on importation of such products or remission of duty on exportation, in so far as they apply in intra-Community trade, must conform with the principles of Articles 95 to 98 of the Treaty. Once tax frontiers have been removed—and before then, in the case of new duties introduced subsequent to the Directive—only those duties may be retained which affect only one product or group of products and which do not involve border tax adjustments and border controls. Such duties as might be retained would consequently have to be relatively light in order to be effective at all, since there would clearly be an incentive to engage in cross-border shopping in the absence of border controls.[95] Thus, although Member States would still retain a measure of freedom in this respect, there might well be a move towards "spontaneous harmonisation"[96] leading to the gradual elimination of all excise duties other than those on tobacco, mineral oils and alcoholic drinks.

**225**   The proposed "framework" Directive was considered by the Economic and Social Committee and by the Parliament in 1973 and, in general, was approved by these bodies. The Economic and Social Committee concurred with the overall approach and favoured restricting the number of excise duties, whilst emphasising their regressive nature, urging that they be reduced in level and that greater consideration be given to their economic and social effects.[97] The Parliament, too, generally welcomed the proposal and urged prompt action to harmonise rates of duty, though it expressed reservations regarding the imposition of excise duty on wine.[98] Nevertheless, despite this favourable reception, little if any progress has been made in the Council despite the fact that it was originally intended that the Directive should be adopted by the end of 1974.[99] In August 1977 the Commission, in a communication to the Council,[1] urged that work should resume on the various proposals but so far the problems of harmonising the duties on alcoholic beverages have proved intractable and have prevented further real progress.

## (iii)  Tobacco

**226**   Prior to the proposed "framework" Directive the Commission had, in 1967, submitted a proposal for the harmonisation of taxes affecting manufactured

---

[95] *e.g.* German consumers might buy their coffee in France or the Netherlands : see Dodsworth, (*op. cit.* n. 73) at p. 62.

[96] *Cf.* the solution suggested with respect to the harmonisation of VAT rates, Chapter 2, para. 146, above.

[97] O.J. 1973, C. 36/34.

[98] O.J. 1974, C. 48/6. The Artzinger Report (E.P. Doc. 342/73) also doubted whether the retention of duty on beer could be justified. This question is discussed further below, at paras. 240–242.

[99] See E.P.W.Q. 580/77, O.J. 1978, C. 30/14.

[1] (EC) Bull. 7-8/77, p. 35. The Council resumed work on the alcohol proposals in October, 1979.

tobacco as part of a programme of measures to be taken in the tobacco sector.[2] Four regulations and a resolution were proposed, concerning:

(a) the Common Agricultural Policy—a proposed Regulation on the establishment of a joint market organisation for unmanufactured tobacco. Approximately one-third of the (original six) Member States' processing requirements is provided by Community-grown tobacco, largely concentrated in a few regions of France and Italy.

(b) Adjustment of national monopolies—a proposed regulation governing commercial monopolies in manufactured tobacco, notably those of France and Italy.

(c) Associated overseas countries and territories—a proposed regulation regarding unmanufactured tobacco originating in those States. Much of the Community's imported tobacco comes from the Yaoundé, and now Lomé, States and from associated countries such as Greece and Turkey.

(d) Tax harmonisation—a proposed Regulation governing taxes other than turnover taxes levied on the consumption of manufactured tobacco.

227        The above gives an indication of the scope of the problem: tax harmonisation cannot be viewed in isolation but must be considered in conjunction with the agricultural and regional issues, the question of national commercial monopolies and the Community's relations with associated states. In particular, the objective of removing obstacles to the interpenetration of national tobacco markets by harmonising taxes on these products is unlikely to be achieved so long as national monopolies exist and remain free to fix prices.[3]

Even without these additional considerations, the harmonisation of taxes affecting manufactured tobacco is no easy matter. Taxes on tobacco constitute an important source of revenue in most Member States, though there is a wide variation in the levels of taxation imposed.[4] Moreover, tax structures in the Member States vary, some taxes being calculated upon the specific tobacco component (e.g. weight) and others being imposed on an ad valorem basis. These differences tend to distort competition, a specific tax favouring the more expensive tobaccos and an ad valorem tax favouring the cheaper brands.[5] In addition, Italy has had to contend with a not inconsiderable problem of contraband cigarettes.[6]

228        The Commission's original proposal was that taxes on tobacco should be

---

[2] (EEC) Bull. 9-10/67, pp. 13–18. These proposals were submitted to the Council on July 4, 1967.

[3] See the Council Resolution of April 21, 1970, proposing that such monopolies be phased out by the end of 1975 : J.O. 1970, C. 50/2. This has not been achieved and Member States remain free to regulate prices provided this is done in conformity with Art. 30 and with Dir. 70/50 of December 22, 1969. See also Case 13/77 *Inno* [1977] E.C.R. 2115, and EPWQ 319/78 : O.J. 1978, C 251/8.

[4] App. A, Table 4.

[5] For a comprehensive study, see *Cigarette Tax Harmonisation,* Comm. Study, Taxation Series 1975, No. 2 (the *'Metra' Report*). See also Dodsworth (*op. cit.* n. 73) at pp. 68–73.

[6] "Metra" Report, p. 69.

based upon retail selling price, actual rates to be freely determined by each Member State. In the case of cigarettes a degressive scale of tax could be applied,[7] in order to avoid undue discrimination against higher-quality cigarettes. Tobacco products were divided into a number of groups— cigarettes, cigars, pipe tobacco, etc.,—and Member States would be required to apply the same tax rates to all products within a particular group. The major reaction to the proposal came from the Parliament[8] and was concerned less with the actual content (though in view of the serious budgetary consequences for some Member States it was urged that the new system be phased in gradually) but rather with its form. The Commission had proposed a Regulation, based upon Article 99 of the Treaty, but the Parliament urged, both for policy and judicial reasons, that action should rather be taken by means of a Directive.[9] Although the Commission had initially taken the view that Article 99 permits a choice of instrument, the recommendation of the Parliament was accepted and, in 1970, a revised proposal was submitted, this time in the form of a Directive pursuant to Articles 99 and 100.[10]

This proposal, with some modifications, found acceptance and was adopted in 1972.[11] The Directive requires the harmonisation by stages of the structure of excise duties on manufactured tobacco, *i.e.* on cigarettes, cigars and cigarillos, smoking tobacco, snuff and chewing tobacco.[12] Such tobacco may be subjected only to excise duty and to value added tax.[13] In the case of cigarettes, the excise duty has two components: a proportional duty cal-culated on the maximum retail selling price, the rate of which must be the same for all cigarettes,[14] and a specific duty calculated per unit of produc-tion, which must also be the same for all cigarettes.

**229**    According to the First Directive, the harmonisation of tax structures on cigarettes[15] is to proceed by stages. Initially, the first stage was to last until June 30, 1975 but, by a series of subsequent Directives,[16] it was extended a further three years. During the first stage, the required "mix" of *ad valorem* and specific components permitted a specific duty of between 5 per cent.

---

[7] *i.e.* above a certain minimum level the rate of tax would reduce.

[8] J.O. 1969, C 97/66.

[9] For an analysis of the juridical question, see the Artzinger Report, E.P. Docs. 224/68. See also para. 00, above.

[10] Proposed Directive, transmitted to the Council on November 20, 1970 : J.O. 1971, C 4/22.

[11] Dir. 72/464 of December 19, 1972.

[12] *Ibid.* Art. 3.

[13] *Ibid.* Art. 2.

[14] *Ibid.* Art. 4(2). By virtue of Dir. 77/805, Art. 3, the United Kingdom is permitted temporarily to derogate from this rule and to impose an additional duty, for health reasons, on cigarettes whose tar yield is 20 mg. or more : for a comment, see G. Morse, (1978) 3 E.L.Rev. 155.

[15] Art. 3(2) of the Dir. requires further proposals to be made dealing with the other categories of manufactured tobacco.

[16] Dir. 74/318 of June 25, 1974 : Dir. 75/786 of December 18, 1975 : Dir. 76/911 of December 21, 1976 and Dir. 77/805 of December 19, 1977.

and 75 per cent. of the aggregate amount of duty.[17] For the second stage, which is to run from July 1, 1978 to December 31, 1980, the permitted range has been narrowed to that between 5 per cent. and 55 per cent.[18] At the final stage, whenever this may be reached, the "mix" should be the same in all Member States.[19]

At this final stage, at the latest, the rules for collecting the excise duty are to be harmonised.[20] Meanwhile, the First Directive envisages that the normal method of collection of the duty will be by means of tax stamps, made available to manufacturers and dealers in other Member States.[21] Member States are, however, permitted to adopt other methods of collection provided these give rise to no obstacle, administrative or technical, affecting trade between Member States.[22] The use of the tax stamp system explains the provisions of Article 5 of the Directive: this permits manufacturers and importers to fix a maximum selling price for each of their products.[23] Tax is levied on the basis of that maximum price (and the appropriate stamp affixed) and cannot, consequently, be avoided by retailing at a higher price.

**230**   The fixing of a maximum price is subject to the proviso that it may not hinder implementation of national systems of legislation regarding the control of price levels or the observance of imposed prices and Member States are permitted, subject to a number of conditions, to fix a scale of retail selling prices, for each group of tobacco products, applicable to all products belonging to the particular group.[24] The effect of Article 5 would therefore appear to be that, whilst manufacturers or importers may, subject to national price regulation and provided Article 86 of the Treaty is not infringed, fix maximum prices, this constituting an essential fiscal guarantee, they are not authorised to impose fixed, or minimum, retail prices, since there would be no tax loss if a retailer were to sell at a price lower than that on which the tax had been calculated. Member States, by contrast, do have the power to fix a scale of maximum and minimum retail prices,[25] provided the scale makes no distinction as to quality, presentation or origin of the

---

[17] Dir. 72/464, Art. 8. Special transitional provisions were made in the case of the United Kingdom and Ireland, postponing implementation to the end of 1977 and permitting until then the retention of customs duties of a fiscal nature, or the fiscal element of such duties, on imported tobacco : Act of Accession, Art. 37 and Decs. 73/199, 200 of February 27 and March 6, 1973.

[18] Dir. 77/805, Art. 3. Ireland is permitted to go to 60 per cent.

[19] Dir. 72/464, Art. 4(3), as amended by Dir. 77/805, Art. 1.

[20] Dir. 72/464, Art. 6. Importers and national manufacturers will be subject to the same system as regards payment : Art. 6(2).

[21] This is necessary, as the normal method is for the tax stamp to be affixed to a packet of cigarettes beneath the exterior cellophane wrapper. Thus it is the exporting manufacturer, rather than the importer, who normally affixes it : see Case 13/77 *Inno* [1977] E.C.R. 2115.

[22] Dir. 72/464, Art. 6(1).

[23] Such a maximum price, fixed by a manufacturer or importer, is prima facie valid, though it could in certain circumstances constitute an abuse of a dominant position and be prohibited by Art. 86 of the Treaty : see Case 13/77 *Inno*, above.

[24] Dir. 72/464, Art. 5.

[25] Or, it would seem, a single fixed price for a particular product.

products or of the materials used. Whereas a system of price controls is, in general, capable of constituting a measure having equivalent effect to a quantitative restriction— maximum prices may have the effect of excluding higher cost imports and minimum prices of removing the price advantage of lower cost imports[26]—the Court held, in *Inno*,[27] that a legislative provision,[28] which prohibited resale of cigarettes at a price other than that declared by the manufacturer at the time of affixing the tax stamp, was not prohibited by Article 5 of the Directive. Such a provision, at least where the fixed price has been freely determined by the manufacturer or importer, would seem to be valid provided it applies equally to imported and domestic products and, taking into account the obstacles inherent in the different methods of fiscal control, is not likely to hinder intra-Community trade. As the Court explained:

**231**
> "In all the Member States, taxes on manufactured tobacco are an important source of revenue, so that the competent authorities must possess effective means of ensuring that they are collected. In the present state of Community law, it is for each Member State to choose its own method of fiscal control over manufactured tobacco on sale in its territory. Because of the need to satisfy the demands of the rigorous and often complicated controls—which differ moreover from one Member State to another—the import and export of manufactured tobacco at present come up against inevitable obstacles and in these circumstances trade between states in this product requires considerable resources and skill."[29]

As we have seen, the First Tobacco Directive deals only with cigarettes and anticipated a further measure in which other types of manufactured tobacco would be defined and classified in groups.[30] This has now been achieved by the Second Directive,[31] which defines and distinguishes between cigars and cigarillos, cigarettes, smoking tobacco, chewing tobacco and snuff. Certain special derogations are permitted,[32] and the definitions are stated to be without prejudice to the choice of system or the level of taxation

---

[26] Case 65/75 *Tasca* [1976] E.C.R. 291 : Cases 88–90/75 *SADAM* [1976] E.C.R. 323 : Case 82/77 *Van Tiggele* [1978] E.C.R. 25.

[27] Case 13/77, above.

[28] The question was referred under Art. 177 by the Belgian Hof van Cassatie, arising out of a challenge to the validity of the Belgian law by a supermarket chain charged with selling cigarettes at a price lower than that stated on the tax label. An apparent aim of the legislation was to protect small retailers from undue competition on the part of supermarkets. See further the note by D. Wyatt, (1978) 3 E.L.Rev. 308.

[29] [1977] E.C.R., at p. 2142.

[30] Dir. 72/464, Art. 3(2).

[31] Dir. 79/32 of December 18, 1978.

[32] These apply to Denmark and Germany. The distinction between cigars and cigarettes is not easy to make in some cases, *e.g.* rolls of tobacco without binder. The derogations apply to products peculiar to those national markets.

which shall apply to the different groups of products.[33] As such, the directive constitutes merely a preliminary step towards the harmonisation of the structures of taxation to be applied to each group. Nevertheless, as will be more apparent when the problem of taxation of alcoholic drinks is considered,[34] classification and definition of products is one of the most essential and difficult aspects of harmonisation.

### (iv) Mineral oil

**232**     Of the major excise duties by far the most important, in terms of national revenue and of the effects upon costs of production and transportation, competition and the cost of living generally, is the duty on mineral oils, in particular the duties on petrol, diesel and heating oils. One of the fundamental objectives of the Treaty was the adoption of a common transport policy[35] and the events of 1973 and subsequently have emphasised the need for a common energy policy. Harmonisation of the taxes affecting oil must therefore proceed with regard not only to the progress made in respect to other excise duties but also to the evolution of the Community's transport and energy policy.

Prior to the proposal for a "framework" Directive for excise duties, the Commission had proposed a Directive for the harmonisation of specific taxes on consumption imposed upon liquid hydrocarbons used as fuels.[36] The preamble to this proposal recites the need to develop a common energy policy and emphasises the effects of the difference in levels of taxation from one Member State to another upon the conditions of competition. As a first step, the draft Directive proposed a harmonisation of structures, classifying hydrocarbon fuels into two basic categories[37] and also proposed that prescribed maximum rates of tax should be applicable after the end of 1975. The reaction to the proposal was unenthusiastic. In particular the Parliament regretted the partial character of the proposal and urged the adoption of an integral approach to the harmonisation of taxes on all sources of energy, including coal, electricity and natural gas.[38]

**233**     A further proposed directive on the harmonisation of excise duties on mineral oils was submitted to the Council in August, 1973.[39] This again emphasised the effects upon competition and proposed a progressive har-

---

[33] Dir. 79/32, Art. 1(2). But since these products are probably competing products, it may be that Art. 95(2) of the Treaty requires that the relative level of taxation of each group of products is such that it does not afford protection to another : See above, paras. 44–55.

[34] See also the discussion of the concept of "similar products" in Chapter 1, paras. 33–43, above.

[35] Art. 3(e), and see below, paras. 252-254.

[36] Proposed Directive submitted to the Council on December 28, 1970 : J.O. 1971, C 14/25.

[37] These categories followed those set out in Chap. 27 of the Common Customs Tariff.

[38] J.O. 1971, C 55/14, and see the De Broglie Report, E.P. Docs. 43/71.

[39] O.J. 1973, C 92/36.

monisation, concentrating during the first stage upon the structures of the duties. The draft Directive is therefore concerned with the definition and classification of mineral oils, the chargeable event giving rise to the duty, the permissible exemptions and the collection of duty. The Commission considered that a specific consumption tax should not have the effect of a production tax, which could distort the conditions of competition, and consequently proposed that mineral oils used as raw materials or as manufacturing agents should have no excise duties imposed upon them and that industrial heating oils should similarly be exempted to secure as far as possible a neutral tax system with regard to all the sources of primary energy. Member States would remain free to fix their own rates of duty but any preferential treatment granted to certain categories of consumers would be subject to a consultation procedure. Although the proposed Directive was generally welcomed by the Parliament,[40] no action has yet been taken[41] and none appears to be imminent.

Reasons for the lack of progress are not hard to find. From a national budgetary point of view, revenue from duties on mineral oils accounts for between one-half and two-thirds of all excise duty revenue. Rates of duty are high[42] and vary widely from one state to another and from one product to another.[43] As regards a common energy policy, there is general agreement only that consumption of oil throughout the Community should be reduced. This would suggest that oil be taxed considerably more heavily than alternative sources of energy yet one of the avowed aims of the 1973 proposal was to secure neutrality as between different sources of energy. Progress may be further complicated by the prohibition, in paragraph two of Article 95 of the Treaty, on the taxation of one product so as to afford protection to some other, competing, product,[44] bearing in mind that some Member States produce, and export, significant quantities of oil and others do not. Nevertheless, this ought not to prevent a harmonisation of tax structures and methods of collection in order to at least achieve a measure of transparency and to permit the accurate calculation of border tax adjustments.

## (v) Alcohol

**234** Although less important from a budgetary point of view than the excise duties on oil, harmonisation of the various duties on alcoholic drinks pre-

---

[40] O.J. 1975, C 32/9. The Report of the Committee on Budgets (the Petre Report : E.P. Docs. 401/74) contains a valuable analysis of the problem and much useful information on the different national systems.
[41] The proposed Directive aimed at implementation before 1975.
[42] *e.g.* for regular petrol, tax (including VAT) accounts for from 48 per cent. to 72 per cent. of the selling price : see EPWQ 908/78, O.J. 1979, C 79/11, and see App. A, Table 4.
[43] Thus duty on petrol is three times higher in Italy than in Britain whereas, for diesel, British rates are five times greater than those in Italy : see EPWQ 397/78, O.J. 1979, C 5/3, and App. A, Table 4.
[44] See above, paras. 52, 54.

sents even greater problems. As with tobacco, agricultural policy must also be taken into account[45] and the problems associated with national commercial monopolies have also to be considered.[46] Rates of tax vary widely from One Member State to another and these disparities have increased dramatically since the Commission's original 1972 proposals as a result of the accession of Denmark, Ireland and the United Kingdom.[47] National treatment of different types of alcoholic beverages also varies considerably and frequently discriminates in practice against products imported from other Member States. Indeed, there is probably no other sector of economic activity which has given rise to so many complaints of discrimination and of contravention of Article 95.[48] The patience of the Commission, and of taxpayers, would now seem to have been exhausted and the recent proceedings against offending Member States,[49] and in national courts by taxpayers,[50] are probably only the first of many unless a solution can be found through the harmonisation of these taxes.

In 1972 the Commission submitted, together with its proposed "framework" Directive on excise duties and its proposed decision establishing a Committee on Excise Duties,[51] four specific draft Directives dealing with alcoholic beverages.[52] These were as follows:

## (a)  Spirits

235      The draft Directive constitutes a preliminary step and is concerned primarily with the harmonisation of the structure of taxes on ethyl alcohol,[53]

---

[45] See the Commission's Action Programme, *"Progressive establishment of balance in the market in wine,"* (EC) Bull. S. 7–78 and Reg. 337/79 of February 5, 1979.

[46] See, for example, Case 13/70 *Cinzano* [1970] E.C.R. 1089; Case 45/75 *Rewe* [1976] E.C.R. 181; Case 91/78 *Hansen* [1980] 1 C.M.L.R. 162.

[47] The three new members tax spirits between two and a half and five times more heavily than any of the original members—Denmark taxes brandy 40 times more heavily than Italy. Wine is taxed three to four times more heavily than in any of the original "six" and beer from three to seven times more heavily. See App. A, Table 4.

[48] This has been a recurring theme in the Commission's annual reports : see (EC) Third General Report (1969), p. 77; (EC) Tenth General Report (1976), p. 109; (EC) Eleventh General Report (1977), p. 117. Questions in the Parliament frequently draw attention to such discrimination : for recent examples, see O.J. 1978, C 64/10, C 88/4, C 175/12, C 251/24, C 282/25; O.J. 1979, C 68/26, C 79/15, C 178/18.

[49] Cases 168–171/78 *Commission* v. *France, Italy, United Kingdom and Denmark*; Case 55/79 *Commission* v. *Ireland*, see above, Chapter 1.

[50] Case 127/75 *Bobie* [1976] E.C.R. 1079; Case 148/77 *Hansen & Balle* [1978] E.C.R. 1787; Case 68/79 *Just*; (not yet reported), above, Chapter 1.

[51] Above, paras. 220–225.

[52] Proposals transmitted to the Council on March 7, 1972 : J.O. 1972, C 43, and see (EC) Bull. S. 3–72.

[53] It does not deal with other forms of alcohol—amyl, methyl, propyl, etc.—which cannot normally be used in beverages. It proposes the exemption from duty of ethyl alcohol used industrially for non-human uses and for the manufacture or production of perfumes, vinegar, medicines, etc. (Art. 7).

with methods of assessment, collection[54] and control. It does not apply to beers, ciders or to wines of less than a prescribed alcohol strength.[55] It is proposed that alcohol shall not be subjected to any indirect taxation other than VAT and the harmonised excise duty, save that Member States may apply other taxes provided that these do not give rise, in intra-Community trade, to border tax adjustments.[56] The amount of the harmonised duty is to be fixed per hectoliter of pure alcohol[57] and, within each Member State, alcohol is to be subject to one single excise rate, which cannot differ according to the national origin of the materials used, the size of the production company or any other criteria.[58] Reduced rates would, however, apply to certain quality or fortified wines, liqueur wines, vermouths and similar beverages.[59] The great advantage of the proposal is that it automatically abolishes (except perhaps in the case of the intermediate fortified or liqueur wines) the discriminations which result from the application of different rates of duty to different categories of alcohol, classified according to alcoholic content or according to the material from which produced, e.g. distinctions between spirits produced from grapes and from grain, which give rise to discrimination in favour of domestic akvavit or against imported whisky.[60]

The reaction of the Parliament to this proposal was generally favourable.[61] The need to retain the duty, for budgetary reasons and from the point of view of public health, was acknowledged and its effect, in removing discrimination and distortions to competition, welcomed. A number of reservations were expressed and the Commission now proposes that the special category of fortified and liqueur wines be removed from the Directive and instead be included in a special category in the wine Directive.[62]

(b) *Wine*

236    The second of the Commission's draft Directives proposed a harmonised system for the taxation of wine. Wine was distinguished from alcohol on the

---

[54] Art. 21 of the proposed Dir. permits the deferral of payment of tax by producers, apparently for up to 12 weeks, without payment of interest. In the light of the Court's decision in Case 55/79 *Commission* v. *Ireland* [1980] 1 C.M.L.R. 734, it would seem that this will have to be revised.

[55] Proposed Dir., Art. 2.

[56] *Ibid.* Art. 35. Examples of such other taxes include special taxes imposed on sales in public houses or by retailers, though these may not discriminate against imported products.

[57] At a temperature of 15°C : Art. 4.

[58] Art. 5. Member States would be free to fix their own rate.

[59] Art. 6. It is now proposed to delete this article : see below.

[60] See Cases 168, 169 and 171/78, above, n. 49.

[61] O.J. 1974, C 48/6, and see the *Artzinger Report,* E.P. Docs. 5/74.

[62] Communication to the Council of June 22, 1979 : Doc. COM (79) 261 final. It also proposes that a less restrictive approach be adopted towards other special excises, *e.g.* those applying to liqueur chocolates.

basis of a prescribed maximum alcoholic strength and the Commission proposed that there should be two categories—sparkling wines and other wines[63]—though it is now proposed to add a third category, that of fortified and liqueur wines.[64] It was proposed that Member States should be free to fix a standard rate of tax applicable to each of these categories, levied on the basis of volume, the same rate applying to all wines in any one category.[65]

This proposal has encountered numerous obstacles. Of the original Member States, Italy imposes no excise duty on wines,[66] Germany imposes duty only on sparkling wines and France imposes duty at a very low rate.[67] The Benelux states now have a partially harmonised system,[68] which in a number of respects does not conform with the draft Directive, whilst Denmark, Ireland and the United Kindgom impose heavy duties.[69] Introduction of a duty on wine in Italy and Germany would be politically difficult, especially as the wine-producing countries take the view that the high levels of duty in the new Member States is unjustified and operates as a form of tariff barrier.[70] Following the report of its Committee on Budgets,[71] the Parliament recommended that all excise duties on wine should preferably be abolished or, at any rate, that Member States should not have to introduce one.[72] The Commission, however, has taken the view that, as all alcoholic drinks are more or less in competition, an excise duty on wine is a necessary complement to the duties on alcohol and beer, both from the standpoint of competitive neutrality and for the protection of tax revenue from the duties on alcohol and beer. Whilst a reduction in the overall level of taxes on wine would be of assistance in reducing the recurring wine surplus in the Community,[73] the abolition of duty in those countries presently taxing wine would be politically difficult (and contrary to what some would regard as the interests of public health) and would probably also necessitate massive reductions in the duties levied by those countries on alcohol and beer, thus causing serious budgetary difficulties.

---

[63] Most Member States tax sparkling wines at higher rates than ordinary table wines. Germany taxes only sparkling wines.

[64] See above, n. 62.

[65] Draft Dir., Art. 5. Higher rates would, however, be permitted for certain "quality wines" produced in specified regions. Under the revised (1979) proposals, the third category, of fortified, etc., wines, might be sub-divided by reference to alcoholic strength.

[66] VAT applies in all Member States.

[67] A higher rate is applied to champagne.

[68] See H. G. M. Wardenier, "Benelux : Excise Tax Convention" (1977) Intertax 351.

[69] On ordinary still table wines these duties are three to four times higher than the maximum Benelux rate and 60 to 75 times higher than the French rate.

[70] Italy supported the Commission in the proceedings against the United Kingdom in Case 170/78.

[71] The Gerlach Report, E.P. Docs. 26/74.

[72] O.J. 1974, C 48/6.

[73] See the Commission's Recommendation 76/2 of December 5, 1975 : O.J. 1976, L 2/13.

**237**    In an attempt to resolve the impasse,[74] the Commission has recently
advanced a compromise solution,[75] whereby
- —— the draft Directive would be adopted, with amendments:
- —— derogations would permit, until the abolition of fiscal frontiers at
  the latest, Italy and Germany to defer introduction of the excise
  on wines not already taxed and the Benelux states to retain, subject to conditions, their existing regime :
- —— fortified, liqueur and quality wines would comprise a new
  category:
- —— those Member States taxing wine would do so on the basis that
  the ratio of the excise levied on a given quantity of typical wine to
  that levied on a given quantity of typical beer should not exceed
  the ratio (roughly wine 3 : beer 1) between the alcoholic strengths
  of those drinks:[76]
- —— each Member State would apply the same VAT rate to both beer
  and to wine.

These proposals, whilst creating difficulties for the United Kingdom in
particular, would appear to meet most of the objections of the wine-
producing members, though they appear to achieve little real harmony.
Their compatibility with Article 95 of the Treaty will be considered later.

### (c)   Beer

**238**    Unlike wine, excise duty is levied upon beer in all of the Member States,
though, again, duty is considerably heavier in Denmark, Ireland and the
United Kingdom than elsewhere in the Community. The main problems
with which the proposed Directive had to deal concerned the classification
of, and application of different rates of duty to, beers of different alcoholic
strengths and the basis for the assessment of the duty. The draft Directive
proposes[77] that there should be four categories of beer. Member States
would be free to fix a basic rate of duty for "standard" beers,[78] with
increased and decreased rates for stronger and weaker beers, the same rate
applying to all beers in the same category.
    By way of temporary derogation, some Member States would be per-
mitted to retain a system of progressive rates linked to the volume of
production of the particular brewery or producing concern.[79] In view of the

---

[74] Due to the divergent views in the Council, work on the proposed Dir. had been
suspended in 1974.

[75] See above, n. 62.

[76] The United Kingdom presently taxes a typical wine approximately five times more
heavily (on a volume basis) than a typical beer. Either wine duties would halve or beer duties
would double!

[77] Prop. Dir., Arts. 5 and 6.

[78] Beers with an original extract of 11 to 13.5 per cent. by weight, according to the Plato
method.

[79] Arts. 13 and 17.

Court's decision in *Bobie*[80] it would seem that such a system is only permissible, within the terms of Article 95, so long as it is non-discriminatory and applies equally to imported beer. The proposed derogation is, perhaps, unfortunate: although it may be justifiable to accord preferential treatment to small producers,[81] it hardly seems appropriate to tax imported beer according to the volume of production of the exporting brewery and to do so may distort the conditions of competition between different imports. If preferential treatment is necessary, it would seem better to accord it by means of a reduction of the tax borne by the domestic producer[82] rather than of the tax imposed on the product.

As regards the basis of assessment of the duty, two methods have commonly been used in the Community.[83] According to one system duty is assessed on the basis of the quantity and alcoholic content of the musts or worts used in the production of beer. The other method bases duty upon the alcoholic content of the finished product. The latter method is preferred by the Commission,[84] in part because the former method can result in variations from one brewery to another according to the extent of losses occurring in the transformation of the musts into beer, but chiefly because, where duty is assessed on the finished product, the basis of taxation is the same for imports as for domestic beer and any possible discrimination is therefore avoided.

### (d)   Mixed beverages and other alcoholic drinks

**239**      The Commission originally submitted, in 1972, a further proposed directive dealing with "mixed beverages," This has since been withdrawn.[85] It would seem that duties on certain alcoholic drinks, such as cider,[86] perry and mead, can be retained without the need for harmonisation. Some mixed drinks, where ethyl alcohol is added, fall by definition within the "alcohol" proposal. Other mixtures are probably not significant in terms of intra-Community trade — the more bizarre combinations are normally concocted immediately prior to consumption and after duty has been paid—and harmonisation is unnecessary, though whatever system of taxa-

---

[80] Case 127/75 [1976] E.C.R. 1079. See above, Chap. 1, paras. 30–33. In the view of the Commission, a graduated system can be compatible with Art. 95, but it is disliked as non-neutral : see EPWQ. 861/77, O.J. 1978, C 64/10.

[81] The purposes of the progressive scales is apparently to enable small breweries to compete against the larger concerns and to counter the tendency towards concentrations in the brewing industry—an aim which would surely be applauded by discerning consumers.

[82] *e.g.* a reduction in business profits tax.

[83] See further, J. Dodsworth, (*op. cit.* p. 127, n. 73) at pp. 73–76.

[84] (EC) Bull. S. 3–72, pp. 62–64. See also the report to the Parliament of the Committee on Budgets (the Rossi Report) : E.P. Docs. 378/73.

[85] Doc. COM (74) 712 of May 17, 1974.

[86] Apparently, strong cider will be placed in the same category as wine : see EPWQ 554/79, O.J. 1980, C 66/4.

tion is applied must be non-discriminatory in accordance with the principles of Article 95.

(e)   *The proposed directives and the principle of non-discrimination*

**240**     If it is accepted that measures adopted for the harmonisation of laws must be in conformity with the basic provisions of the Treaty, and in particular with Article 95,[87] then the validity of the Commission's proposals with regard to excise duties on alcoholic beverages must be called into question.

In the case of alcohol, *i.e.* spirits, the proposed directive treats all such products as essentially "similar," to be differentiated only on a related basis of alcoholic strength and without regard to such matters as the habits of consumers or the raw materials from which they are produced. This appears to be consistent with the jurisprudence of the Court. The respective treatment of wine and beer in the proposals, in particular in the Commission's recent compromise solution, is more difficult to justify. The Commission has long been of the view that wine and beer, though not "similar" products within the meaning of the first paragraph of Article 95, are competing products and are subject to the provisions of the second paragraph of that Article.[88] Certain Member States, notably Italy, have insisted that the proposals for wine and beer must be considered together. This relationship now seems to have been confirmed by the Court in the recent proceedings against the United Kingdom,[89] which at least establishes that a duty on wine, which is disproportionately heavy in comparison to the duty on beer, may have the effect of discriminating against imported wine and of affording protection to domestically produced beer. It is no doubt for this reason that the Commission now proposes that the ratio of the duty levied upon a given quantity of typical wine to the duty levied upon a given quantity of typical beer shall not exceed the ratio (roughly three to one) between the alcohol strengths of these drinks.

This seems reasonable enough in order to prevent discrimination on the part of those Member States which produce little or no domestic wine against wine imported from other Member States. But if wine and beer are in competition then it ought not to be permitted to discriminate against beer so as to afford protection to wine, which would be the case if the ratio of the wine duty to the beer duty is considerably less than three to one or if, as the compromise solution would permit, wine is exempt from duty and beer is

[87]   See above, para. 66. It seems to be accepted by the Commission in principle : see the reply to EPWQ 554/79 (above). See also Case 21/79 *Commission* v. *Italy.*
[88]   See (EC) Bull. S. 3–72, p. 46 and the explanation of its compromise solution given in Doc. COM (79) 261. Much earlier, this view was referred to in the Deringer Report, at p. 63. By contrast, the Parliament seems to have considered that very little competition exists between the two : see the Gerlach Report, at pp. 14, 15.
[89]   Case 170/78, above, paras. 46–50.

taxed.[90] It may be objected that the purpose of Article 95 is to prohibit the discriminatory taxation of imported products and that nothing in the Treaty prevents a Member State from discriminating between different products, even if the products are competing, so long as this discrimination is not based upon the national origin of the products in question. Thus Germany or Italy would doubtless argue that for them to tax beer and to exempt wine is legitimate, since both countries produce substantial quantities of both products : imported beer would be taxed in the same way as domestic beer and imported wine would be exempt in the same way as domestic wine. Nevertheless this argument may be objected to on a number of grounds :

(1) The second paragraph of Article 95 states that "no Member State shall impose on the products of other Member States any internal taxation of such a nature as to afford indirect protection *to other products.*"[91] It does not say "to other *domestic* products." Thus, according to the plain wording of the provision,[92] if a tax on beer affords protection to wine, an importer of beer would seem to be entitled to challenge its validity, even though a domestic beer producer cannot complain.

(2) To permit a country which has a substantial domestic production of both of the products in question to discriminate between them, but to deny this privilege to a country which produces substantial quantities of only one of the products is contrary to the basic principle of the equality of all Member States.

(3) A major element of uncertainty would be introduced, namely what constitutes a "substantial" proportion of consumption or production. To hold that the United Kingdom, which produces only a small proportion of the wine consumed there, protects beer, which is mainly produced domestically, but that Italy does not protect wine (in such a way as to contravene Article 95) because it also produces most of the beer consumed there, requires a distinction to be drawn between "negligible" and "substantial." Such a distinction must perforce be arbitrary and unsatisfactory.

(4) Whether or not a tax system which discriminates between two competing products is likely to afford protection to the relatively less heavily taxed product is not necessarily related to the level of domestic production of the less favoured product. A tax system which discriminates against beer and in favour of wine may have the effect of discouraging the importation of beer, regardless of whether domestic production of beer is substantial or not. Removal of the discrimination might well lead to an overall increase in the level of beer consumption, to the benefit of domestic producers and producers in other Member States alike.

[90] See the question of M. Cousté in the Parliament : EPWQ 702/77, O.J. 1978, C 42/24. The Commission's reply, that its proposals are based upon expediency and practicability, must be regarded as unsatisfactory.
[91] Italics added.
[92] Though such literal interpretations rarely find favour with the Court.

(5) Article 95 has been stated, by the Court, to be a "fundamental" provision of the Treaty.[93] Like Article 40(3), this appears to be but one example of the "general principle of equality" which is one of the "fundamental principles of Community law."[94] As has been held, notably in the isoglucose and starch cases,[95] Community legislation which offends against this principle is invalid: products which are in competition and which may be substituted for each other must be treated in the same manner, at any rate unless the differentiation is objectively justified.

**241**    The solution proposed by the Commission in the draft Directives and in its new compromise proposal are open to criticism, in that in attempting to remedy one type of discrimination it apparently permits a reverse discrimination. One must therefore ask whether this defect affects the validity of the proposal. It may be argued that, since the Treaty itself contains a clear directly-binding and fundamental obligation to abolish discrimination, then it is not for the Commission and Council, by means of secondary legislation, to seek to attain objectives for which provision is already clearly made in the Treaty.[96] However, the existence of a clear obligation in the Treaty does not prevent or invalidate harmonisation measures designed to attain this objective. For example, a harmonisation Directive may prescribe detailed rules to this end, adding flesh to the bare bones of the Treaty,[97] provided always that these rules are consistent with the basic principles enshrined in the Treaty. Moreover, where the objective may be attained in a variety of ways—thus the discrimination between wine and beer can be cured either by abolishing all duties on both products or by requiring a proper relationship between the respective duties—it is permissible to adopt one of these methods in the context of harmonisation, provided that the harmonised method is not contrary to the Treaty provision in question. But since a fundamental Treaty provision overrides a secondary provision contained in a Regulation or Directive, a Member State which is in breach of a Treaty obligation cannot justify this on the ground that its action is consistent with, or not contrary to a harmonisation Directive. Distinctions must therefore be drawn between those provisions of a Directive which are mandatory and those which are permissive, and between the provisions of the directive itself and the action which a Member State might take pursuant to the Directive.

[93] Case 171/78 *Commission* v. *Denmark*, para. 20 of judgment : see above, Chapter 1, para. 66. And see Case 21/79 *Commission* v. *Italy* (1980) 2 C.M.L.R. 613 at p. 627.
[94] Case 124/76 *Moulins et Huilèries de Pont-a-Mousson* [1979] 2 C.M.L.R. 445, at para. 16 of judgment.
[95] Cases 103, 145/77 *Scholten Honig* [1979] 1 C.M.L.R. 675; Case 117/76 *Ruckdeschel* [1979] 2 C.M.L.R. 445.
[96] As the Commission itself emphasised, in the proceedings against France (Case 168/78, above, Chapter 1, para. 38) it would be improper to subordinate the prohibition against fiscal discrimination constituted by Art. 95, a provision having direct effect, to the adoption of *règles d'exècution* by means of Directives under Art. 99.
[97] *e.g.* Dir. 64/221 in relation to Art. 48 of the Treaty : see Case 41/74 *Van Duyn* [1974] E.C.R. 1337.

242     Viewed in this light, the only mandatory provisions in question are that beer must be subject to duty and that that duty may not be less than one-third of any corresponding duty on wine.[98] There is nothing here which must necessarily result in a violation of Article 95. A Member State is, however, permitted by the Directive to determine its own rate of duty for wine (provided this does not exceed the stipulated ratio) or, in the case of Germany and Italy, to exempt certain wines from duty altogether. This permission, it is submitted, is subject to the provisions of Article 95, so that a Member State which exempts wine, or taxes it in relation to beer in such a manner as to afford it a protection against imported beer, will be in contravention of the Treaty, notwithstanding that such action is not prohibited by the Directive.

To this extent, then, it appears that the proposed Directive permits, though it does not expressly require, that beer and wine be taxed in a manner contrary to Article 95 and that such permission may not validly be given to a Member State by means of a directive for the harmonisation of laws. This also points to a major difficulty which may be encountered in the future. If the eventual aim is to achieve a completely harmonised system of excise duties with uniform, or closely approximated, rates of duty, then it must be remembered that such a system would necessarily be of a mandatory nature. It would therefore not be sufficient simply to secure general agreement among the Member States as to the appropriate rates of tax for each category of alcoholic beverages but it would also be necessary to ensure that these rates, in relation to each other, were compatible with the provisions of Article 95 of the Treaty.

### (vi)   The abolition of fiscal frontiers

243     The ultimate aim to abolish fiscal frontiers and the system of border tax adjustments in intra-Community trade has already been discussed in Chapter 2.[99] As has been emphasised, there would seem to be little point in removing these frontiers with respect to value added tax so long as they are required to be retained for excise duties[1] or for other purposes.[2] Thus, parallel progress must be made with respect to both value added tax and to excise duties. To achieve the necessary degree of harmonisation many difficulties will have to be overcome. Much of what has been said in relation to value added tax applies equally to excise duties but the problems associ-

---

[98] This is, of course, an over-simplification : only two Member States are to be permitted not to tax wine, and the one-third figure is approximate.

[99] Above, paras. 136–150.

[1] See the passage quoted from the Deringer Report, at p. 113, above.

[2] *e.g.,* for the administration of the system of monetary compensation under the common agricultural policy.

ated with excise duties may be even more difficult to solve.[3] This appears to be so for a number of reasons.

### (a)  The allocation of tax revenues

As has been suggested, the application of a pure "origin principle" is inappropriate in the case of value added tax since the tax is imposed at the final stage, *i.e.* sale to the consumer. Thus some or all of the tax revenue will accrue to the "destination" country, depending on whether the system adopted allocates tax to the country in which the value is added[4] or follows a modified "destination" principle with a system of accounting and settlement between Member States for tax paid in the exporting country and credited in the importing country. Excise duties, by contrast, are not levied at the retail stage[5] and the abolition of fiscal frontiers would seem to require the adoption of the "origin" principle, so that the products would be taxed in the country of production. This would have serious budgetary consequences for net importing countries, which would no longer derive revenue[6] from tobacco, oil and alcohol imported from other Member States. It would also cause considerable difficulties where dutiable goods are re-exported to third countries.[7]

### (b)  The need for approximation of rates

**244**   Again, as value added tax applies at the retail stage and as the rate then applied determines the total tax burden, a difference in tax rates from one country to another ought not to distort intra-Community trade, except in the case of sales made directly to a consumer resident in another Member State. As suggested,[8] it may consequently be possible to abolish VAT-frontiers without full harmonisation of tax rates, though a greater degree of alignment would be necessary than at present exists. In the case of excise duties virtually complete harmonisation would be essential since the total

---

[3] See, for example, the Neumark Report (p. 76, n. 23), at p. 127, and the Andel Report (p. 101, n. 83) at p. 82.

[4] The *Wertschöpfungslandprinzip,* above, p. 101, n. 83.

[5] *e.g.* the duty on alcohol and wine would be payable when the product was cleared for home use, and on beer when it leaves the brewery. The proposed Directives would permit additional duty to be imposed at the retail stage, *e.g.* on sale in a public house, such a duty involving no border tax adjustments.

[6] Other than that deriving from the VAT. It might, however, be argued that those countries which produce little or no domestic wine and tax it heavily—Denmark, Ireland and the United Kingdom—would no longer need to worry about the rate of tax since they would not receive the revenue anyway. Moreover, they might be compensated by a corresponding increase in revenue from oil exported to other Member States. There may, after all, be some justice in the way nature has allocated her resources!

[7] See above, para. 148.

[8] Above, para. 144.

tax burden[9] would be determined by the rate of duty applicable in the country of production.

## (c)   National diversities

Just as the need to harmonise excise duty rates is greater than is the case with value added tax, the difficulties in agreeing upon a common scale of rates are also more apparent. Rates of excise duty are, generally, much higher[10] and differences between national rates far more extreme.[11] To harmonise rates of duty on alcoholic beverages, for example, at somewhere near the Community mean, would involve massive reductions in revenue and consumer prices in Denmark, Ireland and the United Kingdom and large increases in France and Italy.

## (d)   The selective nature of excise duties

Excise duties are, by their nature, selective, applying only to a restricted number of products, whereas value added tax is intended to be a general tax, applying to almost all products at a uniform rate or, at most, at either a standard or a reduced rate. In the case of excise duties this gives rise to two further problems. First in view of the nature of the products to be taxed, harmonisation of excise duties can only take place within a general framework of harmonisation of legislation and policies applying to other sectors of economic life.[12] Secondly, it involves the making of certain value judgements as to what should be the appropriate level of taxation on each product. Are wine and beer luxuries or necessaries? Should smoking and drinking be discouraged by high taxes? Should the tax system be employed in an attempt to reduce dependance upon oil as a source of energy? And what should be the proper relationship between the taxes on these products and those affecting other, competing, products, particularly in view of the prohibition upon discrimination contained in Article 95 of the Treaty?

## C.   TAXES AFFECTING THE PRIVATE IMPORTATION OF GOODS

**245**   Under the value added tax system the importation of goods constitutes a chargeable event[13] and, in the case of excise duties, countervailing duties are

---

[9] Apart from the VAT element and any special retail duty (above n. 5), neither of which would be permitted to discriminate on the basis of national origin.

[10] In the case of petrol, for example, excise duties account for between 48 and 72 per cent. of the selling price : expressed in *ad valorem* terms, this is equivalent to a tax rate of from 92 to 257 per cent.

[11] See App. A, Table 4.

[12] Notably agricultural and energy policy : on this point, see M. Prouzet, "La Politique de la CEE en matière d'Harmonisation des Impôts Indirects" (1972) 49 R.D.I.D.C. 151.

[13] Dir. 77/388, Art. 2 : see above, Chap. 2. para. 116.

normally imposed upon imported products which are subject to those duties. Thus, where goods are imported privately into a Member State from another Member State, there is a likelihood of double taxation. The goods will have been purchased from a retailer in the exporting state and will have borne value added tax[14] and excise duty there and will then be subjected to further taxes on entry into the importing state, unless exempted by reason of a duty-free allowance. A variety of measures have been introduced, or proposed, in order to remove this element of double-taxation and to harmonise the levels of duty-free allowances accorded by each Member State.

### (i) Goods imported by travellers

**246**     The first measure to be adopted was the Directive of May 28, 1969,[15] on the harmonisation of provisions laid down by law, regulation or administrative action relating to exemption from turnover tax and excise duty on imports in international travel. As recited in the Preamble, it was considered desirable, even before the abolition of imposition of tax on importation and remission of tax on exportation, that the populations of the Member States should become more strongly conscious of the reality of the Common Market and also that double-taxation should be avoided or minimised. The Directive provides that goods of a non-commercial character (defined as goods for personal or family use or intended as presents) imported in the personal luggage of a traveller[16] shall be exempted from turnover tax and excise duties, up to a value of 50 units of account.[17] This limit has since been increased and now stands at 180 units of account.[18] Personal effects, *e.g.* a traveller's camera, which are imported temporarily or are reimported after temporary absence, are not to be taken into account for this purpose. In addition the Directive prescribes the quantities of tobacco, alcoholic beverages, perfumes, coffee and tea which may be imported free of tax and duty by travellers,[19] the value of which is not to be taken into account for the purposes of the general exemption. A reduction in the duty-free

---

[14] In some cases, goods purchased by a visitor, on production of a passport or other satisfactory evidence of non-residence, may have had the VAT remitted.

[15] Dir. 69/169. It should be noted that this Dir. was adopted, pursuant to Art. 99, without prior consultation of the Parliament and ESC. These bodies have been consulted on all subsequent measures. See the discussion of this issue, above, at para. 206.

[16] *i.e.* a visitor entering a Member State or a resident returning from abroad.

[17] This amount may be reduced for children. In the case of importation from a third country, an amount of 25 u.a. was fixed. If the total value of such goods exceeds this amount the exemption still applies, but the value of an individual item cannot be split.

[18] Dir. 78/1032. It had previously been raised to 125 UA, by Dir. 72/230. A proposed fifth Directive would further increase the limit to 210 UA : O.J. 1979, C 318/5.

[19] These limits were raised by Dir. 72/230 and, again, by Dir. 78/1032. Provision is made, in Dir. 78/1032, for the amounts expressed in the new EUA to be rounded-off, within limits, when converted into national currencies. The tobacco, alcohol and coffee exemptions do not apply to children under the age of 15 years.

allowances may be made in the case of frontier-zone residents and workers and international transportation workers.

The duty-free exemptions are thus largely standardised throughout the Community.[20] Initially, some difficulty was caused by the application, by some Member States, of a "24 hour rule," but after the Commission had initiated proceedings under Art. 169 of the Treaty this practice was abandoned.[21] A more serious problem related to Article 6 of the Directive. The aim of the Directive was to eliminate, or mitigate, the double-taxation of goods, rather than to render them tax-free. Article 6 therefore required Member States to take appropriate measures to avoid remission of tax being granted for travellers residing in another Member State who would benefit from the exemptions on importation into their own countries. This gave rise to administrative difficulties[22] and the Commission was asked to re-examine the question.[23] As a result, Article 6 was amended,[24] so that it is now permitted to remit, in retail sales to residents of other Member States, value added tax, but not excise duties.[25] This is without prejudice to any rules which may apply in duty-free shops at airports and on board aircraft.

### (ii)    Small consignments of goods

247    A further Directive was adopted, on December 19, 1974,[26] concerning the tax reliefs to be allowed on the importation of goods in small consignments of a non-commercial character within the Community. It was considered that tax impediments hindering the despatch of packages of goods between private individuals in different Member States constitutes an obstacle to the creation of an economic market with characteristics similar to those of a domestic market. To grant relief from taxation on importation would remove the element of double-taxation, would promote personal and family contacts between private persons in different Member States and constitutes a necessary corollary to the freedom of movement and of establishment of persons within the Community.

The Directive therefore provides that small consignments of goods, of a non-commercial character, which have been acquired within the Community subject to the normal taxes and are not sent for payment, shall be allowed relief from turnover tax and excise duty on importation up to a

---

[20] Dir. 78/1032 provides that under no circumstances may the limits be exceeded. However, a number of derogations have been permitted, notably to Denmark : see Act of Accession, Annex XI(V) (1), and Dirs. 76/134, 77/82, 77/800, 78/1032.

[21] See (EC) Fifth General Report (1971), pp. 80, 106 : Sixth General Report (1972) p. 68.

[22] See the examples given in the Memmel and Koch Reports to the Parliament : E.P. Docs. 248/71.

[23] (EC) Fourth General Report (1970), p. 40.

[24] By Dir. 72/230 and, again, by Dir. 78/1032.

[25] The remission of tax is subject to a number of conditions and may not be made in respect of items whose value exceeds the prescribed limits.

[26] Dir. 74/651.

value of 40 units of account[27] for each consignment. This exemption may be reduced or excluded in the case of certain products, *e.g.* alcohol or perfume.

### (iii)  Goods imported from third countries

**248**     For administrative reasons the harmonisation of tax-free allowances in respect of goods imported from non-member states was also felt to be desirable. In particular, the psychological gains derived from granting tax exemptions for imports from other Member States would have been substantially lessened if it had been permitted to grant larger exemptions for travellers returning from third countries.[28] Directive 69/169 consequently prescribed the exemptions, in terms of value and quantities of specified articles, to apply to similar goods imported in the personal luggage of travellers from non-member states.[29] These limits are lower than the corresponding limits in intra-Community travel.[30]

Unlike the 1969 Directive, Directive 74/651 (on the transmission of small consignments of goods) contained no exemptions in the case of packages received from third countries. However, this is now provided for in Directive 78/1035.[31] Moreover, since goods entering from third countries may be subject to import duties (customs duty or agricultural charges), corresponding exemptions from such duties are provided in the case of non-commercial goods contained in travellers' personal luggage or sent in small consignments.[32] Thus, the exemptions for goods coming from third countries in travellers' luggage are governed, as to taxes,[33] by Directives 69/169 and 78/1033 and, as to import duties, by Regulations 1544/69 and 3061/78 : goods sent in small consignments are governed, as to taxes, by Directive 78/1035 and, as to import duties, by Regulation 3060/78.

### (iv)  Temporary visitors and immigrants

**249**     Normally, personal goods imported into a country by a temporary visitor

---

[27] Raised to 60 EUA by Dir. 78/1034. Rounding-off and adjustments for changes in national conversion rates is provided for.

[28] Thus Dir. 78/1035, Art. 2(3) provides that "under no circumstances shall tax exemption granted for small consignments from non-member countries exceed that applicable to small consignments sent within the Community." It is strange, therefore, that "personal luggage" is defined more widely in the case of travellers coming from third countries : see Dir. 78/1033, Art. 1(3).

[29] Dir. 69/169, Arts. 1 and 4.

[30] They have recently been revised by Dir. 78/1033.

[31] Of December 19, 1978.

[32] Regs. 3060 and 3061/78, of December 19, 1978 (the latter amending Reg. 1544/69). It is significant that, given a choice of instrument—the Regs. were adopted pursuant to Arts. 28, 43 and 235 of the Treaty—these measures were adopted by way of Regulation rather than by Directives. It is also rather confusing that Dirs. 69/169, 72/230, 78/1032, 78/1033 and 78/1035 were adopted pursuant to Art. 99 alone, whereas Dirs. 74/651 and 78/1034 were adopted pursuant to Arts. 99 and 100.

[33] VAT and excise duties.

who is in transit or on a holiday or business trip are not subject to tax or duty in the country visited.[34] Problems do arise, however, in the case of extended stays or where a person comes to settle, more or less permanently, in a country, bringing with him goods which will normally already have been taxed in the country of origin. Two proposals of the Commission attempt to deal with these problems.[35]

The first of these proposes tax exemptions for certain means of transport—motor vehicles (other than commercial vehicles), trailers, caravans, pleasure boats, private aircraft, bicycles and riding horses—temporarily[36] imported into one Member State from another. It is proposed that such means of transport be exempted from turnover tax, excise duty and other taxes, provided that the importer has his principal residence in another Member State and employs the means of transport for his private use or for a business use, other than for hiring the vehicle out for reward or for the transportation of goods.[37]

The second proposal is concerned with similar tax exemptions for personal property which is not of a commercial or speculative nature, on the permanent importation from another Member State by an individual intending to take up residence in the country of importation. The property must be for the personal use of the individual or members of his family and must have been acquired in another Member State and not been subject to any exemption or refund of tax granted because the property was being exported, nor have been acquired for importation. These conditions are to be deemed to be satisfied if the article shows signs of use and was acquired at least three months (or six months, in the case of motor vehicles, boats, aircraft, etc),[38] previously. Somewhat similar exemptions are proposed in the case of personal property imported on marriage or acquired by inheritance. An avowed object of the proposal is, of course, to remove obstacles to the free movement of persons and to allow workers migrating within the Community to take their personal effects with them.

These proposals have not yet been adopted by the Council though the Parliament and the Commission have urged prompt action to put an end to the numerous complaints which have been received from individuals.[39]

---

[34] This appears to be assumed by Art. 3 of Dir. 69/169.

[35] Proposed Directives, submitted to the Council on October 30, 1975 : O.J. 1975, C 267/8, 11.

[36] This is defined as being for a period not exceeding 6 months in any 12 months.

[37] "Goods" do not include portable tools, sales literature or trade samples, which would similarly be exempt.

[38] The inclusion of such vehicles makes the further requirement, that the article be imported for the purpose of installation in a dwelling, rather curious—see the comments of the ESC, which also considered the proposal "very generous" and open to abuse : O.J. 1976, C 131/49.

[39] See EPWQ 1019/78 : O.J. 1979, C 118/2. The Council resumed examination of these proposals during 1979.

### (v)  Duty-free sales

**250**     One of the main objectives of the measures and proposals considered
above has been to eliminate the double-taxation which may occur when
goods, which have been taxed at the time of purchase, are subjected to
further taxation on importation into another Member State. The intention of
the exemptions is not to render such goods entirely duty-free,[40] and it would
seem to follow from this that the practice of making tax-free sales in duty-
free shops at airports and on board aircraft and ferries should be dis-
continued, at least in the case of intra-Community travel. The Commission
did submit a proposal to this effect in 1972,[41] but this encountered considerable opposition[42] and has since been withdrawn,[43] though the Parliament
has urged the Commission to submit fresh proposals.[44]

### (vi)  Conclusions

**251**     Relief from double-taxation is always to be welcomed and the measures
discussed above constitute a small but significant step towards the creation
of a single market so far as private individuals are concerned and doubtless
have a valuable psychological effect without causing any appreciable reduction in tax revenue. In practice, travellers are rarely checked at frontiers at
all[45] and it may be questioned whether it is really necessary to impose limits
at all for bona fide travellers.[46]

This, of course, raises again the question of the abolition of fiscal
frontiers.[47] It will be observed that, within the limits of the "personal goods"
Directives, the "origin" principle of taxation applies and tax frontiers disappear.[48] The real objection to increasing the existing limits, or abolishing
them entirely, relates to excise duties, since these apply specifically to the
types of product commonly imported by individuals, frequently constitute
the major portion of the total tax burden and vary greatly from one country

---

[40]  Though Art. 6 of Dir. 69/169 (as amended) would seem to facilitate this in the case of
VAT.
[41]  Proposed Directive, transmitted to the Council on September 22, 1972 : J.O. 1972, C
113/18.
[42]  It has been rumoured that some airlines make enough profit on their duty-free sales to
balance the losses they make on carrying passengers!
[43]  O.J. 1978, C 33/4.
[44]  O.J. 1977, C 133/44 and see EPWQ 577/78 and 1057/78 : O.J. 1978, C 307/14; O.J.
1979, C 172/6 (which refers to the practice of taking "duty-free excursions" on cross-channel
ferries!). A new proposal has been submitted concerning exemption procedures applicable to
the stores and provisions of ships, aircraft and international trains : O.J. 1980, C 31/10.
[45]  It is the Commission's policy that travellers should be checked at internal frontiers only
in exceptional cases : (EC) Bull. 8–68, p. 32; 4–72, p. 58.
[46]  As Mr. Dondelinger points out, real smugglers operate on a totally different scale :
EPWQ 623/77, O.J. 1978, C 30/17.
[47]  See above, Chapter 2, para. 136.
[48]  On this point, see P. Derouin, *"La Taxe sur la valeur ajoutée dans la Communauté
Economique Européenne"* (1977), at pp. 378–386.

to another. In one sense, the exemptions may be seen as an incentive towards the alignment of rates of excise duties[49] : on the other hand, it may be argued that they serve only to distract attention from the basic problem of harmonising excise duty rates.[50]

## D.   TAXES AFFECTING TRANSPORT

**252**   The authors of the Treaty regarded the creation of a common transport policy as one of the "foundations" of the Community,[51] comparable in importance with agriculture and with the free movement of goods, persons, services and capital. Article 75 empowers the Council to lay down common rules applicable to international transport to or from the territory of a member State or passing across the territory of a Member State, the conditions under which non-resident carriers may operate transport services within a Member State, and any other appropriate provision. It is further provided, by Article 76, that no Member State may, without the unanimous approval of the Council, make its existing provisions governing transport less favourable in their direct or indirect effect on carriers of other Member States as compared with its own nationals. This, therefore, prohibits the introduction of any *new* measures which discriminate against carriers from other Member States (and would seem to apply to any discriminatory tax provision), though action is required in order to abolish those discriminations already in existence when the Treaty came into force. However, as the *Schöttle* case[52] demonstrates, in certain instances a tax imposed on a carrier may be considered to be a tax upon the goods carried and be consequently within the scope of Article 95.

**253**     A set of policy guidelines was adopted by a Decision of the Council[53] taken in 1965. This provided that, with effect from the beginning of 1967, double taxation of motor vehicles when such vehicles are being used for carriage in a Member State other than that in which they are registered shall be abolished and that the provisions regarding the duty-free admission of fuel contained in the fuel tanks of commercial motor vehicles and inland waterway vessels shall be standardised.[54] With regard to the double taxation of commercial motor vehicles, the Commission had submitted a proposed Regulation in 1964,[55] whereby such vehicles would be required to be registered in one Member State only. However, it proved impossible to reach

---

[49] See the comments of the ESC : J.O. 1972, C 29/17.
[50] *Cf.* the opinion of the Parliament : O.J. 1977, C 133/44.
[51] Art. 3(e) and Arts. 74–84.
[52] Case 20/76, [1977] E.C.R. 247; see Chap. 1, paras. 27–28, above.
[53] Dec. 65/271 of May 13, 1965.
[54] *Ibid.* Art. 1.
[55] The text is set out in (EEC) Bull. S. 5–64, pp. 27 *et seq.*

agreement on the proposal, which was finally withdrawn in 1976.[56] As to the duty-free admission of fuel contained in fuel tanks of commercial vehicles, a Directive was adopted in 1968[57] providing for the minimum duty-free admission of 50 litres of fuel. A proposal to increase this limit to 100 litres was submitted in 1974[58] but has yet to be adopted. The 1965 Decision also provided[59] that the common system of value added tax should apply to the carriage of goods by rail, road and inland waterway[60] and should replace specific taxes applying to such carriage.[61]

**254** This apart, little real progress has been made. In a memorandum to the Council on the Common Transport Policy,[62] the Commission pointed out that the large variations in taxation of transportation, both as regards licence and registration duties and taxes on fuel, create obstacles to the free movement of goods and distort the conditions of competition.[63] This raises the issue of the harmonisation of excise duties on oil[64] and of the desirability of using taxation as an instrument for charging for the use of transport infrastructures, which may in turn involve environmental questions. A more precise programme was set out in the Commission's communication of October 25, 1973,[65] in which it was recommended that the same rate of value added tax be applied to all modes of transportation to avoid distortion of competition and that specific taxes be harmonised and used as instruments of transport policy and be linked with the question of harmonising duties on oil. In line with this programme, a proposed Directive was submitted, in 1971,[66] providing for a common framework of tariff systems for usage of transport infrastructures. The aim of the proposal is to promote the optimum utilisation of existing infrastructures and to ensure that costs of construction and operation are borne by the users. This would require the adjustment of national tax systems for commercial vehicles and a deter-

[56] O.J. 1976, C 130/3, cf. the proposed Directive relating to the temporary importation by visitors of non-commercial vehicles submitted in 1975 : O.J. 1975, C 267/8, above, para. 249. A proposed Directive is also being prepared, relating to motor vehicle taxes payable by persons in border regions : see the Commission's reply to EPWQ 373/77, O.J. 1977, C 259/20.
[57] Dir. 68/297 of July 19, 1968.
[58] O.J. 1974, C 104/56. The Parliament urged that all fuel contained in fuel tanks be admitted free, thus avoiding the need for measurement : O.J. 1974, C 155/78. Dir. 78/1033 (above, para. 249) provides for duty-free admission of fuel up to 10 litres in cars of visitors from non-member states. See also the new proposal concerning stores and provisions in international travel (above, n. 44).
[59] Arts. 3 and 4.
[60] See the Sixth VAT Directive : Dir. 77/388, Arts. 9, 15, 16.
[61] See Case 9/70 *Grad* [1970] E.C.R. 825, the effect of which is to render such specific taxes invalid.
[62] (EEC) Bull. S. 3–67.
[63] For recent details, see EPWQ 397/78 and 164/79 : O.J. 1979, C 5/3 and C 178/13. It has been asserted that the total tax burden on a heavy vehicle of 16 tons, covering 50,000 km. a year, is nine times higher in Germany than in Italy.
[64] Above, paras. 232, 233.
[65] *Common Transport Policy : Objectives and Programme* : (EC) Bull. S. 16–73.
[66] J.O. 1971, C 62/15. See also the proposed Directive, submitted on July 17, 1968, concerning national tax systems on public vehicles (*e.g.* buses) : J.O. 1968, C 95/41.

mination of the proper relationship between taxes on fuel and specific registration taxes on vehicles, based upon engine size or axle weight. It would appear that the Council has now reached agreement in principle on the proposal, though still with some reservations, and that adoption may be anticipated in the near future.[67]

The question of taxes in transport has also recently been considered in the Economic and Social Committee,[68] which recommends that, apart from the value added tax, the only taxes on transport should be the duty on fuels and the motor vehicle registration tax, though it advocates that in the case of private motor vehicles the complete charge for the use of roads should be included in the duty on fuels.[69] It would therefore recommend the abolition of road tolls, which are regarded as tantamount to the erection of new barriers, though in the view of the Commission such tolls are not incompatible with the aims of the Treaty so long as all users are treated equally.[70]

### E.   TAXATION AND THE CAPITAL MARKET

#### (i)   The Treaty provisions

**255**      One of the fundamental aims of the Community, as set out in the Treaty, is the abolition as between Member States of obstacles to freedom of movement for persons, services and capital.[71] The free movement of persons and services includes freedom of establishment : the right to take up and pursue activities as self-employed persons and to set up and manage undertakings, in particular companies and firms, in another Member State under the same conditions as are laid down for nationals of that state.[72] And the free movement of capital requires the abolition of all restrictions on the movement of capital belonging to persons resident in Member States and of any discrimination based on the nationality or on the place of residence of the parties or on the place where such capital is invested.[73]

Obstacles to such free movement may take a variety of forms — provisions of company law, the licensing of particular occupations or professions, restrictions upon the exportation of currency, etc.—some of which may be fiscal in nature. For example, the discriminatory taxation of foreign-owned businesses or of foreign-source investment income may constitute such an

---

[67]  See the reply to EPWQ 410/79 : O.J. 1979, C 275/10.

[68]  Fredersdorf Report, paras. 4.1.4., 4.2.4. : Doc. CES 846/78.

[69]  A standard registration fee, regardless of the size of the vehicle, favours larger vehicles (and would be contrary to the aim of energy conservation), whilst a progressive scale of fees only accomplishes the same purpose as the tax on fuel and could, perhaps, operate in a discriminatory manner, e.g. by discouraging the importation of larger cars into a country which produces only small cars.

[70]  EPWQ 410/79, above, n. 67.

[71]  Art. 3(c).

[72]  Art. 52.

[73]  Art. 67.

obstacle, as may the fact that the same business or income is taxed in two or more Member States in such a way as to impose a burden of double taxation.

**256**    The Title of the Treaty which is addressed to the free movement of persons, services and capital[74] does not expressly concern itself with obstacles of a fiscal nature and contains no provisions dealing with taxation as such. Nevertheless, certain of these provisions may be applicable : discriminatory taxation might fall within the prohibitions on discrimination contained in Articles 52 and 67, and the general powers bestowed on the Council to take measures to remove obstacles and restrictions to free movement could properly be exercised in respect of obstacles or restrictions of a fiscal nature.[75] Recourse may also be had to other provisions of the Treaty.[76] Article 100 provides a basis for the adoption of Directives for the approximation of legislation or administrative provisions which directly affect the establishment or functioning of the Common Market and, since differences in national tax laws affecting enterprises and capital may create distortions in the conditions of competition, resort may also be had to Article 101. In addition, Article 220 requires that Member States shall, so far as is necessary, enter into negotiations with a view to securing for the benefit of their nationals the abolition of double taxation within the Community and Article 221 provides that Member States shall accord nationals of other Member States the same treatment as their own nationals as regards participation in the capital of companies or firms.[77]

### (ii)  The Segré Report

**257**    The desirability of harmonising taxes affecting business profits was recognised at an early stage in the development of the Community. In particular, it was perceived that such taxes may distort the conditions of competition between enterprises located in different Member States. The Neumark Committee[78] recommended that the first phase of tax harmonisation should deal not only with indirect taxation but also with the methods of taxing dividends and interest and with the problem of double taxation, and that the second phase should include the reform of systems of company taxation.[79] The emphasis here was essentially upon competition but in 1963 the Com-

---

[74] Title III : Arts. 48–73.
[75] Notably Art. 54(3) (c), (f) and (h), and Art. 69.
[76] Generally, see P. M. Storm "Companies and the Common Market" in *Branches and Subsidiaries in the Common Market : Legal and Tax Aspects* (2nd ed.) (European Association for Legal and Fiscal Studies, 1976) : U. Anschutz, "Harmonisation of Direct Taxes in the European Economic Community" (1972) 13 Harv. Int. Law Jo., 1.
[77] Art. 221 would appear to be capable of producing direct effects and might be invoked against discriminatory tax treatment of foreign investors.
[78] Report of the Fiscal and Financial Committee in *The EEC Reports on Tax Harmonisation* : see above, Chapter 2, paras. 109 *et seq.*
[79] *Ibid.* pp. 118–120, 139–141, 154.

mission appointed a committee of experts to study specifically the problems confronting the establishment of an integrated capital market within the Community. This committee, under the chairmanship of Professor Claudio Segré, delivered its report in 1966.[80]

The committee considered a wide range of subjects—company laws, stock exchange regulations, exchange controls and the like—but also dealt extensively with fiscal obstacles to the free movement of capital.[81] It concluded that the realisation and proper functioning of a European capital market require that fiscal systems do not obstruct the creation of conditions similar to those of an internal market. This neutrality will be achieved when tax considerations no longer influence the choice of location of investments or transactions, nor the choice of an investor between direct investment and investment through an intermediary. The chief obstacles to the attainment of the desired neutrality were identified as the international double taxation of investment income, the existence of tax advantages or disadvantages affecting investment in certain countries and the different attitudes of Member States with regard to the fiscal treatment of investment income payable to non-residents and to corporate investors. The following solutions were proposed:[82]

  (i)  the replacement of existing bi-lateral double taxation agreements by a multi-lateral Community convention;
 (ii)  the extension of tax credits (for tax paid by corporations) to non-resident shareholders;
(iii)  the abolition of retention at source of tax on interest payments, or the use of common rates of withholding tax;
 (iv)  the harmonisation of tax rules governing institutional investors;
  (v)  the removal of discrimination against the use of financial intermediaries; and
 (vi)  the harmonisation of taxes on the formation of capital.[83]

The report recognised, however,[84] that to the extent that differences in the incidence of taxation have a permanent character their effect upon the functioning of the capital market may be minimal: the market will normally

---

[80] *Le Developpement d'un Marché européen des capitaux* : rapport d'un groupe d'experts constitué par la Commission de la CEE (Brussels, 1966), referred to hereafter as the *Segré Report*. For a review of the fiscal aspects of the report, see "The Taxation of Dividends and Interest in the EEC and resulting obstacles to Free Capital Movement" (1967) 7 E.T. 212 and J. Van Hoorn Jr., "Les obstacles fiscaux aux émissions internationales de titres de sociétés et a leur négociation," in *Les Emissions de Titres de Sociétés en Europe et aux Etats-Unis* (Institut d'Etudes Européennes, Université Libre de Bruxelles, 1970). For a more general appraisal, see P. Leleux, "European Integration and the reconciliation of Legislation," in *Ten Years of European Integration* (papers presented at a colloquium of the CEDE, Montréal, 1968), at pp. 37 *et seq.*

[81] Especially in Chap. 14, which contains a comprehensive review of the different national tax legislations.

[82] *Ibid.* pp. 34 *et seq.*

[83] A Directive to this effect had already been proposed by the Commission : see below.

[84] At pp. 310 *et seq.*

adjust to such differences so that, for example, higher taxes upon interest or dividends may be compensated for by higher interest rates or larger returns on capital.[85] It therefore recommended that Member States should in future refrain from unilateral modifications of the tax incidence—a recommendation which has certainly not been generally observed.[86]

### (iii)  The Commission's programme for the harmonisation of direct taxes

**258**   Many of the recommendations in the Segré Report were adopted by the Commission in the following year when it formulated a programme for the harmonisation of direct taxes.[87] In the long term the Commission envisaged that tax revenue would be derived, in all Member States, from three major sources : (1) the value added tax, harmonised to the necessary degree, and some major excise duties also harmonised; (2) a general tax on company profits, having the same structure throughout the Community and based upon broadly similar methods of assessment and rates; and (3) a single comprehensive personal income tax which would differ from one Member State to another for a long time to come. More urgently, action was perceived as being necessary to attain the following objectives:

**259**   **(a) Liberalisation of capital movements.** Taxation constitutes a major obstacle to the free movement of capital and the interpenetration of capital markets and is one of the main causes of "abnormal" capital movements, *i.e.* movements springing from other than the traditional economic or financial considerations. In part this is due to the simultaneous or combined application of the tax rules of two or more countries to one and the same transaction, resulting in double or multiple taxation or in the creation of tax havens, but the mere existence in certain Member States of tax rules favouring certain groups of taxpayers or types of investment more than do the corresponding rules in other countries may also have a distorting effect. The long-term solution lies in the alignment and harmonisation of national tax systems to create conditions of complete fiscal neutrality. As a first step, however, the Commission considered it necessary to deal with the following matters:

(1)  The systems of withholding tax charged on dividends and interest;
(2)  Methods of reducing the economic double taxation of dividends;

---

[85] Thus it would seem that the integration of capital markets and the harmonisation of taxes affecting investment decisions can only properly take place within a comprehensive programme for economic and monetary union : see P. Wooley, "Integration of Capital Markets," in G. Denton (ed.), *Economic and Monetary Union in Europe* (1974), Chap. 3. Conversely, the creation of a single capital market would lead to tax-induced movements of capital in the absence of harmonisation of taxes : see P. B. Musgrave "Harmonisation of direct business taxes : a case study," in Shoup, *Fiscal Harmonisation*, Chap. 10.

[86] Arguably, Art. 102 might apply to such modifications.

[87] Memorandum to the Council of June 26, 1967 : (EEC) Bull. S. 8–67. See also the further memorandum, on taxes affecting the capital market, of March 5, 1969 : (EC) Bull. 5–69, p. 21.

    (3) Discrepancies in the tax arrangements applicable to holding companies; and

    (4) The tax treatment of investments handled by financial intermediaries, in particular by the various types of investment company.

**260**  **(b) The removal of fiscal obstacles to industrial and combinations.** Mergers between companies in different Member States and the acquisition by one company of a holding in a company situated in another Member State should not be impeded by fiscal considerations. Fiscal neutrality, as between purely domestic and intra-Community combinations, should be sought, both as to the tax costs of merger transactions and as to the subsequent treatment of related enterprises.[88]

**(c) The approximation of the bases of assessment for taxes on company profits.** Distortion of the conditions of competition and of capital movements may be caused not only by differences in the systems and rates of taxing company profits and distributions but also by differences in the methods of computing those profits for tax purposes. In particular, the Commission considered harmonisation to be necessary in such matters as the rules governing the depreciation of capital assets, the valuation of stocks and the granting of investment incentives.

These matters were listed, by the Commission, as questions to be solved before July 1, 1968. More than a decade later solutions (though several have been proposed) have yet to be agreed upon and adopted.

### (iv)  Taxes on company capital

**261**    Even before the publication of the Segré Report and of its own programme for the harmonisation of direct taxes, the Commission had decided to press ahead with proposals on what it termed "indirect" taxes on capital movements. These it divided into two categories—those on capital contributions and those on transactions in securities. It is questionable whether such taxes should properly be described as "indirect," at least as that term is used in Article 99 of the Treaty.[89] Certainly such taxes would not seem to be "indirect" for the purposes of Articles 96 and 98.[90] Nevertheless, the problem of classification can be, and was, avoided by recourse to both Articles 99 and 100 as a juridical basis for harmonisation.[91]

---

[88] *e.g.* transfers of profits and losses, payment of inter-corporate dividends, etc.

[89] This point is considered by R. Oberson, *Harmonisation fiscale dans la CEE : droits de timbre et droits d'apport* (1972), Chap. 1, and see also the Hesse Report, Commission: Série Concurrence-Rapprochement des Législations, No. 13 (1970), at p. 18.

[90] See Case 45/64 *Commission* v. *Italy* [1965] E.C.R. 857 and the comments in Chap. 1, 26–28, 91, above.

[91] See the report of the Parliament's internal market committee (the Seuffert Report) : E.P. Docs. 1965–66, No. 64, at p. 1.

(a)  *The Commission's proposed Directive*

**262**     In 1964 the Commission published and submitted to the Council a proposal for a Directive concerning indirect taxes on capital contributions,[92] with the intention of preparing a further proposal dealing with taxes on transactions in securities. Priority was given to taxes on capital contributions because it was felt that these have the most perceptible effects upon the free movement of capital. Under the national laws then existing,[93] there were various instances of double taxation and of discrimination. Stamp duties might be charged when foreign securities were offered or issued on the home market, without any refund of duty paid in the home country of the issuing company, and in some cases the bases of assessment, rates of duty and special regulations varied according to the nationality of the company or security. Differences in these rates and in the rates of duty might influence how[94] and where capital should be raised.

The Commission considered various methods of dealing with these problems and would clearly have preferred to abolish entirely all duties on capital contributions, stamp duties on securities and similar taxes,[95] though such a solution was regarded as being unacceptable to some Member States.[96] Instead, the Commission proposed that stamp duties on securities representing a company's own share capital or loan capital should be abolished, whatever the country of issue, and that capital duties be maintained (at least for the time being) but be harmonised at as low a level as possible. As the Commission explained:

"If shares and similar securities issued by residents of Member States are to move freely throughout the Community without countervailing charges being levied at national frontiers, care must be taken to ensure that they are all taxed in the same degree, irrespective of their origin. In other words, firms seeking capital in any one Member State must not be placed at a disadvantage, even on their home market, compared with firms in other Member States where taxes are lower."[97]

(b)  *The capital duty Directive*

**263**     With some amendments, the proposed Directive was adopted by the

---

[92] Proposal transmitted on December 16, 1964. The text and an explanatory memorandum were published in (EEC) Bull. S. 2–65, pp. 8 *et seq.*

[93] See R. Oberson, (*op. cit.* above, n. 89) Chap. 2, and the Seuffert Report (above, n. 91).

[94] *e.g.* share capital or loan capital.

[95] This solution had also been favoured by the Neumark Committee, *The EEC Reports on Tax Harmonisation*, pp. 131–132.

[96] As pointed out in the Seuffert Report, however, these taxes had minimal budgetary significance : in no Member State did the revenue amount to much more than one-half of 1 per cent. of total tax revenue.

[97] (EEC) Bull. S. 2–65, p. 10.

Council in 1969.[98] The Directive provides that Member States shall charge on contributions of capital to capital companies a harmonised duty, to be known as "capital duty."[99] Transactions subject to capital duty are to be taxable only in the Member State in whose territory the effective centre of management of the company is situated at the time when such transactions take place.[1] "Capital company" is defined in the Directive[2] to include the various types of share- and limited-liability companies and other types of company, firm, association or legal person whose shares or assets may be dealt in on a stock exchange or, if they operate for profit, whose members are entitled to dispose of their shares to third parties without prior authorisation and are only responsible for the debts of the enterprise to the extent of their shares.[3] Member States are also free to impose the duty on any other company, firm, association or legal person operating for a profit.[4] Chargeable transactions include[5] the formation of a capital company, the conversion of some other company, firm, association or legal person into a capital company, an increase in the capital of a capital company by the contribution of assets of any kind or an increase in the assets of the company by a contribution of assets in return for voting or other participating rights,[6] and the transfer from a third country to a Member State of the effective centre of management or registered office of a company, etc., which is considered in that state to be a capital company or a similar transfer from one Member State to another where the company, etc., is considered to be a capital company in the latter state but not in the former. The formation of a capital company does not include the conversion of a capital company into another type of capital company, the transfer of the centre of management or registered office from one Member State to another of a company, etc., which is considered to be a capital company in both states, or any change in the constitution or objects of a capital company or extension in its period of existence.[7] The intention of these provisions is thus to ensure that a particular contribution of capital is taxed only once. Member States are further permitted to apply the capital duty to certain other increases of

---

[98] Dir. 69/335 of July 17, 1969. For a detailed examination, see R. Oberson (*op. cit.* above, n. 89) Chap. 3 and see also P. Leleux and G. Hutchings, in *Les Emissions de Titres* ... (above, n. 80), Part V, Chaps. 1 and 2.

[99] Dir. 69/335, Art. 1.

[1] *Ibid.* Art. 2. If the effective centre of management is situated in a non-member state but the registered office is within a Member State, the transaction is taxable in the country of the registered office. If both centre of management and registered office are situated outside the Community, the supply of fixed or working capital to a branch within a member state may be taxed by that State.

[2] *Ibid.* Art. 3(1), as amended by the Act of Accession, Annex I (VI)(1).

[3] Certain types of limited partnership are consequently within the definition.

[4] Art. 3(2).

[5] Art. 4(1).

[6] It would seem that a gift of assets is not a chargeable transaction : see J. G. Monroe and R. S. Nock, "Stamp Duties" (1973) B.T.R. 368, 377.

[7] Art. 4(3).

capital or assets, *e.g.* by capitalisation of profits or reserves or by certain types of loan which have the same function as an increase in capital or carry participating rights.[8]

**264**    Capital duty is charged upon the actual value of the assets contributed by the members of a company on the formation of a capital company or on an increase of its capital or assets.[9] In computing this value, there is deducted any liability assumed or expense borne by the company as a result of the contribution. Such a liability must be an actual, quantifiable, liability and not merely a potential unascertained, liability. Thus in a recent case referred to the Court,[10] a Danish company claimed that, in determining the actual value of assets transferred from an existing business to the company (which was formed to take over the business), it ought to be entitled to deduct from the value of stocks and orders transferred an amount representing the potential liability to tax on its profits which could be anticipated to arise when those stocks were sold and the orders were fulfilled.[11] This claim was contested by the Danish government, which maintained that there was no way of measuring such an alleged potential tax liability, which had not yet arisen and might never arise. In the view of the Commission sums deductible may only be taken into consideration to the extent to which the national law itself treats them as being of such a kind as to be regarded as "liabilities or expenses" and, thus, a tax which under national law is merely "potential" cannot be a debt which is ascertained and payable and which ranks as a liability or expense. The Court upheld these latter contentions and declared:

> "The need . . . to base the taxation of capital which has been raised on criteria which are objective and uniform within the Community in fact precludes the book value of the assets contributed and also of potential tax liabilities chargeable on the profits of the company from being taken into consideration."[12]

As originally adopted, paragraph two of Article 5 of the Directive provided that the amount on which duty is payable should not in any event be less

---

[8]  Art. 4(1).

[9]  Art. 5(1). In the case of conversion into a capital company or transfer of the effective centre of management or registered office, duty is charged on the value of the assets at the time of such conversion or transfer. Special rules apply to those transactions which may be charged under Art. 4(2).

[10]  Case 161/78 *Conradsen* [1980] 1 C.M.L.R. 121 : see the note by H. Rasmussen in (1979) 4 E.L. Rev. 488.

[11]  Such a situation may easily arise where there is a "roll-over" of unrealised profits or gains when a business is incorporated, *i.e.* instead of the business being taxed on the difference between the original cost of the assets and their value at the time of incorporation, the assets are deemed (for income tax purposes) to have been disposed of by the business, and acquired by the company, at cost, so that the tax is deferred and the entire profit or gain is taxed in the hands of the company.

[12]  It would seem to follow from this that Art. 5(1) of the Directive is capable of having direct effect, *e.g.* a Member State may not charge duty on an amount greater than the actual value of the assets (subject to Art. 5(2)), or refuse a deduction for a valid liability or expense, or charge duty in respect of an amount coming within Art. 5(3).

than the actual value of the shares in the company allotted or belonging to each member or the nominal value of such shares if the latter exceeded their actual value.[13] This gave rise to some difficulties and to the possibility of taxation in excess of that intended. For example, if a company makes a "rights issue" whereby existing shareholders are entitled to subscribe for additional shares,[14] it is frequently the case that the actual value of the new shares exceeds the cash contribution of the shareholders[15] though the true aim of the directive was to tax only the actual amount of capital contributed.[16] The paragraph was consequently amended in 1974,[17] and now provides that Member States may base the amount on which duty is to be charged on the actual value of the shares allotted or belonging to each member but that this shall not apply to those cases where contributions are made only in cash.[18] Member States are permitted to exclude from the dutiable amount the amount contributed, or share of assets, of a member whose liability is unlimited.[19]

265     The Commission originally proposed that a uniform rate of capital duty of 1 per cent. be charged.[20] This encountered opposition, notably from Germany,[21] and as eventually adopted the Directive provided for a rate of duty not exceeding 2 per cent. and not less than 1 per cent., but that further proposals be submitted with a view to establishing a common rate.[22] This common rate was subsequently fixed, at 1 per cent., with effect from January 1, 1976.[23] It was further provided that the rate of duty should be reduced by 50 per cent. or more[24] where all the assets or capital of one or more capital companies are transferred to one or more capital companies which are in the process of being formed or which are already in existence,

---

[13] In the United Kingdom, for example, duty had formerly been payable on the nominal value of shares allotted. It had commonly been the practice to allot shares with a nominal value considerably lower than their true value in order to minimise duty : see L. C. B. Gower, *Modern Company Law* (4th ed. 1979), at pp. 221, 240. The Directive removed this advantage by requiring duty to be paid on whichever was the higher of nominal value or actual value : see further B. J. Sims, "Capital Duty—a first real step in Tax Harmonisation" (1976) B.T.R. 33.

[14] Normally in proportion to their existing shareholdings : see the Second Company Law Directive, Dir. 77/91, Art. 29.

[15] *i.e.* there is a "watering-down" of the value of the original shares but, if the new shares were allotted or offered *pro rata*, this is of no consequence.

[16] See the comments of the ESC (O.J. 1974, C 109/35), which had pointed this out when the proposal was originally debated (J.O. 1965, p. 2227). See also (EC) Seventh General Report (1973), p. 165.

[17] Dir. 74/553 of November 7, 1974.

[18] The rule is retained whereby in no case shall the chargeable amount be less than the nominal value of the shares allotted or belonging to each member.

[19] Art. 6.

[20] Subject to certain reduced rates, considered below.

[21] See the Seuffert Report, E.P. Docs. 1965–66, No. 64.

[22] Art. 7(1)(a); 7(2).

[23] Dir. 73/80 of April 9, 1973, Art. 1. The Directive is notable as the first instance of harmonisation of tax rates.

[24] Dir. 73/80, Art. 2, now provides that the reduced rate shall be any rate between 0 per cent. and 0.50 per cent., *i.e.* complete exemption, as in the United Kingdom, is permitted.

provided that the consideration for the transfer consists exclusively of the allocation of shares in the acquiring company or companies and the companies taking part in the transaction have their effective centre of management or registered office within a Member State.[25] The rationale for the reduction is that, in certain mergers and corporate reconstructions, the capital of the acquired or extinguished company will already have been subject to duty and that, in such situations, no new capital is being contributed. In its original form the Directive accorded relief only to certain types of reconstruction and did not extend to others, such as the take-over by acquisition of shares, common in the United Kingdom.[26] The scope of the relief was widened to include these transactions by an amendment adopted in 1973.[27]

**266** Member States are permitted to grant partial or total exemption to certain companies[28] and may, subject to consultation with the Commission, introduce other exemptions, reductions or even increases in rates in order to achieve fairness in taxation, for social considerations or to deal with special situations.[29] The capital duty is intended to be the only tax applied to capital contributions and Member States are thus not permitted to subject chargeable transactions to any other form of taxation or to charge registration taxes on formation of capital companies.[30] Nor may any tax be imposed on the creation, issue or admission to stock exchange quotation of shares, stock, loans, debentures or similar securities.[31] However, it is still permitted to charge duties on the transfer of securities and on the transfer of certain types of assets, or when assets are transferred to a capital company for a consideration other than shares.[32]

The Directive required Member States to bring into force, by January 1, 1972, the measures necessary to comply with its provisions. Some difficulty was experienced by Belgium, France and Italy but by mid-1973 the Directive had been implemented by all members, including the three new Member States.[33]

---

[25] Art. 7(1)(*b*). Member States are permitted to extend the reduction to cases where the consideration consists of shares together with a payment in cash not exceeding 10 per cent. of the nominal value of the shares.

[26] Techniques of merger and reconstruction vary from one Member State to another, largely due to differences in national company laws : see further C. M. Schmitthoff, *European Company Law Texts* (1974), at pp. 15–18.

[27] Dir. 73/79 of April 9, 1973. See further B. J. Sims, (*op. cit.* above, n. 13).

[28] *e.g.* those supplying public services and those with cultural or charitable objectives : Art. 8.

[29] Art. 9.

[30] Art. 10. It would seem that registration and stock exchange fees may still be charged : Art. 12(1)(*e*).

[31] Art. 11. An exception is made in the case of certain types of loan, by Art. 4(2).

[32] Art. 12. There may consequently still be a double imposition of tax, as where land registration tax is imposed on real property transferred to a company and capital duty in respect of the shares allotted in return.

[33] (EC) Sixth General Report (1972), p. 70 : Seventh General Report (1973), p. 165. As to implementation in the United Kingdom, see J. G. Monroe and R. S. Nock, (*op. cit.* n. 6).

### (c)   Transactions in securities

**267**     The Commission's 1964 proposals anticipated that a further Directive would deal with the taxation of transactions in securities.[34] However, it was not until 1976 that the Commission was able to present its proposals.[35] The Commission's preferred solution would have been to abolish such taxes entirely and this would appear to remain the eventual aim.[36] At present, Luxembourg levies no tax on such transactions and rates of tax are very low in all Member States with the exception of Ireland and the United Kingdom.[37] Only in the United Kingdom could the tax be said to have any real budgetary significance. Nevertheless, the existence of these taxes may lead to discrimination and to double-taxation due to the differences in national legislation. Some Member States apply a single tax, others tax both the disposal and the acquisition of shares, whilst Ireland and the United Kingdom have registration-based systems in which stamp duties play a role in the control of companies and securities.[38]

The Commission's proposal is therefore a compromise which does not aim at strict harmonisation. Member States which wish to do so may abolish the tax and Luxembourg will not be required to introduce one. Where the tax is retained the Commission has preferred the dual system of taxation : tax is imposed on both the disposal and the acquisition. This has the advantage, in international transactions, of permitting the tax to be shared between the countries involved. Ireland and the United Kingdom, however, are permitted to derogate from this rule and to continue to treat the transfer as a single transaction, taxable on registration, subject to the granting of relief for tax payable in another Member State.[39] It is proposed that the maximum rate of tax applicable should be 0.3 per cent. of the consideration for the transfer,[40] and transactions carried out by intermediaries would be exempt.[41]

The proposals have been criticised as being imprecise and leading to anomalies[42] and are likely to be revised before final adoption, unless it

---

[34]  (EEC) Bull. S. 2–65, p. 8.

[35]  Proposed Dir. submitted to the Council, April 2, 1976 : O.J. 1976, C 133/1.

[36]  Concurred in by the Parliament : O.J. 1976, C 259/43.

[37]  For details, see the Opinion of the Confédération Fiscale Européenne to the Commission (referred to hereafter as the CFE Opinion) : 1979 *Intertax* 400.

[38]  See G. Morse, note, in (1976) 1 E.L. Rev. 564 and the report of the Parliament's Committee on Economic and Monetary Affairs (the *Dykes Report*) : E.P. Docs. 315/76.

[39]  As presently drafted, this gives rise to a number of difficulties and anomalies : see the *CFE Opinion*, 1979 *Intertax*, at pp. 406–407.

[40]  Applicable to each transaction (disposal and acquisition), the rate being reduced by half in the case of bonds. These rates would be doubled in the case of Ireland and the United Kingdom, by virtue of the transfer being treated as a single transaction. Even so, this would necessitate a substantial reduction in rates for those countries. Gifts would appear to be exempt.

[41]  *e.g.* where shares are purchased by a broker for re-sale to a client, the intermediate purchase and sale would be ignored.

[42]  In the Dykes Report and in the CFE Opinion.

should prove possible to reach agreement on the complete abolition of such taxes.

## (v) Taxes on corporate profits and distributions

**268**    The need to harmonise the systems of taxing company profits and distributions was clearly recognised in the Segré Report[43] and the intention to do so had been proclaimed in the Commission's General Programme of 1967.[44] Indeed, a number of commentators considered that action in this regard was at least as important as in the case of turnover taxes.[45] Differences in the effective tax burden on company profits may distort the conditions of competition between enterprises situated in different Member States and may influence the decision as to where an enterprise should be located, especially in the case of branches or subsidiaries of multinational enterprises.[46] Similarly, investment decisions may be influenced or distorted. A free capital market requires that tax factors do not interfere with an investor's choice of where to invest his capital and that tax rules do not discriminate between investors from different countries investing in a particular enterprise.[47] Moreover, tax systems should be neutral as between direct investment and investment through intermediaries.

### (a)    The choice of corporation tax systems

**269**    The first problem to confront the Commission, in formulating proposals for the harmonisation of company taxation, concerned the choice of system. Just as in the case of turnover taxes, the need for a common system is an essential prerequisite to any further harmonisation of the bases of assessment or of tax rates. A variety of corporation tax systems existed, and still exists, in the Member States of the Community and the very existence of these different systems renders it almost impossible to make any valid comparison of the relative fiscal burden on enterprises in different Member

---

[43] Above, para. 257.

[44] Above, paras. 258–260.

[45] The Neumark Committee's timetable envisaged parallel action (above, para. 110) and see the "Debatin-Schink debate" in B. Börner *et al, Die Harmonisierung der Unternehmensbesteuerung im Gemeinsamer Markt* (1972) *K.S.E.,* Vol. 14, and the note by E. Grabitz in (1970) 6 EuR 79. For a comprehensive study of the subject, see B. Snoy, *Taxes on Direct Investment Income in the EEC : a Legal and Economic Analysis* (1975).

[46] See Snoy, Chaps. 27, 28 and J. H. Dunning and G. Yannopoulos, "The Fiscal Factor in the location of affiliates of Multinational Enterprises," in *Vers une politique fiscale Européenne a l'égard des sociétés multinationales,* Centre d'Etudes Européennes, Louvain (1973), (referred to hereafter as *Vers une politique fiscale . . .*). For an interesting empirical study, see A. E. Scaperlanda and L. J. Mauer, "The Determinants of U.S. Direct Investment in the EEC" (1969) 59 *American Economic Review,* 558.

[47] See Snoy, Chap. 3.

States.[48] Corporation tax systems fall esentially into three major categories[49]:

**270** **(1) The "classical" system.** The so-called "classical" system[50] treats the company as a legal and taxable entity distinct from its shareholders. The company is taxed on its profits, whether distributed or not, normally at a single flat rate. Distributions to shareholders are treated as the personal income of the shareholders just like any other income received by them.

The system has the advantage of being comparatively simple. It is, however, open to two principal objections : on the one hand it discriminates between retained profits (taxed only once) and distributed profits (taxed twice) and, on the other, it involves the economic double taxation of distributions and thus discriminates between investment in company securities and other forms of investment.[51] The classical system is therefore non-neutral in a number of respects :

   (a)   as between incorporated and unincorporated businesses;
   (b)   as between share capital and loan capital[52];
   (c)   as between financing out of retained profits and by raising fresh capital.

In international terms, the profits of the company will be taxed in the country in which the company is resident (subject normally to some form of relief for foreign taxes paid by the company in respect of profits earned abroad) and distributions paid to an investor will be taxed, as the personal income of the investor, in the country where he or she resides, though frequently some tax will be withheld by the paying country in respect of such distributions.

**271** **(2) Partial integration.** The non-neutral features of the classical system may be mitigated, though they are not entirely eliminated, by adopting a system whereby there is a measure of integration of the tax on the profits of the company and the tax on distributions received by investors. There are two basic methods of achieving this :

---

[48] *"Rapport sur le choix des méthodes de comparaison de la charge fiscale effective que supportent les entreprises dans les divers Etats membres de la CEE"* : Commission, Etudes : Série Concurrence, 1967 No. 7 (the *Zeitel Report*). See also P. B. Musgrave, (*op. cit.* p. 159, n. 85).

[49] For descriptions and analyses of the different systems, see *"Corporation Tax and Individual Income Tax in the European Communities"* : Commission Studies : Competition—Approximation of Legislation Series, 1970 No. 15 (the *Van den Tempel Report*) : J. Chown, *The Reform of Corporation Tax* (Institute for Fiscal Studies, 1971). The various national tax rules are described in *Branches and Subsidiaries in the European Common Market* (above, p. 157, n. 76) and in *The Taxation of Companies in Europe* (I.B.F.D., Amsterdam, 1972- ).

[50] Applied in the United States, in Luxembourg and the Netherlands (and in the United Kingdom from 1965 to 1973).

[51] This may not be entirely correct. Many studies suggest that the burden of tax on company profits is, to a large extent, shifted forwards in the form of higher prices and does not fall upon the shareholders : see the Van den Tempel Report, at p. 14.

[52] Interest on loans is normally deductible as a business expense in computing profits and is therefore not subject to double taxation.

(a)   *The "two-rate" method.* Under this method[53] company profits are subject to different rates of tax according to whether or not they are distributed. Thus, assuming an average personal income tax rate of 30 per cent., retained profits might be taxed at 50 per cent. and distributed profits at 20 per cent. The investor would then be taxed in the normal manner on the distributions received.

(b)   *The "imputation" or "tax credit" method.* By this method the company's profits are taxed at a single rate but the investor is given a credit, in respect of part of the tax paid by the company, to set against his liability for personal income tax. Thus, using rates equivalent to those under the two-rate system, the company would pay tax at 50 per cent. on all its profits and the investor would receive a credit equivalent to the personal tax liability at a rate of 30 per cent. If this was indeed his personal tax rate he would pay no additional tax in respect of his dividends.

In a purely domestic situation the two methods produce similar results.[54] The discrimination in favour of retained profits is removed[55] and that between incorporated and unincorporated businesses and between share and loan capital is reduced. The methods may, however, produce different results internationally.[56] Assuming that, as with the classical system, the tax on the company accrues to the country where the company is resident and that distributions are taxed in the country where the investor resides, the two-rate method will have the result (according to the rates employed above) that profits paid to a non-resident will be taxed at only 20 per cent. in the paying country, whereas under the imputation system they will be taxed at 50 per cent. This position is, of course, modified if either dividends paid under the two-rate method to a non-resident are subject to an additional withholding tax or if, under the imputation system, the tax credit is extended to the non-resident investor in such a way that he is entitled to a refund of tax wherever he does not have other income taxable in the paying country against which to set the credit.

**272**   **(3) Full integration.** Only if there is complete integration between corporate and personal taxation are the distortions mentioned above entirely eliminated.[57] The most feasible method of achieving complete integration is to give shareholders a tax credit for the full amount of corporation tax paid

---

[53] Formerly applied in Germany : see the Van den Tempel Report and J. Chown, *op. cit.* above, n. 49.

[54] The imputation method may have advantages for governments, since the company will in effect make an advance payment of tax on behalf of the shareholder, which also reduces the possibility of tax evasion.

[55] If the difference between the two rates or the size of the tax credit is sufficient.

[56] See J. Chown, "The Reform of Corporation Tax : some International Factors" (1971) B.T.R. 215 : N. I. Miller, "Some tax implications of British Entry into the Common Market" (1972) 37 L. & C.P. 265.

[57] However, if the corporation tax rate is higher than the average personal tax rate, as will commonly be the case, this may give rise to a new distortion in that retained profits may effectively be taxed more heavily than distributed profits. It may therefore be cheaper to finance expansion by raising fresh capital rather than out of retained earnings.

by the company in respect of distributed profits.[58] An alternative would be not to tax the company at all on its profits but to allocate the profits among the shareholders and to tax them, whether or not the profits were actually distributed. Such a method seems inappropriate in the case of large public companies, which commonly retain a considerable proportion of their profits and in which the ordinary shareholder has little influence as to how much of the profits will be distributed, but may be a realistic alternative in the case of small private companies.[59] Internationally, the effect is essentially similar to that of the imputation method under a partial integration system, the major difference being that the credit, being a full credit, will be larger. Thus, if the foreign investor is not able to take full advantage of the credit the discrimination against him is increased, but if he does benefit fully from the credit, and is entitled to a refund of tax, the country in which the company is resident receives no tax revenue at all.

273     The Neumark committee[60] initially favoured the adoption of a common system of partial integration, employing the two-rate method. The Van den Tempel Committee[61] preferred the "classical" system, in part because of its simplicity but mainly because it presents fewer difficulties from an international point of view. The Commission, however, eventually decided in favour of a system of partial integration using the tax credit method and it is this system which is advocated in the proposed Directive concerning the harmonisation of systems of company taxation and of withholding taxes on dividends.[62] In spite of the technical problems which the operation of such a system gives rise to in international transactions it was considered that the greater degree of neutrality which the system achieves in domestic situations justifies its preference over the "classical" system. In reaching its decision, the Commission may well have been influenced by what appeared to be a growing preference among the member states for the tax credit system[63]: moreover, whilst the "classical" system might ensure neutrality between

---

[58] For proposals on these lines, see W. Stützel, "Participant Tax" (1970) 10 E.T. 142 : "Teilhabersteuer—ein realisticher Reformvorschlag?" 1969 *Steuer-Kongress-Report* 319, and the proposals of the Canadian Royal Commission on Taxation (Carter Report), 1966. The new German corporation tax system employs a combination of the two-rate method and full credit : see H. J. Ault and A. J. Radler, *The German Corporation Tax Reform Law 1977* (1976), pp. 11–13.

[59] Especially where it is an optional alternative, as with the "partnership option" in the United States.

[60] *The EEC Reports on Tax Harmonisation*, at pp. 122–123, 139.

[61] Above, n. 49.

[62] Proposal transmitted to the Council on August 1, 1975 : O.J. 1975, C 253/2 and see (EC) Bull. S. 10–75 for the Commission's explanatory memorandum. Among the many works discussing the proposed Directive, see H. J. Ault, "International Issues in Corporate Tax Integration" (1978) 10 L.P.I.B. 461; J. Chown, "The Harmonisation of Corporation Tax in the EEC" (1976) B.T.R. 39; Th. W. Vogelaar, "Ein Anrechnungssystem für Europa" (1974) 16 D.St.Z. 291, and see the special number of *European Taxation* (1976) 16 E.T. 39.

[63] The United Kingdom had, for example, changed from the classical to the tax credit system in 1973 : see J. Chown and P. Rowland, "The Finance Bill—the reform of Corporation Tax" (1972) B.T.R. 133; A. R. Prest, The Select Committee on Corporation Tax" (1972) B.T.R. 15.

different national capital markets, the greater internal neutrality of the partial integration system would seem more appropriate to a common, Community, capital market, especially within the context of the proposed Economic and Monetary Union.[64]

The proposed Directive consequently provides that the Member States shall adopt a common imputation system of corporation tax.[65] Each Member State is required to apply a single rate of corporation tax to the profits, whether distributed or undistributed, of its corporations, this normal rate being not lower than 45 per cent. nor higher than 55 per cent.[66] A dividend distributed by a corporation of a Member State confers on its recipient a right to a tax credit,[67] the rate of credit to be fixed by each Member State but determined in such a way that it shall neither be lower than 45 per cent. nor higher than 55 per cent. of the amount of corporation tax at the normal rate on a sum representing the distributed dividend increased by such tax.[68]

(b)    *The tax credit and withholding tax*

**274**        It should initially be noted that the proposed Directive is concerned only with a dividend distributed by a company : "dividend" is defined as that part of the profits of a corporation, other than a corporation in liquidation, distributed by it by virtue of a proper decision of its competent authorities and divided among its members in proportion to their rights as members of the corporation; distributions of bonus shares are not regarded as dividends within the meaning of the proposed Directive.[69] The Directive is therefore not concerned with the payment of interest, *e.g.* on loan capital, except in so far as such payments may be considered to be dividends under the legislation of the Member State in which the company is resident.[70] Whilst it is true that the tax credit reduces the extent of the discrimination between equity- and loan-financing which exists under the "classical" system, it seems surprising that no attempt was made in the proposed Directive to harmonise

---

[64] M. Soldati, "Taxing Corporate Income : European Harmonisation and the Italian Experience" (1976) 24 A.J.C.L. 246.

[65] Proposed Dir., Art. 1.

[66] *Ibid.* Art. 3. By way of derogation it is proposed that Member States may, in particular cases and for well defined reasons of economic, regional or social policy, apply a rate different from the normal rate or complete exemption, subject to consultation with the Commission.

[67] *Ibid.* Art. 4.

[68] *Ibid.* Art. 8. The tax credit rate (expressed as a percentage of the amount of the dividend) is arrived at by applying the formula

$$\frac{a}{100-a} \times b$$

where "a" is the rate of corporation tax and "b" is the rate referred to in Art. 8, i.e. between 45 and 55 per cent.

[69] Art. 2.

[70] Art. 7. Thus, in certain cases, payment of interest may be deemed to be a dividend but it is only treated as such by the Directive if it confers the right to tax credit : *cf.* the distinction between qualifying and non-qualifying distributions in the United Kingdom.

the tax treatment of distributions other than dividends. The Commission's *Programme for the Harmonisation of Direct Taxes*[71] considered it necessary to deal with the systems of withholding taxes on both dividends and interest and took the view that withholding taxes on the latter should be as low as possible, and preferably not exceeding 10 per cent. Subsequently, the Commission went further and proposed the abolition of withholding taxes on bond interest.[72] Such a solution, however, seems unacceptable for two reasons. First, if interest is paid without withholding tax to foreign bondholders there will be a grave danger of tax evasion through the non-reporting of such income.[73] Secondly, the proposed Directive would achieve, in the case of dividends, a reasonably equitable sharing of tax revenue between the countries where the company and the investor respectively reside. Profits are earned in part through the efforts of the company's management and workers and in part through the investment of capital. In the case of dividends, tax revenue is shared by subjecting the profits of the company to taxation and by giving a credit *for a part only* of such tax to the investor.[74] It would consequently seem proper that a similar sharing should occur in the case of interest income, *i.e.* that the country in which capital is invested should impose some tax upon the income earned thereon by means of a withholding tax, for which the investor should receive a credit against the tax payable on his income in the country in which he resides.[75] In order to reconcile the need to discourage tax evasion with the desire to allocate tax revenue equitably, it might consequently be necessary to have a two-tier system of withholding tax on interest : one part being retained by the country from which payment is made and the other part being refundable through some form of "clearance" system.[76]

275     In the case of dividends the draft Directive proposes that a dividend distributed by a corporation of a Member State shall confer on its recipient a right to a tax credit provided that he is a resident in a Member State and that he is subject to a tax on income or profits in such a way that the full amount of the dividend (increased by the tax credit) is taken into account in

---

[71] Above, paras. 258–260.

[72] Memorandum to the Council of March 5, 1969; see (EC) Bull. 5–69, pp. 22–23. This solution was also favoured in the Segré Report (above, para. 257), and see M. Sarmet, "Harmonisation fiscale et integration des marchés de capitaux," in *Vers une politique fiscale* . . . , Chap. 6.

[73] J. Jansen, "Harmonisation of Corporation Tax in the European Countries," in G. W. Keeton and S. N. Frommel (ed.), *British Industry and European Law,* Chap. 5, and see B. Snoy (*op. cit.* n. 45), Chap. 2. The Commission apparently now accepts the need for a substantial withholding tax on bond interest : see (EC) Bull. 11–73, p. 23.

[74] If it is objected that the profits earned by the efforts of management and workers are taxed in the form of income tax on salaries, then this equally would be an argument in favour of full integration.

[75] As is commonly the practice under international tax treaties and with respect to other types of investment income, *e.g.* rental income. See further M. Norr, "Jurisdiction to Tax and International Income" (1962) 17 *Tax Law Review*, 431 and B. Snoy *op. cit.* Chap. 5.

[76] See below.

arriving at the amount of his taxable income or profits.[77] A credit may also be granted, pursuant to a double taxation agreement, to a person resident in a third country, provided that such a person may in no circumstances be treated more favourably than a person resident within the Community.[78] The tax credit, to a Community resident, is to be set off against the amount of tax on income or profits to which the recipient of the dividend is liable and, where the credit exceeds that amount, the excess is payable to him by the Member State which charges that tax.[79] However, the budgetary cost of the tax credit is to be borne by the country of the corporation which distributes the dividend, by means of a "clearance" system of financial compensation between the Member States concerned.[80]

The proposed tax credit has an effect similar to a withholding tax, there being a payment (by the company) on account of the recipient's final tax liability. However, the effective rate of the tax credit, as a percentage of the gross dividend, will not always be sufficiently high to prevent tax evasion.[81] The Directive therefore proposes that an additional withholding tax be imposed of 25 per cent. of the dividend distributed, no matter who is the recipient of the dividend.[82] Like the tax credit, the withholding tax is set against the final tax liability of the recipient, or repaid to the extent that it exceeds the amount of tax payable by him.[83]

The granting of the tax credit—both for a part of the tax paid by the corporation on its profits and for the withholding tax—may be withheld from the recipient in accordance with national provisions whose purpose is to prevent the recipient from obtaining an unjustified advantage[84]; thus the proposed Directive acknowledges that certain national anti-avoidance rules may continue to be necessary. However, the penultimate article of the proposed directive lays down a principle of non-discrimination that is of wide and general application, requiring that a dividend distributed to a person resident in a Member State by a corporation of another Member State shall not be subjected, in the first state, to any less favourable taxation treat-

---

[77] Art. 4. By way of derogation, a tax credit may be granted to a non-taxable person, being an "institution which is of public interest," *e.g.* a charity.

[78] Art. 6.

[79] Art. 5, *i.e.* the excess is refundable by the Member State where the recipient is resident.

[80] Art. 13. Member States may, however, agree to share the budgetary cost between them, provided that the shareholder's entitlement to a full tax credit is not affected. For an analysis of the proposed "clearance" system, see B. Bracewell-Milnes, "Tax Credits under the proposed EEC Directive on Company Taxation" (1976) *Intertax,* 277.

[81] According to the rates of tax and credit prescribed by the Directive, the effective rate will lie between (approx.) 27 and 40 per cent. : see B. Bracewell-Milnes, (*op. cit.* above) at p. 278.

[82] Art. 14. This is stated to be subject to the provisions of the conventions concluded between Member States and third countries. A Member State will be free not to impose the withholding tax on distributions made to its own residents. Special rules apply to distributions between associated companies : see below, paras. 289, 290.

[83] Art. 16. The system of financial compensation between Member States similarly applies.

[84] Art. 19.

ment or to any more burdensome requirement[85] than if that dividend had been distributed by a corporation of the first state.[86]

*(c) The proposed Directive : an appraisal*

276      The proposed Directive constitutes a first step towards the comprehensive harmonisation outlined in the Commission's *Programme for the Harmonisation of Direct Taxes.* As such, it follows the pattern adopted with the value added tax of first harmonising the system of taxation and, subsequently, the basis of assessment. However, it seems unlikely to be adopted in the near future, or in its present form,[87] and it therefore seems inappropriate to consider the provisions of the draft in any greater detail than has already been done. Nevertheless, a number of more general comments seem to be called for :

(1) **Rates of Tax.** Unlike the procedure adopted with the value added tax, which has regarded the harmonising of tax rates as the final stage to be accomplished, the proposed directive does prescribe a permissible range, both with regard to the corporation tax and to the tax credit, within which rates of tax must fall. This appears to be necessary, given the choice of a system of partial integration, for the degree of integration is itself a function of those rates and of their relationship. The "classical" system is characterized by a relatively low rate of corporation tax, with no credit for such tax at all. Full integration would seem to require a high rate of corporation tax, with, as the name implies, a full tax credit. Thus a Community system which made no provision whatsoever as to rates would, in effect, be no system at all.[88] Rate bands must be sufficiently wide to allow Member States adopting the common system to do so without substantial loss of tax revenue,[89] but not so wide as to be capable of accommodating systems which are not really partial integration systems at all.[90]

277      (2) **The basis of assessment.** This, however, renders the proposal open to the criticism that it is misleading, and perhaps dangerous, to attempt any harmonisation of rates without at the same time achieving equivalence of the basis of assessment.[91] Major differences exist among the various national

---

[85] Other than a requirement relating to a refund of tax.

[86] Art. 21. This is stated to be without prejudice to the application of the provisions of Art. 92 of the Treaty, relating to state aids.

[87] See the comments of Mr. Nyborg in the debate of the Parliament on May 7, 1979 : E.P. Debs. 1979, reproduced in (1979) *Intertax*, 384.

[88] See the address of Mr. Burke (Member of the Commission) to the first Congress of European Tax Consultants, Strasbourg, October 1978 : (1979) *Intertax* 46, at p. 52.

[89] It is also desirable that Member States (such as the United Kingdom) which have a standard rate of personal income tax, for administration convenience, should be able to align that rate with the tax credit : see J. Chown, "The Harmonisation of Corporation Tax in the EEC" (1976) B.T.R. 39, at p. 42.

[90] *e.g.* the recently introduced German system.

[91] See the Interim Report of the Parliament's Committee on Economic and Monetary Affairs : E.P. Doc. 104/79 (the Nyborg Report).

legislations with regard to the computation of the taxable income of companies, making any comparison of effective rates of tax almost impossible.[92] Different rules concerning the computation of profits, deductability of expenses, valuation of stock, depreciation of assets, and the treatment of losses, reserves and capital gains will mean that the "normal" corporation tax rate[93] will be applied to entirely different tax bases in the Member States. Distortions are created by the differences in investment incentives offered by Member States to attract foreign capital[94] : in part, these incentives raise issues of regional policy, but there is a more general danger of Member States competing with each other to attract investment from multi-national enterprises by offering bigger and better incentives.[95] It is clear that, in the long term, a substantial degree of harmonisation will be required in order to ensure neutrality, both as regards competition between enterprises and as regards the integration of capital markets[96], and the harmonisation of the bases of assessment will probably also require the harmonisation of accounting standards.[97] This would become even more important should a harmonised corporation tax ever constitute a part of the Community's "own resources" and finance the Community's budget.[98] Given the present wide variations in the bases of assessment it must therefore be questioned whether the proposed Directive should attempt to secure any approximation of tax rates.[99] The answer to this would seem to be that the Directive does not aim at an approximation of rates as such,[1] but that the proposed rate bands are an essential element in the adoption of a common system of taxation.[2]

[92] For a comprehensive study, see B. Snoy (*op. cit.*), and see A. Mennel, "Internationaler Vergleich der Steuerlichen Abschreibungen und Investitionsvergünstigungen" (1976) 6 R.I.W. 321.
[93] Prescribed by Art. 3 of the proposed Directive.
[94] *e.g.* special "tax holidays," reduced tax rates and other concessions, such as accelerated depreciation, loss relief, etc. For an extensive analysis, see *Tax Policy and Investment in the European Community,* Commission Studies, Taxation Series, 1975 No. 1 (the Christiaanse Report).
[95] B. Snoy, "Politiques fiscales nationales et stratégies des sociétés multinationales dans la CEE," in *Vers une politique fiscale . . .* , Chap. 2.
[96] Commission's *Programme for the Harmonisation of Direct Taxes,* (EEC) Bull. S. 8–67, pp. 8, 19–20, and see the Fredersdorf Report, para. 4.2.6.1.
[97] A. F. Conard, "Corporate Fusion in the Common Market" (1966) 14 A.J.C.L. 573, at p. 600. Appreciable progress has been made to this end with the adoption of the Fourth Company Law Directive, Dir. 78/660 of July 25, 1978, regarding the disclosure of financial information and the contents of annual accounts, and the proposed Eighth Directive (proposal transmitted April 24, 1978 : O.J. 1978, C 112) seeks to lay down rules as to the persons entitled to audit company accounts and the qualifications which they must hold. However, it would appear from the Court's decision in Case 161/78, *Conradsen* [1980] 1 C.M.L.R. 121, that Dir. 78/660 has no application to questions of taxation.
[98] See below, Chap. 4, paras. 437, 438.
[99] See the conclusions of the Nyborg Report (*op. cit.* above, n. 91).
[1] Thus, Art. 3(2) would permit derogations from the normal rate in many circumstances. This, too, was criticised in the Nyborg Report.
[2] This is the view of the Commission, expressed by Mr. Burke in the debate in Parliament on May 7, 1979 (above, n. 87) and in his address to the Parliament's Economic and Monetary Committee on October 18, 1978 : see 1979 *Intertax* 240.

**278    (3) Neutrality as between forms of business enterprise.** The proposed Directive applies to the taxation of all companies which are subjected to corporation tax under national law.[3] Member States would presumably remain free to determine whether or not the harmonised system of coporation tax should apply also to the small private company or to the "incorporated partnership." Moreover, the derogation permitted by the Directive[4] would seem to allow for the application of special rules to small companies, such as a reduced tax rate or a "partnership option."[5] Although it is true that the partial integration system reduces the extent of economic double taxation of dividends (in comparison with the "classical" system), it does not eliminate it and this consequently has an effect upon the choice of business medium. Private companies may be large or small : large private companies compete with, and may be alternative to, public companies : small private companies are frequently comparable to unincorporated businesses. Furthermore, business structures vary considerably from one Member State to another and the incorporation of small businesses may be far more common in one country than in another. Ideally, the tax system should be neutral as to the different legal forms of enterprise but in practice it would seem to be virtually impossible to achieve complete neutrality,[6] and the partial integration system is probably the best available compromise, both domestically and for the Community as a whole. However, it may become necessary to define with greater precision the scope of the proposed common Community system, in particular with regard to the definition of those small or private companies which may be accorded special treatment. This would be especially so if the corporation tax were ever to constitute a part of the Community's own resources.[7]

**279    (4) International aspects.** As already mentioned, the proposed Directive requires that the tax credit, and credit for the withholding tax, be given to all recipients of distributions resident in a Member State and taxable there.[8] Tax credits may be granted to residents of third countries, pursuant to double taxation agreements, provided that such persons are in no way treated more favourably than are Community residents.[9] The chief problem, in relations with third countries, is that a change from the "classical" system to a tax credit method of partial integration will normally involve an

---

[3] The definition of "corporation" in Art. 2 of the proposed Directive refers to Art. 2 of the proposed Directive relating to the taxation of parent companies and their subsidiaries (O.J. 1969, C 39/7), see below, para. 289. This applies to all companies subject to corporation tax, *i.e.* Impôt des sociétés, Körperschaftssteuer, etc.

[4] Art. 3(2).

[5] The Van den Tempel Report, at p. 8, envisaged that the harmonised system would essentially apply only to public companies and would not preclude special arrangements for private companies.

[6] Unless a fully integrated system were adopted, which is unlikely for economic reasons.

[7] See D. Dosser, "Future Tax Policy of the United Kingdom as a Member of the EEC," in D. Dosser (ed.), *British Taxation and the Common Market* (1973), Chap. 7.

[8] Art. 4(1).

[9] Art. 6.

increase in the standard rate of corporation tax, to prevent an overall loss of revenue. This will be detrimental to the foreign investor unless he is entitled to benefit from the tax credit. Within the Community this will be the case, according to the Directive, and it is the state which imposes the corporation tax which ultimately bears the cost of the credit. But this is unlikely to be so in the case of an investor from a third country. Such an investor will either be denied the tax credit, and thereby be treated less favourably than an investor resident in a Member State, or will receive a credit under the tax laws of his own country,[10] in which case the cost of the credit will be borne by that country, resulting in a re-allocation of total tax revenue between the two countries. Thus, where a Member State changes from the "classical" to the partial integration system,[11] without there being any corresponding change in that country's existing double taxation agreements, this is prejudicial to the foreign investor or to the exchequer of his country of residence, or both.[12] This may place that country in the position of suppliant, with regard to re-negotiation of the agreement, and, since double-taxation agreements commonly adopt a "mirror-image" (each party according similar treatment to income originating in the other), there is considerable potential for discrimination where a non-Member State applies the "classical" system (*e.g.* the United States) and the Community adopts an integration system.[13] Moreover, as Member States may differ as to the extent to which they wish to encourage investment from outside the Community, it may be difficult to secure the adoption of a common position on the extension of tax credits to third-country investors.[14]

**280**    **(5) Prospects for adoption and implementation.** As required by Article 100 of the Treaty, the proposed directive was referred to the Economic and Social Committee and to the Parliament for their opinions. The Economic and Social Committee generally welcomed the proposal whilst expressing a number of reservations and proposing amendments.[15] The Committee approved the adoption of the partial integration system and considered that the proposed rate bands represented a necessary, and largely satisfactory, compromise. It considered that derogations as to the normal rate of corporation tax should be more strictly controlled and was less than enthusiastic over the proposed additional withholding tax. Its major worry

---

[10] Including any existing double-taxation agreement.

[11] Or, as in the case of the recent German reform, from partial to full integration : see H. J. Ault and A. J. Radler, *The German Corporation Tax Reform Law 1977* (1976), Chap. 4; S. N. Frommel, The new German Imputation System and Foreign Investors" (1976) B.T.R. 269.

[12] H. J. Ault, "International Issues in Corporate Tax Integration" (1978) 10 L.P.I.B., 461; C. Sivaprakasam, "The Impact of the proposed EEC Directive on non-EEC Countries" (1977) 17 E.T. 120.

[13] See P. T. Kaplan, "European Discrimination and American Retaliation" (1978) B.T.R. 206.

[14] As required by Art. 6 of the proposed Directive.

[15] O.J. 1976, C 278/6.

concerned the economic effects which adoption of the directive might have in some Member States, especially those in which foreign investment is a major factor. These states might suffer a significant reduction in tax revenues, which would have to be recovered from other taxes and might require adjustments to the rates of personal income tax.

The response of the Parliament has been somewhat less favourable. The initial recommendations of the Committees on Budgets and on Economic and Monetary Affairs[16] endorsed the proposal, subject again to various reservations.[17] The Parliament, however, rejected the motion for a resolution contained in the report.[18] A subsequent interim report, drawn up on behalf of the Committee on Economic and Monetary Affairs,[19] though apparently accepting that the common system of taxation should be one of partial integration, considers that more comprehensive proposals are necessary, laying down a strategy for the overall harmonisation of company taxation and in particular of the bases of assessment which should be harmonised at the same time as the rates of corporation tax and of the tax credit. Rejecting the suggestion that the Parliament was delaying progress, the rapporteur[20] urged that a proposal to harmonise rates, with no guarantee that the bases of assessment could be harmonised in the near future, would inevitably be rejected in the Council.

**281**    The choice, then, is not whether the Community should choose the classical system or the partial integration system but the exact form which the common partial integration system is to take.[21] Of the present Member States, Luxembourg and the Netherlands alone retain the classical system. It is unlikely that either would strongly resist a change to partial integration but both countries would prefer to wait until agreement is reached on a common Community system before embarking upon a major tax reform. Of the other Member States, Belgium and France have applied the tax credit method for a number of years. The United Kingdom changed from the classical system to the tax credit method in 1973,[22] and subsequently Denmark,[23] Ireland[24] and Italy[25] have followed suit. Only Germany has moved away from the proposed Community system, abandoning its two-

---

[16] E.P. Docs. 291/77 (the van Aerssen Report).

[17] Like the ESC, they wished to restrict derogations but, by contrast, they considered the withholding tax essential.

[18] On December 14, 1977.

[19] E.P. Docs. 104/79 (the Nyborg Report).

[20] Mr. Nyborg, in a speech in the Parliament on May 7, 1979.

[21] It is assumed that, for economic reasons, full integration is not feasible.

[22] At a time when it appeared, following the Van den Tempel Report, that the Community might adopt the classical system! See above, p. 168, n. 49.

[23] See (1976) 16 E.T. 342; (1977) 17 E.T. 134.

[24] See (1976) 16 E.T. 138.

[25] See A. Fantozzi, "Italy : the new method of taxation of dividends" (1978) 18 E.T. 260; A. Lovisolo, "Italy : the new Imputation System" 1979 *Intertax* 10; M. Soldati, "Taxing Corporate Income : European Harmonisation and the Italian experience" (1976) 24 A.J.C.L. 246.

rate method of partial integration and adopting what is virtually a fully integrated system.[26]

With the possible exception of Germany, therefore, it would seem that agreement already exists as to the type of common system to be adopted. It is in matters of detail and, especially, of the permitted rate bands, that difficulties remain. A possible compromise might be to provide immediately for the adoption of the tax credit method of integration, stipulating only a minimum rate of tax credit.[27] The second stage would then involve the harmonisation of the bases of assessment in parallel with a closer approximation of rates, both of the corporation tax and of the tax credit.

### (d)   The treatment of intermediaries

282      The need to remove discriminations against the use of investment intermediaries and to harmonise the rules governing institutional investors was emphasized in the Segré Report.[28] Such institutions perform a valuable function in permitting small investors to spread their risk, and should therefore be encouraged rather than penalised. In its *Programme for the Harmonisation of Direct Taxes*,[29] the Commission recommended a system of fiscal transparency, whereby investment through intermediaries should be treated as if it had been made directly.

In a recent proposal for a Directive,[30] the Commission has proposed that the principles of the company taxation Directive be extended to income received through the intermediary of a collective investment institution.[31] Where such an institution acts as an intermediary between a distributing company and the final recipient of the dividend a problem arises under the company taxation Directive in that the tax credit[32] is only available, as a general rule, to a recipient who is liable to tax on the dividend. Thus the body receiving the dividend (the institution) and the person liable to tax (the investor) are different persons. The new proposal seeks to remedy this by providing for the transfer of the tax credit to the final recipient by way of the

---

[26]  H. J. Ault, "Germany : the new Corporation Tax System" (1976) *Intertax* 262; S. N. Frommel, "The new German Imputation System and Foreign Investors" 1976 B.T.R. 269; A. J. van den Tempel, "EG und Deutschland : Vorschläge für das Körperschaftssteuersystem" (1974) *Intertax* 59.

[27]  A rate of 40 per cent. is suggested. It might also be necessary to prescribe minimum and maximum rates of corporation tax (say from 40 to 60 per cent.), though this appears less of a problem.

[28]  Above, para. 257.

[29]  Above, paras. 258–260.

[30]  Submitted to the Council on July 24, 1978 : O.J. 1978, C 184/8.

[31]  As defined in Art. 2 and the Annex to the proposed Directive. In the United Kingdom the rules will apply to authorised unit trusts and approved investment trusts. For a comment on the proposal, see G. Morse, (1978) 3 E.L. Rev. 409.

[32]  And similarly, the credit for any withholding tax.

institution. The provisions whereby the credit is transferred are complex.[33] Since the proposed Directive is complementary to the company taxation proposal,[34] its adoption, and any amendments which might be made to it, depend upon what happens to the earlier proposal and it therefore seems unnecessary to consider these complexities further.

### (vi) Fiscal obstacles to industrial combinations

**283** As already observed,[35] one of the declared objectives of the Commission's *Programme for the Harmonisation of Direct Taxes* was the removal of fiscal obstacles to industrial combinations : mergers between companies in different Member States and the acquisition by one company of a holding in a company in another Member State should not be impeded by fiscal considerations. This policy may be considered in both its passive and its active aspects : the desire to achieve fiscal neutrality, so that considerations of taxation do not distort business decisions, and the desire actively to promote a Community industrial policy.

Fiscal neutrality requires that national tax rules do not impede the freedom of establishment, the freedom to provide services and the free movement of capital across frontiers.[36] Tax obstacles may hinder, and indeed render almost impossible, mergers between companies situated in different Member States, thereby encouraging concentrations within a Member State rather than combinations across national frontiers, or may make the companies of one country an easier target for takeovers than those of another country.[37] And even if transnational combinations succeed in coming into existence, tax rules governing the transfer of dividends, profits or assets between associated companies in different countries may interfere with the normal conduct of the business of the group and distort the conditions of competition.[38] Differences in these rules may encourage the companies of one country to "go international" and to acquire control over foreign subsidiaries, whilst this may be discouraged in other countries,[39] or

---

[33] Especially where, for example, a dividend paid by a company in state A to an institution in state B is redistributed to an investor in state C. See the Commission's explanatory memorandum, Doc. COM(78) 340 final, reproduced in (1978) *Intertax* 342.

[34] It is intended that the two proposals should be adopted together.

[35] Above, para. 260.

[36] Th. W. Vogelaar, in the Foreword to the special number of *European Taxation*, (1969) 9 E.T. 145.

[37] G. Brosio, "National Tax Hindrances to cross-border Concentrations in the European Economic Community" (1970) 11 Harv. Int. Law Jo. 311.

[38] For considerations of these problems, see G. Brosio, *op. cit.* above; M. Burgio, "Le transfert des bénéfices entre diverses unites des sociétés multinationales et le probleme de l'harmonisation fiscale dans la CEE," in *Vers une politique fiscale* ..., Chap. 8; A. F. Conard, "Corporate Fusion in the Common Market" (1966) 14 A.J.C.L. 573.

[39] It is perhaps not solely due to their greater enterprise and experience that American companies have been dominant in transnational merger activity : see G. Brosio, *op. cit.*; J. M. Hollrah, "Taxation of cross-border concentrations in the EEC" (1974) 9 Texas Int. Law Jo. 313.

may affect the choice of location of holding companies with foreign subsidiaries.[40] Another aspect of fiscal neutrality is that the profits of a transnational undertaking should be taxed once[41] and once only : differences in tax rules should not result in double taxation but neither should they facilitate tax avoidance or evasion.[42]

**284**    A further incentive towards the removal of fiscal obstacles to transnational combinations is afforded by the Community's industrial policy.[43] The Commission sees this as being complementary, rather than contradictory, to its policy on competition :

> "The intensification of measures to combat cartels and the efforts made to eliminate the abuse of dominant positions are essential to supplement the encouragement that the Community must give to the cross-frontier harmonisation of undertakings ... The setting up of transnational European undertakings can increase competition ... Transnational groupings offer the possibility of combining fair competition and economies of scale."[44]

This policy is based upon two assumptions. First, the larger European market calls for larger companies in order to compete with multinational enterprises from outside the Community and to promote greater efficiency and the sharing of technology and research costs. Secondly, in the interests of competition and, no doubt, of European integration, such concentrations should not dominate a single national market but should be genuinely European, *i.e.* transnational.[45] A major concern of the Commission has been that the greater part of merger activity within the Community has either been purely national, *i.e.* involving companies within the same country, or, if not, has involved companies from without the Community, in particular from the United States.[46] Relatively few mergers have taken place between companies established in different Member States of the Community.[47] Thus technical, legal and, above all, fiscal obstacles to such mergers must be removed.

---

[40] *e.g.* special rules relating to holding companies in Luxembourg and the Netherlands : see below.

[41] The tax may of course be shared among the countries concerned.

[42] The problem is discussed in the Commission's memorandum, "Multinational Undertakings and the Community," (EC) Bull. S. 15–73, and see U. Immenga, "Transnationale Kooperation," in *Möglichkeiten und Grenzen einer Europäischen Union* (1974), at pp. 46 *et seq.* See below, para. 304.

[43] Resolution of the Council, December 17, 1973 : (EC) Bull. 12–73, p. 63. This is based upon the Commission's "Action Programme for industrial and technological policy," submitted on October 30, 1973.

[44] Commission memorandum : (EC) Bull. S. 7–73, p. 10.

[45] C. Layton, *Cross Frontier Mergers in Europe* (1971), Chap. 1.

[46] (EC) Third General Report (1969), p. 36, and see C. Layton, (*op. cit.* above) especially Chap. 5.

[47] See P. C. Canellos & H. S. Silber, "Concentration in the Common Market" (1970) 7 C.M.L. Rev. 5, 138 : C. M. Schmitthoff, "Multinational Companies" 1970 J.B.L. 177.

(a)  *The proposed Directives of 1969*

285        To this end the Commission submitted, in 1969, two proposals for
Directives[48] concerning, respectively, the tax treatment of mergers and the
taxation of parent companies and their subsidiaries in different Member
States. Although the proposals were generally welcomed by the Economic
and Social Committee and by the Parliament,[49] little progress has since been
made. The Council, in its Resolution of December 17, 1973,[50] envisaged
that action would be taken by the end of 1975 if possible, but the proposals
appear subsequently to have been shelved, although the Council did resume
work on the merger proposal during 1978.[51] Reasons for this delay are
readily apparent : the proposals must be viewed in the context of the work
which has been undertaken in other areas of taxation, notably the taxation
of company profits and distributions, and in company law in relation to
mergers, associated companies and the proposed European Company.
These various proposals are to a large extent interdependent and solutions
must be found to a wide variety of problems before action can be taken in
respect of any one of them.

(b)  *Mergers*

        As the Commission has explained,[52] the main tax obstacle to mergers, the
splitting up of companies and transfers of assets between companies of
different Member States lies in the cost of the operation. The preferential tax
treatment granted by most Member States if the operation involves domestic
companies only does not normally apply if assets are transferred to a
foreign company. For this there are good reasons. Where a company
transfers its assets to another company in return for shares in that company,
or to a new company formed for the purpose of absorbing one or more
existing companies, there are a number of tax consequences. In terms of
taxes on capital transactions, assets have been transferred and shares issued.
As regards the taxation of income it will frequently be the case that the
assets transferred have a value in excess of their original cost and conse-

[48] Proposals submitted to Council on January 16, 1969 : J.O. 1969, C 39. A working
party had been set up to examine these problems in 1961 ((EEC) Bull. 1–62, p. 52) and the
intention to propose measures expressed in the Commission's memorandum, "Concentration
of Firms in the Common Market," (EEC) Bull. 2–66, p. 16. For an analysis of the proposed
directives, see the special number of *European Taxation* (1969) 9 E.T. 144, and see J. H.
Christiaanse, *Tax Harmonisation in the European Common Market* (1971), Chap. 5; G.
Gosset, "Les Propositions de directives de la Commission pour lever les obstacles fiscaux aux
concentrations internationales" (1969) 33 Fisc. M.C. 27.
[49] J.O. 1969, C 100/4; J.O. 1970, C 51/6.
[50] Above, n. 43.
[51] (EC) Twelfth General Report (1978), p. 121.
[52] (EC) Bull. 3–69, p. 40.

quently include unrealised capital gains. Similarly, the assets may include reserves which have not been subject to corporation tax. Where the merger takes place between two companies within the same jurisdiction this is commonly permitted without taxing the transfer of assets, the previously unrealised capital gains or untaxed reserves. Since the assets, and the new owner, remain within the jurisdiction, tax liability may safely be deferred until such time as the assets are realised or the reserves are distributed. But where assets are transferred to a new owner who is not resident within the jurisdiction there is a danger that the tax will not merely be deferred but will be lost altogether. Consequently, the reliefs given in the case of a domestic merger are commonly withheld where assets are transferred to a non-resident. Hence the heavy cost of transnational, as opposed to domestic, mergers.[53]

**286**     The proposed solution is founded on three basic principles:
(1)  no tax is to be levied at the time of the merger;
(2)  the interests of the state of the absorbed company are not to be prejudiced, and its rights must be safeguarded for the future;
(3)  the tax system applicable to companies with a permanent establishment in another country must be improved and harmonised.[54]

The proposed Directive consequently provides that, in the case of a merger[55] or of a division[56] involving companies of two or more Member States, no tax shall be imposed in respect of any capital gains arising in respect of assets which have been contributed in so far as such assets are allocated to the permanent establishment which the receiving company maintains in the country of the contributing company.[57] Provisions and reserves of the contributing company which have been constituted under a partial or total tax exemption may be carried over tax-free to the books of the permanent establishment of the receiving company, which thus takes over the rights and obligations of the contributing company[58] and unrelieved losses may similarly be carried over to the permanent establishment of the receiving

[53]  For more detailed consideration of these problems, see A. F. Conard *op. cit.* n. 38; A. D. Lawton, "Tax aspects of Company Mergers in Europe" (1974) 124 New L.J. 1153; C. Layton, (*op. cit.* n. 45) at Chaps. 2, 3; B. Snoy, *Taxes on Direct Investment Income in the EEC* (1975), at pp. 12 *et seq.*
[54]  It should be noted that, whilst ownership of the assets of the absorbed company is transferred, the assets themselves will normally remain within the original jurisdiction as part of the permanent establishment there of the new owner.
[55]  As defined in Art. 2, *i.e.* when the assets of one or more companies are transferred, following a dissolution without liquidation, to another company which is either in existence or is formed for the purpose, against an allotment of shares in that company. Thus the Directive does not apply to the "takeover," where it is the shares of the absorbed company which are acquired.
[56]  Where the assets are transferred to two or more existing or newly formed companies against an allotment of shares : Art. 2.
[57]  Art. 4.
[58]  Art. 5.

company.[59] Assets which are contributed, *i.e.* are transferred from the contributing to the receiving company in return for the allotment of shares, are to be taxed according to the provisions of the Company Capital Duty Directive[60] and no transfer duty or similar tax is to be imposed in respect of such contributions.[61] Similarly, the allotment of shares to members of the contributing company ought not normally to result in any tax liability.[62] Special rates apply where the receiving company already owns shares in the contributing company, in particular where such shares must be cancelled as a consequence of the rule, applicable in some Member States, that a company may not hold its own shares, giving relief against capital gains liability on the cancellation of shares.[63]

287       The interests of the state of the absorbed company are protected by the "permanent establishment" rules. Since the tax liabilities in respect of capital gains, reserves, etc., are rolled-over to the receiving company, it is essential that the state in which the contributing company is situate should not lose the ability to tax those gains or reserves when realised by the new owner. As has been observed, the assets which have been transferred will normally remain, physically, in the original country[64] and will form part of the permanent establishment of the receiving company in that country.[65] That permanent establishment is, in effect, treated as a taxable entity in the country where it is situate, its profits are taxed there and are not to be taxed in the country of the company whose establishment it is, *i.e.* they are not taxed in the country of the receiving company.[66] An exception to this rule is made where the profits of that company are taxed on a "world-wide profits" system.[67] The permanent establishment of a foreign company may not be taxed more heavily in a Member State than would a domestic company of that state exercising the same activity.[68]

---

[59] Art. 6. This does not apply to losses arising from a permanent establishment (of the contributing company) abroad. The right of the receiving company to set such losses against the future profits of its permanent establishment are governed by the tax laws applying to the permanent establishment. Thus it would be subject to provisions designed to prevent the abuse of "tax loss companies". See also Art. 10(2).

[60] Dir. 69/335, see above paras. 263–266.

[61] Art. 7. Thus, apparently, no real estate transfer tax or similar tax would be imposed, *cf.* the position under Dir. 69/335, above para. 266.

[62] Art. 9.

[63] Art. 8.

[64] Member States are not required to exempt assets which are transferred out of the country. It would seem that difficulties might well arise in the case of movables, such as inventory, and intangible assets, such as patent rights and know-how.

[65] The definition of "permanent establishment," contained in the Annex to the proposed Directive, follows closely that adopted in the OECD model convention for the avoidance of double taxation.

[66] Art. 12.

[67] Such a system is applied in some Member States, notably in France. Essentially, the company is taxed in the country of its registered office, or its *siège réel*, on its global profits with a reduction to take account of foreign taxes : see (1969) 9 E.T., at p. 158. Further proposals are required, by Art. 12(5), to harmonise these rules.

[68] Art. 13.

**288**    Apart from the technical difficulties which it presents—Member States
will be unwilling to assent to its adoption unless quite certain that they are
protected against loss of tax revenue—a number of other obstacles must be
overcome. Transnational mergers are hindered not only by fiscal considerations but also by legal obstacles. Progress in this regard has recently been
achieved with the adoption of the Third Company Law Directive,[69] co-
ordinating the provisions regulating internal mergers within a Member State.
Nevertheless, mergers between companies in different Member States still
encounter serious legal difficulties.[70] Although the Commission has
expressed the hope[71] that the adoption of the tax Directive should not
become linked with other, essentially political, issues (such as that of worker
participation on the boards of companies), it is difficult to see how this can
be avoided. Member States will scarcely be willing to take any step to
facilitate mergers whilst there remains a danger that these may be employed
to evade provisions of national law. A similar objection may be expressed
with respect to the harmonisation of corporation tax : so long as corporate
tax systems, and effective tax burdens, remain significantly different, there
will be a danger that companies will emigrate, by way of merger, to lower-
tax States.[72] Thus it may well be that the harmonisation of corporation tax
is a necessary prerequisite to the liberalisation of the merger rules.[73]

### (c)  Parent companies and their subsidiaries

**289**    Industrial combinations may be created either by merger, where one company transfers its assets to another, is dissolved and, in effect, absorbed into
the receiving company, or, alternatively, by one company acquiring the
shares of another to an extent sufficient to give it a controlling, or a significant, interest in that other.[74] Similarly, a company may expand its operations into another country either by opening a branch or permanent
establishment there or by incorporating there a company which it owns and
controls. The choice of method—merger or takeover, branch or subsidiary—commonly depends upon the tax and other legal rules of the
countries involved.[75] As a general rule, the takeover or incorporation of a

[69] Dir. 78/855 of October 9, 1978. In addition, Dir. 77/187 deals with the safeguarding of
employees' rights in the event of transfers of undertakings.
[70] It is largely for this reason that the creation of a "European Company" has been
proposed : see below.
[71] R. Burke, "Harmonisation of Taxation in Europe," (1979) *Intertax 46*.
[72] The permanent establishment rules may protect existing tax liabilities but cannot, by
themselves, protect future revenues.
[73] U. Anschutz, "Harmonisation of Direct Taxes in the European Economic Community"
(1972) 13 Harv. Int. Law Jo., 1, and see the remarks of R. Burke, "Harmonisation of
Corporation Tax" (1979) *Intertax* 240.
[74] The "take-over" being a common example.
[75] See further P. B. Musgrave, "Harmonisation of Direct Business Taxes : a Case Study,"
in Shoup *Fiscal Harmonisation*, Chap. 10, at pp. 302–309; P. M. Storm *et al.*, in *Branches
and Subsidiaries in the European Common Market : Legal and Tax Aspects* (2nd ed., 1976).

subsidiary presents fewer problems, from the point of view of tax or company law, at the time of creation of the combination.[76] It is in the subsequent conduct of the business of the combination that difficulties commonly arise, in particular in the transfer of profits from the subsidiary to the parent company. There is potential economic double taxation where dividends are paid by the subsidiary to its parent company and are subsequently redistributed by the parent to its own shareholders.[77] In a purely domestic situation relief is commonly given in one of two ways : either the dividend is taxed when paid by the subsidiary and may be redistributed by the parent tax-free,[78] or the dividend may be paid tax-free by the subsidiary to its parent but is taxed when distributed to the shareholders of the parent.[79] If the dividend is redistributed in full by the parent the result will be the same, but if it is not it will have borne tax in the former case but not in the latter. In an international context, double taxation may occur where the countries concerned have adopted different rules.[80]

**290**    The solution proposed in the draft Directive requires that dividends from a subsidiary[81] are not to be treated as a part of the profits of the parent company.[82] Profits distributed by a subsidiary to a parent are not to be subject to withholding tax, *i.e.* the dividend is paid tax-free to the parent and is taxed only on redistribution.[83] A parent company which holds at least 50 per cent. of the capital of its subsidiary would be permitted to opt for taxation according to a system of consolidated profits, under which the profits and losses of the subsidiary are included in the computation of the profits and losses of the parent, with allowance made for the fact that the subsidiary's profits have already been taxed.[84] Details of the common system of consolidated profits remain to be worked out.[85]

As with the proposed Directive on the taxation of mergers, this proposal cannot be viewed in isolation. In particular, it must be considered in relation to the proposed Directive on the taxation of company profits and

---

[76] The provisions granting relief from Company Capital Duty, under Dir. 69/335 (as amended) have already been considered : above, para. 265.

[77] The problem is in some respects similar to that where dividends are channelled through an investment institution to the original investor : see above, para. 282.

[78] *Cf.* the treatment of "franked investment income" in the United Kingdom.

[79] As happens in the United Kingdom when the dividend is paid between "associated companies."

[80] There may also be a problem where, as in the United Kingdom, the latter treatment applies only to associated companies and not to dividends generally, and the definitions of "association" differ from country to country.

[81] "Parent" and "subsidiary" corporations are defined in Art. 3. Any company holding a participation of at least 20 per cent. of the capital of another company is treated as a parent (Member States may impose a qualifying period not exceeding two years), but Member States are permitted to apply more liberal rules.

[82] Art. 4.

[83] Arts. 5, 6.

[84] The chief advantage of the consolidated profits system is to permit the parent to take advantage of the ability to deduct from its own profits the losses of its subsidiary.

[85] Art. 7.

distributions.[86] Thus, although the dividends of a subsidiary will have been paid to the parent free of withholding tax, the profits of that subsidiary will have been subjected to corporation tax in the normal manner and the question of the parent's entitlement to a tax credit in respect of a part of that corporation tax also arises.[87] Likewise, the treatment of dividends received by a company from investments in non-affiliates must be considered. It therefore seems clear that the proposals for parent companies and their subsidiaries will have to be reviewed, and probably revised,[88] in the light of whatever decisions may eventually be reached with regard to company taxation generally. Additionally, the proposed consolidated profits system would seem to be dependent upon there being a proper, harmonised, system of accounting for group profits.[89]

*(d)   The European Company*

**291**     A more radical solution for the removal of obstacles to the creation of industrial combinations at Community level was the proposal, initiated by Professor Sanders,[90] for the creation of a new form of incorporation—the European Company. The idea was adopted by the Commission, which submitted in 1970 a proposal for a Regulation[91] incorporating a Statute for a European Company. The main features of the proposal are that a European Company may be incorporated by registration in a European Commercial Register, maintained by the Court in Luxembourg. Such a company will be given legal recognition in all Member States and will have the same rights and powers as a company incorporated under national law : a European Company may be established when two or more companies, each incorporated under the law of a Member State, and of which at least two are subject to different national laws, merge or form a holding company or joint subsidiary.[92]

---

[86] Above, paras. 273–281.

[87] Art. 10 of the proposed company taxation Directive.

[88] For example, Art. 5(2) of the proposal provides for the case where a Member State employs the two-rate method of partial integration. This would not be permitted under the company taxation Directive.

[89] The Fourth Company Law Directive, Dir. 78/660 of July 25, 1978, prescribes rules concerning the disclosure of financial information and the contents of annual accounts. A further proposal, for a seventh Directive, provides for the submission of consolidated accounts for groups of companies and associated undertakings : proposal transmitted May 4, 1976; O.J. 1976, C 121/2.

[90] P. Sanders, *European Stock Corporation* (1969). The idea originated in a speech made by Prof. Sanders in 1959, though a similar suggestion was made, roughly simultaneously and apparently quite independently, by a French lawyer, M. Thibierge.

[91] Submitted June 30, 1970 : J.O. 1970, C 124/1.

[92] The original Sanders proposal would have permitted a single national company to transform itself into a European Company and would also have allowed companies from non-member states to adopt this form by incorporating a holding company or subsidiary jointly with a company from a Member State.

The proposal has met with a relatively lukewarm reception[93]: several commentators have indeed questioned whether there is any real need for such a form of incorporation.[94] A major difficulty is that the provisions of the Statute will have to be sufficiently attractive to induce enterprises to adopt the European form, whilst being sufficiently stringent to prevent the "emigration" of national companies which wish to escape from the regulations imposed upon them by domestic laws. To a great extent the debate on the proposal has focussed upon issues such as whether or not worker participation in the boards of directors of European Companies should be mandatory. However, similar considerations apply in the case of taxation. If the European Company is subjected to a heavier tax burden than a corresponding national company, there will be little incentive to adopt the form : if it is taxed less heavily, there will be a serious risk of the emigration of companies and the loss of tax revenue. Thus the adoption of adequate tax provisions is a pre-requisite to the creation of the European Company.[95]

**292**     The original Sanders proposal, whilst recognising the importance of taxation, gave very little indication as to how these problems might be solved. The Commission's proposal, especially in its amended form, does attempt to deal with the question.[96] By Article 275,[97] the allotment of shares in the European Company on its formation to the shareholders of the national companies, in return for their shares in those companies, is not to give rise to any tax liability. The European Company will be treated as resident, for tax purposes, in the Member State in which the centre of its effective management is located.[98] Where the company has a permanent establishment in another Member State only that state will have the right to tax the profits of the establishment.[99] Losses of a permanent establishment will be deductible from the profits of the company in the State in which it is resident.[1] The tax treatment of a permanent establishment maintained in

---

[93] The Commission has since submitted an amended proposal : (EC) Bull. S. 4–75.

[94] F. A. Mann, "The European Company" (1970) 19 I.C.L.Q. 468; Y. Scholten, "The European Company" (1968) 5 C.M.L. Rev. 9. See also the comments of J. van Hoorn Jr. (1968) 8 E.T. 75, who takes the view that the chief obstacles to European combinations are fiscal ones and if these are solved, which they would have to be in any event, the European Company would probably be unnecessary.

[95] Similar considerations apply in the case of the proposed Convention on the International Merger of Companies : (EC) Bull. S. 13–73. See especially Joint Declaration No. 3, at p. 99.

[96] For a comprehensive review, see G. Sessa and A. Vitali, *La Politica Fiscale della Communita Economica Europea* (1969), Chap. 11, and for a review of the Commission's tax proposals, see H. C. Ficker, "The Proposed Statute of a European Corporation" (1971) J.B.L. 167.

[97] References are to the amended proposal submitted on May 13, 1975 : (EC) Bull. S. 4–75.

[98] Art. 276. This may be determined by agreement of the competent authorities of the Member States concerned or, in default of agreement, by the Court.

[99] Art. 278.

[1] *Ibid.* Subsequent profits of the permanent establishment will be taxed in the country of residence up to the amount of the loss allowed.

another Member State is not to result in a greater charge to tax than would arise in the case of a company which carries on a business of the same nature and is resident for tax purposes in that state.[2] Provision is also made for the deduction of losses of a subsidiary of a European Company from the profits of that company in the state in which it is resident.[3]

The provisions are somewhat rudimentary and follow closely the principles incorporated in the proposed directive on the tax treatment of mergers, with regard to the taxation of permanent establishments,[4] and in the proposed Directive on the taxation of parent companies and their subsidiaries, though the provisions relating to the relief of losses are more extensive. Distributions of profits to a European Company from a subsidiary would presumably be governed by the directive on company taxation. Thus, adoption of the proposed European Company Regulation would seem to require also the adoption of the three proposed Directives and to be confronted with similar obstacles. So long as significant differences remain in the systems and levels of corporate taxation under national laws, investment and location decisions will be distorted and there will be dangers of manipulation to secure tax advantages. In particular, the allocation of profits among parent companies and their subsidiaries or permanent establishments in different Member States is likely to give rise to difficulties. A more radical solution, which avoids the need for such allocation, would be to subject European Companies, and their subsidiaries and branches, to a Community corporation tax which would constitute an additional part of the Community's own resources.[5] This, however, would probably require a complete harmonisation of the rates and bases of assessment of national corporation taxes, which would have to be virtually identical with the Community corporation tax system : otherwise, the decision whether or not to adopt the European Company form would be unduly influenced by tax considerations. Moreover, the Member States would have to be convinced that this method of augmenting own resources would be more equitable and less undesirable than any alternative. There would be fears that the companies of one Member State might be more likely to adopt the European form than those of another and any merger with, or takeover by, a European Company, since it would result in a decrease in national tax revenue, would be likely to meet with resistance in various forms, thus increasing the very obstacles which the European Company was designed to overcome.[6]

[2] Art. 279.
[3] Art. 281. For these purposes, a subsidiary is a company of whose capital the European Company holds not less than 50 per cent.
[4] The definition of "permanent establishment" in Art. 280 is virtually identical with that in the Annex to the proposed Directive.
[5] D. Dosser, *British Taxation and the Common Market*, (1973), pp. 166–167.
[6] Thus Professor Dosser regarded this only as a step towards an eventual Community corporation tax embracing the entire corporate section, and considered that some system of equalisation might be needed during this transitional stage.

### (vii)  International double taxation

**293**     According to the OECD Draft Convention,[7] "the phenomenon of international double taxation ... can be generally defined as the imposition of comparable taxes in two (or more) states on the same taxpayer in respect of the same subject matter and for identical periods." This is an over-simplification : international double taxation may also occur where two or more states seek to tax the same transaction or the same item of income or profit in the hands of different taxpayers.[8] The causes of such double taxation are numerous. In some cases it may result from the deliberate policies adopted by states, either to deter an outflow of capital by reason of their own residents investing abroad or to discourage investment in the country by foreigners. In other cases it results purely from fiscal greed. As one commentator has remarked:

> "In practice, there is a constant struggle between states as regards initial access to tax sources. And the struggle does not take the form of a dialogue designed to achieve an equitable balance, but rather the form of a one-sided and total exploitation of the sources of taxation at their disposal. Regardless of whether states proceed in such cases on the basis of residence or of territoriality, or of both, they will always seek to secure their share of the tax revenue and will often take more than other states are prepared to concede."[9]

And in other cases, double taxation is a more or less unintended consequence of the application of different tax rules and principles by the states concerned : differences in the bases of assessment of profits, of the categorisation of receipts or the deductability of expenditures, of the allocation of items to particular fiscal periods, and of the interpretation of tax provisions. Such differences may, though for obvious reasons they less commonly do, result not in double taxation but in the absence of taxation.

Whatever the reasons for, and causes of, international double taxation it is objectionable on the following grounds :

(1)  it violates the basic principles of fiscal justice;

(2)  it frequently provides an incentive to tax avoidance or evasion,[10] thus undermining tax morality and resulting in budgetary losses;

(3)  it distorts capital movements, the choice of location of enterprises and the conditions of competition.

---

[7] Model Double Taxation Convention on Income and on Capital, OECD, Paris, 1977. The passage quoted is taken from the General Remarks.

[8] *e.g.* associated enterprises or persons, transferor and transferee, etc. An example already considered (above, para. 267) occurs in the case of taxes on transactions in securities.

[9] Mr. Ritter, General Reporter of the 1975 International Fiscal Association Congress, in a speech quoted by B. Runge, "International Double Taxation with regard to Transnational Companies," (1977) *Intertax* 180.

[10] International double taxation and international tax avoidance are frequently two sides of the same coin. Many of the comments in this and the following sections of this chap. apply equally to both.

Its existence is consequently incompatible with the principles of the Common Market and action is necessary to achieve its elimination.

(a)   *The elimination of international double taxation*

**294**     As early as 1961 a Commission Working Group was set up to consider various problems in international taxation[11] and the subject has been almost constantly under consideration ever since. Essentially there are three approaches to the elimination of international double taxation, which are in some senses alternatives but in others are complementary :

**(1) Unilateral relief.** Virtually all national tax legislations contain provisions giving relief in respect of foreign taxes borne by taxable persons and in respect of the taxable income of non-residents. Thus a person resident in one state who derives income from another state will commonly be allowed a credit, in the state in which he resides, in respect of tax paid in the state from which the income is derived, to set against the tax levied in his home state upon that income. Such credit may be for the full amount of the foreign tax or may be partial only.[12] Similarly, income accruing in a country to a non-resident is frequently taxed at a lower rate than would be the case had it accrued to a resident of that country,[13] and is sometimes entirely exempted from tax.[14] Measures of this nature may be described as "unilateral," in that the relief is granted regardless of which other country the income is derived from, or paid to, and is not dependant upon the existence or otherwise of any agreement with that country.

Much of the potential for international double taxation is eliminated by these means and the combination of reduced rates of withholding tax and oredits for foreign tax also achieves, in many instances, a reasonably equitable division of tax revenue between the states concerned. However, differences in national tax legislation—rates of taxes and of withholding taxes, bases of assessment, extent and availability of credits, etc.,—prevent the complete elimination of double taxation.

**295**     In the context of the Community, the solution to many of the problems may be found in the harmonisation of tax legislation and practices. A major objective of many of the measures, adopted or proposed, which have already been discussed in this chapter, has been the elimination of double-taxation and it is unnecessary to consider these further. Additional har-

---

[11] (EEC) Bull. 1–62, p. 52. In particular, the Group was instructed to study double taxation and tax avoidance by use of tax havens.

[12] In most cases the credit may not exceed the amount of tax imposed in the home state in respect of that income. In some cases an exemption, rather than a credit, is given in respect of foreign-source income : *e.g.* certain holding companies in Luxembourg and the Netherlands (see below).

[13] Thus withholding taxes on dividends and interest may be imposed at lower rates than would apply to a resident.

[14] Income from government bonds are commonly exempted and some countries, *e.g.* Luxembourg, impose no withholding tax on bond interest generally.

monisation Directives might deal with matters such as the receipt, from a source in another Member State, of bond interest, royalties and similar forms of income by companies. The harmonisation of the bases of assessment of company profits would also help to eliminate one of the most persistent causes of double taxation. It may, however, be difficult to move much further in this direction without embarking upon the harmonisation of personal income taxes—a subject which, to date, the Commission has shown little intention to tackle.[15]

296    **(2) Bilateral agreement.** Harmonisation of tax legislation within the Community could (though it would not necessarily do so) eliminate double taxation in respect of transactions involving only states which are members of the Community. It would not do so where non-member states were involved.[16] Unilateral relief measures are commonly augmented by bilateral tax treaties, entered into between states, and such treaties will continue to be necessary between Member and non-member states. Assuming also that there will be no substantial harmonisation of personal income taxes in the foreseeable future, they will also remain necessary between Member States, unless replaced by a multilateral convention.[17]

The objectives of the Community would therefore appear to be twofold : first, to eliminate double taxation in transactions involving only Member States and, secondly, to achieve conditions of neutrality (and if possible to eliminate double taxation as well) in transactions involving non-member states. This would seem to require that all 36 treaties between Member States should be substantially the same, as should each group of nine treaties between the Member States and any particular non-member. To achieve this, however, two difficulties must be overcome. The tax systems of the Member States must be harmonised to a degree sufficient to ensure that similar treaties achieve similar results.[18] Secondly, although the Community clearly has competence to require that the treaties between Member States be identical,[19] it has no such competence[20] with regard to treaties made with non-members. Thus other means of international co-operation are necessary

[15] See below paras. 315–327.
[16] It might, however, create conditions of neutrality. Thus, if the relevant tax laws of all the Member States were identical, an American company could invest in any of them upon the same conditions (assuming also that each Member State had a similar tax treaty with the United States). The extent of the double taxation, if any, would be the same in each case.
[17] Below.
[18] The problem caused by a treaty between one country with an integrated corporation tax system and another country with a classical system has already been referred to : above, para. 279.
[19] e.g. a Directive could require the adoption of identical treaties by all Member States with fellow members.
[20] Since the elimination of international double taxation could be regarded as being a matter of Community policy, it may be proper for the Community to be involved in the negotiation of new treaties with non-members and to prevent a member from negotiating with a non-member a treaty which might create non-neutral conditions. But the Community has no power to compel a non-member to renegotiate an existing treaty with a member or to adopt any particular form of new treaty.

in order to achieve neutrality *vis-à-vis* non-Member States. An obvious example of such co-operation is the adoption, within the framework of the OECD, of a new model convention in 1977.[21] The Commission, however, can do little more than attempt to co-ordinate national policies with regard to renegotiation of treaties and to encourage Member States and non-members to adopt promptly the new model convention. Alternatively, the Community itself might enter into an agreement with a non-Member State, the provisions of which could be made binding upon all Member States and upon the non-member.[22]

**297**  **(3) Multilateral conventions.** An obvious alternative to a series of similar bilateral intra-Community treaties is a single Community convention, as envisaged by Article 220 of the Treaty.[23] This solution was advocated in the Segré Report[24] and by the Neumark Committee.[25] It is understood that a working group of the Commission prepared a draft convention as early as 1968, but as yet no formal proposal has been made. Again, it would seem desirable, if perhaps not essential, to first achieve a satisfactory measure of harmonisation of national tax legislation.[26]

A single convention, adopted by the Community and ratified by the Member States,[27] could therefore replace the existing bilateral treaties between Member States. It would not, of course, be applicable in instances involving non-Member States though there would seem to be nothing to prevent other states from acceding to it.[28] However, there has recently been proposed, within the Council of Europe,[29] a European multilateral agreement on co-operation between the Member States of that body against international tax avoidance and evasion. A similar measure would no doubt be possible to deal with the problem of international double taxation. This, of

---

[21] Above, n. 7.
[22] An example is afforded by the proposed Code of Principles for Multinational Enterprises and Governments, to apply between the Community and the United States : O.J. 1977, C 118/16.
[23] See I. Claeys-Bouuaert, "Ou en est le droit fiscal européen?" (1966) 2 C.D.E. 251, at pp. 268 *et seq.*
[24] Above, para. 257.
[25] *The EEC Reports on Tax Harmonisation*, pp. 141–145. The Committee proposed that such a convention should be based upon the OECD model, but that a number of amendments should be made.
[26] It has been suggested that one reason for the inactivity in this regard has been a fear, on the part of the Commission, that the premature adoption of a convention, though it might succeed in eliminating many instances of double taxation, might also lessen the incentive for the harmonisation which is necessary for other reasons : B. Snoy, *Taxes on Direct Investment Income in the EEC* (1975), p. 14.
[27] As with other conventions under Art. 220, *e.g.* on mutual recognition of companies and reciprocal enforcement of judgments. Precedents for such a tax convention may be found in that (of 1953) between the Benelux states, for the enforcement of tax claims, and the Nordic Convention of 1972.
[28] As has been the case with the convention on patents.
[29] Recommendation of the Parliamentary Assembly, No. 833, adopted April 24, 1978 : see (1978) *Intertax* 251.

course, requires that work within the Community be co-ordinated with that of other organisations, such as the Council of Europe and the OECD.

## (b)   Transfer pricing

**298**     A significant proportion of international transactions in goods and services takes place between associated enterprises established in different countries.[30] In a transaction between associated enterprises the price paid in respect of a supply of goods or services will frequently not be the same as that which would have been paid had the enterprises been entirely independent of each other. For such a difference in price there may be a number of reasons. Assuming, for example, that a subsidiary company supplies goods to its parent at a lower price than that which it would have charged an independent purchaser, that may simply be to offset the fact that it receives raw materials from its parent at a reduced price, or receives services or the benefits of research expenditure from the parent without payment. Or where the parent company pays a high price to its subsidiary for goods, or charges a low price for services, the explanation may be that the parent wishes to subsidise the offspring during its early years in order to encourage its attainment of self-sufficiency. Considerations of taxation may be entirely absent. In other cases the motivation may be regarded as an entirely legitimate form of tax planning. Thus, where tax rules prevent the losses of a subsidiary being set against the profits of the parent it may be quite proper to eliminate those losses, and correspondingly reduce the parent's profits, by over-paying the subsidiary for what it supplies to the parent and under-charging it for what it receives. In yet other cases pricing policy may be motivated by what is commonly regarded (at least by tax authorities) as improper tax avoidance or evasion. Thus, if the subsidiary is established in a low-tax country and the parent in a high-tax country, the price at which the subsidiary supplies the parent may be artificially inflated, increasing the profits of the subsidiary which will be taxed at a low rate and decreasing the profits of the heavily-taxed parent.[31] Opinions differ greatly as to the extent to which transfer pricing is determined by legitimate commercial considerations as opposed to the desire to reduce or evade taxation.[32] In any event it is clear that transfer pricing does result,

---

[30] A United Nations study has estimated that some 50 per cent. of all exports from the United States, and some 30 per cent. of British exports, represent intra-group transactions : see K. Messere, "OECD : Report on Transfer Pricing and Multinational Enterprises" 1979 *Intertax* 288.

[31] Various aspects of the use and abuse of transfer pricing are examined in detail in the chapters by B. Snoy (Chap. 2), J. H. Dunning and G. Yannopoulos (Chap. 3), G. Hutchings (Chap. 5) and M. Burgio (Chap. 8) in *Vers une politique fiscale* ...

[32] See, for example, T. Neilsen, "The Arm's-length Test : a Rule of Law or an Excuse for Arbitrary Taxation" (1979) *Intertax* 296; *cf.* the works of K. Messere and B. Runge referred to above, at nn. 9, 30.

occasionally or frequently, in tax avoidance or evasion and that the measures which are taken by most states to counteract this may, and commonly do, result in international double taxation.

### (c)   Double taxation

**299**      The problem of international double taxation was neatly summarised, in a report to the European Parliament, thus :

> "The interdependence of enterprises within the Community, resulting particularly from the activities of many transnational companies, facilitates artificial transfers of profits between associated enterprises operating in different countries.
>
> These transfer operations lead to tax evasion which the tax authorities counter by raising the taxable profits of the enterprise concerned to the level they would have reached if these transactions had been carried out between independent enterprises. However, these adjustments give rise to double taxation if the tax authorities of the other Member State do not make a corresponding adjustment of the taxable profits of the enterprise established in that state . . ."[33]

Double taxation, then, is a consequence of the measures adopted to combat tax avoidance or evasion.[34] Most countries have adopted such measures, which normally take the form of substituting a hypothetical "arms-length" price for the actual price charged in the transaction in question.[35] This may be done by increasing the amount of the actual receipt or by reducing the amount of allowable expense : if the other country does not make a corresponding adjustment, double taxation will result.[36] How can this be eliminated?

**300**      One possible approach would be to ignore the problem, on the basis that, as artificial pricing is due to an attempt to avoid or evade taxes, those who practice it are undeserving of sympathy. As was remarked in one English case, "[i]t scarcely lies in the mouth of the taxpayer who plays with fire to complain of burnt fingers . . ."[37] However, as has been suggested, there may

[33]  Report of the Committee on Economic and Monetary Affaris, E.P. Doc. 126/77, at p. 7 (the Couste Report).

[34]  It may, of course, also result from differences in national tax laws which are not specifically directed against avoidance, *e.g.* a payment is treated as a taxable receipt in one country but not as a deductible expense in the other.

[35]  For a survey of anti-avoidance measures in the Member States, see J. F. Avery-Jones (ed.), *Tax Havens and Measures against Tax Evasion and Avoidance in the EEC* (1974). See also J. Strobl, "Tax treatment in the Federal Republic of Germany of International Transactions between Affiliated Companies" (1974) B.T.R. 219, 312.

[36]  It may be observed that the interests of different tax authorities within the same country may also be in conflict. Thus, if goods are imported into a country at an inflated price, this may be challenged by the income tax authorities but be entirely acceptable to those who administer the value added tax.

[37]  *Per* Lord Greene M.R., in *Lord Howard de Walden* v. *I.R.C.* [1942] 1 K.B. 389 (Court of Appeal).

be entirely legitimate reasons for a price to differ from that which might have been charged in an arm's length transaction and to deny relief altogether might be regarded as an open invitation to national tax authorities to engage in arbitrary tax assessments.[38] At the other extreme, adjustments on an arm's length basis might be eliminated, at least with respect to transactions taking place wholly within the Community. This might be justified on the ground that, in so far as such adjustments are unnecessary within a single national market,[39] they should similarly not apply in the wider, Community, capital market. Such a solution might be possible, but only when a sufficient degree of harmonisation—of rates of corporation tax and of the bases of assessment—had been reached so that any "artificiality" in price would be for legitimate business reasons, since no tax advantage would be obtainable. Another alternative, which avoids the problem of double taxation, would be to tax "Community Multinationals" on a global profits basis, allocating those profits among the Member States concerned in an agreed manner.[40] In the long term this may be the most appropriate solution : meanwhile, however, Member States will continue to make tax assessments based upon adjusted prices and there is a need to mitigate the resulting double taxation.

### (d)   The proposed arbitration procedure

**301**     The solution commonly adopted in double taxation agreements is a "mutual agreement" procedure between the countries concerned.[41] This requires the competent authorities of those countries to attempt to resolve problems of double taxation by consultation and mutual agreement, in particular by establishing an acceptable "arm's length price." The procedure, however, is neither automatic nor comprehensive and there is no guarantee, to the taxpayer, that agreement will be reached and that an upward adjustment of profit in one country will be matched by a corresponding downward adjustment in the other.

The Commission has consequently proposed a Directive,[42] setting up an "Arbitration Procedure" for the purpose of eliminating double taxation in connection with the adjustment of transfers of profits between associated

---

[38] T. Neilsen, *op. cit.* above, n. 32.

[39] Though arms-length adjustments are sometimes necessary even in wholly domestic situations, in order to counter tax avoidance or evasion. To that extent they would need to be retained.

[40] See G. Hutchings; *op. cit.* n. 31; K. Messere, *op. cit.* above, n. 30. See also the proposed tax treatment of the European Company and that in the draft Directive on parent companies and their subsidiaries; above, paras. 289–292.

[41] See the OECD 1977 Model Convention, Art. 25. Similar provisions are found in Arts. 31–34 of the EEC/United States Draft Code (above, n. 22). For a comprehensive review of the procedure, see D. A. Waardenburg, "Transfer Pricing Arbitration Procedure" (1978) 18 E.T. 144.

[42] Proposal transmitted to Council on November 25, 1976 : O.J. 1976, C 301/4.

enterprises.[43] The proposal provides that where the amount of the taxable profits of an enterprise is increased or is likely to be increased by the tax authority of a Member State, as a result of conditions agreed in a transaction with an associated enterprise which differ from those which would have been agreed between independent enterprises, and double taxation results or is likely to result from the increase, each of the associated enterprises may present its case to the appropriate tax authority with a view to eliminating the double taxation.[44] That authority is required to inform the other national authority concerned without delay. The Directive is intended to apply both to transactions carried out directly with an associated enterprise established in another Member State and through a permanent establishment of such an enterprise situated in another Member State.[45] Enterprises are considered to be "associated" where one of the enterprises participates directly or indirectly in the management, control or capital of the other enterprise or where the same persons participate directly or indirectly in the management, control or capital of the enterprises.[46]

**302**    If neither of the tax authorities is able on its own to arrive at a satisfactory solution of the problem,[47] the two authorities are to endeavour to reach mutual agreement with a view to avoiding double taxation.[48] Failing such agreement, the tax authorities are required to present the case to an arbitration "commission," whose decision they must agree from the outset to accept.[49] The arbitration commission is to consist of an equal number of representatives from each of the tax authorities concerned plus an uneven number of independent persons, selected from a list of persons of standing nominated by the Member States.[50] The independent members are

[43] Although the proposed Directive differs in substance from the normal harmonisation Directives, it requires Member States to adopt the necessary laws, regulations and administrative provisions to comply with the Directive (Art. 9), and would seem to be properly founded upon Art. 100 of the Treaty.

[44] Proposed Directive 1(1). This is stated to be notwithstanding the remedies provided by the national laws of the Member States concerned. However, in some Member States the tax authorities have no power to depart from decisions of judicial authorities. The enterprise may therefore be placed in a dilemma—to appeal under national law or to resort to the arbitration procedure—since an unsuccessful appeal might preclude adjustments following arbitration : see the comments of the Parliament (O.J. 1977, C 163/24) and see Art. 3(2) of the proposed Directive.

[45] The procedure is also to apply to the allocation of the total profits of an enterprise between its headquarters in one Member State and its permanent establishments in other Member States : Art. 8.

[46] Art. 1(2). The definition is much wider than that used elsewhere to define parent companies and their subsidiaries.

[47] Presumably this means satisfactory to itself and to the enterprise?

[48] Art. 2. Thus far, the procedure is similar to the normal mutual agreement procedures under most tax treaties.

[49] Art. 3(1). This may be waived by mutual agreement and with the agreement of the enterprises concerned : Art. 3(3). The case must be presented to the commission within two years of its first being raised, if previous agreement has not been reached. It is not clear whether the enterprises must also agree to accept the decision : this is stated to be so by Art. 3(2), but it is also provided that the national authorities may agree otherwise.

[50] Art. 4.

appointed by mutual agreement or, in the absence of agreement, by the drawing of lots, in which case either authority may, in certain circumstances, refuse to accept a particular appointment.[51] The expenses of the arbitration proceedings are to be borne by the states concerned.[52] The commission may request that the associated enterprises appear or be represented before it and that they, and the national authorities, provide such information and produce such evidence and documents as may be of use in reaching a decision.[53]

**303**        The decision of the commission is to relate to the amount of double taxation which remains unrelieved by prior action or agreement. It may relate to the increase in taxable profits in one member state, the corresponding adjustment in the other Member State, or to both. The Directive requires that the decision "shall eliminate the said double taxation,"[54] Thus the main object of the procedure would seem to be to apportion taxable income between the national authorities and to resolve any dispute between them : nevertheless it is proper that the enterprises should themselves have a right to appear, since this apportionment may still affect the total amount of tax payable even though double taxation is eliminated.[55]

The proposal constitutes an important step towards the elimination of double taxation. It does, however, have a number of limitations. The way in which "double taxation" is defined[56] restricts its scope essentially to those cases in which an adjustment of profits is made by one national authority without a corresponding adjustment in the other. Thus it would not appear to apply to other instances of double taxation caused by differences in the bases of assessment of profits or in the categorisation of various receipts or expenditures.[57] This is primarily a matter for harmonisation, but meanwhile the availability of an arbitration procedure might be valuable. Secondly, it assumes the continued application of the "arms-length" principle without giving guidance as to how this principle should be applied.[58] Finally, of course, it will not be of assistance where one of the enterprises concerned is established in a non-member state.

### (viii)   Tax avoidance and evasion

**304**        The inter-relationship between international double taxation and tax avoidance and evasion has been commented upon in the preceding part of

---

[51] Art. 4(2). The enterprises apparently have no right to object to any member : see the comments of the Parliament, O.J. 1977, C 163/24.

[52] Art. 4(6). Apart from expenses incurred by the enterprises themselves.

[53] Art. 5. It would seem that the enterprises have a right to appear or to be represented and to present evidence : cf. the comments of the ESC, O.J. 1978, C 18/27.

[54] Art. 6.

[55] Depending upon how much of the profit is allocated to the higher-tax country and how much to the lower.

[56] Art. 1 (2)(c).

[57] See the comments of the ESC : O.J. 1978, C 18/27.

[58] Such guidance may, however, be derived from the published decisions of the arbitration commission.

this section of the chapter, in particular in the context of the transfer-pricing problem. Differences in national tax laws which give rise to instances of double taxation may equally well create opportunities for avoidance or evasion.[59] The immorality on the part of national tax authorities in taxing the same profit or transaction twice provides an incentive, and even a justification, for enterprises to seek to avoid as much tax as possible.[60] Conversely, the attempt to eliminate tax avoidance and evasion by greater co-operation between national tax authorities may itself result in an increase in double taxation : thus one reason given for the proposed arbitration procedure to eliminate double taxation was that such double taxation was likely to be increased as a result of the "mutual assistance" Directive[61] to control tax avoidance and evasion.[62]

### (a)  The distinction between avoidance and evasion

**305**      Thus far, the terms "avoidance" and "evasion" have been used together and indiscriminately. Some attempt should be made to distinguish between the terms for, together, they comprise various types of activity, varying from entirely legitimate "tax planning" to outright fraud which, in so far as they should be eliminated at all, may require very different forms of remedial action.

It is first of all necessary to draw a basic distinction between those activities which are illegal, commonly termed "evasion," and those which, whether they are undesirable or not, involve no breach of the law. Tax evasion, or tax fraud, may take various forms : the failure to file tax returns when required to do so, the deliberate understating or omission of receipts or the overstating of expenditures, the false claiming of allowances or deductions, the falsification of books of account or invoices, and so on. If detected, such activities are punished by the law. To eliminate them requires vigilance on the part of the authorities : to eliminate them in an international context requires co-operation on the part of the national authorities of the states concerned.

By contrast, it is impossible satisfactorily to define "tax avoidance," and difficult to draw the line between legitimate "tax planning" and undesirable avoidance. Most countries start out from the proposition that planning to secure the most favourable tax position attainable is perfectly proper. To repeat the oft-quoted statement of Lord Tomlin in the English House of Lords :

---

[59] See above, para. 293.
[60] B. Runge, "International Double Taxation with regard to Transnational Companies" (1977) *Intertax* 180.
[61] Dir. 77/799, discussed below.
[62] This appears in the Commission's explanatory memorandum accompanying the proposed arbitration procedure Directive. See also the Resolution of the European Parliament : O.J. 1977, C 163/24.

"Every man is entitled if he can to order his affairs so that the tax attaching under the appropriate Acts is less than it otherwise would be. If he succeeds in ordering them so as to secure this result, then, however unappreciative the Commissioners of Inland Revenue or his fellow taxpayers may be of his ingenuity, he cannot be compelled to pay an increased tax."[63]

**306**     Clearly, the taxpayer is entitled to take advantage of whatever concessions are offered to him by the tax system : indeed, that is normally the reason for the existence of concessions. It is only when a taxpayer seeks to avail himself of a concession, or to take advantage of some anomaly in the system, for a purpose or in circumstances not envisaged or intended by the legislature, that his conduct is considered to amount to tax avoidance. At that point, national tax authorities, and legislation, adopt a variety of means to counteract or nullify what is regarded as an abuse.[64] Special rules are commonly adopted to apply in the case of non-arm's-length transactions, regard may be had to the true substance of a transaction rather than to its form, powers may be given to counteract "artificial" transactions or those which are considered to constitute an *abus de droit*. The borderline between an artificial transaction, lawful, but the tax advantages of which are liable to be nullified by anti-avoidance measures, and a "sham" which, in so far as it may involve deliberate misrepresentation, constitutes evasion and may incur penal sanctions, is not always easy to discern and the location of this borderline may vary from one national tax system to another, as may the degree of artificiality or the extent of abuse which is tolerated.

However, the principal cause of tax avoidance lies in the non-neutrality of tax laws. Artificial transactions can only succeed in reducing tax liability if essentially the same transaction can be carried out in a variety of ways which produce different consequences. Thus, the best method of eliminating tax avoidance is through the harmonisation of tax laws. Harmonisation secures neutrality as between the tax laws of different Member States, thereby eliminating one form of international tax avoidance.[65] This, in itself, is not sufficient. The particular harmonised system must also endeavour to ensure that the system itself is neutral, as between different types of transaction, forms of enterprise, methods of financing and the like.[66]

---

[63] *Inland Revenue Commissioners* v. *Duke of Westminster* [1936] A.C. 1.
[64] For a comprehensive study of anti-avoidance measures, see J. F. Avery-Jones (ed.), *Tax Havens and Measures against Tax Evasion and Avoidance in the EEC,* (1974).
[65] *e.g.* the location of a holding company in one Member State rather than in another, for tax reasons.
[66] In this respect harmonisation also has a role to play in the prevention of tax evasion. The chosen system should be one which lends itself less easily to evasion. Thus, a value added tax, being to some extent self-enforcing, is preferable to a single-stage retail sales tax and a withholding tax on dividends and interest is desirable for the same reason.

(b)  *International co-operation and the "mutual assistance" Directive*

307     The Council Resolution of February 10, 1975[67] had called attention to the dangers, to the Community, of international tax avoidance and evasion. Not only do such practices lead to budgetary losses and violate the principles of fiscal justice, but they also create distortions of capital movements and of the conditions of competition. Action was called for to secure the mutual exchange of information necessary for making correct assessments of taxes on income and profit, co-operation in carrying out investigations, the provision of facilities for assistance between tax officials of different Member States and collaboration in all these respects with the Commission. Pursuant to this instruction the Commission submitted, in 1976, a proposed Directive[68] which was adopted by the Council in the following year.[69]

308     The Directive provides that the competent authorities of the Member States shall exchange any information that may enable them to effect a correct assessment of taxes on income and on capital.[70] Such taxes include all taxes imposed on total income, on total capital, or on elements of income or of capital, including taxes on gains from the disposal of movable or immovable property, taxes on the amounts of wages or salaries paid by enterprises, and taxes on capital appreciation.[71] Three types of exchange of information are provided for : these are referred to in the Directive as exchange on request, automatic exchange and spontaneous exchange. The competent authority of one Member State may request that of another Member State to forward information necessary to make a correct assessment of tax in a particular case.[72] The state receiving the request need not comply if it appears that the requesting authority has not exhausted its own usual sources, unless to do so might endanger the attainment of the sought-after result.[73] Thus, Article 2 allows an authority to seek assistance in a specific case where there is reason to believe that there may be tax avoidance or evasion, but does not authorise it to engage in a "fishing

---

[67] On measures to be taken by the Community in order to combat international tax evasion and avoidance : O.J. 1975, C 35/1.
[68] Doc. COM (76) 119 final.
[69] Dir. 77/799 of December 19, 1977 : O.J. 1977, L 336/15. For an analysis, see C. S. Salomons, "The EEC against Tax Evasion" (1978) 18 E.T. 136.
[70] Art. 1(1).
[71] Art. 1(2). The national taxes intended to be covered are listed in Art. 1(3). In the United Kingdom these are : income tax, corporation tax, capital gains tax, petroleum revenue tax and development land tax (but not capital transfer tax). Essentially similar taxes introduced subsequently are intended to be covered : Art. 1(4). The list does not appear to be comprehensive and contains some anomalies, *e.g.* the inclusion in some Member States, but not others, of what are essentially property taxes : see the Opinion of the Economic and Social Committee (O.J. 1977, C 56/66), which considered that death duties and gift taxes should also be included.
[72] Art. 2.
[73] *e.g.* by forewarning the suspected tax evader that investigations were being undertaken.

expedition." Article 3 provides that, in certain categories of cases, information is to be exchanged automatically, on a regular basis, without prior request. These categories are not set out in the Directive but are to be determined by consultation between the national authorities.[74] In its explanatory memorandum to the proposed Directive,[75] the Commission indicated that it had in mind categories such as the payment of dividends and royalties and the salaries of frontier-workers.[76] Article 4 provides for the supply of information, without prior request, in a number of other specified circumstances. This applies where one authority has grounds for supposing that there may be a loss of tax in another member state[77]; where a taxable person obtains a reduction in or an exemption from tax in one state which would give rise to an increase in or liability to tax in another Member State; where business dealings between persons in different Member States are conducted through one or more other countries in such a way that a saving in tax may result in either Member State or in both[78]; where there is reason to suppose that a saving of tax may result from artificial transfers of profits within groups of enterprises and where information received from another authority has enabled information to be obtained which may be relevant to the assessment to tax by the supplying authority. These categories may be extended to other cases by agreement and authorities may supply information in any other case, without prior request, if they so wish, if that information would be helpful in arriving at a correct assessment of taxes.[79]

**309**        An authority which is called upon to furnish information is required to do so as swiftly as possible.[80] If it encounters obstacles in furnishing the information, or refuses to do so, it must inform the requesting authority[81] to this effect, indicating the nature of the obstacles or the reasons for the refusal. The Directive permits an authority to refuse to supply information in a number of cases, *e.g.* where the information is required for purposes or in circumstances for or in which it would not be permitted, under its own national legislation, to make disclosure,[82] if its national legislation prevents it from collecting or using such information for its own purposes[83] or if the

---

[74] Arts. 3, 9.

[75] Doc. COM (76) 119 final : also set out in E.P. Doc. 67/76.

[76] It might have been preferable to specify these categories and make it obligatory throughout the Community to supply such information, rather than to leave it to agreement between national authorities.

[77] It is not clear what is intended by "loss of tax." Presumably the Directive does not apply to a reduction of tax by legitimate tax planning? See the comments of the E.S.C. : O.J. 1977, C 56/66.

[78] Again, it is not clear if this applies to entirely open and legitimate, as opposed to artificial, transactions : *cf.* the following category.

[79] Art. 4 (2), (3).

[80] Art. 5.

[81] This is confusing. Art. 5 refers to information "called for under the preceding articles," *i.e.* Arts. 2, 3 and 4, and thus appears to apply whether or not a request has been received. If so, there may be no "requesting" authority.

[82] Art. 7(2).

[83] Art. 8(1).

provision of such information would lead to the disclosure of a commercial, industrial or professional secret or of a commercial process, or of information whose disclosure would be contrary to public policy.[84] It is unclear what would be the effect of a refusal to furnish information on some other ground[85]: certainly, the Directive provides no sanction in the case of such refusal though it is submitted that a refusal, other than for a permitted reason, would constitute a breach, on the part of the Member State, of its obligations under Community law.[86]

Information received by one authority from another may be transmitted to a third authority with the consent of the authority which originally supplied it.[87] Provision is made in the Directive for the preservation of secrecy and confidentiality,[88] for collaboration by officials of national tax authorities,[89] for consultations between national authorities[90] and for the pooling of experience.[91]

**310**     The Directive applies only to direct taxes. However, a subsequent Directive[92] has now extended its field of application to include value added tax. This was felt to be necessary, not only because it was suspected that illegal practices, such as the fraudulent importation of goods and the issuing of false export invoices, are prevalent in some Member States, but also because VAT-fraud and the failure to collect taxes results, under the "own resources" system,[93] in a loss of revenue to the Community.[94] Moreover, co-operation with respect to VAT can be expected to facilitate, by means of cross-checking, the proper assessment of taxes on income and profits.

---

[84] Art. 8(2). The term "public policy" is rather vague here. It has been suggested that it ought to be interpreted in the more restrictive sense of "ordre public" : see the comments of the ESC.

[85] Art. 8(3) appears to permit refusal on the ground of lack of reciprocity, *i.e.* where the requesting authority would be unable, for practical or legal reasons, to provide similar information.

[86] *Cf.* the report of the Parliament's Committee on Economic and Monetary Affairs : E.P. Doc. 372/76 (the de Broglie Report). The permitted grounds for refusal are, however, sufficiently wide and nebulous to make this unlikely.

[87] Art. 7(4).

[88] Art. 7. The Parliament suggested that there should be an appeals procedure, at Community level, available both to national tax authorities and to individuals, in respect of decisions to, or not to, disclose information : O.J. 1976, C 293/34.

[89] Art. 6. By agreement, a Member State may authorise the presence within its jurisdiction of an official of another Member State in connection with the conduct of investigations.

[90] Art. 9. This envisages that consultations will be essentially bi-lateral. The Commission is not involved in the process and is only required to be informed of agreements which have been reached. It is therefore entirely possible that the level of co-operation between the authorities of any two Member States will be greater, or lesser, than between others.

[91] Art. 10. This is stated to apply in particular to questions of transfer pricing.

[92] Dir. 79/1070, of December 6, 1979.

[93] Above, Chap. 2, para. 124.

[94] (EC) Bull. 4–78, p. 42. It also results in a misallocation of the burden of financing the Community, to the detriment of those Member States whose administrations are most efficient.

Mutual assistance in this field would also seem to be an essential pre-requisite to any possible abolition of fiscal frontiers.[95]

These Directives have application only as between the authorities of Member States and are additional to any existing arrangements for co-operation contained in double taxation treaties.[96] Tax avoidance and eva-sion, of course, also occur between enterprises established within the Com-munity and associated enterprises in third countries, or by the use of "tax havens" situated elsewhere.[97] The Community, naturally, also seeks to participate in wider, international, efforts to counter tax abuse and mention may be made, in particular, of the proposed European multi-lateral agree-ment on co-operation between Council of Europe Member States against international tax avoidance and evasion.[98] This proposal goes considerably further than the Directives, in calling not only for mutual exchanges of infor-mation and co-operation between authorities, but also assistance in the recovery of tax debts, the abolition of unduly strict rules on bank secrecy, the study of various forms of economic crime and the promotion of an effec-tive system for taxing multinational companies.[99]

### (c)   Holding companies and tax havens[1]

311          One problem of special concern to the Community is the use of holding companies by multinational enterprises to secure tax advantages. Holding companies are commonly established in countries which afford special tax advantages : in some cases these take the form of generally low rates of tax or total exemption from tax.[2] More commonly, the advantages consist of special privileges accorded to certain types of company, in particular those which carry on business only abroad,[3] or in respect of income earned abroad.[4] Privileges of this sort exist in countries which would not commonly be regarded as "tax havens" at all.[5] A holding company established in such a country may be used to collect income, in the form of dividends, interest, royalties or licence fees, from associated companies in other countries : the

---

[95]   Above, Chap. 2, paras. 147, 150.

[96]   The directives are without prejudice to any wider obligations contained in a treaty, *e.g.* Art. 26 of the OECD Model : Dir. 77/799, Art. 11. Several of the Nordic Countries have expressed a wish to participate—(EC) Bull. 2/80, p. 43.

[97]   See below.

[98]   Recommendation of the Parliamentary Assembly, No. 833 (1978).

[99]   See the explanatory memorandum (the Pettersson Report), reproduced in (1978) *Intertax* 253, 298.

[1]   See J. van Hoorn Jr., "The Use and Abuse of Tax Havens," J. F. Avery-Jones (ed.) *Tax Havens and Measures against Tax Evasion and Avoidance in the EEC*, (1974), Chap. 1.

[2]   *e.g.* such exotic tax havens as the Bahamas, Bermuda, the Cayman Islands, etc.

[3]   Privileges of this type exist in countries such as Gibraltar, Liechtenstein and the Netherlands Antilles.

[4]   Preferential treatment of foreign-source income is relatively common and may be desig-ned to subsidise exporters, in which case it may be contrary to the GATT rules : see the note, "GATT : DISC and other discriminatory income taxes" (1977) 11 J.W.T.L. 546.

[5]   Thus, Luxembourg and the Netherlands are otherwise comparatively high-tax countries.

income received may be accumulated with little or no tax liability or may be redirected, often in the form of loans, to other members of the group. The result is tax avoidance (or at least the lengthy deferral of tax liability) and the distortion of the capital market and of conditions of competition.[6]

For the Community, the problem is twofold. The existence within the Community of these partial "tax havens" should be eliminated to achieve neutrality of tax conditions. The special advantages which exist, notably in Luxembourg[7] and in the Netherlands,[8] should be removed by the harmonisation of the tax treatment of foreign-source income and of withholding taxes on bond interest.[9] The difficulty, apart from persuading those countries to abandon practices which attract to them much international business, is that the inevitable result would be a flight of international capital from the Community to those non-Member States which offer, or would be prepared to offer, similar privileges.[10] Parallel action would consequently be required in a wider, international, context.[11] However, some small countries derive a substantial part of their national incomes from their status as international tax havens and these countries have, in the past, shown an understandable reluctance to co-operate in measures to eliminate tax avoidance and evasion. This leaves the possibility of the adoption by the Community (and by other countries whose interests are similar) of special provisions designed to deprive enterprises resident or operating within the Community of the tax advantages which they enjoy by virtue of having established a holding company or affiliate in a tax haven country. One solution which has been advocated[12] is to deny to companies making use of tax havens the right to open new establishments within the Community. This, however, seems somewhat arbitrary[13] and would also discriminate in favour of those enterprises which already have the good fortune to be established in most Member States as well as in a tax haven country. A more feasible, and reasonable, alternative would be for Member States to charge a special

[6] Commission Report on the Tax Arrangements applying to Holding Companies : Doc. COM (73) 1008 EEC.

[7] See A. Elvinger, "The position of Luxembourg within the EEC," J. F. Avery-Jones (ed.), *op. cit.* above, n. 1. The Luxembourg problem was acknowledged in the Commission's *Programme for the Harmonisation of Direct Taxes* : (EEC) Bull. S. 8–67, p. 14.

[8] M. A. Wisselink, "Tax Haven Companies and Dutch Tax Law" (1978) *Intertax* 211.

[9] This raises the issue of the special role of Luxembourg in the Eurobond market : see M. Sarmet, "Harmonisation Fiscale et Intégration des Marchés de Capitaux," *Vers une politique fiscale . . .*, Chap. 6.

[10] *e.g.* to Liechtenstein and Switzerland.

[11] As contemplated within the Council of Europe. The Pettersson Report (above, n. 99) considers the problem of tax havens within Europe.

[12] See the questions in Parliament of MM. Edwards and Notenboom, EPWQ 660/77, 343/78 : O.J. 1978, C 30/23, 251/10.

[13] It also raises the questions of which countries are to be considered to fall within the tax haven category and whether any use of a tax haven, for whatever reason, will result in reprisals.

increased rate of withholding tax on interest, royalties and similar payments remitted to companies which, by virtue of the tax laws of the countries where they are established, pay little or no tax on such income.[14]

### (d) Tax administration

**312**     Tax avoidance and evasion result in part from differences and anomalies in national tax legislations. Of perhaps equal importance are differences in the standards of administration and enforcement of tax laws. Once the Community has harmonised taxes beyond mere structures and has harmonised rates of tax to ensure equality of competition it will not be possible to ignore the question of fiscal control.[15] Mere "paper harmonisation" will not be sufficient, and it is necessary to distinguish between real and apparent tax burdens. As was said in the *Fredersdorf Report* :

> ". . . even laws that make the law completely identical on paper will not by themselves produce uniform taxation, if owing to differences of personnel, organisation or procedure or excessive differences of mentality in taxpayers the system of tax administration does not permit or ensure this."[16]

Differences exist in the structure and functions of tax authorities, the allocation of responsibility for particular parts of the tax system, the qualifications, training and conditions of work of the personnel.[17] Measures designed to approximate legislation or align underlying tax theory will not be fully effective unless the measures of inspection, verification and collection are also harmonised.[18] This applies, of course, to tax harmonisation generally, but is especially important in the context of the elimination of tax avoidance and evasion. Community legislation may succeed in eliminating certain abuses, but could conceivably give rise to a new type of tax haven—one which does not enforce its laws. As the Fredersdorf Report points out, it is not only differences in the efficiency of national tax administrations which

---

[14] This is proposed in the Commission's report on the tax treatment of holding companies : see above, n. 6. Also suggested by the Commission is a provision, modelled upon the Belgian rule, whereby the burden of proof is shifted so that a Community company, making any payment or transfer to a tax haven affiliate, must justify the transaction before being entitled to a tax deduction.

[15] Th. W. Vogelaar, "Die Entwicklung des Europäischen Steuerrechts" (1972) 55 F.M.C./E St. Z. 105.

[16] Report of the Section for Economic and Financial Questions of the Economic and Social Committee on Tax Harmonisation, Doc. CES 846/78, at para. 2.2.8.

[17] *Ibid.* para. 2.3.3.

[18] The need for parallel action in this field has long been recognised by the Commission : see (EEC) Ninth General Report (1966), p. 106; (EEC) Bull. S. 8–67, p. 7. More recently, the Economic and Social Committee doubted whether, at the present state of development of the Community, it is possible to achieve any great measure of harmonisation of official tax conduct : O.J. 1977, C 56 at p. 69.

cause the problem, but also differences of mentality in taxpayers. The standards of "tax morality" vary from one country to another[19] : in one country, tax avoidance and evasion may be regarded as a serious form of fraud, in another as a national sport.

#### (ix)  Other taxes affecting the capital market

**313**     Having considered the most important of the taxes which have an impact upon capital movements and the proper functioning of the capital market it remains to consider briefly some other taxes which may require to be harmonised or, perhaps, eliminated.

#### (a)  Taxes on transactions

As was seen in considering the Companies' Capital Duty,[20] Directives have been adopted or proposed with respect to the formation of company capital and to transactions in company securities. These measures do not apply to taxes or stamp duties on the transfer of business assets or of real estate, or on transactions such as mortgages. Taxes of such a nature, provided the rates are low as is generally the case, are unlikely to cause severe distortions of the market. Nevertheless, in so far as they affect the costs of incorporation, major differences in these taxes from one Member State to another may influence the conditions of competition in much the same way as differences in capital duty. Taxes are commonly also imposed on financial instruments, such as bills of exchange, cheques and contract notes. Such taxes are similar in effect to those upon company securities and, when employed in international trade, instruments of this type are frequently subject to double taxation. Consequently it seems appropriate that they should be harmonised or eliminated.[21] Of greater importance are the various taxes on insurance contracts. These vary widely and may affect not only the conditions of competition between insurance companies but also the choice of insurer.[22] An alternative, with many of these taxes, is to incorporate them

---

[19] See A. Dale, *Tax Harmonisation in Europe* (1963), Chap. 3, and the comments of M. Krauss, *Fiscal Harmonisation in the Benelux Economic Union* (1969), at pp. 49 *et seq.*
[20] Above, paras. 261–267.
[21] The matter has been under consideration by the Commission for some years : see (EC) Third General Report (1970), p. 82.
[22] The question has been under consideration by the Commission since 1962 : (EEC) Bull., 6–62, p. 29. A draft Directive was prepared in 1967, but has not been formally presented : (EEC) Tenth General Report (1967), p. 113. See further I. E. Schwartz, "Creating a Common Market for Insurance : the Harmonisation of EEC Insurance Legislation," G. W. Keeton and S. N. Frommel (ed.), *British Industry and European Law* (1974), Chap. 13. Another issue, recently raised, concerns the practice of some Member States, notably the United Kingdom, of giving tax relief for insurance premiums paid to domestic (but not foreign) insurance companies : see EPWQ 644 /79 and 1045/79; O.J. 1979, C 328/16, O.J. 1980, C 15/4. This might be contrary to Art. 67 of the Treaty?

into the value added tax.[23] However, as observed in Chapter 2,[24] the treatment of real estate transactions and of financial services presents considerable technical difficulty.

## (b)   Taxes on businesses

**314**      There are in addition, in some Member States, special taxes upon businesses, of which the German "Gewerbesteuer" and the French "Taxe Professionelle" are probably the best-known examples. Such taxes may be imposed upon business profits, turnover, capital assets, capital yield, or payroll : although the bases of assessment may be different, the effect is broadly similar to an additional imposition of corporation tax. At the present stage of the proposed harmonisation of corporation tax it seems unnecessary to consider these additional taxes, but when the rates of corporation tax and the bases of assessment are eventually harmonised it will be necessary to take them into account.[25]

One difficulty is that some of these taxes, notably the Gewerbesteuer, are local or municipal taxes. Although local taxes are clearly within the jurisdiction of the Community it is generally assumed that they cause no significant distortion in the functioning of the Common Market and that harmonisation will not be necessary. However, where these taxes are substantial and overlap with national taxes which are to be harmonised, their existence can scarcely be disregarded.[26] But whereas in one Member State municipalities may raise revenue by means of a tax on business profits, in another this may be done through taxes on real property.[27] These may impose just as heavy a burden on businesses and have a similar effect upon their competitive position. The Community would surely be most reluctant to intervene in the allocation of tax revenue and taxing powers between the central and local authorities of a Member State or to preclude local authorities altogether from imposing any tax which has been harmonised or overlaps with a harmonised tax.[28] Nor is it possible to ignore the fact that the level and type of services provided by municipalities varies from one municipality, and Member State, to another and that, to a large extent, local taxes represent a payment for these services. It therefore seems that, when rates of taxes (such as the corporation tax) are eventually harmonised, the impact of the more important local taxes should be taken into account in fixing the national rate

---

[23] (EC) Fourth General Report (1970), p. 41, and see the comments in the *Fredersdorf Report*, at para. 4.2.5.2.

[24] Above, para. 122.

[25] In answer to a question in the Parliament, the Commission stated that these taxes would only be considered at a later stage : O.J. 1979, C 57/6.

[26] Fredersdorf Report, para. 4.1.7.

[27] Local property taxes are especially heavy in Ireland and in the United Kingdom.

[28] Thus, in the case of excise duties on alcohol, the Commission accepts that purely local taxes on the consumption of alcohol may be retained : see p. 139, n. 56, above.

within the prescribed limits,[29] but that otherwise local taxes should not be subject to harmonisation.

### F.   Taxation of Personal Income and Wealth

#### (i)   The harmonisation of direct personal taxation

**315**    The Commission's *Programme for the Harmonisation of Direct Taxes*[30] envisaged that tax revenue in the Community would derive from three major sources—taxes on consumption (the value added tax) and some major excise duties, which would be harmonised to the necessary degree : a general tax on company profits, also harmonised : and a single comprehensive personal income tax, which would differ from one Member State to another for a long time to come. Having considered the first two of these sources it is necessary, briefly, to advert to the third. Also to be considered are those other forms of direct personal taxation, such as taxes on capital gains, on transfers of wealth (gift and inheritance taxes and estate duties) and on net wealth. Finally, the relationship between personal income taxes and social security contributions must be taken into account.

Personal income tax varies greatly from one Member State to another, as to its application to individuals and families, as to rate structures and as to effective tax burdens when account is taken of the various allowances and deductions which may be permitted. In some Member States each individual is taxed separately,[31] in some the incomes of husband and wife are aggregated, in others the incomes of dependent children are also aggregated into the family income. The threshhold at which income tax becomes payable varies,[32] as does the initial rate of income tax,[33] the maximum rate,[34] and the point at which the maximum rate is reached.[35] Such comparisons may, of course, be misleading since income levels also vary widely. However, a single person earning the average male industrial wage of a country

---

[29] This could be done according to a formula to be agreed between the Member State and the Commission.

[30] (EEC) Bull. S. 8–67 : above, paras. 258–260.

[31] Or, as in the United Kingdom, may elect to be taxed separately on earnings.

[32] A married couple with two children may earn over 5,000 EUA in Luxembourg before becoming subject to tax. At the other end of the scale a similar family in France would commence to pay tax at about 1,300 EUA. These, and the following figures on income tax, are taken from the replies of the Commission to questions raised in Parliament by Mr. Howell : EPWQ 230, 232, 1217, 1218/77; O.J. 1977, C 233/6, O.J. 1978, C 175/16. Recent tax changes in some Member States will have altered them to some extent. See further, App. A, Table 6.

[33] From 5 per cent. in France to 41 per cent. in Denmark.

[34] From 56 per cent. in Germany to 83 per cent. in the United Kingdom (this has now been reduced to 60 per cent. The maximum rate remains above 70 per cent. in several Member States).

[35] From 1.34 × average earnings in Denmark to 14 × in Italy.

may pay as much as 38 per cent.[36] or as little as 7 per cent.[37] of his earnings in income tax. Similarly when deductions are made for family benefits received, a married couple with two children and with average earnings may pay 28 per cent. of this in taxes[38] or, in four countries, be a net recipient.[39]

Capital gains are taxed in all Member States, either as part of income or separately (and commonly at a lower effective rate than other forms of income) but their definition and the extent to which they are taxed varies considerably.[40] Major differences exist in the systems and burdens of gift and inheritance taxes and estate and succession duties,[41] and personal wealth is taxed in four Member States[42] but not in the others.

### (a)   The Need for harmonisation

**316**          Given these major differences, the question arises whether there is any need for harmonisation. Justification for harmonisation may be found on a number of grounds :

(1) The requirements of a free capital market. A completely unified capital market might require that all investors, wherever resident within the Community, should receive similar treatment. A free, or "neutral," market simply requires that tax considerations do not distort the choice of where, or in what, to invest. Thus personal income tax rates may vary, provided that no discrimination exists as to the source of the income. This the proposals for the harmonisation of taxes on company profits and distributions and for the elimination of double taxation seek to achieve. It may be, however, that differences in wealth and estate taxes, especially in so far as a distinction is made between domestic and foreign wealth, or different types of wealth, have an impact upon investment decisions.

(2) The freedom of establishment. One of the major aims of the proposal for the harmonisation of corporate taxation is to achieve neutrality with respect to the choice of location of business enterprises. Execessive differences between Member States in the levels of income tax upon the profits of unincorporated businesses may also influence that choice and, similarly, differences within a Member State in the taxation of the profits of companies and of unincorporated businesses may affect the choice of the

---

[36]  In Denmark. The United Kingdom ranks second at 27 per cent.
[37]  In Italy.
[38]  In Denmark. The United Kingdom again ranks second at 16 per cent.
[39]  In Belgium, France, Italy and Luxembourg. The French family would receive an additional 8 per cent.
[40]  EPWQ 273/78 : O.J. 1978, C 282/8.
[41]  EPWQ 274/78 : O.J. 1978, C 238/24.
[42]  Denmark, Germany, Luxembourg and the Netherlands : EPWQ 273/78, above n. 40. For comprehensive details of wealth taxation, see the report of the OECD Fiscal Affairs Committee, *The Taxation of Net Wealth, Capital Transfers and Capital Gains of Individuals,* OECD, 1979.

legal form of an enterprise.[43] It has also been suggested that unusually high marginal rates of personal income tax, which might apply to the salaries of senior executives, may influence a company's choice of location.[44]

(3) Competition. Differences in the taxation of profits of unincorporated businesses may distort the conditions of competition. The levels of taxation on wages and of social security contributions have an effect upon labour costs. Frequently, of course, there will be compensating factors, such as higher social security benefits or greater state aids to industry.[45] Tax on profits and wages is one element only of the cost of production and to attempt to harmonise taxation without harmonising other important elements, some of which may not be susceptible to harmonisation,[46] may actually create greater distortions. But where a particular market is already subject to a high degree of Community regulation,[47] differences in taxation may cause distortions which cannot be countered by other market forces.

(4) The free movement of workers. Taxation is probably a very minor element in determining one's choice of workplace.[48] Other factors are normally far more important—the existence of cultural or language barriers, the availability of employment and housing, the cost of living, the level of real wages and of social security benefits. It therefore seems unnecessary to harmonise personal income tax in order to facilitate the free movement of workers : indeed, it may be questioned whether the objectives of the Community extend to the encouragement of labour mobility[49] rather than simply to removing discriminations against those workers who do choose to migrate. Where differences in personal taxation do result in discriminations some harmonisation seems to be called for.[50]

(5) The level and funding of social security benefits. A close relationship exists between personal taxation and social security contributions, and between personal tax allowances and social security benefits. This issue is discussed below.

[43] This was recognised in the Van den Tempel Report and was a factor in the Commission's choice of the "imputation," rather than the "classical," method of taxing companies : see above, para. 278.

[44] J. H. Dunning and G. Yannopoulos, "The Fiscal Factor in the Location of Affiliates of Multinational Enterprises," *Vers une politique fiscale* . . . , Chap. 3, at pp. 109–110 : J. M. Hollrah, "Taxation of Cross-border Concentrations in the EEC" (1974) 9 Texas Int. Law Jo. 313, 337. If an executive moves to a country where his marginal tax rate is 75 per cent. or higher, it may be prohibitively expensive to match his former salary and constitute a great inducement to tax avoidance by means of "fringe benefits." It is sometimes suggested that the high rates in the United Kingdom have deterred enterprises from locating there, *cf.* K. Exley, "U.K. Destination London—What Tax Bill will arise?" 1979 *Intertax* 424, who suggests that an executive posted to the United Kingdom may well (now) enjoy "a mild tax holiday."

[45] State aids, however, may be subject to review under Arts. 92, 93 of the Treaty.

[46] *e.g.* climate, distance from markets, the availability of skilled workers, labour relations.

[47] *e.g.* agriculture : see below.

[48] Except perhaps in the case of highly paid executives; above.

[49] Assimilation of personal income taxes might tend to intensify the migration of labour and to aggravate the problems which are thereby created : R. Regul and W. Renner, *Finances and Taxes in European Integration* (1966), Chap. 3.

[50] See below.

(6) Social justice. The personal tax system performs, or may perform, an important function in the redistribution of wealth. This is discussed in Chapter 4.[51]

(7) The ratio between direct and indirect taxation. This is an important aspect of economic policy and is considered in Chapter 4.[52]

### (b)   Proposals for the harmonisation of personal taxation

317        It is clear that the harmonisation of personal direct taxation, of incomes and of wealth, in so far as it has been considered to be necessary at all has been perceived as being of a far lower priority than that of indirect taxes and taxes on companies. The Neumark Committee[53] considered that, during the second phase, some harmonisation of personal income tax would be necessary and that there would be a need to study taxes on wealth and inheritances.[54] It was suggested that a certain degree of approximation of taxation structures, with respect to the balance of direct and indirect taxation, would be desirable and that the same type of single tax on income, with a similar structure of scales, though not necessarily with similar rates, should be levied in all Member States.[55] A wealth tax, at low rates, was recommended and, in so far as estate or inheritance taxes may lead to a transfer of capital or of domicile, some approximation might be required.[56]

More recently, the Fredersdorf Report has raised again the question of the balance between direct and indirect taxation.[57] It considers that harmonisation of income tax on wages and salaries will not be essential, although really large differences would definitely be undesirable, especially in connection with cross-frontier movements of labour.[58] The harmonisation of wealth taxes and estate and succession duties is also felt to be unnecessary, except where these taxes have business implications which interfere with competition. Some alignment, however, is required between taxes on company profits and those on unincorporated businesses.[59]

318        As already observed, the Commission envisages, as one of the three major sources of tax revenue, a single comprehensive personal income tax, though this would differ from one Member State to another for a long time

---

[51]  Below, paras. 429–430.
[52]  Below, paras. 407, 429.
[53]  *The EEC Reports on Tax Harmonisation* (1963), pp. 97 *et seq.*
[54]  *Ibid.* pp. 154–155.
[55]  *Ibid.* pp. 117–119. In particular, any remaining schedular income taxes should be assimilated into a single structure. The Committee also considered that capital gains should receive the same treatment in all Member States and that a common system of taxing the family unit would be desirable : p. 120.
[56]  *Ibid.* p. 127.
[57]  Information Report of the Section for Economic and Financial Questions of the Economic and Social Committee on Tax Harmonisation : Doc. CES 846/78, paras. 3.1.2 and 5.
[58]  *Ibid.* para. 4.1.6.
[59]  *Ibid.* para. 4.2.6.2.

to come and would remain under the control of the Member States.[60] The possible need for some measures with respect to income taxes has been acknowledged, in order to facilitate the free movement of frontier and migrant workers.[61] This apart, the Commission has repeatedly asserted[62] that, at the present stage of development of the Community, the harmonisation of personal taxes is not envisaged. As a member of the Commission recently stated :

> ". . . it is not our ambition to harmonise personal income tax in general, which is an important instrument of national policy and should be left to member states even when the Community achieves a much higher degree of integration than at present. But there are certain features of national income tax systems which may make it difficult for citizens of one Community country to work or settle in another—although such an effect was probably never intended. We are therefore examining the field of income tax in order to identify such obstacles or hindrances and see what can be done about them."[63]

**(ii) Frontier and migrant workers**

**319**     The Commission, as Mr. Burke explained, is presently examining income tax legislation with a view to eliminating obstacles or hindrances to the free movement of workers, and has been doing so for some time.[64] These obstacles appear to fall into three main categories :

*(a) Double or discriminatory taxation*

A person who resides[65] in one country and earns income in another country, by performing work or providing services[66] there, is commonly liable, under national tax legislation, to tax on that income in both countries. The one country seeks to tax its own residents upon their global income, the other to tax income earned there. Commonly, relief against double taxation is afforded, either by national legislation which allows a credit for foreign tax

---

[60] (EEC) Bull. S. 8–67, p. 8 : (EC) Bull. 9, 10–69, p. 9.

[61] Attainment of the Economic and Monetary Union, (EC) Bull. S. 5–73, p. 14. See below.

[62] In reply to questions in the Parliament : see EPWQ 672/76, O.J. 1977, C 27/31; EPWQ 1/77, O.J. 1977, C 148/77; EPWQ 273/78, O.J. 1978, C 282/8.

[63] R. Burke, "Harmonisation of Taxation in Europe" 1979 *Intertax* 46, 48.

[64] (EC) Sixth General Report (1972), p. 71; (EC) Seventh General Report (1973), p. 168; (EC) Twelfth General Report (1978), p. 122. A proposed Directive on the taxation of frontier and migrant workers was submitted to the Council on January 28, 1980 : O.J. 1980, C 21/6.

[65] Frequently a person will be held to be resident in a country if he maintains a home there for his family. Thus it is not only the frontier worker but also the married migrant worker who may be affected.

[66] In the case of provision of services the question also arises as to where the services are performed. A similar problem exists under the value added tax system : see above, Chap. 2, paras. 123, 127, 134.

paid or by means of bi-lateral conventions, which attempt to resolve questions of dual residence[67] and to ensure that earnings are taxed in one or other country but not in both.[68] However, although double taxation conventions now exist between all Member States of the Community, the treatment of migrant and frontier workers varies considerably from one convention to another.[69] And even though double taxation may be eliminated, discriminations may persist according to which of the two countries taxes the income. Problems arise with regard to the aggregation, or non-aggregation, of income earned in the one country with other income of the worker, or with the income of his spouse,[70] with regard to the rate of tax payable in each country,[71] or with regard to the deductions which are permitted from taxable income or from tax.[72] In some cases this may be to the advantage of the migrant worker : more often it is not. In any event, the result is that the migrant and non-migrant worker receive different treatment, contrary to the spirit of the Treaty.[73] The solution would appear to lie in the adoption of uniform provisions, by amending existing bi-lateral conventions, by adoption of a multi-lateral convention, or by means of a Directive.[74]

### (b) Taxation of social security benefits

**320** Under legislation governing national social security systems, entitlement to, and the level of, benefits may depend upon the payment of qualifying contributions and upon the residence of the beneficiary within the jurisdiction. Both types of restriction may be entirely justifiable : under some systems benefits are in effect "purchased" by the contributions made by employer and employee,[75] and in some cases it may be unreasonable to expect benefits to be paid to a worker's dependants who reside in another

---

[67] The frontier or migrant worker may be resident in one country, by virtue of having a home there for himself and his family, and in the other, by virtue of his length of stay there. The OECD Model Treaty, Art. 4, resolves the question of "fiscal domicile," according to various criteria—permanent home, centre of vital interests, nationality or, in the last resort, by mutual agreement between the countries.

[68] Earnings from long-term employment being taxed in the country where the work is performed, and from short-term employment in the country of fiscal domicile : OECD Model Treaty, Art. 15.

[69] See the Opinion of the Economic and Social Committee on the problems of frontier workers : O.J. 1979, C 128/41. This points out eleven possible variations.

[70] Thus affecting the marginal rate of tax payable.

[71] The income of a non-resident may be taxed at a special flat rate of tax, often higher than that which would apply to a similar resident worker.

[72] See below.

[73] And perhaps contrary to Art. 48 of the Treaty and to Art. 7(2) of Reg. 1612/68 : see below.

[74] The provisions would have to be more comprehensive than those of the OECD Model Treaty, and deal with the problems of aggregation, rates and deductions.

[75] e.g. earnings-related pensions or unemployment benefits and redundancy payments based upon length of service.

country.[76] Nevertheless, the non-transferability of qualifying contributions or qualifying periods of service and territorial restrictions upon the payment of benefits constitute a major obstacle to the free movement of workers and tend to put the migrant worker at a disadvantage compared to the worker who remains in his home country. The Community has attempted to resolve these problems by co-ordination of national policies, providing for the aggregation of qualifying periods and for the payment of benefits to persons resident anywhere within the Community.[77] The object is to ensure that as regards entitlement to receive social security benefits, the migrant worker and his family are placed in the same position as national workers.

With regard to personal income tax this may give rise to difficulties where social security benefits are treated as tax-free receipts in one country but as taxable income in another. Thus, an individual may work in country A and, as a result, benefits may be paid to him or to his family, in country B. Such benefits may be tax-free in country A, but taxable in country B. Consequently the net benefits received would be lower than would be those received by an equivalent worker or family resident in country A, and lower than had been intended by the authorities in country A.[78] The position, of course, might be reversed if benefits, which would normally be taxable in the paying country are not taxed there[79] and are treated as non-taxable income in the country in which they are received. In some cases it is even possible that, due to *lacunae* in the relevant tax treaties, a benefit is taxed in both countries.[80]

**321**    A solution to these problems is not easy to find. Clearly, instances of double taxation should be eliminated by improving existing tax treaties, or replacing them with a multi-lateral convention. Otherwise, however, it appears that no discrimination is practised against the migrant worker in the country in which he works if he is taxed, or not taxed, there in the same way as a national worker. Nor is he, or his family, discriminated against in the country of residence by virtue of the fact that he works elsewhere, provided

[76] Such benefits may derive from contributions or may be provided as part of a non-contributory social assistance programme, in which the work relationship is non-existent. Moreover, the dependants may reside in a country in which living standards and cost of living are much lower.

[77] By action taken under Art. 51 of the Treaty, notably in Reg. 1408/71 : see D. Wyatt, "The Social Security Rights of Migrant Workers and their Families" (1977) 14 CML Rev. 411.

[78] See the decision of the Netherlands Hoge Raad, in *Re Tax Assessment of Social Security Benefits of Frontier Workers* [1971] C.M.L.R. 462. Sickness benefits and child allowances paid by the Belgian Government to a worker who worked there but resided in the Netherlands were held to be properly taxable in the Netherlands, although they would not have been taxed in Belgium. The Court held that Reg. 3 of 1958 (J.O. 1958, p. 561), the forerunner of Reg. 1408/71, was concerned only with social security schemes and had no application to taxation. This view appears to be supported by the Commission : see the reply to EPWQ 310/77, O.J. 1977, C 246/15.

[79] By virtue of provisions in a double taxation treaty, under which the recipient is taxable only in the country of residence.

[80] EPWQ 310/77, above n. 78.

of course that relief is given in respect of any tax imposed in the paying country. Indeed, it would be contrary to principles of horizontal equity to tax foreign-source pensions or benefits differently from those with a domestic source. And even were it to be agreed, for example, that all Member States would regard social security benefits as taxable income, such benefits would be taxed at different rates in different states. In so far as migrant workers are influenced at all by questions of taxation and social security they would still tend to seek work in the country in which the net benefits were greatest.[81] Thus, apart from eliminating double taxation, it would appear that action is neither necessary nor feasible.

### (c)  Tax allowances and deductions

**322**    A single wage earner has, all other factors being equal, greater discretionary spending power than has a worker with a dependant spouse, infant children or other dependants. This fact is recognised in all Member States, either by the payment of social security benefits, such as children's or dependants' allowances, or through the taxation system, by applying lower tax rates or by giving deductions from taxable income, or commonly by a combination of both methods. Much of what has been said above in relation to social security benefits applies equally to tax allowances or deductions. However, a further problem exists when a migrant or frontier worker is taxed upon his earnings in the country in which he works if he is denied allowances or deductions from tax for his dependants, because they are resident elsewhere, which would be permitted to an equivalent national worker. For example, a Dutch national working, and taxable, in Germany may be denied the normal deduction for a dependant relative, or his marital status may not be recognised, because the relative or spouse is not resident in Germany.[82] This appears to be a clear instance of discrimination, since the migrant worker does not receive the same treatment as the national worker in the country in which he works.

**323**    Article 48 of the Treaty provides that the freedom of movement of workers ". . . shall entail the abolition of any discrimination based on nationality between workers of the Member States as regards employment, remuneration and other conditions of work and employment." It is further provided, in Council Regulation 1612/68,[83] that:

> "1. A worker who is a national of a Member State may not, in the territory of another Member State, be treated differently from national workers by reason of his nationality in respect of any conditions of

---

[81] Though there are exceptions, high benefits tend to go with high wages, high wages with high taxes, and both with available employment.

[82] EPWQ 977/76, O.J. 1977, C 148/41 : EPWQ 908/78, O.J. 1979, C 133/4. This is not an uncommon situation and is not restricted to the two countries mentioned.

[83] Reg. 1612/68 of October 15, 1968, Art. 7.

employment and work, in particular as regards remuneration, dismissal and, should he become unemployed, reinstatement or re-employment;

2. He shall enjoy the same social and tax advantages as national workers."

It may be objected that "remuneration and other conditions of work," or "any conditions of employment and work," do not extend to the conditions of taxation of income. However, the Court of Justice has held[84] that the Regulation applies to allowances whose payment is related to employment,[85] regardless of whether it is based on a statutory or contractual obligation. Moreover, the Regulation expressly refers to social[86] and tax advantages. A further objection is that to deny a tax deduction for a non-resident dependant is not a discrimination based on nationality : a national worker whose spouse or dependant lived elsewhere might similarly be denied the deduction. Nevertheless, a rule based upon residence may conceal a discrimination based upon nationality[87] and the Court considered that there could be discrimination if the grant of an allowance were conditional upon being resident.[88]

**324**     It is therefore unclear whether or not a restriction of this nature is, by virtue of the Treaty and of the Regulation, necessarily invalid.[89] If the requirement that dependants be resident within the country applies equally to nationals and to non-nationals it may be entirely valid[90] : indeed, if the migrant worker has other income taxable in his home country he may well be entitled to a deduction or allowance there in respect of his dependants. Moreoever, such allowances commonly take into account any income of the dependant and further complications arise from the fact that differences exist, from one Member State to another, in the tax treatment of the family unit. In many cases it would therefore be preferable to assess the total tax liability of the family in the home country, according to the normal rules of that country, allowing a credit for the tax paid by the migrant worker in the host country. Unfortunately, the families of many migrant workers have little or no income other than that earned by the migrant and to deny an

[84] Case 152/73 *Sotgiu* |1974| E.C.R. 153. The case concerned a "separation allowance" payable to a worker who is separated from home and family. The allowance was restricted to cases where the home was situated elsewhere within Germany.

[85] This is not to be construed narrowly. Thus, members of a worker's family—his widow and children—are protected even after the employment has ceased : Case 32/75 *Christini (Fiorini)* |1975| E.C.R. 1085.

[86] In Case 32/75, above, this was held to apply to the right to reduced rail fares.

[87] See the remarks of Advocate General Mayras in Case 152/73, |1974| E.C.R. at p. 173.

[88] *Ibid.* at p. 166.

[89] See the replies of the Commission to EPWQ 977/76 and 908/78, above, n. 82. In its earlier reply, the Commission took the view that there was no infringement of the Treaty : in the later reply it considered that there might be, and stated that it intended to submit proposals.

[90] One problem, in granting deductions for non-resident dependants, is to verify that they actually exist. The automatic exchange of information concerning frontier workers, under Dir. 77/799 (above, paras. 307–310), should help to prevent abuse.

immediate tax deduction in the host country might cause hardship and administrative difficulties and delays, even if full tax credit were eventually to be given.

### (iii)  Social security systems[91]

325       Differences in the provision of, and levels of, social security benefits may have an influence upon the free movement of workers and the choice of workplace. Similarly, differences in benefits, and in the way in which they are funded, affect labour costs and may influence decisions as to the location of enterprises, as well as affecting conditions of competition between enterprises. Major differences exist within the Community, as to the absolute levels of social expenditures, the types of benefits which are provided, the manner in which they are provided,[92] and the means by which they are funded.[93] Such differences commonly reflect the overall level of prosperity of a country and its social and political traditions, philosophies and priorities.

The Treaty[94] envisages some approximation of social policies, but does so only in the most general terms. The Commission's *Social Action Programme* of 1973[95] scarcely mentions the levels of social security benefits or the means of financing them and makes no proposals for harmonisation. Priority has been given to more pressing issues—unemployment, inflation and the participation of workers in decision-making processes—and it is generally concluded that overall harmonisation of social security systems is simply not feasible at the present stage of development of the Community.[96] The most that might be expected, in the medium-term, is a gradual levelling upwards of benefits by the adoption of certain minimum standards.[97] Nor is any great need for harmonisation perceived. The level and availability of benefits is simply one of the many factors which influence the movement of workers, some of which are not capable of being harmonised.[98] The cost of providing benefits is only one of the elements in labour costs, which cannot be isolated from other elements.[99] Thus, in the view of the Commission,

---

[91] This topic will be dealt with very briefly. For comprehensive analyses, see N. Andel, "Problems of Harmonisation of Social Security Policies in a Common Market," Shoup : *Fiscal Harmonisation,* Chap. 5; P. R. Kaim-Caudle, *Comparative Social Policy and Social Security : a Ten Country Study* (1972).

[92] *i.e.* by cash allowances, which may be "earned" by contributions or be based primarily upon need, or by tax deductions.

[93] Out of general tax revenues or by contributions from employer and/or employee. See App. A, Table 8.

[94] Art. 117.

[95] (EC) Bull. S. 2–74.

[96] M. Shanks, "The Social Policy of the European Communities" (1977) 14 C.M.L. Rev. 375.

[97] A. Dale, *Tax Harmonisation in Europe* (1963), Chap. 11.

[98] Above, para. 316.

[99] N. Andel, (*op. cit.* n. 91) at pp. 380–383.

widely differing patterns of social security financing are perfectly viable at the present stage of integration.[1]

**326**    Nevertheless, some consideration must be given to the fiscal aspects of social security systems in relation to existing measures and proposals for tax harmonisation. Benefits are commonly funded in part out of general tax revenues and in part from specific contributions : the respective proportions vary considerably from one Member State to another.[2] Wide variation also exists in the proportion of those receipts derived from contributions made by employers.[3] Where contributions are paid by individuals these may simply be regarded as an alternative form of personal income taxation.[4] Where they are paid by enterprises, they may constitute an additional tax on profits, at least to the extent to which the burden is not shifted to employees.[5] Thus, an enterprise in one Member State may bear a heavier tax burden than a corresponding enterprise in another country because, in the latter, a higher proportion of contributions is paid by the employee or a higher proportion of social expenditure is funded out of general tax revenues. This would normally be unimportant, but may become significant when, or if, the actual rates of corporation tax are harmonised.[6]

### (iv)    The income of farmers

**327**    It has been suggested above that national differences in personal income taxation (and in social security benefits) may be unimportant where taxation is but one of a number of variables which may affect the conditions of competition. But when one or more of these other factors ceases to be a variable, harmonisation may become necessary. Such may be the case in the agricultural sector. The income of farmers is, to a major extent, determined by the farm policy of the Community in fixing guaranteed prices for agricultural produce. However, there are major differences in the way in which the income of farmers is taxed, from one Member State to another and as between the income of farmers and of other individuals.[7] Various tax

---

[1] Reply to EPWQ 533/78, O.J. 1978, C 310/3. Substantial progress towards economic and monetary union may alter this.

[2] From 84 per cent. out of tax revenue in the Netherlands to 79 per cent. from contributions in France : reply to EPWQ 533/78, above. And see App. A, Table 2.

[3] From 6 per cent. of total receipts in Denmark to 48 per cent. in Italy : *Ibid.*

[4] D. W. Williams, "National Insurance Contributions—a Second Income Tax" (1978) B.T.R. 84. It may also constitute a relatively regressive form of income taxation.

[5] It may be that contributions on behalf of an employee are another form of wages and that, if the employee had to pay the full contribution, larger wages would have to be paid. The possible shifting to the consumer is unimportant, since this would apply equally to taxes on business profits.

[6] Large employer contributions would also seem to impose a disproportionate burden upon labour-intensive enterprises, which is a tendency also of the value added tax system. This may be inappropriate in times of high unemployment.

[7] In most Member States it is exceptional for farmers to be taxed according to normal rules. They are frequently taxed on the basis of the size or value of the holding or on an imputed yield : see EPWQ 23/79, O.J. 1979, C 164/5.

concessions, such as flat-rate schemes and special exemptions, constitute a form of state aid[8] and are likely to distort the conditions of competition, thus necessitating action under Article 40 of the Treaty. Further distortion may arise from different tax treatment, within the Member States, of amounts, such as levies, refunds and special grants, paid to or received from the agricultural funds by farmers.[9] If a sum received by a farmer under a common agricultural market organisation is taxable in one Member State but not in another, it is arguable that this constitutes a discrimination between producers within the Community, contrary to Article 40. It is, however, difficult to see what co-ordinating action might be taken. For a variety of reasons, some member states find it administratively or politically difficult to apply normal tax rules in the agricultural sector[10] : yet a uniform system under which farmers receive treatment more favourable than that accorded to other individuals or enterprises is hard to justify and would be unacceptable to those Member States which have achieved some measure of success in subjecting farmers to the normal disciplines of their tax systems.

### G.   THE DYNAMICS OF HARMONISATION

**328**   Tax harmonisation in the Community is a dynamic and continuing process. It is necessarily so.[11] If one accepts that tax policy performs a secondary or complementary role, subordinate to the major policy objectives of the Community,[12] then tax harmonisation can only respond to, or at best anticipate, developments in other areas of policy. Thus tax legislation will be harmonised only when it becomes necessary to do so. Moreover, few areas of national sovereignty are as jealously guarded by the Member States as that over fiscal policy : it will only be surrendered when this becomes essential and inevitable.

Consequently, tax harmonisation is also a slow process. It may take several years for the Commission to formulate a proposal, having studied an issue, identified the problems, solved the technical difficulties and arrived at a solution which has some chance of being acceptable to the Member States. Securing adoption in the Council involves lengthy negotiations, balancing national interests and persuading the Member States of the desirability of,

---

[8] These may fall within Arts. 92, 93 of the Treaty : see EPWQ 755/77, O.J. 1978, C 150/3.

[9] Whether or not such payments fall within the national tax systems of Member States seems to vary : see EPWQ 96/76, O.J. 1979, C 150/16. The English High Court, in *White* v. *Davies* [1979] 2 C.M.L.R. 620 (Ch.D), held that a lump sum payment to a farmer in connection with the conversion from dairy herds to beef herds, under Reg. 1353/73, constituted business income of the farmer rather than a capital receipt. No question was raised as to how such payments are treated in other Member States or were intended to be treated by the Council.

[10] In the context of value added tax, see above, Chap. 2 paras. 121, 131, 135.

[11] A. Barrere, "The Influence of Economic Growth of the Member States on Problems of Tax Harmonisation," App. E of the *EEC Reports on Tax Harmonisation.*

[12] Above, para. 210.

and necessity for, a particular measure. Further delays occur before measures are implemented in the Member States and then constant vigilance is required to ensure that those measures are observed. As this and the preceding chapter have demonstrated, the Commission is sometimes criticised for not being sufficiently ambitious, yet its more realistic proposals have been largely unrealised.

The process of tax harmonisation, however, is not restricted to the formulation, adoption and implementation of Directives. There are other forces at work, which will be examined briefly in the remainder of this chapter.

### (i) The role of the courts

329    Once a Directive has been adopted, the Court of Justice has an obvious role to play—to ensure that Member States comply with their obligation to enact the necessary measures for its implementation and enforcement. Failure to do so will constitute a breach of its duty on the part of the Member State, which may be censured by the Court, under Article 169 of the Treaty,[13] and the Member State may be ordered to take the necessary measures to comply with the judgment of the Court.[14] Moreover, since it is now established that the provisions of a Directive may, in certain circumstances, have direct effect and confer enforceable rights upon individuals,[15] compliance may be secured through action in the national courts.

However, the role of the courts is not restricted to the enforcement of obligations which arise from the adoption of a Directive. An impetus may be given to adopt and implement a proposal of the Commission, or even for the Commission to present a proposal. Where national tax legislation or practice is contrary to the principles of the Treaty itself, decisions of the courts which hold such legislation or practice to be invalid or inoperative provide a powerful incentive to take common measures to remedy the situation. It is surely no coincidence that the Value Added Tax Directives of 1967 were adopted quite soon after the Court of Justice had demonstrated, in *Lütticke*,[16] that existing turnover-tax systems were essentially incompatible with the Treaty and that individuals could properly refuse to pay taxes assessed upon them. The confusion created by this decision, the prospect of litigation on an unprecedented scale and the fear of major losses of revenue constituted a major inducement to adopt a more compatible tax system. It remains to be seen whether the recent decisions of the Court, in relation to excise duties on alcohol,[17] will similarly provide the necessary spur to at last take action to achieve the harmonisation of excise duties.

[13]  Or under Art. 170, though this is unlikely.
[14]  Art. 171.
[15]  Above, paras. 214–216.
[16]  Case 57/65 [1966] E.C.R. 205 : above, Chap. 1, pp. 72–75.
[17]  Above, paras. 38–55.

### (ii)   The inter-relationship of taxes

**330**      The "salami" approach to harmonisation necessitates that one tax be
tackled before another. Yet different taxes interact and inter-relate with each
other within the tax system as a whole. Value added tax and excise duties
are both taxes upon consumption, but value added tax may also be regarded
as a form of taxation of business profits.[18] Corporation tax and personal
income tax must be integrated at least to some extent, in so far as they relate
to the taxation of various types of investment income and to the profits of
incorporated and unincorporated businesses. Changes made with respect to
one tax may therefore bring about a corresponding need to act in respect of
some other tax. As Doctor Hallstein has explained :

> "Every tax system is an integrated whole. Changes in turnover tax,
> which is so important an element of indirect taxation, must lead to
> other changes, in direct taxation too. What is more, by losing national
> control of turnover taxes, the Member States lose financial
> flexibility—which has an important effect upon budget policy. In short,
> the truly free movement of goods within a community means that the
> Member States must accept not only a good deal of interference in their
> administrative processes but also even a restructuring of their taxation
> and budget policies."[19]

Community policies, therefore, have a cumulative effect. Once the
traditional methods of protecting a national market—customs duties,
quantitative restrictions and discriminatory taxes—have been abolished,
disparities which exist in taxation, which hitherto have not been apparent or
had been regarded as unimportant, assume a much greater significance.[20]
Differences, from one Member State to another, in indirect taxation may be
compensated for by differences in direct taxation : when the former
differences are eliminated the latter may give rise to distortions which previously did not exist.[21] As already seen in this chapter, the measures adopted
to counter tax avoidance and evasion necessitated the proposed arbitration
procedure to eliminate double taxation,[22] the harmonisation of corporation
tax rates may necessitate action with regard to the funding of social security
systems[23] and to certain types of local taxes,[24] and harmonisation of taxes

---

[18] Above, para. 107.

[19] W. Hallstein, *Europe in the Making* (1972), p. 25.

[20] G. Close, "Harmonisation of laws : use or abuse of the powers under the EEC Treaty"
(1978) 3 E.L. Rev. 461; P. Nasini, "The Reconciliation of Fiscal Legislation," in *Ten Years
of European Integration,* CEDE, Montréal, 1968, at p. 49.

[21] A. J. Easson, "Tax Policy in the European Economic Community" (1977) 1 RIE/JEI,
31, 40–44. See also the statement of H. von der Groeben to the Parliament, on March 6,
1966 : (EEC) Bull. 5–66, p. 15.

[22] Above, paras. 307–310.

[23] Above, para. 326.

[24] Above, para. 314.

generally will also require an alignment of the methods of tax administration, collection and control.[25]

These forces, however, do not always operate in favour of increased and accelerated harmonisation. From a technical point of view, progress in one area may be delayed because harmonisation there would be ineffective without corresponding measures being taken with respect to some other tax.[26] And Member States may be reluctant to adopt an otherwise inoffensive proposal because they recognise that this will lead inevitably to a loss of fiscal sovereignty over some other form of taxation.

### (iii)   Spontaneous harmonisation

**331**      This leads one to a further issue. Given that the harmonisation of one part of the tax system may result in a need for changes in, or the alignment of, other parts of the system, to what extent does this require action on the part of the Community and to what extent may such action be left to the Member States themselves?

Member States may, and sometimes do, react of their own accord to the needs of the Community. They will support proposals for changes which they themselves wish to make, though having unanimously adopted Directives in the Council one may wonder why they so often delay implementation. If the reform is one which is desired by a Member State it may adopt the Commission's proposal, or implement the Council's Directive, before it is legally required to do so.[27] It may defer a domestic reform until it knows the form of the Commission's proposed solution, as did some Member States in the case of the corporation tax system, or it may even try to influence that solution by anticipating it with a unilateral reform.[28]

Assuming that, even when full economic union is eventually achieved, the Member States will continue to enjoy a certain measure of fiscal autonomy, just as do provinces within a federal system, it would seem to be necessary to rely to a considerable extent upon spontaneous and voluntary harmonisation to attain the desired degree of integration. Harmonisation, at the Community level, of some parts of the tax system will, it may be argued, compel or induce Member States to make corresponding adjustments to other parts of the system, so that alignment will come about gradually and

---

[25]  Above, para. 312.

[26]  *e.g.* the proposed Directives on mergers and associated companies must await the approximation of corporation tax systems : above para. 290.

[27]  Thus the German adoption of value added tax : see D. J. Puchala and C. F. Lankowski, "The Politics of Fiscal Harmonisation in the European Communities" (1977) 15 J.C.M.S. 155.

[28]  *e.g.* by adopting a partially-integrated corporation tax system at a time when it was thought that the Commission favoured the classical system : see D. Dosser, "The Corporation Tax," and K. Schneider, "Tax Harmonisation Policy from the point of view of the Commission," D. Dosser (ed.), *British Taxation and the Common Market*, Chaps. 4, 6.

automatically.[29] On the other hand, it may be that, as Member States are deprived of freedom to manoeuvre in respect of an increasing number of taxes, disparities will be concentrated into those taxes over which sovereignty is retained and will actually widen. The manner in which Member States may exercise what remains of their fiscal sovereignty would seem to depend upon three factors :

332   (a) **Internal consistency.** If the example is taken of the harmonisation of taxes on company profits and distributions, then it appears that, though the Commission has no plans for the harmonisation of personal income taxes generally, various adjustments will be necessary in order to achieve or preserve internal consistency, or "horizontal equity." A reasonable degree of neutrality must exist as between the taxation of profits of incorporated and unincorporated businesses and of dividends, interest and other forms of investment income.[30] Not only does fiscal justice require this but a tax system which lacks such neutrality openly invites tax avoidance and risks excessive losses of revenue. Thus national self-interest would seem to impel Member States towards the adoption of broadly similar solutions.

(b) **International competition.** If some part of the total tax burden on goods or enterprises is fixed, by measures taken at the Community level, but the remainder may be freely determined by each Member State, then those Member States are subject to conflicting pressures. The budgetary requirements of the state demand tax at one level, but the need to compete, within the Community and in external trade, may require a lesser burden. If, for example, fiscal frontiers were to be abolished without approximation of the rates of value added tax, a Member State wishing to encourage exports or discourage imports would impose rates lower than those of its neighbours. A neighbour, if the effects of this competition became too severe, would reduce its own rates, and so on. Eventually a state of equilibrium would be reached, in which rates were approximated to a sufficient degree, i.e. disparities were within tolerable limits.[31] Similarly, if the rates of corporation tax were harmonised but not the bases of assessment, some Member States would seek to give their enterprises a competitive advantage by adopting generous rules for the computation of profits. Again, a sufficient degree of harmonisation should ultimately result. This process may be objected to, however, on a number of grounds. First, there is the danger that equilibrium would not be attained, or if so only occasionally and temporarily, and that instead there would be a continuous state of "tax war" between the Member States. Secondly, some forms of competition might be regarded as fair, others as unfair. Competition in tax rates is at least overt, whereas conces-

---

[29] Th. W. Vogelaar, "Tax Harmonisation in the European Community" (1970) 7 C.M.L. Rev. 323, 328.

[30] Some departure from neutrality may be justified, e.g. to encourage small businesses or certain types of investment.

[31] See above, Chap. 2, para. 146.

sions offered by means of disparities in the bases of assessment are less readily apparent, less easy to compare and potentially more discriminatory. Member States might be tempted to resort to concealed discriminations, even relaxing standards of equity and of administration to create a "tax haven" where taxes are easily avoided or evaded. Finally, Member States would tend to bow to the pressures of those with most power to exert them. Normally, these would be enterprises seeking to achieve an advantage over their competitors in other Member States. The result might be not only a tax war, but a regressive tax war.

**333** **(c) National fiscal policy.** The potential tax war, as described above, is limited by the overall fiscal policies of the Member States. Tax cuts in one sector must be paid for, either by raising other taxes (or resorting to other sources of revenue) or by reducing government expenditure. In many cases tax concessions and government expenditures are simply two methods of attaining the same result : to the extent that this is so, Member States should normally remain free, within the limits imposed by the Treaty,[32] to determine which method to apply. Moreover, as many governments have discovered, reductions in expenditure are not easy to make and the capacity to increase taxes is restricted. Where the yield from certain taxes is aligned, as a result of the harmonisation of rates and bases of assessment, a Member State will obtain an increase, or suffer a decrease, in the revenue from those taxes. Unless that state wishes to increase, or is able to reduce, expenditure, then it must make corresponding adjustments to those other taxes over which it retains control. Where two states have broadly similar overall levels of taxation, the alignment by harmonisation of the yields from some taxes, *e.g.* taxes on consumption and company profits, should automatically result in the spontaneous alignment of the remaining taxes, *e.g.* taxes on personal incomes and wealth. Where, however, the overall levels of taxation differ significantly, the effect may be the opposite, since the whole of the difference will be concentrated upon the non-aligned taxes.

In conclusion it may be suggested that, under a process of gradual harmonisation, certain forces operate in favour of spontaneous harmonisation on the part of the Member States, whilst other forces are exerted in the opposite direction. In determining the extent of harmonisation and the speed at which it should progress, the Commission must necessarily attempt to predict and anticipate such reflex reactions. The harmonisation of one tax, however desirable in itself, may be counter-productive if it results in the creation of fresh divergences elsewhere and may therefore have to be postponed until a sufficient degree of co-ordination of economic conditions and policies is achieved throughout the Community.[33]

---

[32] *e.g.* the provisions on state aids, in Arts. 92, 93.
[33] See further, Chap. 4, paras. 414–416.

### (iv)  The external effects of harmonisation

**334**  The Community constitutes one of the world's major trading blocks and capital markets. Tax changes within the Community necessarily have important effects upon the Community's neighbours and trading partners, effects which cannot be disregarded in the process of harmonisation.

In some cases action by the Community may lead to a spontaneous harmonisation at the international level. The adoption of the common system of value added tax has been followed, or even anticipated, by its introduction in a number of other states.[34] In part this has been because certain features of the tax have been regarded as desirable[35] : in other cases it appears to have been adopted to facilitate trade with the Community.[36] Sometimes the possible international repercussions exert an influence or impose a restraint upon Community action. For example, the changes resulting from the harmonisation of the systems of taxing company profits and distributions will necessitate the re-negotiation of some double taxation treaties. One reason for preferring partial integration over the classical system was that Member States would not be placed at a disadvantage in such renegotiations.[37] By contrast, the desire of the Community to take action against tax avoidance and evasion, especially with respect to the use of holding companies established in tax havens, is hindered by the fear that, without increased international co-operation, a flight of capital from the Community to more accommodating locations might occur.[38]

**335**  Finally, the adoption of measures which appear to be advantageous to the Community may result in countervailing action on the part of other states, either by adopting similar measures which nullify the advantage or by introducing retaliatory measures of some other kind. The United States, in particular, has expressed concern as to the effects both of the value added tax and of the changes in the corporation tax system. The value added tax, as we have seen,[39] was selected to replace cumulative turnover taxes largely because it is better adapted to the system of border tax adjustments permitted by the Treaty and by the provisions of the GATT. One result, however, was that countervailing duties on imports from without the Community increased, in some cases by as much as two or three times, as did the remission of tax on exported goods. This led to American claims that the

---

[34] See M. Norr and N. Hornhammar, "The Value Added Tax in Sweden" (1970) 70 Columbia L. Rev. 379.

[35] *e.g.* the ability to raise large amounts of revenue, its self-enforcing nature and its advantages in international trade.

[36] This appears to have been a relatively minor factor in Sweden, but a major one in Austria : see C. S. Shoup, "Experience with the Value Added Tax in Denmark and prospects in Sweden" (1969) 28 *Finanzarchiv* 236; H. Lober, "Survey of Austrian Tax Law," (1978) 18 E.T. 40.

[37] Above, paras. 273, 279.

[38] Above, para. 311.

[39] Above, Chap. 1, paras. 83–85.

value added tax constitutes an undue subsidy to Community exports, albeit one which is apparently permitted by the GATT.[40] This sense of grievance has been further exacerbated by the changes in corporation tax, which are perceived to discriminate against Amercian enterprises and investors,[41] resulting in various suggestions that the United States might itself adopt a value added tax in partial replacement of corporate income tax,[42] might unilaterally take countervailing action[43] or might seek a revision of the GATT rules.[44] The fear has been expressed that the policies of the Community might thus lead to a "countervailing tax war,"[45] to the detriment of world trade in general.

### [The Next Paragraph is 401]

[40] M. B. Krauss, "Border Tax Adjustments : a potential Trans-Atlantic Trade Dispute" (1976) 10 J.W.T.L. 145; M. von Steinaecker, *Domestic Taxation and Foreign Trade : the United States—European Border Tax Dispute* (1973).

[41] P. T. Kaplan, "European Discrimination and American Retaliation" (1978) B.T.R. 206; A. R. Prest, "GATT and Company Taxation" (1977) B.T.R. 201.

[42] R. W. Lindholm, *Value Added Tax and other Tax Reforms* (1976) : R. W. Rosendahl, "Border Tax Adjustments : Problems and Proposals" (1970) 2 L.P.I.B. 85.

[43] The DISC legislation, whereby favourable tax treatment is accorded to Domestic International Sales Corporations, whose income is largely derived from exports, may be regarded in this light : see A. R. Prest, *op. cit.* n. 41, and the note, "GATT : DISC and other Discriminatory Income Taxes" (1977) 11 J.W.T.L. 564.

[44] J. J. Barcelo, "Subsidies and Countervailing Duties—Analysis and a Proposal" (1977) 9 L.P.I.B. 779 : G. M. Grossman, "Alternative Border Tax Policies" (1978) 12 J.W.T.L. 452.

[45] M. B. Krauss *op. cit.* n. 40 : R. W. Rosendahl *op. cit.* n. 42.

# CHAPTER 4

# FISCAL ASPECTS OF COMMUNITY POLICIES

## A. THE OBJECTIVES OF THE COMMUNITY

**401**     The objectives of the Community, and the activities prescribed to attain these objectives, are set out in Articles 2 and 3 of the Treaty.[1] As already observed,[2] these activities do not specifically include the formulation of a fiscal policy as such: rather, the approximation of laws, including tax laws, is prescribed "to the extent required for the proper functioning of the common market."[3] But since fiscal measures are essential to the attainment of the Treaty objectives and all the prescribed activities of the Community have fiscal implications, then it may fairly be said that "all of the objectives of the Treaty are made in varying degrees easier to achieve by appropriate progress in tax harmonisation."[4]

Tax policy is consequently regarded as an essential tool for achieving the real objectives of the Treaty. As such, its use must be directed towards one or more particular ends but must also be consistent with, and complementary to, other objectives and activities. Fiscal solutions designed with one end in mind should not conflict with other policies of the Community. Tax provisions intended to promote the free movement of goods, such as the harmonisation of excise duties on particular products, must also have regard to agricultural policy,[5] energy policy,[6] transport policy,[6] and external policy in relation to the associated states.[7] Provisions for the removal of obstacles to the free movement of workers must take into account social policy; those designed to assist the freedom of establishment and the free movement of capital must also consider competition and economic policy. Taxes applied to transport must serve the ends not only of transport policy but also of energy and environmental policy.[8] And environmental policy itself raises questions of who should bear the costs of pollution, and how?[9]

Problems of this nature have been considered in various parts of earlier Chapters : in the remainder of this chapter it is intended to examine the fiscal implications of some specific aspects of Community policy which, thus far in this work, have received little attention.

---

[1] Above, Chap. 1, para. 3.
[2] Above, Chap. 3, paras. 202, 210.
[3] Art. 3(h). Arts. 99 and 100 contain similar limitations.
[4] Fredersdorf Report, para. 2.2.1.
[5] Duties on tobacco and alcohol.
[6] Duty on mineral oil. See Case 21/79 *Commission* v. *Italy.*
[7] Duties on tobacco and alcohol.
[8] (EEC) Bull. S. 3–67, p. 17; (EC) Bull. S. 16–73, p. 12. And see Case 21/79 (n. 6, above).
[9] (EC) Bull. S. 5–72, and see G. Close, "Harmonisation of Laws : Use or Abuse of the Powers under the EEC Treaty" (1978) 3 E.L. Rev. 461, at p. 468–470.

## B.    Economic and Monetary Policy

### (i)    The economic objectives of the Community

**402**    By Article 2 of the Treaty, the Community has as its task, "by establishing a common market and progressively approximating the economic policies of Member States, to promote throughout the Community a harmonious development of economic activities, a continuous and balanced expansion, an increase in stability, an accelerated raising of the standard of living and closer relations between the states belonging to it."

Two means of achieving the objectives are thus provided : the establishment of a common market and the progressive approximation of national economic policies. Whether any meaningful distinction may be made between these two means is not clear, since the concept of a "common market" and what it comprises is not defined in the Treaty.[10] Schematically, the Treaty appears to provide for a common market, involving the abolition of obstacles to the free movement of goods, persons, services and capital and the creation of a common market in agricultural products and of a common transport policy.[11] The "common rules,"[12] on competition, tax provisions and the approximation of laws, relate to the establishment and functioning of the common market.[13] Economic and social policy,[14] by contrast, appear to be matters primarily of national concern and distinct from the common market, though required to be approximated or co-ordinated in order to attain the objectives of the Community.

**403**    If such a distinction, between the establishment of the Common Market and the approximation of economic policies, can be drawn, the question arises as to which instruments are available for the latter purpose.[15] In the context of fiscal policy, indirect taxes may be harmonised "in the interest of the Common Market,"[16] other taxes which "directly affect the establishment or functioning of the Common Market" may be approximated,[17] and the residual power to take appropriate measures also relates only to "the operation of the "Common Market"."[18]

---

[10] *Cf* Art. 4 of the ECSC Treaty. However, the common economic market is clearly broader in scope than the common coal and steel market.

[11] Arts. 9–84.

[12] Title I of Part III, Arts. 85–102.

[13] See esp. Arts. 85, 86, 91, 92, 99, 100, 101.

[14] But commercial policy appears to be an adjunct of the customs union, and thus of the Common Market.

[15] See further, P. Leleux, "Le Rapprochement des Législations dans la Communauté Economique Européenne" (1968) 4. C.D.E. 129, especially at pp. 132 *et seq.*; Th. W. Vogelaar, "The Approximation of the Laws of Member States under the Treaty of Rome" (1975) 12 C.M.L. Rev. 211, at pp. 218 *et seq.*

[16] Art. 99.

[17] Art. 100.

[18] Art. 235 : see R.H. Lauwaars, "Art. 235 als Grundlage für die flankierenden Politiken in Rahmen der Wirtschafts—und Währungsunion" (1976) 11 EuR. 100.

In practice this distinction may be less important than it appears, at least as regards the approximation of fiscal policy.[19] As Professor Leleux has pointed out,[20] once economic policies are "translated" into legal rules, differences in such rules may well have an incidence on the functioning of the Common Market and thus become the proper subject for harmonisation. It would seem, therefore, that tax harmonisation has at least some role to play in achieving the economic policies of the Community.

(a)   *Economic policy in the Treaty*

**404**     The activities of the Community are stated to include "the application of procedures by which the economic policies of Member States can be co-ordinated and disequilibria in their balances of payments remedied."[21] The Title of the Treaty devoted to "Economic Policy"[22] is divided into three chapters, but really falls into two parts, the latter dealing with "Commercial Policy" and being essentially concerned with trade relations with third countries. The two chapters dealing specifically with economic matters are entitled respectively "Conjunctural Policy" and "Balance of Payments," which is in itself confusing since the meaning of "conjunctural" is far from clear and since the second chapter is not in any way restricted to balance of payments problems.[23]

The first chapter is contained in a single article, Article 103, which provides :

"1.   Member States shall regard their conjunctural policies as a matter of common concern. They shall consult each other and the Commission on the measures to be taken in the light of the prevailing circumstances."

The term "conjunctural" policy is a literal translation of the terms used in the original versions of the Treaty (politique de conjoncture, Konjunkturpolitik, etc.) and, apparently, is intended to refer to "short-term economic policy," "business cycle policy," or "cyclical policy."[24] The aim of conjunctural policy is to achieve conditions of stable growth with the emphasis, it would seem, upon stability, but though this aim is a long term one the policy itself is primarily concerned with short-term measures. The second

[19] The question whether the Treaty as it stands provides the necessary juridical basis to achieve all the objectives of the proposed economic and monetary union is considered below.
[20] *Op. cit.* n. 15, at p. 142.
[21] Art. 3(g). Additionally, the creation of a European Social Fund and European Investment Bank is designed to achieve economic objectives : Art. 3(i),(j).
[22] Arts. 103–116.
[23] For comprehensive analyses of these Chapters, see J. Mégret *et al., Le droit de la Communauté Économique Européenne* (1976), Vol. 6; H. Smit and P.E. Herzog, *The Law of the European Economic Community : a Commentary on the EEC Treaty*, Vol. 3.
[24] In addition, it applies to situations of shortages in the supply of particular products : Art. 103(4).

chapter has a broader scope, as can be seen from Article 104, which provides :

> "Each Member State shall pursue the economic policy needed to ensure the equilibrium of its overall balance of payments and to maintain confidence in its currency, while taking care to ensure a high level of employment and a stable level of prices."

It is further provided, by Article 107, that :

> "1. Each Member State shall treat its policy with regard to rates of exchange as a matter of common concern."

Thus the Treaty encompasses virtually all aspects of economic policy—growth, balance of payments, exchange rates, unemployment and inflation.

### (b) The instruments of economic policy

**405**    Though economic policies are a matter of "common concern," the Treaty makes it clear that, essentially, each member state is to pursue its own economic policy.[25] The objectives which it is required to pursue are clearly set out, albeit in general terms, in Article 104, but the means of ensuring that these objectives are sought, let alone attained, are not provided. It is true that Article 103 imposes an obligation upon Member States to consult each other, and the Commission, on measures to be taken in the light of prevailing circumstances, but, as one commentator has observed, consultation in practice means comparing notes rather than deciding in common.[26] The Article does provide for "measures" to be decided upon and for directives to be issued to give effect to such measures.[27] The scope of this power is unclear[28] and the actions taken thereunder have tended to be of a procedural nature, setting up various mechanisms for co-ordination, or temporary in effect and in derogation of other Community rules.[29] Article 105 provides that the Member States shall co-ordinate their economic policies in order to facilitate attainment of the objectives set out in Article 104, whereas Article 145 provides that the Council shall, in accordance with the provisions of the Treaty, ensure co-ordination of the general economic policies of the Member States. A distinction appears to be drawn, in Article 145, between the co-ordination of economic policies and the power to take decisions, from which

---

[25] By Art. 6 it is the member states which, in co-operation with the institutions of the Community, shall co-ordinate their respective economic policies. See also Art. 105.

[26] A. Szasz, "The Monetary Union Debate" (1970) 7 C.M.L. Rev. 407, 408.

[27] Art. 103(2), (3). It seems strange that the measures must be decided upon unanimously, but a qualified majority only is needed to issue the directives.

[28] See U. Everling, "L'Aspect Juridique de la Co-ordination de la Politique Economique au sein de la Communauté Economique Européenne" (1964) 10 A.F.D.I. 576 : H. H. Maas, "The Powers of the European Community and the Achievement of the Economic and Monetary Union" (1972) 9 C.M.L. Rev. 2.

[29] e.g. authorisations for the temporary limitation of exports or imports.

it might be inferred that no such general power exists in the field of economic policy. Certainly, the measures envisaged by Article 105 appear to be restricted to the provision of means of co-operation between national administrative departments and central banks, and the establishment of a Monetary Committee with advisory status. In recent years recourse has been had to Articles 6, 105 and 145 for the adoption of economic policy programmes[30] : in these programmes the member states express their intention of acting in accordance with the guidelines contained therein, but it seems clear that no binding obligation to do so is created.[31] Certain additional powers are given to the Commission or Council in Articles 107–109,[32] but these relate primarily to the authorisation of special measures to counter the consequences of changes in rates of exchange or to provide assistance where a Member State experiences serious balance of payments difficulties.

**406**     This brief review of the "economic provisions" of the Treaty seems to confirm that economic policy remains largely in the hands of the Member States and that the powers of the Community to take substantive measures in this field are strictly limited. This, however, is to ignore the effects upon economic policy of those measures which the Community may properly take in pursuit of the objectives of the Common Market and the restrictions which are imposed upon the apparent freedom of action enjoyed by the Member States by other Treaty provisions and by action taken thereunder. When one considers the traditional instruments of economic policy, whereby growth may be stimulated, unemployment and inflation controlled, balance of payments and exchange rates regulated, it is clear that national economic planning can go only so far without coming into conflict with various Community rules. The Court has held, on a number of occasions, that Member States cannot rely upon Article 103 to justify measures which are contrary to the Treaty or to Community law.[33] Thus member states may not, in pursuit of economic policy objectives (even though these are consistent with Article 104), unilaterally adopt customs duties, quantitative restrictions or measures having an equivalent effect, or otherwise seek to regulate the level of imports or exports, when to do so would be contrary to Community law. The regulation of prices is prima facie valid, but is subject to a number of constraints : thus although the Court has recognised that a system of price control may frequently be an instrument of conjunctural policy,[34] it is nevertheless not permitted to encroach upon the Community

---

[30] *e.g.* Dec. 77/294 of March 14, 1977, adopting the fourth medium-term Economic Policy Programme : O.J. 1977, L 101/1.

[31] It is significant that the Decisions are expressed to be taken by the Council and by the representatives of the governments of the Member States, not by the Council alone.

[32] Art. 106 seems curiously out of place and is essentially concerned with the free movement of capital, in particular the liberalisation of payments.

[33] Case 65/75 *Tasca* |1976| E.C.R. 291; Cases 88–90/75 *SADAM* |1976| E.C.R. 323; Case 154/77, *Dechmann* |1976| E.C.R. 1573.

[34] Case 65/75, above, |1976| E.C.R. 291, at p. 300.

sphere.[35] This is especially so in the case of the control of prices of agricultural products and the Court has held that, in sectors covered by a common organisation of the market, and especially when this organisation is based on a common price system, Member States can no longer take action, through national provisions taken unilaterally, affecting the price formation as established under the common organisation.[36] Price controls may also be invalid in so far as they constitute measures having an equivalent effect to quantitative restrictions or are contrary to the rules on competition or state aids.[37] Other measures, to stimulate investment or to aid certain industries or regions, may similarly be contrary to the rules on competition, state aids or discriminatory taxation. Only the powers to adjust exchange rates[38] and to control the supply of money and of credit appear to remain firmly under national control and, as will be seen, these powers would be severely restricted under an Economic and Monetary Union.

At the present stage of integration it thus appears that, whilst the Community has a wide range of powers in relation to the functioning of the Common Market, the exercise of which have considerable impact upon national economic policies, it lacks the competence to develop and impose an overall Community economic policy but, at the same time, the Member States are deprived of a number of important tools which might be used to attain, by themselves and in co-operation with their fellow members, the general objectives set out in the Treaty.

### (c)   The role of fiscal policy

**407**     Fiscal measures constitute an important, if in many respects a controversial, tool of economic planning,[39] though the Treaty envisages the role of fiscal harmonisation as being in relation to the Common Market with the principal objective of removing obstacles to competition and free movement, and appears to ignore its role in economic policy.[40]

If the economic objectives of the Treaty are considered—growth, the combating of unemployment and inflation, balance of payments equil-

---

[35] *Ibid. per* Advocate-General Reischl, at p. 317

[36] Case 31/74 *Galli* [1975] E.C.R. 47, at p. 66. See also the cases cited at n. 33, above, and see P. Baumann, "Common Organisations of the Market and National Law" (1977) 14 C.M.L. Rev. 303.

[37] Case 65/75, Cases 88–90/75 above; Case 13/77 *Inno* [1977] E.C.R. 2115 (see Chapter 3, paras. 229–231, above); Case 82/77 *van Tiggele* [1978] E.C.R. 25.

[38] Cases 9–11 *Cie d'Approvisionnement* [1972] E.C.R. 391. Though this might lead to counteracting measures under Art. 107.

[39] The central importance of fiscal policy is emphasised in *Economic Policy for the European Community : the Way Forward*, Institut für Weltwirtschaft, Kiel (1974), at pp. 49 *et seq.* (the Cairncross Report).

[40] C. K. Sullivan, *The Search for Tax Principles in the European Economic Community* (1963), Chap. 1; B. M. Veenhof, "Harmonisation fiscale et co-ordination des politiques économiques dans les Communautés Européennes" (1972) 53–54 Fisc. M.C. 75.

ibrium, maintaining confidence in the currency and, essential to all of these, economic stability—most would agree that the correct tax policies can further these goals, though there would be less agreement as to which policies are most likely to achieve the desired results or least likely to impede this achievement. Growth may be stimulated by encouraging allocative efficiency, by promoting investment and savings, by rewarding enterprise and endeavour, though whether this should be by establishing conditions of fiscal neutrality or by providing positive incentives is a matter of some dispute.[41] Unemployment may be reduced by stimulating demand and by reducing labour costs,[42] and inflation kept under control by reducing consumer spending (and/or prices), government expenditure and budgetary deficits. The balance of payments may be protected by measures which encourage exports and discourage imports[43] and confidence in currency maintained by controlling inflation and maintaining a balance of payments equilibrium. To some extent these aims may be in conflict : a disproportionate reliance on indirect as opposed to direct taxation may stimulate growth and exports at the cost of increasing inflation. Moreover, some taxes have a long-term effect (the stimulation of investment may not be rewarded for several years), the effects of others may be felt far more quickly (those which affect prices) and these may be more appropriate instruments of conjunctural policy.

What is important here is that fiscal harmonisation, by restricting the freedom of Member States to make adjustments to their tax systems, may have the effect of neutralising certain of the fiscal means of achieving economic policy objectives.[44] In particular, the harmonisation of value added tax and of excise duties, especially if rates of tax become fixed within narrow margins, may deprive Member States of one of the most important tools of cyclical policy.[45] It is this aspect of fiscal harmonisation which to date has received insufficient attention in formulating Community policies and which will become of increasing importance as progress is made towards Economic and Monetary Union.

[41] See generally G.S.A. Wheatcroft, "A Taxation Policy for Growth" |1968| B.T.R. 131; M. Krauss, "Tax Harmonisation and Allocative Efficiency in Economic Unions" (1968) 23 P.F. 367; *Tax Policy and Investment in the European Community* Commission Studies, Taxation Series 1975, No. 1 (the Christiaanse Report).

[42] *e.g.* by reducing employers' social security contributions, or by measures such as the Regional Employment Premium in the United Kingdom.

[43] It has been suggested in earlier chapters that the high level of VAT and the system of border tax adjustments may have this effect. See also D. Dosser, S. S. Han and T. Hitiris, "Trade Effects of Tax Harmonisation : Harmonisation of the Value Added Tax in the EEC" (1969) 37 *The Manchester School*, 337.

[44] This problem is discussed at length in *European Economic Integration and Monetary Unification* (Commission, 1973) (the Bosman Report) especially at pp. 29–30, and by D. Dosser, in Appendix C. See also the *Kieler Diskussionsbeiträge*, No. 38/39 (Institut für Weltwirkschaft, Kiel, 1975), commenting upon the Cairncross Report, in particular the papers by Albers, Neumark, Shoup and Biehl.

[45] Opinions differ as to the extent to which VAT should be used counter-cyclically : contrast the views of Dosser and of Neumark, *op. cit.* above, n. 44.

## (ii)  Economic and monetary union

### (a)  The proposal for EMU

**408**    Although the Commission had on earlier occasions, notably in 1962 and 1964, submitted memoranda concerning monetary policy, the EMU proposal may be said to have originated in the Communiqué of the Conference of the Heads of State or Government of the Member States at the Hague in December, 1969. The gestation period was a little less than two years, the seminal act being a communication from the Commission to the Rome Conference of Finance Ministers in February, 1968, followed, a year later, by the Commission's memorandum to the Council on the co-ordination of Economic Policies and Monetary Co-operation within the Community.[46]

The time for a fresh initiative appeared to be particularly propitious. The customs union had been successfully established, agreement had been reached on the financing of the agricultural policy, the constitutional crisis of 1965–66 had been survived and the economic difficulties of 1968 had demonstrated the Community to be basically sound, though in need of a monetary policy. In a spirit of optimism, the Hague Summit resolved upon a number of vitally important issues—the accession of new members, financing by means of "own resources," increased Parliamentary control over the budget and direct elections. As the Communiqué stated :

> "Assessing the ground covered, and observing that perhaps never before have independent states carried co-operation further, [the Heads of State or Government] were unanimous in the opinion that in view of the progress realized the Community has today reached a turning point in its history."[47]

It continued :

> "They have reaffirmed their wish to carry on more rapidly with the further development necessary to reinforce the Community and its development into an economic union. They are of the opinion that the process of integration should end in a Community of stability and growth. With this object in view they have agreed that, on the basis of the memorandum presented by the Commission on 12 February 1969[48] and in close collaboration with the Commission a plan by stages should be drawn up by the Council during 1970 with a view to the creation of an economic and monetary union."

[46]  The Barre Plan : (EC) Bull. S. 3–69. This contains a valuable review of the earlier tentative proposals.
[47]  The text of the Communiqué, and of other basic documents, is reproduced in (EC) Bull. S. 11–70.
[48]  The Barre Plan, above, n. 46.

**409**     Pursuant to this declaration the Council appointed a committee, under
the chairmanship of Mr. Pierre Werner, to report on the various suggestions
for the realisation by stages of economic and monetary union. The Werner
Report, submitted to the Council in October, 1970,[49] concluded that the
ultimate goal of economic and monetary union implied the following
principal consequences :

> (a) Community currencies would be assured of total and irreversible
>     mutual convertability, with immutable parity rates, or preferably
>     would be replaced by a single Community currency;
> (b) Monetary and credit policy and the creation of liquidity would be
>     centralised;
> (c) Monetary policy in relation to the outside world would be subject to
>     Community control;
> (d) The policies of Member States as regards the capital market would be
>     unified;
> (e) The essential features of national budgets—variations in volume, size
>     of balances and methods of financing—would be decided at Com-
>     munity level;
> (f) Regional and structural policies would no longer be exclusively within
>     the jurisdiction of the Member States;
> (g) New or transformed Community organs would have to be created to
>     which the powers hitherto exercised by national authorities would be
>     transferred.

This ambitious programme was to be achieved by the end of the decade and
by stages, the first stage to extend until the end of 1973, during which the
co-ordination of economic policy would be reinforced. Various mechanisms
would be set up to facilitate this co-ordination, the Council would accelerate
the process of harmonisation and the Central Banks would take action to
limit fluctuations in rates of exchange.

    If the Council was somewhat taken aback by the boldness of the plan, it
did its best not to betray the fact and incorporated most of the proposals
into its Resolution of March 22, 1971.[50] And if the Council did not fully
appreciate the economic consequences of its proposals,[51] it was clearly cog-
nisant of the political effects. The Resolution provides that :

---

[49] (EC) Bull. S. 11–70. See also the interim report, published a few months earlier : (EC)
Bull. S. 7–70.
[50] J.O. 1971, L. 73. The Resolution was stated to be "of the Council and the
representatives of the Government of the Member States," perhaps in recognition of the
restricted juridical basis in the Treaty for such action on the part of the Council alone. The
text is reproduced in (EC) Bull. 4–71, pp. 11 *et seq.*, which also contains a comprehensive
chronology of events. For analysis of the proposals and of the general background, see P.
Coffey and J. R. Presley, *European Monetary Integration* (1971); G. Magnifico, *European
Monetary Unification* (1973).
[51] See the Report of the Study Group, *Economic and Monetary Union 1980* (Commission,
1975) (the Marjolin Report), at pp. 3–4.

" ... the Community shall ... hold the powers and responsibilities in the economic and monetary field enabling its Institutions to organise the administration of the union. To this end, the required economic policy decisions shall be taken at Community level and the necessary powers shall be given to the Institutions of the Community."

It further provides :

" ... the Community policies ... shall be subject to discussion *and control*[52] by the European Parliament."

### (b) Progress towards EMU

**410**    Already by the time the Commission presented its progress report on the first stage in 1973,[53] it had become clear that EMU would be far more difficult to achieve than had originally been anticipated. Now, the decade having ended, EMU should be a reality, yet it can hardly be said that all the tasks set for the first stage have been accomplished. Indeed, by 1975 it was being suggested that in so far as there had been any real movement since 1969 it had been backward.[54]

At the institutional level, initial progress was made in establishing co-ordination procedures by means of various committees and the laying down of economic policy guidelines.[55] The Parliament was given increased control over the budget, by the Second Budgetary Treaty of July 22, 1975, a power which the newly elected Parliament promptly exercised in December, 1979, by rejecting the proposed budget in its entirety. This apart, there has been no real transfer of economic sovereignty from the Member States to central institutions. Various short and medium-term credit mechanisms have been set up to provide financial assistance to Member States which find themselves in balance of payments difficulties, a European Monetary Co-operation Fund has been established and, in 1978, a new borrowing instrument was initiated, empowering the Commission to contract loans for the purpose of promoting investment within the Community.[56]

**411**    In the monetary field the original "snake" ultimately proved a failure[57] but, as a result of a major new initiative, the European Monetary System (EMS) came into being in 1979,[58] adhered to by all member states with the exception of the United Kingdom, and marking the most significant step yet

---

[52] Italics added.
[53] "Attainment of the Economic and Monetary Union" (EC) Bull. S. 5–73. See also G. de Man, "The Economic and Monetary Union after Four Years" (1975) 12 C.M.L. Rev 193.
[54] The Marjolin Report, p. 1.
[55] See para. 405, above.
[56] Dec. 78/870 of October 16, 1978.
[57] See C. J. Oort, "Exchange Rate Policy in the European Communities" (1976) 13 C.M.L. Rev. 301.
[58] Reg. 3181/78 of December 21, 1978. Reg. 1739/79 of August 3, 1979, further provided for interest subsidies on certain loans granted under the EMS to participating Member States.

achieved on the road towards monetary union. Also during the decade the new European Unit of Account (EUA) was gradually introduced,[59] providing a means of accounting at Community level and of conversion of national currencies. Together, the EUA and EMS provide a foundation for progress towards an eventual Community currency.

The other major development during the decade has been the setting up of the European Regional Development Fund (ERDF), to promote the economic expansion of, and assistance to, the less developed regions of the Community.[60] So far as the harmonisation of laws generally, and of tax laws in particular, is concerned progress, as has been said in earlier chapters, has been slow and the abolition of fiscal frontiers, which the Werner Report saw as being necessary in the final phase, is still a long way ahead.

**412**    Reasons for this relative lack of progress are not difficult to find. To achieve economic and monetary union, obstacles of an institutional, economic, technical and political nature will have to be overcome. The Treaty itself has failed to provide a satisfactory juridical or institutional basis for the transfer of the power of decision in economic matters from the Member States to central, Community, institutions[61] and the existing decision-making process, already slow and cumbersome, was further impeded by the enlargement of the Community in 1973. The monetary and energy crises, and the worldwide economic recession of the 1970s, have compelled Member States, in the absence of an established central authority, to give priority to their own economic difficulties. No clear agreement has emerged as to how economic and monetary union should be achieved, whether one should precede the other or progress should be in parallel,[62] or whether monetary union is best achieved by the "apocalyptic approach" —the immediate replacement of national currencies by a Community currency under central control—or more gradually, perhaps in conjunction with a "European Parallel Currency."[63] It is even suggested[64] that the pursuit of the economic objectives of the Community, as stated in the Treaty, is incompatible with the maintenance of fixed exchange rates.

**413**    Above all, the lack of progress has been due to a failure of political will on

---

[59] See H. J. Dixon, "The European Unit of Account" (1977) 14 C.M.L. Rev. 191.

[60] Reg. 724/75 of March 18, 1975. Regional policy is considered in the next section of this chapter.

[61] See, generally, the special issue of the *Common Market Law Review* "The Economic Law of the Member States in an Economic and Monetary Union" (1976) 13 C.M.L. Rev. 147, especially the contributions of Everling, Mosca and Scheuner, and see "The Administrative Implications of Economic and Monetary Union within the European Community" (1973–74) 12 J.C.M.S. 410 (the Wallace Report).

[62] See the Bosman Report (n. 44, above).

[63] G. Magnifico (*op. cit.* n. 50 above) at pp. 199 *et seq.* : *Kieler Diskussionsbeiträge* (*op. cit.* n. 44, above), especially the comments of R. Vaubel : Bosman Report, especially W. Neubauer (App. H.).

[64] *e.g.* B. Balassa and S. Resnick, "Monetary Integration and the Consistency of Policy Objectives in the European Common Market" (1974) 110 *Weltwirtschaftliches Archiv* 564.

the part of the Member States.[65] It may be that the Member States, in 1969, failed to appreciate the essential differences between a customs union and an economic and monetary union and that, when they did, and realised the extent to which sovereignty would have to be transferred to central institutions, they stepped back from the prospect. The impetus towards EMU was, after all, esentially a political one : the Community had reached a "turning point in its history"[66] and must either progress in a new direction or stagnate. By 1975, no doubt in part on account of the international economic situation, the "European concept" had lost a lot of its initial force and impetus[67] and a new initiative had become necessary, this time with the emphasis as much on *political* union as on economic and monetary union. An attempt in 1977, by the President of the Commission, Mr. Jenkins, to revive interest in EMU led to the introduction of the Community lending-instrument and the creation of the EMS,[68] though in the light of the current dispute over the financing of the Community and the impending enlargement of the Community, which can be expected to retard progress at least while initial difficulties are overcome, the prospect of achieving EMU appears bleak.

## (c)  The fiscal implications of EMU

**414**     As envisaged in the Werner Report and in the Council's 1971 Resolution, EMU implies that currencies be totally mutually convertible, with fixed and immutable parities, if not replaced by a single Community currency. This seems inevitably to import the creation of a European Central Bank, or some system such as the United States federal reserve bank system. It would involve the transfer from national to central control of powers over money supply, interest rates and credit facilities. All obstacles to the free flow of capital would be abolished. The essential features of national budgets would be subject to common control. Thus, virtually all the recognised tools for regulating the economy would be taken out of the hands of the national governments, which would be left with the residual powers over the levels of taxation and of public spending.

**415**     Secondly, it is generally assumed that EMU would have the effect of increasing, at least temporarily, the already wide disparities between the richer and poorer regions of the Community.[69] With the elimination of all barriers, capital and, to a lesser extent, labour would flow to the more prosperous and successful regions, the emergence of Community-wide collective bargaining might cause wage differentials to be smaller than productivity differentials, unemployment would increase in the peripheral

[65]  See the conclusions of the *Marjolin Report* (*op. cit.*, n. 51, above).
[66]  Above, para. 405.
[67]  "European Union" (EC) Bull. S. 1–76 (the *Tindemans Report*).
[68]  Above, nn. 56, 58.
[69]  For a penetrating analysis, see H. Giersch, in App. D. to the Bosman Report.

areas, the competitiveness of which could not be restored by currency devaluations. There would thus be an urgent need for large-scale regional policy, at the Community level, to mitigate the effects of EMU upon the less advanced regions, involving substantial transfers of money through a greatly enlarged Community budget.[70] Moreover, as stabilisation policy would largely become a matter for the Community as a whole, further budgetary resources would be needed for this purpose, even if reliance were to be placed primarily upon borrowing powers and grant instruments.[71] The result would be, in effect, the creation of a "federal-type" fiscal policy and budget, albeit a modest one in comparison to that of most federal states.[72] This transfer of resources, from national budgets to the Community budget, would further restrict the economic and fiscal sovereignty of the Member States. The most severe problems might arise during the transitional period to full EMU, as Member States became gradually deprived of more and more of their autonomy at a time when the Community budget was still too small, and the new institutions too weak,[73] to assume responsibility.

**416**         Tax harmonisation, as has already been suggested, will tend further to erode the fiscal sovereignty of Member States and to thus neutralise this, one of the few remaining tools for regulating the economy. The Werner Report regarded fiscal harmonisation as an essential feature of economic and monetary union,[74] both of value added tax and excise duties in order to secure the abolition of fiscal frontiers, and of corporation tax and other taxes affecting the movement of capital. This, as pointed out in earlier chapters, probably requires a fairly close approximation of tax rates, thereby leaving the member States with still less room to manoeuvre.

This raises, finally, the issue of the proper role of tax harmonisation in a developing economic and monetary union. The initial policy of the Community towards tax harmonisation was worked out in relationship to the establishment of the Common Market, when the priorities were perceived as being the elimination of obstacles to competition and to the free movement of goods. Rather later, the creation of the capital market required the

---

[70] Marjolin Report, at pp. 15 *et seq.* For a detailed study as to how this might be done, see the *Report of the Study group on the role of Public Finance in European Integration* (Commission Studies — Economic and Financial Series, 1977) (the MacDougall Report).

[71] MacDougall Report, at pp. 56–59. The central importance of fiscal policy and the need for a common budget is emphasised in the Cairncross Report, at pp. 49 *et seq.* See also G. K. Shaw, "European Economic Integration and Stabilization Policy" in Shoup : *Fiscal Harmonisation*, Chap. 11.

[72] See below, paras. 440, 441.

[73] By virtue of having been given insufficient powers, or due to inadequate decision-making processes. Perhaps worse would be central institutions not subject to proper democratic controls. See H. G. Johnson, "Problems of European Monetary Union" (1971) 5 J.W.T.L. 377; A. Szasz, "The Monetary Union Debate" (1970) 7 C.M.L. Rev. 407; R. Wägenbaur, "Les Fondements Juridiques d'une Politique Fiscale des Communautés Européennes" (1975) 67 *Revue de Science Financiere* 5.

[74] Whether it is really so necessary can be disputed : see the *Report of the Advisory Committee on European Union*, presented to the [Netherlands] Minister of Foreign Affairs, May 1975, at pp. 45 *et. seq.* (the Spierenburg Report).

removal of obstacles to the free movement of persons, enterprises, services and capital. Conditions of fiscal neutrality seemed the obvious and desirable goal. In the light of the proposed EMU it seems proper to re-assess this policy.[75] Whilst neutrality remains a desirable aim whenever there is no good reason for non-neutrality, once harmonised taxes constitute a part of a Community budget and have a role to play in a Community economic policy and in the redistribution of wealth between regions, then a "differentials approach," as long advocated by Professor Dosser,[76] appears more appropriate.

## C.  REGIONAL POLICY

### (i)  Regional disparities within the Community

**417**      It is not suprising that, in a Community of nine, and soon 10 or, perhaps 12 Member States, each with different geography, climate, economies and social and political traditions, there should be wide disparities of wealth from one Member State to another and, within those states, from one region to another. According to the MacDougall Report,[77] these disparities within the Community are far greater than those which exist in most other federal or unitary states which are at a roughly similar stage of economic advancement. In terms of *per capita* personal income, the ratio between richest and poorest region or state in Australia is 1.2 : 1, in Canada 2.2 : 1 and in the United States 2.1 : 1.[78] The corresponding ratio between richest and poorest Member State in the Community is 2.7 : 1.[79] Within each Member State the disparity is less : for France, Germany and the United Kingdom it is in each case approximately 1.7 (between Paris and Midi-Pyrénés, Hamburg and Saar, South-east England and Northern Ireland) and for Italy, 2.2 (Liguria and Calabria). However, the ratio between richest and poorest region in the Community (Paris and Calabria) stands at 4.3.[80] Thus the richest region of the Community is more than four times more prosperous than the poorest and enlargement of the Community will widen the gap still further. Moreover, the degree of economic integration achieved by virtue of the establishment of the Common Market, and still more that which would

[75] See D. Dosser, "Introduction to the Theory and Practice of Tax Harmonization" *British Taxation and the Common Market* (1973), Chap. 1; A. E. Genot, "Fiscal Harmonisation and European Integration : A 1978 Appraisal" (1978) 3 E.L. Rev. 355; M. Soldati, "Taxing Corporate Income : European Harmonisation and the Italian Experience" (1976) 24 A.J.C.L. 246, at p. 264.
[76] See especially App. C of the Bosman Report.
[77] Table on p. 27 of the Report, and see Appendix A, Table 7.
[78] Excluding Alaska. If Alaska is included, the ratio rises to 2.9 : 1.
[79] Between Denmark and Ireland. In terms of purchasing power, however, the ratio is reduced to 2.2 : 1, between Belgium and Ireland. These figures are for various years between 1970 and 1975.
[80] Again, in terms of purchasing power, the ratio is reduced, to 4.0. In terms of GDP the ratio, between Hamburg and Calabria, is still larger, at 4.9.

result from economic and monetary union, is likely to aggravate existing disparities as capital and labour are free to move to the more prosperous regions. As the MacDougall Report explains :

> "Inter-regional differences in output and income can be traced to a variety of causes; for example, unequal natural resource endowment, different degrees of accessibility, different levels of investment in physical and human capital, the different degrees of dependence on industries for whose products demand is growing or declining in the national or world market. The process of capital accumulation and migration frequently tend, in the absence of corrective measures, towards the cumulative distorted reinforcement of these differences."[81]

The social and political difficulties created by the existence of such wide disparities, especially if they are likely to persist or even increase, are obvious. In the view of the Commission :

> "It is difficult to believe that the Community will develop much further towards a real European union of peoples unless its different levels of regional prosperity can be brought within reasonable limits. First, the underprivileged farm-worker of Southern Italy or Ireland, the out-of-work miner or shipyard worker of Scotland—to mention but some of the extreme cases—none of these, all of whom are voters, will have any interest in a Community which condemns them and their families to perpetual poverty as second-class citizens. Second, persistent and growing regional disparities mean that the nine governments cannot possibly follow the convergent, co-ordinated economic policies without which further Community integration simply cannot come about. And third, neither the national nor the Community economy can afford the continued wastage of resources—in terms of people, of money, and of skills—which the present regional inequalities have involved over long years."[82]

### (ii) Regional policies in the Community[83]

**418**    Despite this apparent need to reduce regional inequalities the Treaty is largely silent on the matter. The Preamble recites that the founding members are "anxious to strengthen the unity of their economies and to ensure their harmonious development by reducing the differences existing between the various regions and the backwardness of the less favoured regions."

---

[81] At p. 25. See also M. D. Blechman, "Regional Development in the EEC : A Constitutional Analysis" (1967) 8 Harv. Int. L. Jo., 32.

[82] *The Community and its Regions*, European Documentation, 1977/4, p. 7.

[83] See generally R. M. Bird, "Regional Policies in a Common Market" in Shoup : *Fiscal Harmonisation*, Chap. 6 : M. Sant (ed.) *Regional Policy and Planning for Europe* (1974), and the Commission's *A new Regional Policy for Europe*, European Documentation, 1975/3.

Nevertheless, the Treaty regards regional policy as essentially a matter for the individual Member States,[84] providing only that the European Investment Bank shall grant loans to facilitate the financing of projects for developing less developed regions.[85]

## (a)  *National policies*

**419**    Regional policy was envisaged, and largely remains, a matter for each Member State. Within each Member State measures exist for the transfer of wealth from richer to poorer regions, primarily through the personal income tax system,[86] and to encourage investment and stimulate employment in the less advanced areas.[87] However, as is the case with national economic policy in general, the provisions of the Treaty and the developing rules of the Community impose restrictions upon national sovereignty, thereby preventing certain types of assistance.[88] In particular, Article 92 prohibits the granting of state aids which distort or threaten to distort competition within the Common Market, though providing for the approval, by the Commission and Council, of aids to promote the economic development of areas where the standard of living is abnormally low or where there is serious underemployment.[89] The harmonisation of taxes may further restrict the ability of Member States to grant certain types of regional assistance[90] and, as progress is made, *e.g.* in the harmonisation of tax rates and the bases of assessment of company profits, this will make it more difficult to grant tax incentives for purposes of regional policy.

There is, additionally, the fact that wealth is unevenly distributed among the Member States themselves. The more prosperous Member States have far greater ability to reduce their own regional disparities : thus aid in Denmark or Germany may be granted to regions which are already more

[84] Thus, Art. 92, dealing with state aids, provides that aids to deprived regions may be considered compatible with the Common Market when otherwise they would not be.

[85] Art. 130. There may also be an element of regional aid in various social policies, notably schemes to combat unemployment and assist workers in the coal and steel industries and to re-structure agriculture.

[86] MacDougall Report, p. 36.

[87] Another aspect of this policy is the attempt to restrict expansion in already developed areas : see R.J. Jarrett, "Disincentives : the other side of Regional Development Policy" (1975) 13 J.C.M.S. 379.

[88] Case 47/69 *France* v. *Commission* [1970] E.C.R. 487; Case 173/73 *Commission* v. *Italy* [1974] E.C.R. 709, both concerning assistance to the textile industry. And see Chapter 1, paras. 64, 65, above.

[89] See G. Schrans, "National and Regional Aid to Industry under the EEC Treaty" (1973) 10 C.M.L. Rev. 174 : A Dashwood, "Control of State Aids in the EEC : Prevention and Cure under Article 93" (1976) 12 C.M.L. Rev. 43. For a consideration of British aid measures, see A. Dashwood and T. Sharpe, "The Industry Acts 1972 and 1975 and European Community Law" (1978) 15 C.M.L. Rev. 9, at p. 115.

[90] Reduced VAT rates, but not exemption, would appear to be permitted by the Sixth Directive, and the proposed company tax directive also allows reduced rates for reasons of social and regional policy.

prosperous than the Community average. In the less fortunate Member States, where the disparities tend in any case to be greater, the capacity to reduce these disparities is also considerably less : in Ireland or Italy the transferor regions will themselves be below the Community average.

(b)   Community policy

**420**     The underlying assumption in the Treaty appears to be that regional problems will largely be solved by the creation of conditions of full factor mobility : unemployed or underpaid workers will move to areas where jobs are available or wages are better and investment will flow into areas where labour is plentiful and labour costs are low.[91] Thus, one of the tasks of the European Social Fund is that of rendering the employment of workers easier and of increasing their geographical and occupational mobility within the Community.[92] Unfortunately, it is at least equally likely that capital will tend to flow to the more affluent regions, especially if wage differentials narrow more quickly than productivity differentials, and large scale migration of workers creates social and environmental problems and would be unacceptable to both the regions of origin and of destination. The Community's response[93] to this problem has been threefold :

(1)   The co-ordination of national regional policies, notably by the setting up of a Regional Policy Committee,[94] to examine and make recommendations concerning national development programmes and systems of regional aid. Such co-ordination is doubtless necessary to eliminate the risk of an "incentive war" to attract business to different regions. There is, however, a danger that "co-ordination" may come to mean "approximation," with national aid policies, especially fiscal ones, becoming more similar when, in fact, the problems of an undeveloped German region are very different from those of an Irish or Italian one.[95] On the other hand, major differences in national aid policies may result in the creation of new forms of non-tariff barrier, a problem anticipated by Article 92.[96]

(2)   The financing of development programmes by means of loans. This is already provided for through the vehicle of the European Investment Bank. Further lending mechanisms have been established which, whilst not specifically directed at regional policy, clearly have a role to play in providing assistance for regional development,[97] and aid in the form of low-interest loans may be made under the European Regional Development Fund.[98]

---

[91]   For a critical examination of this theory, see R. M. Bird, *op. cit.* above, n. 83.
[92]   Art. 123.
[93]   Originating at the Paris summit of October, 1972.
[94]   Dec. 75/185 of March 18, 1975.
[95]   See R. M. Bird (*op. cit.* above, n. 83) at p. 418.
[96]   T. Buck, "Regional Policy and European Integration" (1975) 13 J.C.M.S. 368, 374.
[97]   The new "lending instrument" and loans granted under the EMS : Dec 78/870 and Reg. 1739/79, above, nn. 56, 58.
[98]   See below, and Reg. 2364/75 of September 15, 1975.

(3) The support of regional development by financial assistance, which may take the form of grants, under the European Regional Development Fund, established in 1975.[99] The ERDF marks an important stage in the development of a true Community policy towards regional problems in that it provides a basis for the redistribution of wealth between Member States, albeit on a very limited scale.[1] Aid is allocated under the Fund to all Member States, according to specified proportions[2]; thus aid will be given not only to Ireland and to Southern Italy, but to certain regions of Germany, Luxembourg and the Netherlands which are already more prosperous than the Community average. Requests for aid are made by the national governments, so that assistance is closely linked to national regional policies, and must be matched by equivalent amounts of national aid (according to various formulae) so that Community aid may constitute a supplement to, but not a substitute for, national aid. It may therefore not always be possible for a poorer Member State to afford to take advantage of the aid available.

### (iii)   Fiscal aspects of regional policy

**421**      These may be considered under two headings :

### (a)   Regional disparities as an obstacle to tax harmonisation

The existence of regional disparities of such a magnitude within the Community constitutes an obstacle to the achievement of the degree of harmonisation which is desirable for the proper functioning of the Common Market and for the establishment of a true economic union. For a variety of reasons, poorer states tend to rely more heavily upon indirect than upon direct taxes as a source of revenue. Harmonisation of the rates of VAT and excise duties would mean a reduction in revenue for some states, which would find difficulty in making corresponding increases in direct taxation.[3] Moreover, as already pointed out, a conflict exists between the desire to promote regional expansion by means of tax incentives to attract investment and create employment and that to remove differences in tax rules which may distort the conditions of competition and the free movement of capital.

---

[99] Reg. 724/75 of March 18, 1975 : O.J. 1975, L. 73/1. For an analysis see T. Buck (*op. cit.* above, n. 96) and the Commission's *A New Regional Policy for Europe*, European Documentation, 1975/3.

[1] A limit of 300 million units of account was set for 1975, increasing to 500 million for the following year. The budget appropriation for 1979 was 553 million EUA, or approximately 0.05 per cent. of the Community's gross national product and 4 per cent. of the Community's total budget.

[2] Italy and the United Kingdom, at 40 and 28 per cent. respectively, are the largest recipients, though on a *per capita* basis Ireland receives the greatest benefit.

[3] The Fredersdorf Report, at para. 4.2.1.6, concludes that Ireland and Italy would have to reduce excise duties and increase the share of direct taxation. In the case of Ireland it suggests that this would be particularly difficult until incomes go up sufficiently to make higher direct taxes possible. See also W Albers "Steuerharmonisierung in der EWG—Wünsch und Wirklichkeit" (1973) 11 W.D. 593.

(b)   *Expansion of the Community budget*

422     The existing ERDF is both too small and insufficiently selective to make a major impact upon regional disparities. In part this is due to a reluctance on the part of some richer Member States to see established a permanent form of subvention which would merely cushion inefficiency and perpetuate it[4]: in part, to the desire of all member states to secure some aid for their less-favoured regions, thus restricting the Fund's potential for redistribution.[5] It is widely agreed that further economic integration, and in particular the creation of an economic and monetary union, would require redistribution on a much greater scale than at present. As the MacDougall Report explains :

> "The need for redistribution between member states arises partly because the process of economic integration, which may confer net gains in the aggregate, does not necessarily raise the economic welfare in all areas. The changing pattern of production and exchange that characterises an integrating Community typically brings gains to some but losses to others. To make integration acceptable to all participants may then require an explicit redistributive mechanism to divide the gains from integration in a politically acceptable way. Failure to attend to this matter may at the least result in a stagnation of the integration process, and at the worst result in secession and dissolution."[6]

423     The Community's budget at present achieves only about one-fortieth of the redistribution found in maturely integrated economies, such as Canada and the United States. To achieve an acceptable level of redistribution would require a regional fund forty times greater than the present[7] which, without any expansion in other expenditure, would call for a Community budget three times as great as at present. Further, the regional fund would have to be far more "high-powered" than it is now, transferring wealth only to the poorer Member States[8] and only from the richer Member States. Alternatively, a larger fund could be established, whereby the beneficiaries would be the poorer regions but all Member States would contribute to the enlarged budget. Assuming that such redistribution would be made by means of the Community's budget, rather than by direct transfer from one Member State to another, this would necessitate a massive increase in the Community's taxing powers,[9] which would have to be accompanied by a much closer degree of harmonisation of those taxes which would accrue to

---

[4]   See R. Mathews, in the MacDougall Report, Vol. 2, Chap. 13.
[5]   G. Denton, "Reflections on Fiscal Federalism in the EEC" (1978) 16 J.C.M.S. 283.
[6]   At p. 60.
[7]   Approximately 2 per cent. of the Community's gross national product.
[8]   At present Ireland, Italy and the United Kingdom.
[9]   This is considered below, at paras 431-441.

the Community's own resources in order to ensure an equitable apportionment of the increased tax burden as among the Member States.

## D. SOCIAL POLICY

**424**    The Preamble to the Treaty accords a special place to social policy, the founding members 'affirming as the essential objective of their efforts the constant improvement of the living and working conditions of their peoples." This forthright affirmation is scarcely carried over into the body of the Treaty itself. Article 2 declares, as one of the tasks of the Community, the promotion of "an accelerated raising of the standard of living," which is stated as a major objective of the creation of the European Social Fund.[10] But apart from the ESF, the instruments and legal bases provided for attaining this objective are meagre, so that social policy has been described as "the Cinderella of European Community policy."[11] Article 117 speaks of the "harmonisation" of working conditions and the standard of living of workers and of social systems, and of the "approximation" of provisions laid down by law, regulation or administrative action,[12] but it appears from Article 118 that the primary task of the Commission is one of promoting close co-operation between the Member States in the social field.

**425**    The ESF, the budgetary appropriations for which in 1979[13] were a little smaller than that of the ERDF, is given the primary task of "rendering the employment of workers easier and of increasing their geographical and occupational mobility within the Community."[14] This is to be achieved by assisting towards the costs of vocational re-training and re-settlement of workers and of aid for the benefit of workers whose employment is reduced or temporarily suspended as a result of the conversion of an undertaking to other production.[15] Its mandate is thus principally to pay for the social costs of disturbances created by Community policies.[16]

Nowhere in the Treaty is there any specific reference to the objectives of a reasonable distribution of income and wealth among the citizens of the Community and of the elimination of poverty.[17] The Commission's Social

---

[10] Arts. 3(i), 123.

[11] M. Shanks, "The Social Policy of the European Communities" (1977) 14 C.M.L. Rev. 375.

[12] The different texts of Art. 117 contain a profusion and confusion of terms.

[13] 502 million EUA.

[14] Art. 123.

[15] Art. 125.

[16] D. Collins, "Toward a European Social Policy" (1966) 5 J.C.M.S. 26. Similar "disturbance compensation" is provided for under the ECSC Treaty, Art. 55, and under the Guidance section of the Agricultural Fund. This mandate was broadened, under the Second Social Fund, established by Dec. 71/66 of February 1, 1971, to include assistance to categories such as young persons seeking work, handicapped workers and women. For a general survey, see *The European Community's Social Policy* (European Documentation 1978/2).

[17] These objectives are, of course, a major concern of regional policy.

Action Programme of 1973[18] sets out three major objectives—full and better employment in the Community, improved living and working conditions, and the increased participation by both sides of industry in the economic and social decisions of the Community and of workers in the conduct of the enterprise—all of which may be expected to combat poverty and to reduce inequalities in the distribution of wealth. Absent, however, is any clear determination to establish greater equality by means of the harmonisation of social systems or by a redistribution of wealth through the fiscal system.

### (i)  Harmonisation of social systems

426       Until recently it has been widely assumed that the harmonisation of social systems is probably unnecessary, perhaps not desirable and certainly not practicable.[19] Differences in national social systems reflect strong local traditions—social, political and religious, as well as economic—and such diversity may also have the advantage of providing a testing ground for innovation.[20] The demand, as well as the ability to pay, for social benefits tends to rise with income levels, and harmonised social standards would thus likely be considered inadequate for the more advanced Member States and too expensive for the less developed states to provide by themselves.[21] Centralisation, through the Community budget, would provide few if any economies of scale, might impose standardised services which were inappropriate to local conditions, and would involve further transfers on a massive scale.[22] The emphasis, so far, has therefore been upon achieving a measure of co-ordination to permit the transferability of social security benefits and contributions in the case of migrant workers and their families, of eliminating discrimination against such persons and, to a lesser extent, upon a consideration of the social costs imposed upon enterprises.[23]

Appreciation of the full implications of economic and monetary union has led to an acceptance that this attitude must be reconsidered.[24] If accelerated integration leads to an increase in prosperity of the Community as a whole, whilst operating to the disadvantage of some Member States or regions and, more especially, of some individuals, then it would seem proper that the Community, or the beneficiary states, should compensate those to whom there is a detriment. There is, moreover, a growing awareness of the need to give the Community a "human face" : the waning popularity of the Com-

---

[18] (EC) Bull. S. 2–74.
[19] See, *e.g.* N. Andel, "Problems of Harmonisation of Social Security Policies in the Common Market" in Shoup : *Fiscal Harmonisation*, Chap. 5.
[20] MacDougall Report, pp. 51–52.
[21] M. B. Krauss, "The Anti-Economics of the European Common Market : Can British Entry Help? (1973) 7 J.W.T.L. 555, at pp. 565–566.
[22] MacDougall Report (above, n. 20) : M. Shanks (*op. cit.* above, n. 11) at pp. 376–377.
[23] See above, chapter 3, paras. 325, 326.
[24] See the Commission's reply to EPWQ 533/78 : O.J. 1978, C 310/3.

munity will suffer further if the chief beneficiaries of integration are perceived to be the large and affluent enterprises in the central regions and the victims are the underemployed and their families in the outlying regions. Thus both the Bosman and Marjolin Reports envisage a need for some alignment of social benefits and centralisation of social systems, the latter advocating the creation of a Community Unemployment Benefit Fund, funded directly from taxes on profits and wages.[25]

**427**     It seems inevitable that, as economic integration is intensified, there will be a growing demand for the alignment of at least some of the social benefits provided by member states. Full factor mobility will increase the pressure for the harmonisation of employers' social security payments which, one would expect, would result in a "levelling-up" of contributions. As the Bosman Report explains :

> "As social and cultural integration proceeds, there will be increasing emulation effects; people with an inferior social service will view the best standard of provision in the Community with envy. Each state, as now, will be a shining example in one aspect—unemployment benefits, family allowances, pensions, etc.—and form a goal for others."[26]

**428**     However, harmonisation of employers' social security contributions alone will not bring about a major alignment of benefits, given the widely differing levels of economic activity and of unemployment within the Community. But if a Community unemployment benefit fund, on the lines suggested in the Marjolin Report, were established, to provide roughly equivalent levels of benefit (even if only as a proportion of pre-unemployment earnings) this would require a transfer of funds on a major scale.[27] To a considerable extent, of course, such transfers would be a substitute for inter-regional transfers rather than additional thereto. The basic policy question facing the Community is, therefore, not whether large-scale transfers would be necessary in an economic and monetary union but rather whether those transfers, made by means of a regional, social or unemployment fund, should be specifically linked to certain types of assistance programme, in particular in the "welfare" field. With regard to the provision of social and welfare services, the MacDougall Report concluded that[28] :

> "There is no case for any major Community financial involvement in these spending functions as long as two present conditions are maintained : (i) the level of inter-Member State migration remains relatively slight and (ii) the differences in the standard of public services

---

[25] Details of the proposal are set out in the Annex to the Marjolin Report.
[26] At p. 34.
[27] It would, presumably, also result in some "spontaneous" harmonisation of other benefits since unemployment benefits could scarcely be greatly in excess of disability benefits, pensions, etc.
[28] At p. 52 (written in 1977).

are not so great as to constitute a real Community-level political issue. However these two conditions are crucial, and one cannot predict how long they will hold. The Community's objectives and policies are directed towards the day when either or both conditions could cease to prevail. Two deliberate steps are currently being taken in this direction : further enlargement to include one or more less-developed and migration-prone Mediterranean countries, and direct election to the European Parliament, which will increase the political sensitivity to differences in standards in the major public services.[29] A third unintended factor is the continued divergence of economic performance between existing Member States, which means diverging fiscal capacities and ultimately public service standards."

## (ii)   The redistribution of personal incomes and wealth

**429**     As was seen in chapter 3,[30] no substantial harmonisation of the main fiscal instruments for redistributing income and wealth—the taxes on personal income, estates, inheritances and net wealth—is planned or likely, at least for a long time to come. These would, it has generally been thought, remain exclusively within the jurisdiction of the Member States except where some degree of harmonisation might be necessary to secure freedom of movement and of competition. Nevertheless, the distribution of wealth, as among individual citizens as well as among the Member States, may be affected by those Community tax policies which are proposed or which seem more likely to be developed. It is submitted that the achievement of a more equitable distribution of personal wealth is one of the tasks assigned to the Community by the Treaty and is a proper concern and objective of the Community's tax policy, for both economic and social reasons.[31] Thus, in establishing fiscal policies which are primarily directed to other ends, the Community should always take into account the effects of those policies upon the distribution of personal wealth. This applies in particular to :

(a) *The balance between direct and indirect taxation.* It has long been recognised that this balance, within each national system, is a matter of importance for economic reasons.[32] The issue becomes of greater importance in an economic and monetary union, for this would involve the determination at Community level of the essential features of national budgets including methods of financing, so that the appropriate balance between different types of taxation would necessarily become a Community question.

[29] See, on this point, H. Wallace, "Direct Elections and the Political Dynamics of the European Communities" (1979) 17 J.C.M.S. 281, at pp. 285 *et seq.*
[30] Above, paras. 316–318.
[31] See J. E. Meade, in Appendix F of the Bosman Report, at pp. 102–104, and see the Cairncross Report, Chap. 6.
[32] Neumark Report, pp. 113 *et seq.*; Deringer Report, pp. 22 *et seq.* ; Fredersdorf Report, 3.1.

Whilst it would be erroneous to suggest that a heavy reliance on indirect taxation is inevitably regressive or that heavy direct taxes automatically achieve any significant redistribution of wealth, these are undoubtedly tendencies which would have to be considered.

**430**     (b) *Expenditures through the Community budget.* Major increases in Community spending would involve large-scale transfers from the richer to the poorer member states. It is probable that these transfers would mostly follow a·"confederal" rather than a "federal" model, *i.e.* would be made to the governments of the recipient states rather than directly to individuals in those states.[33] Some transfers, however, may be made to individuals, for example by means of a Community unemployment fund, and those transfers which are made to national governments will normally be tied to specific types of expenditure.[34] Greater redistribution of personal wealth could be achieved by concentrating spending upon individuals, directly or indirectly, rather than upon providing assistance to enterprises. A proper balance must consequently be struck between providing immediate relief to disadvantaged citizens (especially when this disadvantage is itself a product of closer economic integration) and providing the means whereby the less developed regions can accelerate growth and bring themselves closer to the general Community standard of prosperity.

    (c) *Revenue accruing to the Community.* An expansion of the budget will necessitate making available to the Community further "own resources," which may have to be derived from tax sources other than the value added tax.[35] Some further degree of redistribution may be achieved if recourse is had to those taxes which are more progressive in effect.[36]

    (d) *Tax harmonisation.* When the time comes for the approximation of the rates of VAT and of excise duties,[37] regard must be had to the fact that high rates of tax would have a regressive effect. Similar considerations should be borne in mind when harmonising the bases of assessment of the corporate income tax, especially in view of its inter-relationship with personal income tax.

    At the present stage of development it cannot be expected that the Community will have any major part to play in the redistribution of individual, as opposed to national, wealth. Nevertheless, it is essential that the Community should not be percieved as being purely a "rich man's club"

---

[33] See W. E. Oates, "Fiscal Federalism in Theory and Practice : Applications to the European Community" in the MacDougall Report, Vol. II, Chap. 10, at pp. 295 *et seq.*

[34] *e.g.* the "matching grant" principle, under the ERDF.

[35] This is considered in the next section of this chapter.

[36] This would be difficult. The strongest candidate to provide additional own resources is the corporation tax, which may be more progressive than VAT, assuming that its burden is not fully shifted to the consumer. A payroll tax, with a progressive structure, might finance an unemployment fund : see below, para. 436.

[37] The latter pose a special problem, *e.g.* high rates of duty on wine would be regarded as progressive in effect in Denmark, Ireland and the United Kingdom but harshly regressive in France and Italy.

and it must therefore ensure that, at the very least, its tax policies do not aggravate existing social and fiscal injustice.

## E.  BUDGETARY POLICY

**431**    The preceding sections of this chapter have demonstrated that the Community's economic and monetary policy, regional policy and social policy are all likely to impose demands on and require a major expansion of the budget. In an economic and monetary union the Community will require the means to exercise some of the counter-cyclical and long-term economic functions at present exercised by national governments and to mitigate or rectify the effects of increased integration upon the less economically advantaged sections of the Community. Even without a significant advance in this direction there is an almost general recognition both that fresh resources will soon be needed to meet existing commitments and that the overall structure of the budget is in need of drastic reform.

### (i)  The need for budgetary reform

The existing budget is small, and has a low potential for redistribution among the Member States, is inefficient and is widely perceived to be inequitable.

The General Budget for the financial year 1979 made provision for a total expenditure of some 13 billion units of account, an amount in the region of only 1 per cent. of the total gross national product of the Member States. Of this amount, almost 10 billion units of account were allocated to agricultural expenditure[38] : by contrast, the regional and social funds together received a little over 1 billion.[39] Guarantee payments in respect of milk and milk products alone comprised almost one-third of total projected expenditure. As a result, the budget may be said to encourage the inefficient allocation of agricultural resources, resulting in "butter mountains," "wine lakes" and the like. Moreover, the bulk of Community expenditure is directed to those Member States with a large agricultural sector and the concentration of

---

[38] 8,773 million EUA to guarantee payments under the EAGGF, 809 million EUA to monetary compensation amounts and 432 million EUA under the guidance section of the fund to the restructuring of agriculture.

[39] 553 million EUA to the ERDF, 502 million EUA to the ESF. Other major items were 832 million EUA for the running of the various institutions (Commission, Council, Parliament, Court and Court of Auditors), 495 million EUA to research. The draft budget for 1980, as proposed by the Commission, would have increased this to 17.9 billion EUA (agriculture 11.8, social 1.1, regional 1.4). The first Council draft reduced this to 16.3 billion (agriculture 11.7, Social 0.8, regional 1.0). The Parliament increased the total to 18.0 billion, with major increases in social and regional expenditure (social 1.1, regional 2.0). The Council removed almost all of these increases in its second draft, and as a result the Parliament rejected the budget in its entirety.

expenditure on dairy products, sugar, cereals and meat favours the more affluent "northern" agricultures disproportionately.[40]

**432**    On the revenue side, slightly less than one-half was derived from the Community's share of VAT and from gross national product-based contributions in lieu,[41] the remainder coming from agricultural and sugar levies and from the common customs tariff.[42] Agricultural levies and customs duties, again, seem to operate in a somewhat arbitrary manner in the sense that they are not in any way related to the ability to pay of the countries whose citizens have to bear them.[43] Customs duties fall most heavily upon those Member States with a high level of imports and of international trade : due to the different components making up the agricultural and sugar levies, on producers and on importers, their overall incidence is almost impossible to calculate.[44] The VAT revenue reflects far more closely the level of economic activity and wealth in each Member State, though even here there is some discrimination against those countries where the level of investment is low.[45]

It is scarcely surprising that some Member States feel that the existing budget, in the allocation of the benefits of expenditure and of the burdens of revenue, operates inequitably as among the Member States. According to Commission estimates, in 1980 the United Kingdom and Germany will be net contributors and the largest benefits will accrue to Ireland and to Italy.[46] Discontent is especially strong in the United Kingdom, which considers that, as one of the poorer members, it should be a net beneficiary rather than a net contributor. As it is, benefits do not correspond with contributions, nor

[40] Among the countries, the Netherlands, Denmark, France and Ireland are the major beneficiaries, Italy, the United Kingdom and Germany the main contributors. In terms of persons employed in agriculture, the Belgian or Dutch farmer receives seven times more than the Italian farmer.

[41] See Chapter 2, para. 124, above.

[42] The amounts in the 1979 General Budget were as follows: VAT (six Member States), 4,323 million EUA; financial contributions (three Member States), 2,097 million EUA; Customs duties, 4,745 million EUA; Agricultural and sugar levies, 2,173 million EUA.

[43] Even the incidence of these levies and duties is difficult to determine : the amounts collected are not necessarily finally paid by the citizens of the State where the collection is made, e.g. goods passing through Antwerp or Rotterdam en route to other Member States. See (EC) Bull. S. 8–78, p.12.

[44] In proportion to national gross national product, customs duties appear to fall most heavily upon Belgium, Netherlands and the United Kingdom and least heavily upon France. Agricultural levies fall heaviest upon Belgium, Italy and the Netherlands and least heavily upon France and Germany : see the tables on p. 12 of *Financing the Community Budget : The Way Ahead*, (EC) Bull. S. 8–78.

[45] There may be other reasons why the proportions of VAT payable diverge from the proportionate share of the Community's gross national product, including, perhaps, inefficiency in collection. The Commission estimates that the VAT-based own resources bear more heavily upon Ireland, Luxembourg and the United Kingdom and less heavily upon Italy : (EC) Bull. S. 8–78, p. 18.

[46] This is strongly disputed by the Italian government, which expects only to break even. In part, the different estimates are due to disagreement as to who actually gains from the "green money" subsidy. This estimate was prior to the agreement of May 30, 1980.

do net contributions accord in any way with ability to pay and the present budget, far from redistributing wealth from the rich to the poor, must be considered regressive in its effects.[47]

Reform of the budget structure would seem to require the following measures :

(a) a real reduction in agricultural expenditure, or a standstill together with some transfer of expenditure from "northern" products, especially dairy products, to "southern" products;

(b) a substantial increase in regional and social expenditure in the less-advantaged Member States;

(c) an increase in revenue, to finance (b), contributed predominantly by those Member States most able to pay, i.e. the notion of a *juste retour* must be firmly rejected.

#### (ii)     The creation of new "own resources"

433     Even without increasing total expenditure on the lines suggested above, the Community is rapidly reaching the point where new sources of revenue will be needed to meet its commitments. Existing own resources are derived from customs duties and agricultural levies and from the application of a VAT rate, which may not exceed 1 per cent. [48] These resources lack buoyancy : the yield from customs duties cannot be expected to increase, especially in times of a world trade recession, the yield from agricultural levies is unpredictable and may fall as world food prices approach the Community level, and the VAT ceiling is likely soon to be reached.[49] By 1982 at the latest, new own resources will be needed : the question is, how are they to be provided?[50]

The main alternatives appear to be as follows :

#### (a)     Customs duties and agricultural levies

Given the existence of the Customs Union and of the Common Market in agricultural products, these are logically "federal-type" revenues. In particular, the appropriation by the Community of customs duties and of levies on agricultural imports avoids the problem of allocation where goods

---

[47] G. Denton, "Reflections on Fiscal Federalism in the EEC" (1978) 16 J.C.M.S. 283; J. R. Dodsworth, "Cost Sharing in the European Communities" (1974) 29 P.F. 131. Probably only Germany and Ireland could be said to respectively pay and receive their proper shares.

[48] Dec. 70/243 of April 21, 1970, Art. 4.

[49] The rate fixed in the 1979 General Budget was 0.72 per cent. The increases for 1980 proposed by the Parliament would have raised the rate to 0.88 per cent., reduced to 0.74 per cent. by the Council. The Commission estimates that the ceiling allows only for an increase of 2,400 million EUA in the total budget and that, unless agricultural expenditure is contained, a VAT rate of 1.25 per cent. will be required in 1982 : (EC) Bull. S. 6–79, p. 116.

[50] For a comprehensive study, see the Commission's *Financing the Community Budget : The Way Ahead*, (EC) Bull. S. 8–78. See also the MacDougall Report, pp. 64 et seq.

are landed in one Member State for transportation to another. They are levied, therefore, primarily for commercial or regulatory reasons and have economic and political, rather than financial, objectives.[51] A unilateral increase in duties would be contrary to world agreements and to the Community's policy of general liberalisation of world trade. Agricultural levies, upon domestic overproduction rather than on imports, already exist and could justifiably be increased to produce extra revenue or reduced expenditure and, hopefully, structural improvements in agriculture.

(b)  *Financial contributions*

**434**     A major reason for providing the Community with its own resources, to replace the financial contributions provided for in Article 200 of the Treaty, was to protect its freedom of action in the use of those resources and to remove the threat that a Member State might withhold its contributions to the budget.[52] This factor may have been somewhat overrated : the Member States still collect the duties and levies on behalf of the Community and account for their shares of the VAT, and a refusal to pay these over to the Community would be as effective, and as much a breach of their obligation, as a refusal to pay the appropriate financial contribution.[53] Nevertheless, a return to financial contributions would be regarded as a retrograde step and contrary to both the letter and the spirit of the Treaty.[54]

(c)  *Value added tax*

An increase in the ceiling on the VAT rate would be by far the simplest solution. The tax base is already harmonised, though some further harmonisation is necessary to achieve a truly uniform basis of assessment.[55] A new ceiling of, say, 2 per cent., would ensure adequate revenue, unless major new expenditures were introduced, probably until the end of the decade. Such an increase might be mildly inflationary and mildly regressive, though as the annual increase in rate would only be in the region of one-tenth of one per cent., it should not cause Member States to make a corresponding increase in the overall rate.[56] The principal objection to this course is that, on the revenue side, it would have no redistributive effect. This could be

[51] (EC) Bull. S. 8–78 p. 10.
[52] G. L. Bustin, "Financing the European Economic Community : Autonomy and the Problem of Parliamentary Control" (1972) 13 Harv. Int. L. Jo. 481.
[53] Witness the British threat to withhold its share of VAT. Of far greater significance, in terms of the independence of the Community, is the power exercised over the expenditure side of the budget by the Parliament.
[54] Art. 201 (EC) Bull. S. 8–78, para. 201.
[55] Above, chapter 2, para. 135.
[56] *i.e.* the rate to the consumer should remain the same, Member States reducing their share of the total proceeds. Those Member States which would be net recipients, taking into account increased Community spending, could clearly afford to do so.

achieved by varying the Community rate from one Member State to another, based upon taxable capacity. There might thus be a neutral tranche of VAT, applicable to all, with an additional indexed rate applying in the wealthier Member States.[57]

### (d)   Excise duties

**435**     Recourse to excise duties appears to offer few, if any, advantages, with the possible exception of an energy tax considered below. Only the duty on cigarettes is harmonised, and that to an insufficient degree. The rate of the community duty would have to be very high to yield sufficient revenue, duties on other tobacco products would have to be harmonised (otherwise pipe-and-cigar-smoking nations would contribute less than their fair shares) and, because of differences in cigarette consumption between Member States, their relative burdens would differ substantially from their relative national incomes *per capita*.[58] Duties on alcoholic drinks would be even less suitable, in view of the formidable difficulties in achieving harmonisation and the widely differing national patterns of consumption. In any event, if the additional revenue is to be derived from taxes on consumption there seems to be no good reason to look beyond the value added tax.

### (e)   Energy tax

**436**     The one exception to this appears to be the possibility of a Community tax on energy, either on consumption or on imports.[59] Such a tax might be consistent with an overall Community policy of energy conservation and self-sufficiency, the development of alternative sources of energy and the removal of one distortion to the conditions of competition within the common market. However, a comprehensive energy policy has yet to emerge, harmonisation of energy taxes presents major problems and a system which discriminated between different forms of energy might be contrary to the Treaty.[60] This would seem to eliminate a Community tax on petrol alone, which might otherwise be feasible, though the rate would have to be high in order to raise adequate revenue.[61]

### (f)   Payroll tax

Though not suggested by the Commission, a payroll tax levied on wages and salaries and borne partly by employers and partly by employees, could,

[57] MacDougall Report, p. 65.
[58] (EC) Bull. S. 8–78, p. 20
[59] The latter might operate unfairly in favour of the oil-producing Member States. The MacDougall Report envisages an oil import levy, in the event of a minimum oil price mechanism being established.
[60] Above, chapter 3, paras. 240-242.
[61] (EC) Bull. S. 8–78, p. 21.

if properly structured, afford a progressive source of revenue without requiring any major degree of harmonisation. Such a tax might be applied only to wages above a certain level, thus exempting the great majority of workers in the poorer Member States, and could if desired be imposed according to a progressively rising scale. A tax of this nature would be especially appropriate for funding a Community unemployment benefit scheme[62] and would be strongly redistributive in nature.

(g)   *Development tax*

**437**      Another tax which conforms with redistributive notions and with the "matching" principle would be a tax imposed upon new development and investment in regions which are already prosperous and overcrowded. As such, it would provide a fiscal complement to regional aid programmes.[63] There would, however, be considerable technical and administrative problems and it is unlikely that any substantial yield could be hoped for.

(h)   *Corporation tax*

Probably the most important alternative to an increase in the VAT rate, a Community share in a harmonised corporation tax would produce adequate revenue[64] and would seem to be progressive and redistributive in nature.[65] Moreover, since it is "business" which is commonly perceived as the major beneficiary of the Common Market, it seems appropriate that "business" should pay.[66] Ultimately, the entire yield from corporation tax might accrue to the Community and provide sufficient revenue to finance the budgetary expansion necessitated by the creation of an economic and monetary union.[67] The immediate prospect of recourse to the corporation tax is, however, very slight, for not only would corporation tax systems have to be harmonised but also the bases for assessment of profits,[68] and other differences in national legislation, such as the way in which partnerships are taxed, would also have to be considered.

----

[62]  See the Marjolin Report, Annex, p. 5 : MacDougall Report, p. 64.

[63]  MacDougall Report, p. 65.

[64]  According to the Bosman Report, the total corporation tax yield would be equivalent of a VAT rate of from 3 to 4 per cent.

[65]  However, as the Commission points out, it would discriminate against countries with relatively large corporate sectors : (EC) Bull. S. 8–78, p. 20. These are not necessarily the richest, as witness the United Kingdom.

[66]  D. Dosser, in App. C of the Bosman Report, p. 47.

[67]  It would be adequate by itself for the "pre-federal phase" envisaged in the MacDougall Report, but would need augmenting to achieve a "small public-sector federation". The report (p. 65) regards the corporation tax as a plausible candidate for a Community tax sharing arrangement only under the hypothesis of a federation.

[68]  See chapter 3, paras. 276-281.

**438**      In the longer term these problems will have to be resolved, especially
since matters such as investment incentives and the treatment of depreciation are highly relevant to regional policy. One other possibility would be to
make over to the Community some other part of the income generated by
corporations : in particular, own resources could be derived from some part
of the withholding tax on dividends, since this would require harmonisation
only of the definition of "dividend," rather than of the entire corporation tax
system. This might be applied to dividends generally[69] or, perhaps, only in
the case of dividends paid to investors in other Member States or in third
countries. Similarly, a Community withholding tax could be applied to bond
interest paid to investors in other countries. Such a tax might be justified on
the ground that investors would be paying a small price for the benefits
derived from the liberalisation of the capital market.

*(i)   Taxes on personal income and wealth*

     Since these are likely to be among the last taxes to be harmonised, if
indeed they ever are, there would seem to be no possibility of the application
of a Community rate to the personal tax base.[70] A parallel Community
income tax with its own definition of the tax base might be possible, but
would create severe additional administrative burdens and there would need
to be arrangements for avoiding double taxation.

**439**      It seems obvious that the only realistic solution, capable of providing the
Community with the additional resources which will certainly be needed by
the end of 1981, is to increase the ceiling on the Community VAT rate. A
budget frozen at its present limit will, with the accession of Greece to the
Community, simply be inadequate even in the unlikely event that agricultural expenditure is contained at its existing level in real terms. An increase
in the VAT ceiling to 2 per cent. would enable the costs of enlargement to be
met and permit a gradual growth in expenditure, perhaps until 1990 or
beyond. On this basis, agricultural expenditure would have to be contained
as much as possible : even so, the accession of Greece, Portugal and Spain,
all countries with a large agricultural sector, would inevitably lead to a sharp
increase, especially if the current pattern of expenditure were changed to
give "southern" farmers a fairer share. The regional and social funds would
also expand as a result of enlargement,[71] but would not greatly increase their
present share of the budget.

     A more dynamic approach would be to proceed more rapidly towards the
2 per cent. ceiling, perhaps by the end of 1986. This would permit a budget

---

[69] It would be difficult to administer a tax credit at the Community level. If the Community withholding rate were low, a credit might be dispensed with entirely. Alternatively, the
investor's home state could grant a credit for the tax paid to the Community.

[70] (EC) Bull. S. 8–78, p. 20 : MacDougall Report, p. 65.

[71] And, presumably, to ensure that the United Kingdom was no longer a major net contributor.

of nearly twice its present size, in real terms, with regional and social expenditure almost equal to that on agriculture.[72] The inequities in the existing budget structure would be largely eliminated and there would be a genuine, if still small, redistribution of wealth from the richer to the poorer Member States.[73] Whichever approach is adopted, the immediate need to raise the VAT ceiling remains : in agreeing to this, Member States would not necessarily be voting in favour of either approach but would permit the appropriate policy to evolve over the next few years.

### (iii)    The budget in an economic and monetary union

**440**      It is generally assumed that the creation of a full economic and monetary union will require a greatly expanded budget. The disruptions caused by EMU will demand increased transfers from richer to poorer regions and the centralisation of economic policy will necessitate the granting to the Community of fiscal instruments to achieve stabilisation.

### (a)    Transfers

The need created by EMU for major transfers of wealth has already been discussed.[74] It is suggested, however, that to a large extent these transfers are already necessary in order to achieve a greater degree of equity in the budget. The need for redistribution exists, regardless of the proposals for EMU, to attain the fundamental objectives of the Treaty. EMU would therefore only increase the need for, and scale of, redistribution in order to compensate for the effects, upon some member states, of greater economic integration. Budgetary reform upon the more dynamic lines suggested above could create the conditions under which the achievement of EMU would become possible : with regional and social expenditure of around 10 billion units of account, it would approximate to the "pre-federal" budget envisaged in the MacDougall Report. This ". . . is small in comparison with that which would probably be required to render full economic and monetary integration acceptable; but it would be an acceptable start."[75]

Full economic and monetary union would require further increases to achieve a "small public sector federation," with a "high powered" (i.e. strongly redistributive) budget, which should be progressive on the revenue as well as on the expenditure side. Additional own resources, in the form of part or all of the corporation tax, an energy tax[76] and a payroll tax to finance an unemployment benefit fund, would then be needed.

---

[72] Such a budget would still be smaller than that envisaged for 1980 in the Bosman Report, pp. 37-41.
[73] Especially if a "taxable capacity" differential is built in to the Community VAT rate.
[74] Above, paras. 414-416.
[75] At p. 69.
[76] Consistent with a Community energy policy.

## (b)  Stabilisation

**441**     One of the greatest problems associated with EMU is that of the allocation of the tools of economic policy. As envisaged in the Werner Report, the
Community would assume many of these—exchange rates, money and
credit supply, interest rates, etc.[77] The question remains as to who should
exercise the fiscal tools : would they remain with the Member States, be
assumed by the Community, be shared, or would they be neutralised as a
result of tax harmonisation?

A Community budget as envisaged above provides little scope as an instrument of stabilisation policy. Reactions to changes in the corporation tax
rate tend to be slow, an energy tax and a payroll tax would have rather
limited use, and the Community VAT rate would be far too small for any
possible change to have much effect. Even if the Community rate were to be
"piggy-backed" on top of the national rate,[78] so that changes made at Community level were automatically reflected in the total rate,[79] it is hard to
believe that there would be any economic reaction to the sort of increase or
reduction which could be made.[80] Moreover, it is far more likely that
economic conditions would vary from one Member State or region to
another, rather than be uniform throughout the Community. A stimulus
might be needed in one area and a brake in another. For this reason it
appears essential that the major fiscal instruments of stabilisation policy
remain in the control of national governments, albeit that consultation be
required before major action. In particular this seems to require that Member States should continue to control those taxes which are most flexible in
terms of economic policy, especially the value added tax. Consequently one
is driven to agree with the conclusions of Professor Dosser[81] that the
corporation tax should eventually provide the main source of revenue for
the Community : a Community rate of VAT would still seem to be
necessary, but VAT should remain primarily a national tax and, in so
far as any harmonisation of rates is necessary, the prescribed rate bands
should be sufficiently wide so as not to deprive the member states of the use
of this tax as an instrument of economic policy.

---

[77]  Above, para. 409.

[78]  For an examination of this suggestion, see W. E. Oates, in the MacDougall Report, Vol.
II, Chap. 10, at pp. 288 *et seq.*

[79]  Unless a member State deliberately made a corresponding reduction in its own rate. At
present, an increase in the Community rate will simply reduce the proportion of the total rate
retained by the Member State.

[80]  In a "small public sector federation," a Community VAT rate of 3 per cent. might
produce one-third of all revenue, a rather larger amount coming from the corporation tax and
the remainder from other sources. A VAT reduction of 1 per cent., which would scarcely
affect spending, would reduce total revenue by more than 10 per cent.

[81]  D. Dosser, in App. C of the Bosman Report, especially at pp. 44, 59–64, and in *British
Taxation and the Common Market* (1973), Chap. 7.

## F.    ENLARGEMENT OF THE COMMUNITY

**442**    Mention has already been made, on a number of occasions, of the additional problems likely to be caused by the enlargement of the Community. With the signing of the Treaty of Accession[82] in May, 1979, Greece will become the tenth member of the Community on January 1, 1981. Negotiations with Portugal and Spain have reached an advanced stage, with the target date for their entry the beginning of 1983. There is yet the further possibility, rather remote at present, of Turkey becoming a thirteenth member.

The increase in membership to 10 and soon 12, will have major political repercussions, which cannot be examined here. However, some brief discussion of the economic and fiscal consequences seems appropriate.

### (i)    The economics of enlargement[83]

Although the economies of Greece, Portugal and Spain differ considerably in many aspects, they share a number of common features. All three are at a level of economic development considerably below the average for the existing Community of the Nine.[84] In terms of gross domestic product, *per capita,* Spain stands slightly below Italy and above Ireland, at a little over one-half of the average for the Nine. Greece stands just below Ireland, at a little under one-half. Portugal stands considerably lower, at less than one-third of the average for the existing Community and less than one-quarter of the six most prosperous states.[85]

Regional disparities are large in all three countries and appear to be growing : thus the disparities between Paris or Hamburg and Andalusia or Braganca are still greater than those between Denmark and Portugal. In each country the agricultural sector is large[86] : agricultural productivity is low, farms tend to be small and only Greece is not a net food importer. Moreover, the type of agriculture and the main products are such as to bring the three countries into competition with some of the least advanced regions of the existing Community.[87]

The three countries share a broadly similar industrial structure (though

---

[82] O.J. 1979, L 291.
[83] See further, W. Wallace and I. Herreman (eds.), *A Community of Twelve? The Impact of Further Enlargement on the European Communities* (1978) (referred to hereafter as *A Community of Twelve?*) : G. Edwards and W. Wallace, *A Wider European Community? Issues and Problems of Further Enlargement* (1976) : A da Silva Ferreira, "The Economics of Enlargement : trade effects on the Applicant Countries" (1978) 17 J.C.M.S. 120 : G. N. Yannopoulos, "The Mediterranean Policy of the EEC" (1977) 11 J.W.T.L. 489 and the Commission's opinions, (EC) Bull. S. 1–78, S. 2–78, S. 3–78.
[84] Annex A, Tables 1 and 7.
[85] The figures quoted are based upon statistics for 1976 : see (EC) Bull. S. 9–78, p. 43.
[86] Agricultural workers, as a proportion of the working population, comprise 28 per cent. in Greece, 33 per cent. in Portugal and 21 per cent. in Spain, compared to 23 per cent. in Ireland, 16 per cent. in Italy, less than 3 per cent. in Britain and 8 per cent in the whole Community of the Nine.
[87] *e.g.* the Mezzogiorno.

Spain has a much larger industrial production and is highly competitive in some sectors) and are competitors in some industries which are already regarded as "problem areas." All three already provide a major source of labour for the existing Community[88] and possess a mobile workforce already accustomed to migration. This, in turn, is due to the fact that the levels of unemployment are relatively high in all three countries.

Enlargement will thus radically alter the existing balance within the Community : the number of agricultural workers will increase by 55 per cent.,[89] the number of "poorer" member states will increase from three to six,[90] the right of workers from the new members to move freely within the Community is likely to impose additional strains and the achievement of EMU may be adversely affected by the new disparities.[91] Alternatively, in so far as EMU is likely to have adverse effects upon some regions, it is in the new Member States that these will be most severe.

### (ii)    The impact of enlargement upon fiscal policy

**443**      This can be considered under the following three headings :

### (a)    Adoption of existing measures

The new Member States will have to adapt their existing tax laws in order to conform with the Treaty and with those directives which have already been adopted for the harmonisation of taxes. This will take time and, as with the previous enlargement in 1973, is likely to result in a relative standstill with regard to existing proposals and new measures to create a breathing-period while the new Member States catch up. Thus one member of the Commission has urged the need to act swiftly on existing proposals lest enlargement cause them to be delayed almost indefinitely.[92]

Under the terms of the Treaty of Accession, Greece will have to modify its existing laws to remove any tax provisions which discriminate against the products of other member states in order to comply with Articles 95-98 of the Treaty.[93] Most of the existing tax directives will have to be implemented

---

[88] Workers in EEC countries from Greece, Portugal and Spain number well over one million and comprise almost 30 per cent. of all non-Community workers.

[89] But production by only 24 per cent. : (EC) Bull. S. 1–78.

[90] The Community "average" will be reduced to somewhere around the present level of the United Kingdom, which may have some effect upon the merits of the British claim to be a net recipient.

[91] See P. van der Bempt, in *A Community of Twelve?* at pp. 247 *et seq.*

[92] R. Burke, "Harmonisation of Taxation in Europe" [1979] *Intertax* 46, at p. 53.

[93] This apparently must be done before accession. By contrast, customs duties on imports and charges having equivalent effect are to be phased-out gradually by 1986 : Treaty of Accession, Arts. 25–29. This will give new importance to the distinction between internal taxation and charges : see Chapter 1, para. 23, above. Note also that Art. 97 will be revitalised : see the amendment to Dir. 68/221 (average rates) in Annex I, Title 6.

by Greece not later than the date of accession, on January 1, 1981,[94] except that Greece, which presently has a form of turnover tax, may delay adoption of the VAT Directives until the end of 1983.[95] Transitional provisions, though not necessarily similar ones, will also be necessary for Portugal and Spain once the terms of entry are finally agreed.[96] It may therefore be as late as 1986 before existing directives are in force in all 12 member states.

### (b)  Progress in harmonisation

**444**    Not only is progress on new measures likely to be reduced to a virtual standstill during the "breathing space" but even thereafter it will be made more difficult. Existing proposals, on which some measure of agreement has already been reached[97] will be thrown open for "re-negotiation," since the new Member States will be entitled to express their views and objections. There will be increased technical difficulties in arriving at acceptable solutions, since there will be 12, rather than nine, different national systems to accommodate within the common solution.[98] Finally, there will be greater institutional problems : the process of making up 12 rather than nine, minds will almost inevitably be a longer one.[99]

### (c)  An enlarged budget

Given the existing budgetary arrangements, and applying the same rules to the three new members, the Commission has estimated that annual expenditure would have to increase by approximately 3 billion units of account.[1] Revenues from customs duties, agricultural levies and the VAT might increase by 2 billion, leaving a shortfall of a billion units of account to be made up by the existing members. Even at this level, the net transfers to

[94] Or as soon as the Council has established the necessary texts in the Greek language : Act of Accession, Art. 146. If the deadline for implementation of an existing directive is later, Greece will have until then to take the necessary measures : Art. 147.

[95] Act of Accession, Art. 145 and Annex XII.

[96] The Commission view is that Spain should adopt VAT before entry : (EC) Bull. S. 9–78, p. 39. Spain apparently proposes to do so as part of a major tax reform : L. Calvo Sotelo, in *A Community of Twelve?*, p. 42. Adoption of VAT by Portugal is likely to be especially difficult since it would replace a wholesale sales tax and greatly increase the number of taxpayers : (EC) Bull. S. 5–78, p. 16.

[97] *e.g.* the harmonisation of corporation tax systems.

[98] Excise duties may be especially difficult to harmonise, in view of the national tobacco monopolies in Portugal and Spain and the fact that all three countries are major wine producers. Generally, too, the three countries rely disproportionately heavily on indirect, as opposed to direct taxation. See Appendix A, Table 2.

[99] Although the Commission suggests that Art. 100 be amended to permit for decisions to be taken by a qualified majority in most cases, it still envisages that *tax* harmonisation under Arts. 99 and 100 would continue to require unanimity : (EC) Bull. S. 2–78, p. 13. See further G. Fitzgerald and G. Olmi, in *A Community of Twelve?*, at pp. 14, 96.

[1] Agricultural guarantee payments would increase by about 1,150 EUA, guidance payments by 400 million EUA and the regional fund by 400 million EUA : (EC) Bull. S. 3–78, p. 37. The increase in staff, particularly those engaged in translation, would be considerable.

the new members would be small, having regard to their relative lack of prosperity.[2] Drastic reform of the budget, as suggested in the previous section of this chapter, would involve an increase in agricultural spending in the new Member States, by favouring Mediterranean agriculture, and very large increases in social and regional expenditure over and above those already projected.[3]

## G.   A FISCAL POLICY FOR THE COMMUNITY?

**445**   Previous sections of this chapter have indicated the serious economic and social difficulties which must be overcome if a true European Union is to be created. At the present time there appears to be a marked lack of political will necessary to solve these problems : the Community is suffering from the loss of a sense of purpose and its very existence, in even its present form, is in some peril. As Prime Minister Tindemans concluded, in 1975,[4] the European concept has lost a lot of its force and initial impetus and the sense of common vision must first be restored if progress is to be made towards European Union.

It might therefore seem a most inopportune moment to consider the formulation of an overall Community fiscal policy. Until this sense of direction is restored—until Europeans know in which direction they are headed—no coherent tax strategy can be devised. The goals of a tax programme must be consistent with the goals of the Community itself[5] : with these now in doubt, the tax programme has inevitably reached a virtual standstill. A certain amount of tidying-up of unfinished business is possible but no major new proposals, or progress on existing proposals of substance, seem likely until there has been an overall re-evaluation of fundamental objectives. Just as the adoption of the Werner Plan in 1971 gave rise to a need for reappraisal of the Community's tax policy,[6] so it must now be asked whether economic and monetary union remains a viable goal at all.[7] Alternatively, it must

[2] In part this is due to the relatively lower level of subsidisation of "southern" agriculture. Spain, in particular, as a large net importer of food, would receive only a small net benefit. The Commission estimates this at 200 million EUA, but it has been suggested that, unless the budget is radically reformed, Spain could be a net contributor : *The Economist*, November 18, 1978, p. 16.

[3] These would, in any event, have to be phased in gradually, otherwise there might be difficulties in absorbing large transfers over a short period : (EC) Bull. S. 1–78, p. 8. For further consideration of the agricultural, budgetary and regional aspects of enlargement, see the chapters by J. Marsh, D. Biehl and M. Abad, in *A Community of Twelve?*

[4] *European Union*, report to the European Council (EC) Bull. S. 1–76. Matters have scarcely improved in the four subsequent years.

[5] A similar conclusion has been drawn from the lessons of the Benelux union : M. Krauss, *Fiscal Harmonisation in the Benelux Economic Union* (1969), p. 84.

[6] Writing in 1973, Professor Dosser considered the existing policy to be "too Neumarkian or pre-Wernerian" : D. Dosser, in *British Taxation and the Common Market* (1973), p. 156.

[7] The dissenting minority of the ESC Section for Economic and Financial Questions considered that future harmonisation should be confined to those measures which are essential for free movement and for preventing distortions of competition, *i.e.* a return to pre-Wernerian policy : *Fredersdorf Report*, para 6.1.

seriously be considered whether a "two-speed" model might be feasible, bringing about a greater degree of integration among certain of the member states and providing for a looser form of association of the others in the short term. According to this model, common long-range objectives would be established, but to be achieved according to different timescales.[8] In this way, those member states which are presently unable or unwilling to move towards greater integration would not be able to impede the progress of the others. The obvious danger of this course is that it might lead to an irrevocable split between the "inner" and "outer" members, widening the gap between them in such a way that it might never be possible to close it.

**446**    It is submitted that, whether according to a one or two-speed model, economic and monetary union must remain the next major objective of the Community. As the Tindemans Report asserts, "an unfinished structure does not weather well."[9] Stagnation may lead to disintegration and thus, however slowly and cautiously, the Community must continue to strive towards this goal.

So far as concerns the Community's fiscal policy it must consequently be asked whether the present rather piecemeal approach to harmonisation will suffice or if there is a need for a comprehensive overall strategy. Given that Member States will be prepared to relinquish last of all their fiscal sovereignty, can tax harmonisation be left in abeyance until progress in economic integration demands action? This passive approach to tax harmonisation largely reflects the Commission's view that there should be no "harmonisation for harmonisation's sake" and that action should be taken only when it proves necessary.[10] On the other hand, the need for an overall blueprint or "master plan" has been widely urged.[11] A dynamic tax policy could help to create the conditions in which EMU would be possible : a federal tax law could come into existence in advance of the federation.[12] In

---

[8] Tindemans Report, (EC) Bull. S. 1–76, pp. 20–21. A precedent for this exists in the form of the Benelux union which, in some respects, constitutes a more closely integrated entity within the Community. There is also the fact that only eight of the present nine Member States adhere to the EMS.

[9] *Ibid.* at p. 11.

[10] See above, Chapter 3 para. 210. Commissioner Burke has recently asserted that " . . . there is at present no question of establishing a Community tax policy analogous to that which exists in the Member States" : "Harmonisation of Taxation in Europe" |1979| *Intertax* 46. But it is understood that the Commission is nevertheless preparing a "Green Paper" on tax policy.

[11] A. E. Genot, "Fiscal Harmonisation and European Integration : a 1978 Appraisal", (1978) 3 E.L. Rev. 355; R. Wägenbaur, "Les Fondements Juridiques d'une Politique Fiscale des Communautés Européennes", (1975) 67 *Revue de Science Financiere* 5, and see especially the *Fredersdorf Report*, 5.1.

[12] See Dr. Vogelaar's suggested "Operation Bulldozer," which in some ways corresponds to the "apocalyptic" approach to monetary union (above, para. 412) : Th. W. Vogelaar, "Die Entwicklung des Europäischen Steuerrechts" (1972) 55 *Fisc. M.C.* 105. The minority, in the Fredersdorf Report (6.2), have warned that such a blueprint might have unfortunate political consequences : a one-eyed Commission may be able to lead the blind Member States, who would not follow if they could see their destination!

any event, the existence of such a blueprint would ensure that such measures as may be taken in the short-term would be consistent with the long-term objectives.

**447**        In conclusion, it seems that two types of strategy may be formulated—a limited short-term programme and a comprehensive long-term programme. Under the limited programme the immediate step would be to increase the Community VAT-rate ceiling to 2 per cent. and to gradually increase and reform the structure of the budget over the next decade. The VAT base would be further harmonised only where essential (allowing the retention of zero rates) and the proposed excise duty framework could be adopted with some harmonisation of structures[13] but not of rates. The structure of corporation tax could be harmonised, perhaps leaving a greater degree of flexibility as regards rates than is presently proposed : this should also permit progress to be made at last on the proposals concerning mergers and associated companies. Co-operation and mutual assistance between national tax authorities should be progressively improved. The question of the abolition of tax frontiers should be re-examined to ascertain if it is possible to remove physical barriers whilst retaining the "destination" principle or, at least, without any close alignment of VAT and excise duty rates.[14]

A more comprehensive programme would call for a genuine "federal" budget, still comparatively small but strongly redistributive in nature. This would require a far-reaching harmonisation of the systems and bases of assessment of corporation tax and some harmonisation of social security systems. The main features of national budgets would be co-ordinated, with particular attention given to the types and levels of expenditure and to the balance between direct and indirect taxation. Tax harmonisation should be viewed as an opportunity for tax reform.[15] The tax system should be made simple, rational and efficient, from the point of view of the tax-paying citizen and of the tax authorities, and should, above all, be fair and equitable and accord with the social aims of the Community. Such a programme would entail a major surrender of fiscal autonomy by the member states to the Community : since there ought to be "no taxation without representation," this would require the full exercise of democratic control by the newly elected Parliament.

Only given the political will to create a new Europe would such a programme be possible.

---

[13] The recent Court decisions in Cases 168, 169 and 171/78 (above, chapter 1, paras. 38–55) seem to make this inevitable, at least in the case of alcohol spirits.

[14] Even the Fredersdorf Report (4.2.2.3.) admits that harmonisation of these rates is unlikely before 1995. The possibility of an "inner Community" without tax frontiers should also be examined.

[15] N. Andel *et al.* "Steuerharmonisierung" in *Möglichkeiten und Grenzen einer Europäischen Union* (1974), pp. 98–99; Th. W. Vogelaar, (*op. cit.* above, n. 12) at p. 108; Fredersdorf Report (2.1.1.8.).

STATISTICAL TABLES

The following statistics have been collected from various sources (European Community, OECD and United Nations statistical publications and Commission replies to questions in the European Parliament). Being derived from different sources and, sometimes, for different years within the period 1974–1978, they may not always provide a true basis for comparison and are intended only as an illustration of the various subjects discussed in this book.

Member States, and potential Member States, are referred to by the following abbreviations :

B – Belgium; DK – Denmark; F – France; G(FR) – Germany (Federal Republic); IR – Ireland; IT – Italy; L – Luxembourg; NL – Netherlands; UK – United Kingdom; GRE – Greece; P – Portugal; S – Spain.

### Table 1: The Community : Population and Standard of Living

|  | B | DK | F | G(FR) | IR | IT | L | NL | UK | GRE | P | S |
|---|---|---|---|---|---|---|---|---|---|---|---|---|
| Population (millions) | 9.8 | 5.1 | 53.1 | 61.4 | 3.2 | 56.5 | 0.4 | 13.9 | 55.9 | 9.3 | 9.7 | 36.7 |
| GDP per capita (US dollars) | 6351 | 7006 | 6356 | 6868 | 2482 | 3134 | 6184 | 6045 | 4064 | 2306 | 1682 | 2902 |
| Estimated real GDP per capita (US dollars)[1] | 3492 | 3636 | 3945 | 3753 | 2512 | 2742 | — | 3312 | 3274 | 2309 | 1504 | 2384 |

[1] Adjusted for exchange rates and purchasing power.

### Table 2: Taxation in The Community

(a)   Total taxation as % of GDP

|  | B | DK | F | G(FR) | IR | IT | L | NL | UK | GRE | P | S |
|---|---|---|---|---|---|---|---|---|---|---|---|---|
| —excluding Social Security contributions | 30 | 41 | 23 | 25 | 30 | 21 | 35 | 29 | 30 | 20 | 19 | 11 |
| —including Social Security contributions | 43 | 42 | 40 | 38 | 35 | 38 | 50 | 46 | 37 | 28 | 27 | 23 |

267

**(b) Tax revenues as % of total taxes**

|  | B | DK | F | G(FR) | IR | IT | L | NL | UK | GRE | P | S |
|---|---|---|---|---|---|---|---|---|---|---|---|---|
| Taxes on income |  |  |  |  |  |  |  |  |  |  |  |  |
| and profits ........ | 40 | 55 | 19 | 37 | 32 | 25 | 45 | 33 | 41 | 15 | 20 | 22 |
| —personal incomes .. | 33 | 52 | 13 | 31 | 28 | 19 | 26 | 26 | 34 | 11 | 10 | 16 |
| —corporate incomes . | 6 | 3 | 6 | 5 | 4 | 6 | 19 | 7 | 7 | 4 | — | 6 |
| Taxes on goods |  |  |  |  |  |  |  |  |  |  |  |  |
| and services ....... | 26 | 35 | 30 | 23 | 45 | 27 | 18 | 24 | 24 | 40 | 39 | 22 |
| —general |  |  |  |  |  |  |  |  |  |  |  |  |
| consumption ...... | 17 | 19 | 21 | 14 | 17 | 14 | 10 | 16 | 8 | 18 | 11 | 7 |
| —specific |  |  |  |  |  |  |  |  |  |  |  |  |
| consumption ...... | 8 | 16 | 8 | 10 | 28 | 12 | 8 | 8 | 16 | 21 | 25 | 20 |
| Taxes on property .... | 3 | 6 | 3 | 3 | 8 | 4 | 5 | 4 | 12 | 12 | 2 | 5 |
| Social Security |  |  |  |  |  |  |  |  |  |  |  |  |
| contributions ...... | 31 | 1 | 42 | 34 | 14 | 44 | 30 | 37 | 19 | 28 | 30 | 50 |
| —paid by employees . | 9 | 1 | 6 | 15 | 5 | 9 | 12 | 16 | 8 | 12 | 10 | 10 |
| —paid by employers . | 20 | 1 | 30 | 18 | 8 | 35 | 17 | 17 | 11 | 14 | 19 | 40 |

## TABLE 3: VALUE ADDED TAX

**(a) VAT as % total tax revenue**

|  | B | DK | F | G(FR) | IR | IT | L | NL | UK |
|---|---|---|---|---|---|---|---|---|---|
|  | 16 | 19 | 21 | 14 | 17 | 14 | 10 | 16 | 8 |

**(b) Rates of VAT %**

|  | B | DK | F | G(FR) | IR | IT | L | NL | UK |
|---|---|---|---|---|---|---|---|---|---|
| Standard ......................... | 18 | 15 | 18 | 11 | 20 | 14 | 10 | 18 | 15 |
| Increased ......................... | 25 | — | 33 | — | 35 | 35 40 | — | — | — |
| Intermediate ...................... | 14 | — | — | — | — | 18 | — | — | — |
| Reduced .......................... | 6 | — | 7 | 5.5 | 10 | 1,3,9 | 5 2 | 4 | — |
| Zero ............................. | 0 | 0 | — | — | 0 | 0 | — | 0 | 0 |

## TABLE 4: EXCISE DUTIES

|  |  | B | DK | F | G(FR) | IR | IT | L | NL | UK |
|---|---|---|---|---|---|---|---|---|---|---|
| (a) | Excise duties as percentage of total tax |  |  |  |  |  |  |  |  |  |
|  | revenue ......................... | 8 | 16 | 8 | 10 | 28 | 12 | 8 | 8 | 16 |
| (b) | Tobacco |  |  |  |  |  |  |  |  |  |
|  | Retail price (20 cigarettes) in EUA ... | 0.83 | 2.01 | 0.40 | 1.08 | 0.66 | 0.52 | 0.60 | 0.77 | 0.81 |
|  | Excise duty as % total retail price .... | 65 | 70 | 47 | 61 | 51 | 58 | 60 | 54 | 63 |
|  | VAT as % total retail price ......... | 6 | 17 | 25 | 11 | 9 | 15 | 2 | 15 | 7 |
| (c) | Alcoholic Beverages |  |  |  |  |  |  |  |  |  |
|  | Duty in EUA per hectolitre pure alcohol. |  |  |  |  |  |  |  |  |  |
|  | —spirits ...................... | 743 | 1844– 2822 | 292– 1039 | 728 | 1539 | 111– | 414 | 752 | 1599 |
|  | —wine ......................... | 121– 243 | 949 | 13 | 0 | 643 | 0 | 0– 122 | 123– 247 | 906 |
|  | —beer ......................... | 96– 152 | 970 | 16 | 92– 115 | 933 | 137 | 70– 115 | 134– 154 | 502 |
| (d) | Mineral Oils |  |  |  |  |  |  |  |  |  |
|  | Duty in EUA per hectolitre |  |  |  |  |  |  |  |  |  |
|  | —petrol (normal) ................ | 19 | 19 | 17 | 16 | 14 | 30 | 13 | 17 | 10 |
|  | —diesel ....................... | 17 | 0 | 8 | 15 | 6 | 2 | 2 | 7 | 10 |
|  | —heating oil ................... | 1 | 0 | 0 | 0 | 1 | 1 | 1 | 1 | 0 |

## TABLE 5: CORPORATION TAX

|  | B | DK | F | G(FR) | IR | IT | L | NL | UK |
|---|---|---|---|---|---|---|---|---|---|
| Corporation tax as % of total tax revenue | 6 | 3 | 6 | 5 | 4 | 6 | 19 | 7 | 7 |
| Standard rate % | 48 | 37 | 50 | 56 | 45 | 25 | 40 | 48 | 52 |

## TABLE 6: PERSONAL INCOME TAX

|  | B | DK | F | G(FR) | IR | IT | L | NL | UK |
|---|---|---|---|---|---|---|---|---|---|
| Personal Income Tax as % of total tax revenue | 33 | 52 | 13 | 31 | 28 | 19 | 26 | 26 | 34 |
| —as % male average earnings —single man | 16 | 38 | 10 | 18 | 25 | 7 | 20 | 18 | 27 |
| —married couple with 2 children (tax less family benefits) | −1 | 28 | −8 | 6 | 13 | −1 | −2 | 6 | 16 |
| Rate of tax % —initial | 10 | 41 | 5 | 22 | 26 | 10 | 18 | 20 | 30 |
| —maximum | 72 | 66 | 60 | 56 | 77 | 72 | 57 | 72 | 60 |
| Income tax thresholds as % of average industrial earnings | 24 | 27 | 21 | 37 | 46 | 58 | 59 | 23 | 51 |

## TABLE 7: REGIONS

|  | B | DK | F | G(FR) | IR | IT | L | NL | UK | GRE | P | S |
|---|---|---|---|---|---|---|---|---|---|---|---|---|
| GDP per capita of Community average[2] | 125 | 141 | 123 | 135 | 47 | 57 | 128 | 121 | 73 | 45 | 30 | 54 |
| —richest region | 191 | 166 | 183 | 213 | — | 77 | — | 139 | 81 | 62 | 44 | 74 |
| —poorest region | 93 | 124 | 95 | 112 | — | 32 | — | 90 | 63 | 26 | 16 | 32 |

[2] Average of Community of the Nine at current prices and exchange rates (1976).

## TABLE 8: SOCIAL CONDITIONS

### (a)  Employment

|  | B | DK | F | G(FR) | IR | IT | L | NL | UK | GRE | P | S |
|---|---|---|---|---|---|---|---|---|---|---|---|---|
| Civilian working population as % of total population | 40 | 50 | 42 | 42 | 35 | 38 | 42 | 34 | 46 | 35 | 42 | 36 |
| —of whom % females | 35 | 42 | 38 | 38 | 29 | 31 | 28 | 27 | 39 | 29 | 26 | 29 |
| % employees | 83 | 82 | 82 | 85 | 71 | 71 | 86 | 85 | 92 | — | 66 | 71 |
| % self-employed | 17 | 18 | 18 | 15 | 29 | 29 | 14 | 15 | 8 | — | 34 | 29 |
| —% employed in agriculture | 3 | 9 | 9 | 7 | 23 | 16 | 6 | 6 | 3 | 28 | 33 | 21 |
| in industry | 38 | 30 | 38 | 45 | 30 | 39 | 44 | 33 | 40 | 30 | 33 | 37 |
| in services | 59 | 61 | 53 | 48 | 47 | 45 | 50 | 60 | 57 | 41 | 34 | 42 |
| —% unemployed | 8 | 7 | 5 | 4 | 9 | 7 | 1 | 4 | 6 | — | — | 8 |

### (b)  Social expenditure

|  | B | DK | F | G(FR) | IR | IT | L | NL | UK |
|---|---|---|---|---|---|---|---|---|---|
| Social expenditure as % of GDP | 24 | 28 | 23 | 28 | 20 | 24 | 24 | 28 | 19 |
| Categories of social expenditure as % of total |  |  |  |  |  |  |  |  |  |
| —sickness, disability and industrial injury | 35 | 41 | 37 | 40 | 41 | 47 | 39 | 47 | 36 |
| —old age and survivor pensions | 40 | 34 | 43 | 43 | 33 | 37 | 52 | 35 | 47 |
| —maternity and family benefits | 15 | 12 | 15 | 10 | 13 | 10 | 9 | 10 | 11 |
| —unemployment | 8 | 10 | 4 | 3 | 10 | 2 | 0 | 6 | 6 |
| —others | 2 | 3 | 1 | 4 | 3 | 4 | 0 | 1 | 0 |

269

APPENDIX B

## SELECTED BIBLIOGRAPHY

**Reports, Studies, etc.**

Andel Report: *Steuerharmonisierung : Bericht der Facharbeitsgruppe Steuerharmonisierung*, in *Möglichkeiten und Grenzen einer europäischen Union* : Baden-Baden, 1975.

Bosman Report: *European Economic Integration and Monetary Unification* : Commission, 1973.

Cairncross Report: *Economic Policy for the European Community — The Way Forward* : Institut für Weltwirtschaft, Kiel, 1974.

Christiaanse Report: *Tax Policy and Investment in the European Community* : Commission Studies — Taxation Series, 1975 No. 1.

Commission: *Programme for the harmonisation of Direct Taxes* : (EEC) Bull. Supp. 8/67.

Commission: *Action programme for taxation* : (EEC) Bull. 7–8/75.

Commission: *Enlargement of the Community* : (EC) Bull. Supps. 1–3/78.

Commission: *Financing the Community Budget : the way ahead* : (EC) Bull. Supp. 8/78.

Deringer Report: *Rapport fait au nom de la Commission du Marché Interieur sur la proposition de la Commission de la CEE au Conseil concernant une Directive en matiere d'harmonisation des législations des Etats Membres relative aux taxes sur le chiffre d'affairs* : E. P. Docs. 1963–4, No. 56.

Fredersdorf Report: *Information Report of the Section for Economic and Social Questions of the Economic and Social Committee on Tax Harmonization* : Economic and Social Committee, 1978.

MacDougall Report: *Report of the Study Group on the role of public finance in European Integration* : Commission Studies — Economic and Financial Series, 1977.

Marjolin Report: *Report of the Study Group "Economic and Monetary Union 1980"* : Commission, 1975.

Neumark Report: Report of the Fiscal and Financial Committee and Reports of Sub-Groups A, B and C, in *The EEC Reports on Tax Harmonization* (trans. H. Thurston) : International Bureau for Fiscal Documentation, 1963.

Segré Report: *Le Développement d'un marché européen des capitaux* : Commission, 1966.

Tinbergen Report: *Report on the problems raised by the different Turnover Tax Systems applied within the Common Market* : E.C.S.C., High Authority, 1953.

Tindemans Report: *European Union* : (EC) Bull. Supp. 1/76.

270

Utrecht Report: *Conséquences budgétaires, économiques et sociales de l'harmonisation des taux de la TVA dans la CEE* : Commission Etudes — Série Concurrence : Rapprochement des Législations, 1970 No. 16.

Van den Tempel Report: *Corporation Tax and Individual Income Tax in the European Communities* : Commission Studies — Competition : Approximation of Legislation Series, 1970 No. 15.

Werner Report: *Report to the Council and the Commission on the realisation by stages of Economic and Monetary Union in the Community* : (EC) Bull. Supp. 11/70.

## Books

Avery-Jones, J.F. (ed.), *Tax Havens and Measures against Tax Evasion and Avoidance in the EEC* (1974).

Biehl, D., *Ausführland-Prinzip, Einführland-Prinzip und Gemeinsamer Markt-Prinzip. Ein Beitrag zur Theorie der Steuerharmonisierung* (1968).

Börner, B. *et al.*, *Die Harmonisierung der Unternehmensbesteuerung im Gemeinsamen Markt* (1972).

Centre d'Etudes Européennes, Université Catholique de Louvain, *Vers une politique fiscale a l'égard des entreprises multinationales?* (1973).

Christiaanse, J.H., *Tax Harmonization in the European Common Market* (1971).

Coffey, P. and Presley, J.R., *European Monetary Integration* (1971).

Dale, A., *Tax Harmonization in Europe* (1963).

Denton, G. (ed.), *Economic and Monetary Union in Europe* (1974).

Derouin, P., *La Taxe sur la Valeur Ajoutée dans la CEE* (1977).

Dosser, D. (ed.), *British Taxation and the Common Market* (1973).

Due, J.F., *Sales Taxation* (1957).

European Association for Legal and Fiscal Studies, *Branches and Subsidiaries in the European Common Market* (2nd ed.) (1976).

Groeben, H.v.d.; Boeckh, H.v.; Thiesing, J., *Handbuch für Europäische Wirtschaft* (1974).

Institut d'Etudes Européennes : Université Libre de Bruxelles, *Les Emissions de Titres de Sociétés en Europe et aux Etats-Unis* (1970).

Ipsen, H.P., *Europäisches Gemeinschaftsrecht* (1972).

Keeton, G.W. and Frommel, S.N. (eds.), *British Industry and European Law* (1974).

Krauss, M., *Fiscal Harmonization in the Benelux Economic Union* (1969).

Layton, C. *Cross Frontier Mergers in Europe* (1971).

Magnifico, G., *European Monetary Unification* (1973).

Meade, J.E.; Liesner, H.H.; Wells, S.J., *Case Studies in European Economic Union : the Mechanics of Integration* (1962).

Megret, J.; Louis, J.V., Vignes, D., Waelbroeck, M. (Eds.), *Le Droit de la Communauté Economique Européenne* (1970–), Vols. 5, 6.

Oberson, R., *Harmonisation fiscale dans la CEE; droits de timbre et droits d'apport* (1972).

Regul, R. and Renner, W., *Finances and Taxes in European Integration* (1966).

Schmolders, G., *Turnover Taxes* (1966).

Sessa, G. and Vitali, A., *La Politica Fiscale della Communita Economica Europea* (1969).

Shoup, C.S. (ed.), *Fiscal Harmonisation in Common Markets* (1967).

Smit, H. and Herzog, P.E. (eds.), *The Law of the European Economic Community: a Commentary on the EEC Treaty* (1976–).

Snoy, B., *Taxes on District Investment Income in the EEC : a Legal and Economic Analysis* (1975).

Steinaecker, M. von, *Domestic Taxation and Foreign Trade : the United States-Europe Border Tax Dispute* (1973).

Strasser, D., *The Finances of Europe* (1977).

Sullivan, C.K., *The Search for Tax Principles in the European Economic Community* (1963).

Sullivan, C.K., *The Tax on Value Added* (1965).

Tait, A.A., *Value Added Tax* (1972).

Van Hoorn Jr., J., McLachlan, K.J. (eds.), *The Taxation of Companies in Europe* (1972–).

Van Hoorn Jr., J. (ed.), *Value Added Taxation in Europe* (1971–).

Wallace, W. and Herreman, I. (eds.), *A Community of Twelve? The Impact of Further Enlargement on the European Communities* (1978).

Wheatcroft, G.S.A. (ed.), *Value Added Tax in the Enlarged Common Market* (1973).

**Articles**

Albers, W., "Steuerharmonisierung in der EWG — Wünsch and Wirklichkeit" (1973) 11 *Wirtschaftsdienst* 593.

Andel, N., "Die Harmonisierung der Steuern im Gemeinsamen Markt" (1971) 30 *Finanzarchiv* 224.

Anschutz, U., "Harmonisation of Direct Taxes in the European Economic Community" (1972) 13 *Harvard International Law Journal* 1.

Antal, K.V., "Harmonisation of Turnover Taxes in the Common Market" (1963–64) 1 *Common Market Law Review* 41.

Ault, H.J., "International Issues in Corporate Tax Integration" (1978) 10 *Law and Policy in International Business* 461.

Barcelo, J.J., "Subsidies and Countervailing Duties — Analysis and a Proposal" (1977) 9 *Law and Policy in International Business* 779.

Barents, R., "Charges of Equivalent Effect to Customs Duties" (1978) 15 *Common Market Law Review* 415.

Bentil, J.K., "EEC Commercial Law and Charges Having Equivalent Effect to Customs Duties" (1975) 9 *Journal of World Trade Law* 458.

Blom, L.A., "Tax Harmonisation in the EEC" [1974/1] *Legal Issues of European Integration* 1.

Bouquin, J.P., "Les Resources Propres des Communautés Européennes" (1978) 218 *Revue du Marché Commun* 321.

Bracewell-Milnes, B., "Tax Credits Under the Proposed EEC Directive on Company Taxation" [1976] *Intertax* 277.

Brosio, G., "National tax hindrances to cross-border concentrations in the European Economic Community" (1970) 11 *Harvard International Law Journal* 311.

Burke, R., "Harmonisation of Corporation Tax" [1979] *Intertax* 240.

Burke, R., "Harmonisation of Taxation in Europe" [1979] *Intertax* 46.

Burki, E.P., "Amélioration ou altération d'une formule de la Cour de Justice" (1978) 14 *Cahiers de Droit Européen* 101.

Chown, J., "The Harmonisation of Corporation Tax in the EEC" 1976 *British Tax Review* 39.

Chown, J., "The Reform of Corporation Tax: Some International Factors" [1971] *British Tax Review* 215.

Claeys-Bouuaert, I., "Ou en est le droit fiscal européen?" (1966) 2 *Cahiers de droit Européen* 251.

Close, G., "Harmonisation of Laws: Use or Abuse of the Powers Under the EEC Treaty" (1978) 3 *European Law Review* 461.

Conard, A.F., "Corporate Fusion in the Common Market" (1966) 14 *American Journal of Comparative Law* 573.

Denton, G. "Reflections on Fiscal Federalism in the EEC" (1978) 16 *Journal of Common Market Studies* 283.

Dodsworth, J.R., "Cost Sharing in the European Communities" (1974) 29 *Public Finance* 131.

Dosser, D., Han, S.S. and Hitiris, T., "Trade Effects of Tax Harmonisation: Harmonisation of the Value Added Tax in the EEC" (1969) 37 *The Manchester School* 337.

Easson, A.J., "Tax Policy in the European Economic Community" (1977) 1 *Revue de l'Intégration Européenne* 31.

Easson, A.J., "The British Tax Reforms — a step towards Harmonisation" (1971) 8 *Common Market Law Review* 325.

Easson, A.J., "The Direct Effect of EEC Directives" (1979) 28 *International and Comparative Law Quarterly* 319.

Ehle, D., "Auslegungsprobleme der steuerrechtlichen Vorschriften des EWG-Vertrags" [1967] *Neue Juristische Wochenschrift* 1689.

Ehring, H., "Zur Abgrenzung der Beihilfsverbot vom Verbot der Zollgleichen Abgaben und der inländischen Abgaben ..." (1974) 9 *Europarecht* 108.

Everling, U., "L'Aspect Juridique de la Co-ordination de la Politique

Economique au sein de la Communauté Economique Européenne" (1964) 10 *Annuaire Francaise de Droit International* 576.

Feller, P.B., "Mutiny against the Bounty: An Examination of Subsidies, Border Tax Adjustments and the Resurgence of the Countervailing Duty Law" (1969) 1 *Law and Policy in International Business* 17.

Genot, A.E., "Fiscal Harmonisation and European Integration: a 1978 Appraisal" (1978) 3 *European Law Review* 355.

Goergen, R., "The Decision of the Council of Ministers of the Community on the Proposal for a Sixth Directive on VAT" (1977) *European Taxation* 48.

Gosset, G., "Les Propositions de directives de la Commission pour lever les obstacles fiscaux aux concentrations internationales" (1969) 33 *Fiscalité du Marché Commun* 27.

Grossman, G.M., "Alternative Border Tax Policies" (1978) 12 *Journal of World Trade Law* 452.

Guieu, P., "L'Uniformisation des Systemes Nationaux de TVA" (1974) 178 *Revue du Marché Commun* 437.

Guillaume, V. and Waelbroeck, J., "Impact of the Added Value Tax on an Economy: The Case of Belgium" (1972) 3 *European Economic Review* 91.

Han, S.S., and Shaw, G.K., "Turnover Tax Harmonisation in the European Community" (1968) 2 *Journal of World Trade Law* 97.

Hellinger, F., "Harmonisierung der Steuern nach allgemeinen Rechts-angleichungs vorschriften des EWG-Vertrags" (1976) 6 *Recht der Internationalen Wirtschaft* 363.

Hollrah, J.M., "Taxation of Cross-border Concentrations in the EEC" (1974) 9 *Texas International Law Journal* 313.

Höppner, H.D., "Die EG-Steuerharmonisierung" (1977) 12 *Europarecht* 122.

Huiskamp, J.C.L., "The Harmonisation of Legislation of EEC Member States Concerning Turnover Taxes" (1967–8) 5 *Common Market Law Review* 177.

Hunnings, N.M., "Value Added Tax and EEC Directives" [1977] *Journal of Business Law* 289.

Kaplan, P.T., "European Discrimination and American Retaliation" [1978] *British Tax Review* 206.

Krauss, M.B., "Border Tax Adjustments: a potential Trans-Atlantic Trade Dispute" (1976) 10 *Journal of World Trade Law* 145.

Krauss, M., "The Anti-Economics of the European Common Market" (1973) 7 *Journal of World Trade Law* 555.

Lawton, A.D., "Tax Aspects of Company Mergers in Europe" (1974) 124 *New Law Journal* 1153.

Leleux, P., "Le Rapprochement des Législations dans la Communauté Economique Européenne" (1968) 4 *Cahiers de droit Européen* 129.

Maas, H.H., "The Powers of the European Community and the Achievement of the Economic and Monetary Union" (1972) 9 *Common Market Law Review* 2.

Meij, A.W.H. and Winter, J.A., "Measures having an effect equivalent to Quantitative Restrictions" (1976) 13 *Common Market Law Review* 79.

Miller, N.I., "Some Tax Implications of British Entry into the Common Market" (1972) 37 *Law and Contemporary Problems* 265.

Möller, H., "Ursprüngs-und Bestimmungslandprinzip" (1968) 27 *Finanzarchiv* 385.

Nasini, P., "Harmonisation of National Systems of VAT" (1973) *European Taxation* 39.

Page, A.C., "The Concept of Measures Having an Effect Equivalent to Quantitative Restrictions" (1977) 2 *European Law Review* 105.

Prouzet, M., "La Politique de la CEE en matiere d'harmonisation des Impots Indirects" (1972) 49 *Revue de Droit International et de Droit Comparé* 151.

Puchala, D.J. and Lankowski, C.F., "The Politics of Fiscal Harmonisation in the European Communities" (1977) 15 *Journal of Common Market Studies* 155.

Reugebrink, J., "The Sixth Directive for the Harmonisation of Value Added Tax" (1978) 15 *Common Market Law Review* 309.

Rosendahl, R.W., "Border Tax Adjustments: Problems and Proposals" (1970) 2 *Law and Policy in International Business* 85.

Salomons, C.S., "The EEC Against Tax Evasion" (1978) 18 *European Taxation* 136.

Shanks, M., "The Social Policy of the European Communities" (1977) 14 *Common Market Law Review* 375.

Sims, B.J., "Capital Duty — a First Real Step in Tax Harmonisation" [1976] *British Tax Review* 33.

Soldati, M., "Taxing Corporate Income: European Harmonisation and the Italian Experience" (1976) 24 *American Journal of Comparative Law* 246.

Stephenson, P., "Problems and Political Implications for the United Kingdom of Introducing the EEC Value Added Tax" (1970) 8 *Journal of Common Market Studies* 305.

Surrey, S.S., "Implications of Tax Harmonisation in the European Common Market" (1968) 46 *Taxes* 398.

Timmermans, C.W.A., "Directives: Their Effect within the National Legal Systems" (1979) 16 *Common Market Law Review* 533.

Vaulont, N., "Die Vereinfachung der Verfahren und Förmlichkeiten im innergemeinschaftlichen Warenverkehr . . ." (1977) 12 *Europarecht* 1.

Veenhof, B.M., "Harmonisation fiscale et co-ordination des politiques dans les Communautés Européennes" (1972) 53–54 *Fiscalité du Marché Commun* 75.

Vogelaar, Th. W., "Evolution du droit fiscal Européen" (1972) 55 *Fiscalité du Marché Commun* 105.

Vogelaar, Th. W., "Tax Harmonisation in the European Community" (1970) 7 *Common Market Law Review* 323.

Vogelaar, Th. W., "The Approximation of the Laws of Member States under the Treaty of Rome" (1975) 12 *Common Market Law Review* 211.

Waardenburg, D.A., "Transfer Pricing Arbitration Procedure" (1978) 18 *European Taxation* 144.

Wägenbaur, R., "Das Verbot Steuerlicher Diskriminierung nach dem EWG-Vertrag (1) im Lichte der Rechtsprechung des Gerichtshof" (1969) 3 *Europarecht* 20.

Wägenbaur, R., "Les Fondements Juridiques d'une Politique Fiscale des Communautés Européennes" (1975) 67 *Revue de Science Financiere* 5.

Wardenier, H.G.M., "Benelux: Excise Tax Convention" (1977) *Intertax* 351.

Wooldridge, F. and Plender, R., "Charges Having an Equivalent Effect to Customs Duties: A Review of the Cases" (1978) 3 *European Law Review* 101.

"The Common System of Tax on Value Added" (1967) 7 *European Taxation* 148.

"The Taxation of Dividends and Interest in the EEC and the Resulting Obstacles to Free Capital Movement" (1967) 7 *European Taxation* 212.

# INDEX